PRAISE FOR VIKTOR SHKLOVSKY

A rambling, digressive stylist, Shklovsky throws off brilliant aperçus on every page. . . . Like an architect's blueprint, it lays bare the joists and studs that hold up the house of fiction. **MICHAEL DIRDA**, Washington Post

Shklovsky is a disciple worthy of Sterne. He has appropriated the device of infinitely delayed events, of the digression helplessly promising to return to the point, and of disguising his superbly controlled art with a breezy nonchalance. But it is not really Sterne that Shklovsky sounds like: it is an intellectual and witty Hemingway. **GUY DAVENPORT**

In their heterogeneity, their subversive undercurrents, their way of achieving inclusion through use of digression while simultaneously using digressions as a means of being pointed, the works of Viktor Shklovsky are so appropriate to our contemporary situation as to seem to have been written for us. His writings do precisely what he has said it is art's goal to do: they "restore . . . sensation of the world," they "resurrect things and kill pessimism." **LYN HEJINIAN**

T0155049

ENERGY OF DELUSION

VIKTOR SHKLOVSKY

ENERGY OF DELUSION
A BOOK ON PLOT

TRANSLATED BY SHUSHAN AVAGYAN

DALKEY ARCHIVE PRESS

First published in Russian as *Energiia zabluzhdeniia;
kniga o siuzhete* by Sovetskii pisatel, 1981
Viktor Shklovsky's Russian text copyright
© 1985 by Varvara Shklovskaya-Kordi
Translation rights into the English language
are granted by FTM Agency, Ltd., Russia, 2004
English translation copyright © 2007 by Shushan Avagyan

First edition, 2007
Second printing, 2011

Library of Congress Cataloging-in-Publication Data

Shklovskii, Viktor Borisovich, 1893–1984

[Energiia zabluzhdeniia. English]

Energy of delusion : a book on plot / Viktor Shklovsky ;
translation by Shushan Avagyan. — 1st ed.

p. cm.

ISBN-13: 978-1-56478-426-1 (alk. paper)

ISBN-10: 1-56478-426-6 (alk. paper)

1. Tolstoy, Leo, graf, 1828–1910—Criticism and interpretation.
2. Fiction—History and criticism. I. Avagyan, Shushan. II. Title.

PG3410.S4713 2007

891.73'3—dc22

2006032805

Partially supported by a grant from the Illinois Arts Council,
a state agency, and by the University of Illinois, Urbana-Champaign

Dalkey Archive Press is a nonprofit organization whose mission
is to promote international cultural understanding and
provide a forum for dialogue for the literary arts

DALKEY ARCHIVE PRESS
1805 S. Wright St., MC-011
Champaign, IL 61820

www.dalkeyarchive.com

Design and composition by Quemadura
Printed on permanent/durable acid-free, recycled paper,
bound in the United States of America, and
distributed throughout North America and Europe

CONTENTS

In one of his earlier works, Viktor Borisovich Shklovsky (1893–1984) wrote: "This book is called *Knight's Move*. The knight moves *sideways*, like this—" and proceeded to draw a diagram of the knight's L-shaped move. The zigzagging diagram was like an epigraph to the book, warning readers to expect unpredictable curves and bends throughout this careful study of the conventions of art.

Energy of Delusion begins in similar fashion, *bokom* or "sideways"—like Tolstoy's house that was part of a once unfinished building, and where everything was arranged unconventionally. In this brilliant synthesis of Tolstoy's biography and critical analysis of his works, Shklovsky shows how to approach literature—and most importantly how *not* to— when trying to understand its essence.

First published in Russia in 1981, *Energy of Delusion* is simply one of the greatest works of literary criticism by the most original critic and theoretician of the twentieth century. As Shklovsky mentions in the preface, he worked on the book for more than ten years (he was 88 at the time of publication). In a way, *Energy* is the return and reinvention of Formalist thought, despite the attacks and censorship by Soviet criticism throughout the 1920s, and by many Western critics professing the surrender of the Formalists to Marxist ideology.

But perhaps the book's greatest contribution is to the highly contested and multifaceted field of comparative literature studies. By opening an especially hospitable space for cultivating multi-perception through comparison and contrast, Shklovsky does a remarkable job demonstrating how Tolstoy's literature both resembles and differs from other literary works. He positions himself—"Viktor Shklovsky"—at the very center of this unique experiment, embodying the very essence of Tolstoyan energy, "the energy of free search," which offers no firm ground underfoot and no fixed road to fully grasp literary meaning. As a comparatist, he takes "free search" as his method, for he is not destined to find a "true" answer or final destination to his quest of mastery; rather, in the unpredictable process of critical investigation, he gains a transformed and transforming perspective—a "sideways" view—that leads to multi-perception.

The most difficult part of translating Viktor Shklovsky is capturing the tone of his voice: at times apologetic, at times ironic, and at times—highly lyrical. One of the more fascinating of Shklovsky's talents is his ability to describe literary phenomena in simple ways, by writing to and addressing the reader directly, and hence doing away with the irritating tone of a scholarly academic. He is constantly negotiating with readers, guiding them through the labyrinths of literature, then leaving them "suddenly" on their own to construe their own ideas based on devices that he, Viktor Shklovsky, has provided. In this, Shklovsky exemplifies the voice of *vdrugoi*, which is composed of three different and contradictory parts: (1) a friend (*drug*) who reinvents himself and appears (2) suddenly (*vdrug*) as (3) an "other" (*drugoi*). Or, vice versa—an "other" who suddenly turns out to be a friend. The elusiveness of this voice is ultimately an illustration of "the contradictory nature of art, the contradictory nature of books and the contradictory nature of love for your own heroes. That's the theme of this book that you're reading."

The text incorporates many quotes from standard translations, some of which are from anthologies that do not include translators' names, as it was common with Soviet publishers. I have used translations from *The Decameron* by G. H. McWilliam, *The Iliad* by Robert Fagles, *Eugene Onegin* by Vladimir Nabokov, *The Captain's Daughter* by Natalie Duddington, *The Diary of a Madman* by Andrew R. MacAndrew, "The Bronze Horseman" by Avrahm Yermolinsky, *Anna Karenina* by Constance Garnett, *War and Peace* by Louise and Aylmer Maude, *The Inspector General* by Andrew R. MacAndrew, *Dead Souls* by Andrew R. MacAndrew, *The Seagull* by Stark Young, and "The Steppe" in Robert Linscott's edition of Chekhov's short stories.

This translation owes much to Terry Myers, who read and provided detailed comments on early drafts, prompting me to rethink and reinterpret; Margaret Meklina whose role was essential in finding references made by the author and citing appropriate sources; and finally, I would like to thank my parents for their constant support and inspiration.

SHUSHAN AVAGYAN

JANUARY 9, 2007

ENERGY OF DELUSION

1

PREFACE

I. TOLSTOY'S HOUSE IN YASNAYA POLYANA STANDS SOMEWHAT SLANTED

The two-story house in Yasnaya Polyana stands with its side facing the road; it's very old. It stands sideways because it's part of a once unfinished house, where the lieutenant colonel's youngest son, Lev Nikolaevich Tolstoy, was born.

It's a comfortable house, but everything in it—the windows, the staircase, even the doors—are arranged oddly, not in the usual places.

This strange, well-known house looks like a traveler, a wanderer, who is resting on the side of the road after a long journey.

There is a room in the basement that remains from the old building. The window here is unusually high up.

The room was intended for storing ham hocks.

Another building stands much farther back, on the side, behind the full-grown trees.

This was the school founded by Lev Nikolaevich, and where he taught; the other teachers were students who got expelled from the university. One of them was Fyodorov's student.

Fyodorov used to say that the dead had to be resurrected; mankind should set impossible tasks for itself, and after its rebirth, mankind would exit earth as if from a waiting room, and leisurely take over the cosmos.[1]

Lev Nikolaevich knew Fyodorov, who worked at the library, which was later expanded and named after Lenin. Fyodorov's student, who taught the peasant children in Tolstoy's school, would become a character in Tolstoy's last novel *Resurrection*, the one who goes into exile with Katyusha Maslova.

She leaves because of someone else—Nekhlyudov, a man she loved and still does; she leaves to forgive him for the love that was stolen from her, for all her suffering and his belated repentance.

The estate is old, and the forest surrounding the house became overgrown after Lev Nikolaevich's death, though it doesn't look sombre. Nobody cuts down trees around here and the forest has spread with bright, joyful birches.

Here, in this quiet underground room that used to be a storeroom, is Lev Nikolaevich's second office. He wrote here, separated from others by a flight of stairs. It was a quiet room.

There is another office where he wrote, too, and received his guests. There is a large print on the wall of orchids in a basket.

Angels and the Sistine Madonna.

Across the print, which with time has turned into wallpaper, hang shelves that hold the volumes of the Brockhaus and Efron Encyclopedia.

In one of the volumes there is an article called "Marxism."

The world in which Lev Nikolaevich lived was unfathomable. Everything kept changing in it.

Everything kept moving. In this world Lev Nikolaevich studied Greek in order to help his son with his studies at the Gymnasium. The son never

---

[1] Nikolai Fyodorov (1828–1903), Russian mystical philosopher whose collection of writings, published posthumously as *The Philosophy of a Common Task* (1906), expressed the belief of man's divine powers to bring about a resurrection of all its kind, and had a major influence on both Tolstoy and Dostoevsky.

finished school, while Lev Nikolaevich read Homer in the original and still found time to browse through the encyclopedia. Everything moved in this unfathomable world, as if entering into the cosmos. Reality itself moved.

Lev Nikolaevich never mishandled books.

He had many books, it was almost impossible to read them all.

He was ahead of his time, like a flag caught in the currents of a favorable wind.

Throbbing between memories and hope—the poet Batyushkov wrote —interrupted only by madness.[2]

By "memories of the future," Batyushkov meant "hope."

With the strong confident hand of a man who knew how to hold both a spade and a pencil, Lev Nikolaevich underlined a section from "Marxism" in his encyclopaedia.

The pencil-marked words read: "social reality determines consciousness."

Social reality is stepped[3]—it is multi-temporal. The epochs existing in it either clash or peacefully coexist.

Lev Nikolaevich had hoped that mankind would leave the old shores and move into the ocean of total knowledge. It would build a new world that had no notion of time. Tolstoy believed in the eternal.

The eternal past is also based on the peasant and his work. The eternal—it's the peasant's yard and his plow. It's villages of harvesters. It's labor that never changes.

Let's go back to man before historic times.

At some point in time, man passed by and left his human footprints.

---

[2] Konstantin Batyushkov (1787–1855), an important precursor of Pushkin, who went mad in the 1820s yet continued to write perfectly metric poems.

[3] The term "stepped" (*stupenchaty*) is a critical concept coined by Shklovsky to designate works of literature that unfold in a linear fashion. Here he is explaining the structure of social reality that develops in a progressive *stepped* narrative or story, the pattern of which follows events as they would occur in real life, bound each to each in a cause-and-effect relationship.

They turned into stone. There were identical footprints next to them, slightly smaller.

The woman and child passed by. Time brings about changes.

It says in the Apocalypse: "There will be a judgement day, and the sky will erupt like a scroll of parchment, and time will cease to exist."

We still exist, and so will our offspring, if we are wise enough and strong enough during times of change.

Lev Nikolaevich, also known as Count Lev Nikolaevich Tolstoy, the owner of Yasnaya Polyana, knew the importance of history.

The old road from Kiev to Moscow went past his gates.

For many centuries, they herded cattle along this road, and pilgrims walked to and from Kiev.

Beggars lazily passed by.

Then cars appeared when Lev Nikolaevich was still living.

He used to come out and talk to the people who rode in these new outlandish vehicles.

It's likely that during his lifetime he even saw airplanes flying over Yasnaya Polyana.

Lev Nikolaevich grew up during the time before railroads, and he didn't like trains. He recorded the Russian saying: "What vast forests were tamed by trains."

For him, this era of railroads was a time of change in things that didn't really need any changing.

This book that I'm writing in the late years of my life is called *Energy of Delusion*.

That's not my phrase, it's Tolstoy's.

He wished for those delusions to never end. They are footprints leading to the truth, the search for the purpose of humanity.

We base our work on rough drafts written by people. Unfortunately, I don't know much about the origins of this art, and I'm too old to start studying them. Time imposes its iron chains.

But I want to look at the history of Russian literature as footprints of a movement, the movement of consciousness—each footprint a negation of the one before. Let's bear in mind one more thing.

There were many circles, steps, and levels in Dante's *Inferno*. Here, people lived in eternal confinement, each punished for a different sin.

But the "circles of the inferno" are not only the ingenious structure of literary creation, they are traces of the various perceptions of time during the era of the great city of Florence.

Even after death, people argue there about their differently inherited experiences from the past.

In Florence, different lifestyles co-existed simultaneously.

Different classes, different guilds, and different relationships to labor. These are the traces of old arguments, traces that have withstood time, because they tried to conceive some of the things that we are trying to conceive today.

It's the same with *The Decameron*—a collection of adventures of people who think in different ways, who relate to the past differently, or who simply want to ignore it. Women and men, telling stories, anecdotes about treachery in love, about shipwrecks, about wars, about separation—they are different, but they all belong to the same milieu. The plague has freed them from the blind impulse to fall under the influence of contemporary laws. The knights, the merchants, the warriors and women, who demand—they each demand a new life.

Lady Filippa was not an exception.

She took part in making the laws. Her speech, according to the story, was given in the city of Prato, not far from Florence. Today there are old museums and some small textile factories.

And the tourists, who keep searching along the paths of delusion, find the pulse of life that keeps slipping from their grip—their hands seem to be frozen.

Tolstoy and his teacher, Pushkin, belong to different epochs at different moments of their lives, with different perceptions of the past and future. This multi-perception of the world is the foundation of what we call literature.

The past arrives not unexpectedly, but in the way spring or winter arrives. Nature is a variety of sensations, the flow of time. The flowers and trees attest to various ways of searching for the sun, of perceiving the earth—varieties of sensations of what we quite simply call life.

The heroes of Dostoevsky and Tolstoy were not created just by these great authors, but are also associated with Pushkin's name.

Blok described Pushkin's name as "joyful."

The tragedies of mankind are joyful because they are the paths from the past to the future. It's difficult to understand this.

Tolstoy's and Dostoevsky's wives were friends. They were learning about publishing.

However, Tolstoy wasn't acquainted with Dostoevsky.

They had never met and hadn't even once shaken each other's hand, even though there was an incident when they both turned up at the same place. The paths for the future don't always intersect.

I don't know how to work on scholarly books and won't have the time to learn. My path is serpentine, and the books that I read—vary.

I thought differently at different times.

I suppose that this book about delusions, about real conflicts between the different ways we perceive life, about the different beliefs regarding duty, has a right to exist. Although I consider my work far from being scholarly, at the same time I fully respect academic work and its difficult means of elucidating truth. This book contains many real things, freed from the pages of oblivion.

The paths of Dostoevsky, Tolstoy, or Chekhov represent to me a road or, to be accurate, paths that don't always intersect, and that have different ways of perceiving life. The path of Tatyana Larina and Eugene Onegin has not come to an end yet. Books aren't always written to their end.

The most difficult thing in the delusion of this search is to find the right way.

When Tolstoy was writing or preparing to write a novel about Peter the Great, he talked about the peasantry, about the static life, about how some time ago in the villages the princes and peasants looked very much alike. He used the old travelers as his witnesses.

Even their outfits hardly ever changed.

Or maybe they did—but for the worse.

The importance of literature lies in the idea that old perceptions, in conflict with new ones, never disappear. Rather, they pave the way to the future.

This is my attempt to collect the footprints from those various paths, those wanderings with different guides.

For many years I have worked in film production and seen more than once how the directors, during the screenings before public release, said that these were just sketches, something that would have to be reworked in the future.

People cringe when showing something that's most precious to them.

Although a sketch—this isn't too bad. They used special ladders when launching an offensive on fortresses.

Otherwise it would be impossible to climb over.

And so, I have already said a few words in my own defense.

It's an old rule. Boccaccio also used to apologize. Everyone does.

II. ABOUT THE TROIKA-BIRD

Forgive me, for I'm going to write another preface and maybe even repeat some of the things I have already said.

The idea that the realm of poetry is as infinite as life itself belongs to Lev Tolstoy; but all themes of poetry are predestined to be placed in a particular hierarchy and the misplacement of the lower with the higher ones, or the perception of the lower as the higher, becomes a major problem.

With the great poets, with Pushkin, a precise harmony in the arrangement of themes is brought to perfection.

It's irritating to read the works of gifted writers—the same goes for composers and painters—who are incapable of creating this harmony. This inability even seems to stimulate an interest in the work and to broaden its scope; this is not correct. The reading of Homer or Pushkin narrows the scope, and if this narrowing arouses interest in the work, then it does so for the right reason.

Pushkin is present and will always be present in our lives. Like the spring —he brings us joy, even when it's late, as it is outside on my street today.

I remember the hall in which Blok joylessly talked about "Pushkin's joyful name": it was in a house on the street that's now named after Nekrasov.

Blok was reading the poems as if they were composed a long time ago or engraved in stone, as if he were delivering something that had already been preserved, but still known and recited.

He read without raising his voice.

He would pause for an instant, just before the rhyme.

The rhyme was felt as a confirmation of the diction.

It takes many attempts to achieve harmony.

In his books, Blok intended to arrange all of his poems in chronological order—like the steps of a staircase.

This was a long time ago.

Many years later—it was the centennial of Pushkin's death—we drove to the village of Mikhaylovskoe with a small group. We had been late for the train and were trailing after it in our car.

There was a forest in Mikhaylovskoe, unlike any other, with its outer parameter cut into logs: tall pines, spruce trees, now all covered in white snow. The pine trees stood encircling a small lake.

The military base, stationed not too far away, and the collective farm had organized a festival in memory of Pushkin.

He is present everywhere here. The forest, the massive pine trees with his humble name at their roots—they co-existed, they were here—and it is as if the memory of him were soaring above. The memory is constant. I was looking at the car parked by the bulging roots underneath the huge trees—it seemed small to me in comparison to his short but grand name.

And so the carnival was taking place on the frozen lake, amid the pine trees.

Ahead of us people walked in carnival costumes: the heroes from "The Tale of Tsar Saltan"—marching in a rhythmic pace, because they were soldiers—thirty-three of them. Then there were the sleighs, harnessed to a troika.

The sleighs carried a girl in a sheepskin jacket and an old bearded Cossack wearing the Annensky band over his shoulder. It was Pugachev, and next to him—Masha Mironova.

They were easily recognizable.

Right after them followed a cart with a machine-gun.

Next to the machine-gun stood Chapaev.[4]

What's he doing here—I asked—at the Pushkin festival?

Bringing everything together is better—they told me. And I thought of the troika-bird.

III. I'M SEARCHING FOR AN OPENING

This is important. I have one more preface. My book is called *Energy of Delusion.*

---

[4] Vasili Chapaev (1887–1919) was a Bolshevik military commander during the Russian Civil War, fighting against the White Guards. His appearance next to the Pushkin characters is an example of how the Soviets conglomerated everything into one homogenized event, however inconceivable and ridiculous such a combination would be.

These are Tolstoy's words; they come from his letter to N. Strakhov[5] from April 8, 1878.

He wrote:

> ... Everything seems to be ready for the writing—for fulfilling my earthly duty, what's missing is the urge to believe in myself, the belief in the importance of my task, I'm lacking the energy of delusion ...[6]

Now I need to bring a quote from Pushkin's poem called "Autumn." This is from the end:

   x
   ....

And here they come—a ghostly swarm of guests
My old acquaintances, the fruits of all my dreams.

   xi
And thoughts stir bravely in my head, and rhymes
Run forth to meet them on light feet, my fingers restive grow,
They boldly seek a pen; the pen—a sheet of paper ...
A moment, and the verse will smoothly flow.
Thus slumbers a quiet vessel on quiet waters. But lo!

[5] Nikolai Strakhov (1828–96), literary critic and philosopher, Tolstoy's friend and editor in the 1870s.

[6] The "energy of delusion" came to replace Tolstoy's inspiration with which he had begun writing *Anna Karenina*. The novel was begun rather loosely, without "scaffolding" and "in ... non-severe style" as he described in his letters to Afanasi Fet, which after some time began to seem revolting to Tolstoy. He wanted to create a real work that would untie the main knot of life, that would uncover something absolutely new and indispensable, but he had no concrete plan of how to write it. This "unstructured" novel was a sort of blind search for truth, but without his "energy of delusion" the real creative work would be impossible for Tolstoy. Shklovsky uses the concept of this energy to show how experimentation and mistakes can lead to rediscovering old forms and reinventing them as new.

....

The ship begins to move—a foaming track behind.

XII

It sails away. But whither shall we sail? . . .

Here is a poem by a person who is full of possibilities to begin something.

Poetry is timeless, or rather, it belongs to a different time—a different clock.

The elements of a work—the "old acquaintances"—they exist outside the whole, outside the existing whole.

Not yet germinated;

not yet sprouted;

they are seeds.

The poetic state doesn't come suddenly.

Neither does inspiration.

It's like the birds, returning to their nests.

—That's how poetry grows, by reconstituting its own origins.

. . . After this poem the author interrupts again and says that he doesn't want to think, he's afraid—the reader might think it is necessary to get deluded, *really* deluded, in order to write.

This is a different kind of delusion.

It's how people get lost in the open sea, when by mistake they discover, instead of India, an island, which they took for India—but they were mistaken—it was only an island, yet somehow they weren't wrong because behind it was the New World.

But stepping back for a moment, let's talk about the feeling of anticipation of the New World.

When Columbus was setting sail, the sailors were singing Roman verses about the existence of a land beyond the northernmost isles, and beyond the island Foula.

They were already prepared for the discovery, they had maps on the ship, they knew what the wind and sails were for.

When the sail bends against the wind, it seems that it's lost.

It's not. It's catching the wind and redirecting it along its own path.

■

Now let's go on and talk about Pushkin's passion—what was it really? Tolstoy initially thought that it was something in the Karamzinian tradition.[7]

And Tolstoy would never get engrossed in reading Pushkin.

In less than a month, unintentionally following his own voice, a reader's intuition—and he knew *how* to read Pushkin's artistic prose—Tolstoy came across a certain work, which at the time wasn't famous at all, but simply known as *The Tales of Belkin*.

We'll talk about Pushkin's notes.

There is a fragment there: "The guests were assembling at the country house."

This immediately drew Tolstoy to Pushkin.

Pushkin turned out to be an "old acquaintance."

At the same time, he turned up rather unexpectedly.

There was a woman's fate in that fragment.

It contained the beginning of an unresolved plot.

No. It contained an already finished plot, only it wasn't recorded yet. There was nothing more than that fragment, well actually two fragments.

Here is the second one: "At the corner of a little square stood a carriage."

The carriage stood in the wrong place. It didn't belong there.

7 Nikolai Karamzin (1766–1826), famous Russian master prose stylist of the Enlightenment era, whose literary tendencies were sentimentalism and didacticism. Shklovsky and other Russian Formalists have argued against Pushkin's affiliation with the Enlightenment and have pointed out, in *The Tales of Belkin*, that the nearly forgotten generic forms of the eighteenth century experienced not a renaissance, but rather a radical reformation that involved irony and parody.

Something unexpected had happened.

Herein lies a story—two fragments from a woman's life, most likely one and the same.

Or the same woman appears in two different dreams.

But look how it's done in Tolstoy's first sketch—the love affair between the future Anna Karenina and the future Aleksei Vronsky is depicted through the rumors among people returning from the theater: two persons are sitting at the table, talking. It's as if someone is beating raucously on the drums in a hall full of people—the music is telling us that something big is about to happen, perhaps something tragic.

Dostoevsky worshipped Pushkin. He was convinced that Tatyana Larina had no other choice but to reject Onegin.

She couldn't have said anything else except for what she had written in the letter.

■

Next to that, Pushkin has another work.

It's about a woman who left her husband.

Because she fell out of love.

She fell in love with someone else, and she is uncompromising.

Tolstoy decided to write a novel as though to finish what Pushkin had set out to do.

But this ladder was difficult to climb even for a giant who wants to reach the sun.

These are the records of Tolstoy's passage through a novel, which he began writing after reading the fragments from Pushkin.

And so how is the novel constructed?

It's done so that somehow it reminds us of Dostoevsky.

Reading the "deathbed" scene in *Anna Karenina*, where the woman is almost dying from postpartum fever—back then this was a certain death—when she is affectionate with both men, Aleksei Karenin and Aleksei Vronsky, Dostoevsky says: see, no one is at fault here.

But everyone stays alive, even Karenin.

According to Tolstoy, marriage shouldn't be the ending of a novel, but its beginning.

And so this scene, this hesitation, the question of who is at fault, why he is at fault. This isn't merely a reconstruction of fiction, but the reconstruction of human consciousness.

When Karenin feels love for the little girl, Vronsky's child, he holds her, smiles at her; even though she isn't his, Karenin is capable of love. He loves his own son Seryozha and someone else's daughter, but he is unable to reconstruct his own life.

Tolstoy is writing about him and judging him. Karenin is being judged by a great person, who wrote profusely about human responsibility. He wrote, he proclaimed that the doors open outward only in taverns—in the human soul they open inward, and Tolstoy, who once used to open his soul inward, found that he was living the wrong life; yet, nobody knew the right one.

Dostoevsky wrote about Don Quixote, that Don Quixote was guilty of one thing: not being a genius.

Tolstoy was a genius.

He was guilty of being a solitary person.

He wished to transform mankind one by one.

No one has ever succeeded in accomplishing that in an epic.

■

It's necessary to speak directly.

I'm searching for a beginning for the exposition—the exposition of my book.

It will discuss various aspects of plot structures in literature.[8]

---

[8] In his essay "Sterne's *Tristram Shandy*: Stylistic Commentary," Shklovsky discusses the structure of a literary novel and the differences between story (*fabula*) and plot (*syuzhet*). In this Formalist approach, story is essentially the temporal-causal se-

How nothing in literature begins from a beginning. Rather it's a collection of various inveterate situations that have a variety of their own expositions and denouements.

When a new machine is invented, its separate parts have been invented a long time ago—they existed long before.

You can see this by looking at the steam engine; it retains the old elements of a pump system, which is subsequently converted into an air-driven machine, a machine that works to create a vacuum. The piston, under the pressure of air, plunges into that vacuum and makes the first step.

Vertically upward.

Then they invented the pump engine.

In the outskirts of London, on one of the streets, there was a water-pump. The water ran on a mill wheel. The mill wheel *was* the engine. Its predecessor, however, was already in use—the knife-sharpening machine, for example, that worked with a crankshaft.

Its axle made a straight, as well as a rotating, movement.

The invention of the steam engine unified all of these existing machines into one, and at the same time added the movement of the piston.

There was no reason to retrieve the water mill from the past.

Next, they loaded the perfected steam engine onto the wagon.

The word *parovoz* (train) somehow reminds or is reminiscent of the word *povozka* (cart).[9] Later, other machines replaced the steam engine.

When Pushkin described the beginning of an inspired work in his po-

---

quence of narrated events. Its formula, capable of infinite extension, is always "because of A, then B." Plot, however, becomes the defamiliarized story that gets distorted in the process of telling. The ways of "plotting" a story are innumerable, but all involve some kind of disarrangement of what is usually considered a natural, or real-life, sequence of events.

[9] In Russian "train" is *parovoz* = par (steam) + o + voz (carriage) and "cart" is *povozka* = po (on) + voz (carriage) + ka. The common root in both words is *voz* (carriage).

ems, the "old acquaintances, the fruits of all my dreams," he wasn't inventing a new structure. He was using his own, already existing, poetic form.

Every invention is like a montage:[10] sometimes the traces of this montage get swept away; a new conversation, a new creative phase begins.

But the history of art is different from the history of technology in the way that its previous creations don't die or turn into mere artifacts. The old is resurrected in a new union.

And so, at some point a bent rod connected with a string was used as a bow, and antiquity remembered the origins of the lyre and the bow.

In modern literature, and particularly in drama, we see various methods for framing the beginning of a work—the creation of conflict.

Let's take *The Inspector General*.

The initial staging of the opening is done through an announcement, the unpleasant news given by the Mayor: "There is a government inspector on his way here."

Second—the appearance of Bobchinsky and Dobchinsky, who tell about a certain man staying at the hotel.

We are told that this man is wearing civilian clothes and is kind of good looking.

The second announcement doesn't contradict the opening yet, but the

10 The French term *montage* was first introduced to film vocabulary in 1914, as a process or technique of selecting, editing, and piecing together separate sections of film to form a continuous whole. The term was first used by Vsevolod Pudovkin in *On Film Technique*, and functioned in association with linkage and unification. However in the early 1920s it became one of the key aspects of Formalist theory that was based on conflict, opposition, and deautomatization. According to Sergei Eisenstein, the filmic image was not to be used only to represent reality; rather it was a bundle rich in material, which could be made to signify the structuring of meaning-forming oppositions. In this context, Shklovsky uses the idea of montage and Tolstoy's term "labyrinths of linkages" to show the interconnections and at the same time contradictions of theme, plot, and movement both within an individual work and for literature as a whole.

second act has already begun by Osip's story and Khlestakov's own monologue. He is already identified by Bobchinsky and Dobchinsky. The inn-
keeper has told him (them) that this man is from St. Petersburg. We are
given a name—Khlestakov—and told that he has been mysteriously held
off in the town.

It's as if the opening required a combination of three elements.

At the same time the opening is a step forward, the first step of the action toward the investigation of the event with the help of the given circumstances, as Pushkin pointed out while analyzing the play.

We have been given a family and the description of Khlestakov.

But then the investigation develops by means of Khlestakov himself
and the town's Mayor.

Khlestakov lies. They feed him and offer him drinks.

He lies compulsively out of hunger, as a hungry man who has suddenly
been fed. He frightens everyone.

The opening starts the movement, a procession of oppositional instances that collide with each other.

The Mayor is afraid of Khlestakov.

Khlestakov is afraid of the Mayor.

They frighten each other.

The Mayor's wife is bored, she's curious, she quarrels with her daughter because, in a way, the daughter gives away the mother's real age.

The lady's character becomes satirical through the conflict with her
daughter—they are jealous of each other.

That's why the opening is almost inseparable from the main act.

There are other types of expositions.

Here's another one: the conversation in an aristocratic house about the
possibility of war, about Napoleon's occupation of new duchies—this
gives you an impression of what's going on and what will happen next.

Pierre Bezukhov's conversation with Andrei Bolkonsky gives you an introduction to Bolkonsky's situation.

He is burdened by a woman whom he once loved.

■

Plays and novels have a whole range of expositions within expositions and denouements within denouements—their own reversals.

Sometimes they unravel from the very beginning. Sometimes this is delayed until almost the middle of the work.

The latter can be seen in *Dead Souls*.

A britzka arrives. It's slightly different from a carriage.

We hear a conversation between two peasants who are astonished by the britzka: sturdy wheels, one can go a long distance on such wheels.

Then we see the man who has arrived in it.

And then his strange behavior begins.

He talks to everybody about the same thing—buying dead souls.

And no one interrupts him. Everyone goes along with it: you can sell serfs even if they're dead, the dead serf is still regarded as a commodity. And only after many chapters, many mysterious chapters, we hear the story of Chichikov, his ideas, and an explanation of what exactly he's trying to do.

■

I am trying to write a book about plot, about the existence of different kinds of plot, about how a plot lives, how it dies, and why it gets revived.

And so I've already started talking about expositions.

We should briefly talk about denouements.

Chekhov said that works usually ended with a person's departure, or death.

Or marriage.

Tolstoy demonstrated that marriage could serve as an opening to a work, the beginning of its construction, rather than its end.

■

I'll try to explain, concisely, and perhaps incomprehensibly, why *traveling plots* exist.

Why they disappear from their previous cultures or epochs.

Traveling plots aren't even formally recorded.

In any case, a new epoch will seek out the same old plot.

However, these plots get transformed.

How they travel and how they get transformed, how they get transformed throughout the epochs and by various authors is what I'll talk about in this concise book, a book that cost me a lot of effort, because I had been writing it in the past as well, while talking to myself about it.

Traveling plots exist like tribes that intermingle or fight each other, and are discovered in their conflicts and transformations.

Some of Boccaccio's stories are repeated anecdotes; others exist as arguments against the plot as an assertion of different values.

Traveling plots show that those people, those individuals who pass for inspector generals or angels, bearing the Last Judgement and bringing retribution, are to a certain degree shameless braggers.

They make mistakes, and even the authors themselves didn't notice their faults for a long time.

In *Anna Karenina*, for example, the address where the tragedy will take place is incorrect.

The novel is not about vengeance, but a judgment about the judgement; the laws are being re-examined. Re-examined rather unwillingly. We see how the autumn leaves fallen from trees decay, how they turn into new soil.

Finally, I will try to write about Chekhov, who died at the age when people today, sometimes mistakenly, want to become members of the Writers' Union. They remind me of the characters in Michelangelo's *Last Judgment*.

The faces that were depicted there apparently belonged to critics whom Michelangelo didn't like.

The most incredible thing for me, though, is that I'm not a young man anymore, I am eighty-eight, and no one offers me a seat in the tram, but that custom has passed, and so has my own habit of walking in the city that I love so much.

But the strangest thing was that I saw myself in my old library, the remains of all my libraries that I once had and lost.

I approach them like my Lutheran grandfather approached the cemetery gates.

It was an Orthodox cemetery with a Lutheran one right next to it. He had requested that Anna Sevastyanovna, an Orthodox, bury their children next to a Lutheran cemetery. He watched over his children's graves from behind the gates—the gates were a product of his own imagination.

Yet the most important thing for me was the discovery that in all those books there was a presentiment, a foretelling, dreams, hints about some mysterious events—it was the same even with Homer.

To take a break, I am inserting here a page from one of my old manuscripts.

■

And so the most incredible thing is that I'm so old that soon I'll start exaggerating my actual age.

But what's even more incredible to me is Chekhov—and I've read him in the light of Marx, in the appendix of the journal *Niva*, those little yellow pamphlets—and I remember how those who used to laugh at Chekhonte[11] and mix him up with Leikin,[12] or if they were writers, they tried to compare themselves to him, they would go up to him, pretend to be something; meanwhile back at home they'd mark the wall to see how much they'd grown.

I'll remind you of the drama at the theater in St. Petersburg, at the per-

[11] Anton Chekhov (1860–1904) first started writing and publishing short humoresques in 1880 under the pen name Antosha Chekhonte.

[12] Nikolai Leikin (1841–1906), Chekhov's first publisher and editor of the St. Petersburg-based humorous journal *Oskolki*.

formance of *The Seagull*, when among the audience some people howled with envy, others smelled the gunpowder that was about to blow them up.

And still others were simply stunned.

These were the years in the life of a person who will someday be compared to Shakespeare, because this guilty man, with his guilty play *The Seagull*, narrates the story of what a person is in nature, in art, and why mediocre people hate the young and perhaps even geniuses.

Treplev was such a person.

I am trying to show that the immortality of art lies in correlations. No, how about this: I will find direct—not traces—buttresses to the arches of *The Seagull*, the lake of the Seagull, the theater by the lake—Treplev and his mother—with Shakespeare's *Hamlet*.

Hamlet is resurrected and he sees how the world has been overturned.

The world, meanwhile, is afraid of even the smallest changes and doesn't like the new.

And so, I'm leaving you. At the threshold of my book.

I need to go rest, and then I still have to correct the proofs and go to the printer.

I wish you happiness.

I wish you restlessness,

alarming dreams.

And a yearning for the future.

So long.

IV. THREE BOOKS—THREE PREFACES: A GUIDE

I have already apologized for the difficult content of this book.

Two books, in fact: one on the history of plot, and the other, let's say, on the history of specific plots, primarily those of Tolstoy, Chekhov, and Pushkin—I am reversing the chronological order.

The two books are unified in one—the third—book.

This required the composition of the order itself in the arrangement of the material.

It required a guide.

First of all, the title, as well as the material that lies in the foundation of the construction, must somehow open the book, whether we want it to or not.

This is why this book opens with the second chapter, the one that's titled "Energy of Delusion."

Before that, we have three prefaces.

If the swan, crab, and pike exist,[13] and if in transforming themselves they also transform their burden, then in the coming chapters you will see the difficulties a great writer must face as he begins and tries to finish his work.

Moreover, it's as if he *needs* those difficulties.

He needs them because in their various forms they are the means through which he is trying to say something that he can say only in one way.

By linking ideas to situations.

And so.

How shall we start? We still have some time.

We must explain how all of this came about, from where all these "delusions" originated.

Whether it was only Tolstoy's phenomenon or a phenomenon on a larger scale, and how it occurred—we're giving the history of linkages, if you will.

Which is why we begin with *The Decameron*.

Tolstoy wasn't too fond of *The Decameron* and used to say that it was the beginning of so-called "erotic literature."

A lifeless phrase, and certainly it didn't start there.

In its structure, *The Decameron* is an assemblage, and it's essential to us

13 Ivan Krylov's (1769–1844) famous fable about a swan, a crab, and a pike pulling a loaded cart; the swan striving to reach the sky, the crab crawling backwards, and the pike dragging it toward the water.

for that reason: it contains the laws of a compositional arrangement, and, moreover, is narrated in a way that protects the author from being held responsible for its contents.

We see how the initial difficulty, the first delusion in almost every story in *The Decameron* is in the conflict.

The conflict that a shipwrecked man, or a man robbed by a prostitute, or, better yet, a man mocked by his own wife, has found himself in.

The most varied difficulties and the suddenness of their resolutions are the basis of the so-called plot; this premise can be readily seen in the work's opening.

Here we talk about the expositions—beginnings and endings of compositions.

Chapter four.

But all of these things change.

The expositions and difficulties for Boccaccio aren't the same difficulties experienced by Pushkin and Tolstoy.

Even though Pushkin says that he is surrounded by his "old acquaintances," he is mainly working on his own material, chiselling it like a mason.

But as a beginning we should mention the fate of the woman, who was sent to her future husband as a bride, but who was passed around from hand to hand and as a result was able to start a happy life.

We'll see that this is not a simple denouement, but the parody of an old plot.

Parody and reinvention of plot—this is the title of the second book within this current one.[14]

Now let's talk about the author's personal affairs.

[14] The term "reinvention" (*pereosmyslivanie*) is used throughout the text to explain the process of recreating or re-conceptualizing a plot that existed in some other form. As Shklovsky paraphrases Chekhov's method: the plot must be new, and the story doesn't matter. A good example of *plot reinvention* is Chekhov's "The Steppe," which as Shklovsky illustrates throughout the book, re-envisions the plot of Gogol's *Dead Souls*, creating a new form.

He does something in the preface; in the first, second, and third parts, he apologizes.

He is imperfect, like any other author.

He is also entangled in this chaos that's called life.

And he is also going through a reinvention.

So, we mentioned parody and reinvention—chapter five.

Let's see how this is done.

Boccaccio started *The Decameron* by giving a description of the plague. This fascinating description was taken from the early writings about the plague in ancient Greece.

Why is this important?

It's explained in the afterword.

The plague has wiped out all prejudices and rules, and the writer is starting with a clean sheet of paper.

He's choosing what to put on that sheet. He's the master, it is up to him to choose any impeded form from a variety of impediments.[15]

It's important for the writer to begin with something that he lived for, something that he was, something that even the plague couldn't destroy.

I'll start with *The Captain's Daughter*.

I will talk about epigraphs, why and how they're used.

This story has a direct association with another story, which I'll provisionally call, as its author did, "The Snowstorm."

---

[15] In his early literary criticism, and mainly in the essay "Art as Technique" (1917), Shklovsky maintained that readers tended to glide blindly over a smooth and familiar verbal surface; to revive their ability to perceive, the Formalists devised a method of distorting ordinary events with such conceptual devices as defamiliarization or estrangement (*ostranenie*) and impediment (*zatrudnenie*). Through an impeded form, the author presents the familiar objects of the real world in great intricacy in order to attract and hold his reader's full attention. Perception, as Shklovsky argued, is an end in itself and literature is successful not by the presence of a certain kind of content or images, but by its ability to make the reader look with an exceptionally high level of awareness—of himself and of the world.

What was the author trying to do?

It's as if he took another author's—the excellent memoirist Aksakov's[16] —description of a snowstorm. A realistic picture, but a picture that was brand-new, that was never described before in this way.

He himself remarks that this was previously written in such and such journal, and points out where to find it.

There are two kinds of people in "The Snowstorm."

The first is a gentleman—he is afraid.

And rightly so.

Then there are the peasant coachmen.

Here, in the second story, originates Tolstoy's "The Snowstorm."

The stoic attitude toward disaster, the re-evaluation of disaster, is rendered in this piece where Tolstoy is returning home in his sleep.

It wasn't really a disaster, it was his estate at Yasnaya Polyana, and we, the reader, partly recognize its ponds.

This work, as we'll show, is connected with Tolstoy's reality and his recollections of literature from the past.

The person who wrote "The Snowstorm" had understood a lot after reading *The Captain's Daughter*.

To be sure, the account of "The Snowstorm," just as the epigraphs in *The Captain's Daughter*, is the history of the search for perspective.

I'll paraphrase—the search for a changing perspective on the changing world.

In Pushkin and in Tolstoy.

Let's see how detail comes into play in all this.

The realistic detail that seems to suddenly enrich the piece and attest to reality, and doesn't seem artificial.

The reality of the existence of elements—in their conflicts.

---

16 Sergei Aksakov (1791–1859), writer best known for his nostalgic descriptions of the Orenburg region. Aksakov's chief work, *Family Chronicle* (1856), is a partly fictionalized picture of country life in the days of serfdom.

Those elements in literature are recounted in various ways.

In early Russian literature, the author pieced together works that were already canonized in the light of tradition.

We could say that this reminds us of the Latin *centones*, poems composed entirely from someone else's lines. A *cento* was a garment patched with various cloths. Later the *cento* becomes *commedia dell'arte*, the unexpected-expected, because, again, it depends on tradition.

But we won't dwell on this for too long.

Everything goes into the work.

The observation made by the traveler in "The Snowstorm" about the calmness of people engaged in work—the coachmen, the calmness of people while they battle the storm—it will recur in Tolstoy. This is the calmness of the soldiers from *War and Peace* and the calmness of Kutuzov.

I'm getting far ahead of myself, but this book is called *Energy of Delusion*.

The writer, the great writer, is working with words created long before him, with instances and images that were created centuries ago, yet he is free—because he is reinventing everything.

Kutuzov is unpredictable.

So is his behavior.

Every literary work is a brand-new montage of the world, a new unpredictability, a new occurrence.

And so after writing stories like "The Raid" and "The Wood-Felling," a system of sketch-writing is developed that appears in a new form prompted as if by Turgenev's[17] *Notes of a Hunter*: I'm talking about *The Sevastopol Sketches*.

Thus I'm like a guide through a museum or a city, who explains why the streets curve. There used to be a wall here, now we have gates, hence the curve of the street. There was a bend behind the wall, too, but that's be-

---

[17] Ivan Turgenev (1818–83), great Russian writer from the Ukraine, author of *Fathers and Sons* (1861). Tolstoy was introduced to Turgenev by his sister, Countess Maria Tolstaya, who was having a lingering affair with the older writer.

cause of the hill. The wall was bent according to the curve of the street; the curve of the street replicated the bend of the hill.

We have reached the history of writing *Anna Karenina*.

Tolstoy placed his epigraph the way he would hang a lock on the gates—an epigraph that's supposed to be the key to his work, the guide.

It turned out to be a riddle.

A detailed discussion of *Anna Karenina*.

The unpredictable metamorphosis of the characters and their values.

The "locks" and riddles of the heroes.

Their topicality.

The novel is written through a method of inner monologues, i.e., the focal point in the novel, the set-up of the camera keeps changing, and so do the ways of relating to the world.

It is the multitude of methods of correlation that reveals the purpose of life.

Art is not just a way of relating to life, but also its montage.

In order to understand it, we'll examine novels: *Anna Karenina* opens as if from the world of Stiva Oblonsky, the world of an estranged person who is made into a parody, a popular character.

But the popularity of this handsome, considerably young man's crisis is juxtaposed with his sister's tragedy.

This is a montage. We'll have to understand it.

At the end of the novel Anna returns to her world, the estranged world of catastrophes. Note how provident, and at the same time how wasteful, art can be.

The heroine from Pushkin's fragment ("At the corner of a little square stood a carriage") doesn't have a surname. She has left her husband and in turn sees her own lover leaving, without turning around, running like a schoolboy from his lesson. It's as if this fragment became the first sketch of Vronsky's departure in *Anna Karenina*.

This observation—be it Pushkin's or Tolstoy's—is the revelation of a single essence.

The heroine of Pushkin's unfinished novel and Anna Karenina both see the same thing—a man who is so easily breaking their life, who is purposefully frivolous.

Now I'm talking about the philosophy of frivolity because *Anna Karenina* is a novel of double-standard morals, the cat-and-mouse game, where the mouse—the woman—is not allowed to pass, while the cat—the man—is so easily and fondly let through.

Schopenhauer held that adultery committed by men was natural, whereas for women—it was unnatural.

A. Fet[18] agreed with him and translated it into Russian.

Which Tolstoy read, although it's more likely that he read it in the original.

But speaking of Tolstoy as a phenomenon of historical continuity, we must decide of which epoch:

—before this epoch; during its collapse; or after.

Each great book and each epoch is a judgment on life, and, incidentally, let's note how the structure of a trial—the speeches of the defendant and prosecutor, the defense of the accused—has left its mark on or has been used in the history of the novel.

Let's not forget that in the classical age, in Greece, the defendant's testimony and the evidence given by the plaintiff were written down by the official scribe by the order of the plaintiff, and then studied only by him, the plaintiff. And then there were orators, speechwriters (logographs), who prided themselves on the excellence of their talent. We even know the name of one such man—Lycaeus.

The elements of a trial are also evident in the big novel *Aethiopica*.[19]

---

18 Afanasi Fet (1822–92), poet, critic and friend of Tolstoy who translated and introduced Tolstoy to the works of Schopenhauer. He and Strakhov were Tolstoy's closest friends in the '70s. Fet later compiled a book of memoirs called *My Recollections*, which contained inaccurate quotations from the letters of Turgenev and Tolstoy.

19 The ancient novel by third-century Greek writer Heliodorus of Emesa, was first brought to light during the Renaissance. The novel, which takes place in

The stories about life are being reinvented.

Then we shift to the period in Tolstoy's life after *Anna Karenina*.

Resurrection.

"The Death of Ivan Ilych," which I'll mention in passing.

"Strider."

Hadji Murad.

Resurrection: the whole novel is based on a trial.

The reversals in this novel occur from a judicial blunder, but behind those blunders are the mistakes of the moral values—the mores of those times, mistakes in justice, and the greatest mistake, which Tolstoy revealed in the novel, was that his intention was to write a novel about the resurrection of a man who had seduced a woman, he was guilty, but seeing *her* being accused in the trial and about to be sent to hard labor, he is as if resurrected and acts in her defense.

But Tolstoy's words—"the energy of delusion"—are highly ironic with regard to himself.

He excuses himself from the agonizing work on *Anna Karenina* with that phrase, he tries to justify himself in front of the publisher, in front of his wife, who is astonished: the novel is hardly moving along and is so strangely interrupted, the author leaves and goes hunting rabbits.

Nekhlyudov who thinks he is a good, kind man, is certain that he will be resurrected; but in the middle of his work Tolstoy realizes—and at first this makes his wife glad—that Nekhlyudov won't marry Katyusha Maslova. Sofia Andreevna agrees, it's right, but it turns out it's not Nekhlyudov who is resurrected, who—as Tolstoy notes in the beginning of the novel—is happy with himself for committing a heroic deed, while this happiness in Tolstoy is somewhat ironically synchronized with the ringing of the bells—it's Easter.

Ethiopia, opens in the middle of the story with a mystery that is solved for the reader only through a complex thread of retrospective narratives or dialogues in which various characters describe their adventures.

The repentance of Nekhlyudov comes almost as a triumph.

However, it's Katyusha Maslova who is being resurrected.

Who refuses to accept the sacrifice offered by a man she loved.

She commits the heroic deed because she still loves.

She doesn't betray her love.

She protects him from making a sacrifice.

But you'll read about all that here in this rather lengthy book.

I myself have wandered, like a traveler who is caught in a snowstorm and who puts his faith only in the strength of the horses and the coachmen's experience.

Which is why at the end I'll repeat the discussion on storyline and plot, on beginnings and endings of works.

I'll try to finish one of my books in this book on the history of plot.

The blizzards of history are powerful and endless.

The fault of people—our ancestors' and our own fault in front of our neighbors—is that we don't speak intelligibly in front of our children, and that we haven't committed enough heroic deeds. The search for truth is through the experience of conflict, through experienced difficulties.

Of course, life is complex.

The snowstorm might turn into a trip in a troika.

It might turn into the troika itself.

And then it will start flying.

Tearing away, it will take off and fly: I am talking about the troika-bird.

We are less sincere and even less eloquent than the old Orlov strider, whom I envision presiding at the Great Judgment over mankind.

■　■　■

So there are two principles by which I'm assembling the material in this book.

The first principle is that I will maintain a general chronology: Pushkin, Tolstoy, Chekhov.

And with each of these I'll maintain his own place in time.

Beside this, I bring in the second principle for organizing the material—
the notion of plot itself;

the transformation of its concept;

the storyline and reversals;

the redundancy of certain elements in plot and the use of fully exhausted plots as parody.

The shift from exhausted plot to parody and the simultaneous reinvention of plot is an important factor. Here we discuss Cervantes.

But we begin with *The Decameron*.

Because with Bocaccio we have a collection of the beginnings of most plots, especially the plots concerning relationships between men and women.

The Decameron is an encyclopedia of various plot constructions.

In different parts of this book we'll mention stories from *The Decameron*: various stories, various ways of constructing relationships, various means to overcome contradictions.

But we need to single out two stories.

The history of Greek novels has had a great number of "storied" reversals that preserve the heroes' virginity.

The Decameron has a story on this topic that stands out as one of the best.

It's about a Sultan's daughter; her name is Alatiel.

Alatiel, with great pleasure, passes from one man to another, and then enters a happy life with her husband.

This is an apparent parody, but at the same time it's a reinvention of plot, the introduction of a new prototype, the hero's relationship with reality and ancient laws.

The second is a story about Lady Filippa from the small town of Prato. Summoned to the trial, the brave Lady announces that she won't comply with the laws because they were written by men, who judge women based on them.

In an entirely transformed version, this subject will appear in *Anna Karenina*.

Just like the subject of old age.

In closing, I'll say this—the difference is between the morals of passion and the morals of convention.

Another parody in *The Decameron* is the story about the old husband, the judge; a pirate has kidnapped his young wife; when the husband comes to take her back, she says: you should have thought about this earlier, I'm staying with the man with the exciting profession.

A reinvented version of this can be seen in Tolstoy's *Anna Karenina*. Anna says that she is happy as a hungry person who finally gets to eat— she's given bread.

It is real life that throbs beneath the rules of moral values. Tolstoy talks about this in a straightforward way.

This is how *traveling plots* emerge.

Motives and situations travel from plot to plot, but even before that, the circumstances of life pass from one epoch to another.

The writer uses plot to cleanse the world.

It's as if the world gets entangled and dusty.

The writer wipes the mirror of consciousness with his plot.

And so it's as if various writers in their own time grope for the same pattern, the same notch in that endless "labyrinth of linkages,"[20] in the chaos that's called life.

It's a rite of passage—the existence of the same circumstances of life.

Thus we arrive at the question of *Anna Karenina*'s historiography, a question which Tolstoy himself called the "energy of delusion." But before that let's note how within *Anna Karenina*'s plot we have Pushkin's plot, the story of his fragment—two fragments: "The guests were assembling at the country house" and "At the corner of a little square stood a carriage."

[20] This is a term that Tolstoy used in one of his letters to Strakhov calling art "a labyrinth of linkages" and discussing how nonsensical is the search for isolate ideas in an artistic work. Shklovsky reinvents this term for his own purposes to show the organic development and changes of plot construction in literature.

The semblance of these plots creates an illusion of plagiarism on Tolstoy's part. But this is not the case. It's just perceiving the same reality.

And so when we begin writing about the epigraph to *Anna Karenina* (it will be the last part of our chapter on the novel), we'll point out how Russian literature has arrived at the question of what is crime and what is necessity.

For that's in Dostoevsky's *Crime and Punishment*.

It's established in Dostoevsky that crime is still a crime; even if we discarded religion, moral values would remain.

From one school to another, generations have conveyed the same themes of love in its extreme forms, desire, wealth, the question of human freedom—the theme of *Hadji Murad*.

And so today's topic is the relationship between a man and a woman, the construction of family, marriage.

Before even starting this book I'll say: the same problem can be solved in various ways by the same author.

In Tolstoy: "The Kreutzer Sonata," "The Devil," *Anna Karenina*.

At the same time, he wrote "Idyll." A pastoral tale about love in the village.

But what's important to us is that Tolstoy talks about infidelity along with the question of property.

A person says "my land," instead of "we are of the land."

Perhaps the phrase will sound odd.

But listen to Nikolai Aseev's verses:

The gulls cried—Whose are you? Whose are you?
We answered—Nobody's.[21]

Now take a look at the real words of the Great Inca, as he stood chained in front of Francisco Pizarro. He said: You, foreigners, say "my land," but you should say, "we are of the land." Words pronounced before he was executed.

[21] From "A Hungarian Song" (1916).

When visitors came to see the great actor Schepkin, his mother would ask: "Whose are you?" The answers varied from time to time: "We are of the state" or "We are of the Morozovs."

And once they even said: "We are of God."

We should talk about Strider here. He thought a great deal about men and property. He pondered to himself:

> At that time I couldn't at all understand what they meant by speaking of *me* as being man's property. The words "*my* horse" applied to me . . . seemed as strange as to say "my earth," "my air," "my water." . . . People considered that I did not belong to God and to myself, as is natural to all living creatures, but that I belonged to the stud groom.

A man says "my wife," even if she's not his wife anymore.

What's important is the fact that there is no single solution here, nothing is brought to a single resolution.

Then we will talk about Chekhov.

Among other things, how *The Seagull* flies over Hamlet's sea.

Right before this we'll talk about Orestes, whose fate Hamlet replicates almost exactly—but with a slight change.

Consequently, the question about plot, the *traveling plot*, emerges again.

Then again the circle comes back to *The Decameron*, where we find various ways of resolving these conflicts.

At this point we need to express a thought. We have been groping, searching for it for a long time now.

It came to us recently.

At the bottom of various approaches to resolve conflicts lie multitudes of moral values.

There are as many values as stars in the sky.

But without the stars, even the birds get lost.

After that, and along with it, the question of storyline and plot arises for the second time, the question about the beginnings and endings of works—compositions.

All of these things have no ending. A happy ending doesn't propose a reformation of the world.

■

In the Roman army, during battles, they would put the veterans in the third row.

Surgery back then was not advanced, people weren't cured properly, there was a lot of work involved in digging the trenches, and the older men weren't happy to be at war.

One of the Roman classics described how an older soldier was sucking on his commander's finger so the commander could regain his senses:

—the old soldier had lost his teeth a long time ago.

But in battles the veterans stood in the ranks, in the third row.

When things would get bad, difficult, when the enemy wouldn't back down, then the older men, experienced in battles, adept in using the sword and shield, would step forward, entering the battleground with a menacing roar: "The third guard is here!"

2

ENERGY OF DELUSION

Going through millions of possible combinations in order to select one out of a million is terribly difficult.
LEV TOLSTOY, from a letter to A. Fet, November 17, 1870

The title of this chapter is used with Lev Nikolaevich Tolstoy's permission. He wrote to N. Strakhov in April, 1878, that he felt unprepared for the work, unprepared for the strain; the real strain comes after the subject has been found and selected.

He consoles Strakhov, who is complaining about the difficulty of work:

I know this feeling very well—even now, I have been experiencing it lately: everything seems to be ready for writing—for fulfilling my earthly duty, what's missing is the urge to believe in myself, the belief in the importance of my task, I'm lacking the energy of delusion; an earthly, spontaneous energy that's impossible to invent. And it's impossible to begin without it.

This is the way they describe the uncontrolled powers of nature, which erupt in various and unpredictable ways, creating the chaos that we call this world.

With a light heart, Vladimir Mayakovsky once wrote about the things of "the other world":[22]

[22] Vladimir Mayakovsky (1893–1930), Shklovsky's close friend and foremost poet of the Futurist movement. *O Mayakovskom* (1940), which was written ten years after Mayakovsky's suicide, is perhaps the best "anti-biographical" biography written by Shklovsky. It gives brilliant insight into the poet's life and art.

It's unknown whose old draft this is.

The first failed draft of the whale.

Nothing happens without effort. Flowers bloom and birds return in time only after many hours of preparation.

The world seems to protest against the first attempts in the plan of creation, that is—coming to terms with it.

Overcoming the past, we move forward, noting the difference between intention and accomplishment.

■

Later, in his article on Maupassant, Tolstoy wrote that talent helped the writer to "see things in their real form."[23]

If he is wrong in his representation of the world, his talent will show the impossibility of that construction, will force him to write the truth.

The energy of delusion—the energy of searching freely—never left Tolstoy.

In his conception of *War and Peace* he begins writing about Kutuzov.

He comes up with a flawed sketch of the character, even though it contains the real facts and the real traits.

But the energy of delusion, the energy of trials, experiments, the energy of investigation compels him to describe again—a different, a real person. This takes him years.

[23] In this review (April 2, 1894) Tolstoy wrote: "In this, indeed, does the remarkable quality of every true talent consist, so long as it does not do violence to itself under the influence of a false theory, that it teaches its possessor, leads him on over the path of moral development, makes him love what is worthy of love, and hate what is worthy of hatred. An artist is an artist for the very reason that he sees the objects, not as he wants to see them, but as they are. The bearer of talent—man—may make mistakes, but the talent, as soon as the reins are given to it, as was done by Maupassant in his stories, will reveal and lay bare the subject and will make the writer love it, if it is worthy of love, and hate it, if it is worthy of hatred."

He wants to understand Alexander I, but the energy of delusion, the energy of search erases the triumphant portrayal of the Emperor, who is thought of as the patron of history—and the heroic character disappears. He is moved to the background of the novel.

Tolstoy then tried to put the aristocrat Andrei Bolkonsky into the center of the novel, someone who would understand and analyze everything. This didn't work either.

He succeeded in something else—the character of Tushin.

Andrei Bolkonsky would have liked to treat Tushin with condescension, call him "Chinese," as if he were a person from a different group, an outsider, whom one shouldn't bother taking interest in.

And this intolerance in the novel, as if without a question, becomes conflicted with truth.

Initially, according to his plan, Tolstoy is examining Prince Anatole Kuragin with much anticipation, wanting to show him among the heroes of the nation. He turns out to be a connoisseur of life. And not only of life, but a connoisseur of living at someone else's expense, a polished liar.

The energy of delusion is the search for truth in a novel.

In the first drafts, Anna Karenina is not beautiful; she is fat and ungraceful, although charming.

She is not too intelligent.

She has a stout, sensible, kindhearted husband; he is much older than she. Karenina falls in love with a younger man, much younger than herself. As a woman, she is guilty in her husband's and society's eye. She is the kind of woman that Dumas called a "female Cain." That was the French verdict. Or at least, Dumas's.

The epigraph to the novel—"Vengeance is mine, and I will repay"—is like an amnesty.

You don't have to kill her; conscience will do it.

But truth is stronger than prejudice.

Gradually, Anna Karenina evolves into a charismatic figure. And Lev

Nikolaevich writes to his aunt and friend, Aleksandra Tolstaya,[24] an eccentric woman with whom he exchanged letters in the manner of Rousseau. He writes that he has adopted Anna as a daughter, she has become his own.

As a result of various trials, or call them rough drafts, Karenin is rehabilitated: the old husband turns out to be not a machine, but a human being. But he is a weak delusion, a person whose kindness and torments aren't necessary.

The history of literature is the history of a search for heroes. One can also say that it's a compilation of the history of delusions.

And no one will contradict the fact that a genius isn't afraid of getting lost, because talent will not only show the way out, but talent, one may say, demands delusions, for it demands strain, nourishment, material, it demands a labyrinth of linkages into which it has been called to investigate.

I have mentioned the *traveling plots*. Plots travel throughout a culture that is changing.

They travel through a changing country.

This is why they are interpreted in various ways. It's as if they are dressed in unrelated pieces of semantic material, different from their original intent. They travel without changing their clothes, through reinvention.

At the turn of the century—an epoch of a fermenting revolution, the discovery of new lands, collapsing monarchies—the desire for change, the search in art amplifies.

Tolstoy's *The Cossacks* is an ingeniously resolved plot of this kind.

And just as a snowstorm can become visible through the blizzard and its "material"—the snow, the whorl, expanding in itself, growing from within, pulling everything into a spiral of great masses, mixing and moving everything—so does *The Cossacks* contain in itself the energy of Tol-

[24] Aleksandra Tolstaya (1817–1904), Tolstoy's first cousin.

stoy's delusion of "that" period, which will be repeated, expanding into *War and Peace*, *Anna Karenina*, *Resurrection*, and *Hadji Murad*.

In order to see the linkage of circumstances, Tolstoy must keep moving.

■

Tolstoy is in the Caucasus.

He left for the Caucasus as a young man without any money or documents. It's almost like the story of Robinson Crusoe.

He wanted to fall in love and make friends.

He did fall in love.

Then got disappointed.

He tried to describe it. Made various notes. Began with the intention of creating a series of sketches, describing the beautiful ancient land—the land of the Terek Cossacks.

The description of the Terek, along which lie the villages, was initially written as a sketch. Later this sketch evolved and became the fourth part of the great short novel *The Cossacks*.

It took him ten years to write the novel. The names of the heroes changed at different stages of the work. The setting shifted. The expositions and denouements changed.

One version replaced another.

What kind of distinction did Tolstoy want to make? What was his first problem, the first observation of a conflict?

In the novel, Tolstoy is describing Olenin's feelings:

> Olenin was a young man who had never managed to complete a university course, who did not work (he held a merely nominal post in some government office), who had squandered half his inheritance, a man who, at the age of twenty-four, had yet to decide on a career. He was what the Moscow society would call *un jeune homme*.

Olenin's friends are disappointed: why is he, a well-to-do person with good connections, leaving for the Caucasus without even the rank of an officer?

He could live in Moscow.

They would find a position for him, and he would marry someone rich, like Tolstoy's father married a rich woman, whom he could even, unexpectedly, love. But Olenin has his own fate—it's nothing new, this isn't the first time it's been described.

But it's described *like this* for the first time.

This is also the fate of Pushkin's Aleko ("The Gypsies"), who ran from his apparently prosperous life to the gypsies, and couldn't live among them.

Olenin wasn't exiled from anywhere, he is a person admired by his friends, and even believes he loves a girl who loves him; it appears that this girl is rich and from a good family.

Olenin leaves his world for a foreign one.

In order to describe failed love, it's necessary to note that someone else loves him. In other words, I'll say this: this story is about something else.

Olenin is almost Tolstoy himself.

Disturbed by Lev's life in Yasnaya Polyana and Moscow, his brother, Nikolai,[25] was calling him to the Caucasus; the request, apparently, was finalised during their meeting in Moscow. In March 1851, Tolstoy writes to Yergolskaya[26] (original in French):

> Nikolenka's arrival was a pleasant surprise for me, since I had completely lost hope that he would come.—I was so glad to see him that I even let go some of my responsibilities ... Now, I am in seclusion once again, and I

[25] Nikolai Tolstoy (1823–60), Tolstoy's eldest brother; of all his brothers, Tolstoy loved and respected Nikolai the most. The portrait of the artillery captain Tushin in *War and Peace* was modeled on Nikolai, as Tolstoy noted in 1908.

[26] Tatyana Yergolskaya (1792–1874), a distant cousin, the grand-daughter of Prince Nikolai Gorchakov, who lived with the Tolstoys and was affectionately called Aunt Toinette. She had fallen in love with Count Nikolai Tolstoy at an early age, and continued to love him even after his marriage and early death. She lived in Yasnaya Polyana throughout her life and took care of the children and household. Toinette's influence on Lev Tolstoy at an important formative period of his life was enormous, as he often recalled later.

mean total seclusion: I don't go anywhere and don't receive anyone. I am making plans for spring and summer, would you approve of them? I will return to Yasnaya Polyana by the end of May for a month or two, in attempt to hold off Nikolenka for as long as I can, and then I will travel with him to the Caucasus (in case I don't succeed in anything over here).

In reality, he was already in Moscow with his brother on April 20 and from there they leave for the Caucasus, through Saratov and Astrakhan. On May 30, the brothers arrive in the Starogladkovskaya village.

Tolstoy noted in his diary the same evening: "How did I get here? I don't know. Why? Don't know either."

Tolstoy writes about Olenin: "At the age of eighteen Olenin was as free as only rich young Russians in the 1840s were . . . He had no relatives, no fatherland, no religion, no needs, no responsibilities."

Tolstoy writes how strange the life of that generation had become. They can't find a place in Nicholas's empire.

They wander on its perimeters.

They want to live, but they don't want to agree.

They can't quarrel either: they already did in December.[27]

It turns out that a person, moreover a person of noble birth, with an estate, horses, hounds, relatives, becomes an outcast—an illegitimate son. He travels to the end of the Russian world; at least that's what it was back then.

He leaves without any hope.

He takes the same road as Tolstoy—through the steppes. He passes from the Volga to the Caucasus and sees the mountains.

[27] On December 14, 1825, around 3,000 officers who had returned from the Napoleonic Wars, and who had brought with them ideals of a democratic republic, revolted against Nicholas I and his monarchy. The Decembrists' revolt was crushed in front of the Winter Palace; some were hanged and others were exiled to Siberia. Although Pushkin didn't take part in the uprising—as he was in a house arrest in Mikhaylovskoe from 1824–6—he was sympathetic to the Decembrist movement and had friends among the leaders.

Passing through this unfamiliar route, he finds a new world.

At first he feels like the mountains are a lie, like love, like everything that he read in books—it all seems unreal. But then he feels—the mountains are turning into his reality. He becomes pensive, he contemplates, assesses his duties, talks about his uncertain hopes. And in chorus of a new tragedy, the words—repeating—resonate: *the mountains!*. . .He sees the approaching mountains, with their defined contour, with their defined character in the chained, convoluted surfaces. The mountains turn into a new reality. These mountains are reality in its purest form, they aren't fictional.

These mountains had imprisoned both those who were exiled and those who came here on their own. The mountains of Pushkin and Lermontov. Through them passed Griboedov.

The Caucasus had often been described in romantic tales and variously discussed. But Olenin will perceive the Caucasus in its reality, its magnificence, and as if never seen before. His impression of the mountains is seconded by his footman Vanyushka, who says: they won't believe it back at home, how beautiful they really are.

Chapter four, as we already said, narrated almost in a geographic language, is about the Terek Cossacks, who they are, how they live, how prosperous they are, how different they are from the Russians. Already in the Caucasus, Tolstoy wrote that there was a reason why abroad the Russians were called "Cossacks." The Cossacks were Russian.

The Cossacks were Russians who couldn't endure serfdom.

Peter the Great fought hard for the port of Azov, but he lost it. The Cossacks took the Azov from the Turks long before Peter because the fort was blocking them from entering the Black Sea.

They wouldn't surrender the Azov for a long time.

Tolstoy understands how the Cossacks fought at the Azov as Russians, not as mercenaries adapted from the German model.

These good soldiers, as though by mistake, bore a comic name.

The name was made up for a game, for the young prince.

The Cossacks were good soldiers with too many shortcomings.

But Napoleon was afraid of them. Later he even wanted to create something of the sort in his own army.

The Cossacks, in essence, fought not only their own wars, but also the wars of other countries; in other words, they had become part of the landscape.

To explain this to a European we could say they were like the "pirates" of young Schiller, or the noble pirates from the Italian Renaissance.

It was out of the question for the Cossackry to leave their lands and go away, because those Cossacks, whom Tolstoy knew, had very good lands that were part of the fertile lands once conquered by the Russians.

The Cossackry is one of Russia's riddles, one that has been poorly studied. Sholokhov tried to figure it out recently in his book of long quests—*And Quiet Flows the Don*.

They are a different kind of people.

Their women are different.

They have different rules, different customs.

This is Yeroshka's Caucasus—the old Cossack, a free man who once had great fame, the best of weapons. Then he realizes: "All of it is false."

The truth is nature.

Meaning, hunting.

The truth is the real Cossackry and the real mountains. Yeroshka isn't overwhelmed by them.

Yeroshka is almost a giant. He is powerful; he has a wide chest, mighty shoulders, hands and legs that still retain muscularity. They conceal the Cossack's height.

The words that Yeroshka pronounces about Olenin's soul—"You're not loved"—are like a verdict.

Yeroshka is a man with his own morals. He has almost no faith in God, but that doesn't bother him.

He doesn't fear judgment after death.

He says: you die, and so what, you turn into grass.

Adopting the Cossack lifestyle, Olenin thinks: So what? I'll turn into grass.

He isn't afraid of the wild boars when hunting: he isn't afraid of death.

The Cossack leaves. The dispatches continue; he is at war. The woman is at home, the household is up to her, she is in charge of the bread, grapes, and cattle. Their women are beautiful, charming. Exquisite, charming creatures. They are, we might say, humans from a different galaxy, but real.

The Cossacks talk of their women with scorn, but at home they are treated with respect: the woman bears the origins of life.

And so Olenin falls in love with Maryana—one of the most beautiful women in the village.

Maryana existed in real life. We even know her name. They called her Sobolka. When she heard about Tolstoy, who was fighting in the war, she "looked at the speaker out of the corner of her eye."

His friends thought it necessary to write about this incident to Sevastopol—she looked so exquisite, smiling at the sound of Tolstoy's name.

Tolstoy, who actually lived many months in that village, was unable to create a plot that would express the essence of that life.

He kept changing one version after another, maturing as a writer.

Here he examined his childhood. Wrote something like the memoirs of a boy. Not as a boy in retrospect, but as a boy, a child, who transcribes everything he sees.

At the Terek, Tolstoy for the first time experienced the intensities of life.

He played cards here, too. He kept losing. He tried to act like the loss of thousands was nothing tragic.

He wanted to save money on bread, wine, clothes.

He found himself a friend—a Cossack resembling Lukashka. This Cossack's image was depicted with great difficulty.

Tolstoy used to say that he couldn't draw a perfect circle in one attempt. He had to spend a long time refining it.

Tolstoy studied his characters for a long time, carrying them not for nine months, like a woman bears a child, but for years.

At first he saw them as if they were his acquaintances, and ascribed to them what is usually ascribed to half-familiar people, and gradually, changing, they would become more recognizable.

The energy of delusion was the energy of studying a person; for in that study the person would undergo various situations taken from real life, and then those situations themselves would enter the personal life of Tolstoy.

He was jealous of the woman.

He didn't want to "live" with her, but he wanted to "experience her life."

And he didn't know how to build a novel that wouldn't age.

He even wanted to construct it in verse and wrote two poems.

They were not in the tradition of the panegyric.

Rather—historical songs.

They tell how the Cossacks cross the river to fight with the mountain tribes. And how some return, while others are brought home wounded or dead.

The Cossack existence is in their work, their revelries, their wars, their love, their simplicity and arrogance; they consider themselves the only real people.

Olenin was a person of his own time. There are things that Tolstoy wrote about him, which later he was forced to take out of the book, probably due to censorship. He wrote:

During the last reign, the Russian youth was being forged to live in a strange way. The entire impetus of their energy that was restrained in their everyday external activity transferred into another sphere of internal activity, and here it evolved with even greater freedom and power. The typical models of Russian youth of the 1840s bear the imprint of this disproportion between their inner development and their capacity for action, between idle philosophizing, unrestrained freedom of thought, cosmopolitism and idle but passionate love without any aim or object.

Olenin was headed into literary Utopia, the worshipped land of freedom and love.

The girl who loved him was made for a different kind of life—different, yet familiar.

He dreamt of the blue-eyed Circassian girl, who is closer to him because she is "a stranger."

This dream was refuted and then elevated by Lev Nikolaevich Tolstoy in his brilliant story "A Prisoner in the Caucasus." A poor Russian officer, a craftsman, a good son, is captured as prisoner. This involved a betrayal: his rich friend could have covered his back with a gun. Zhilin befriends a Circassian girl.

He makes clay dolls for her, he is gentle with her, and in turn she helps him escape.

Love here has nothing to do with it; this is pure friendship and faith in the universal truth of the human heart.

Singling it out from his other works, Lev Nikolaevich considered it his only simply written story.

■

Dropping out of school, young Tolstoy leaves to find his future. He has a flute with him, which he'll learn how to play; an English dictionary; a half-translated book by Sterne; and a very nice suit, made by a French tailor, which he hasn't been able to pay for, but will pay for in the next ten years. He is leaving to grow up and become a writer. But he doesn't know that there exist different kinds of customs and different kinds of freedoms. He is leaving to learn about the differences of the human heart. He is leaving to free himself from illusions.

In ancient times, they used to put Madeira on the deck, and believed that once the ship crossed the equator twice, the wine would be perfect.

I can put this sentence anywhere I like in my book; in fact, I'll put it right here or anywhere—it's like when a person is headed somewhere without having an address.

The poet isn't mad. He knows what he is undertaking. He usually starts out with irony.

How many times has the exhausted human race considered going back to primitive existence, the existence of the happy savages whom we know through isolated encounters? And so in poetry, the savages aren't those people who have wild ideas, but those who don't commit our crimes and who are not tainted by our mistakes. Rousseau acknowledged them in his remarkable book.

Pushkin followed their tracks in "The Gypsies."

The gypsies in Moldavia remember him. They don't remember clearly, but they agree on remembering that a Russian *barin*, the Russian officer Aleksandr Pushkin, could walk with the gypsies, could have a child with a gypsy woman.

In memory of that child, the gypsies almost believe that they carry a part of Pushkin's blood, and it doesn't seem fantastic at all.

To this end, René searched for happiness among primitive people.

The great yet forgotten Chateaubriand wrote about them.

Almost our contemporary—at any rate, the contemporary of all great people—Tolstoy was headed not just toward the peasantry, who were free from knowledge, from lordship, from oppression, who lived in the far steppes, almost on the frontier, the borders of the Russian empire. He was searching for his Olenin, for his René, in the genealogical books of the gentry, in the old legends of the high-born.

He kept hoping that maybe he could find this person.

Not in isolation, but with the culture that he would discover.

■

The first sketch for *The Cossacks* was called "Maryana." Then it changed to "The Fugitive."

A man has arrived in the Caucasus. He is an officer, and he lives in the house of an affluent Cossack. The Cossack's wife sleeps with him.

This is a rather common thing.

It's as though there is no difference between the morals of the officer and the Cossack's wife, who lives close to the war with the mountaineers, on the narrow strip of the Terek's fertile banks.

Here the land is only around six-hundred yards wide. The gardens are planted by these people. There are rich pastures for the cattle. They hunt. Farm.

There is always work—whether the man stays at home or goes hunting.

The more he writes his book, the more divided the world between Olenin and Maryana becomes, the more exact becomes the description of it.

Maryana is not the only one who doesn't understand Olenin.

Young Lukashka, the poor, brave, free Cossack, doesn't understand the newcomer either.

He sees that this man isn't a bad person—he is generous. Lukashka had no horse, and because of that he wasn't "a real Cossack." But his mother was proud of her son. And there wasn't much of a difference in the positions between Maryana, the daughter of a well-to-do Cossack, and Lukashka.

Maryana was a beautiful woman; Lukashka was a handsome Cossack who could earn money by farming or hunting.

The horse was a gift. It brought Lukashka closer to Maryana, but it didn't bring Lukashka closer to Olenin. He is suspicious: why such a present? He is embarrassed and says: the cadet gave me a horse as a present. Meanwhile, Olenin is something between an army volunteer and a cadet, waiting for his promotion.

He is too carefree with his money.

He has servants—domestics, serfs.

One or two of them.

His hounds are brought for him from Russia.

They're good hounds, too, but the whole thing seems suspicious.

Olenin is handsome, young, rich, he's even ready to convert to the Old Faith, which is a difficult thing for an orthodox, particularly one who is also an aristocrat, and could suffer in his post because of it. He proposes to marry Maryana, but he doesn't take part in the Cossack life, and everything is decided with Maryana's words: "Go away, I'm sick of you!" It's as if she were blaming him for the deaths of the Cossacks during their conflict with the Abreks,[28] who had crossed the Terek, maybe trying to recapture a herd of horses. They come across the Cossacks. Lukashka figures out a way to hide behind a hay cart. But still some Cossacks get killed, and Maryana declines the marriage and wealth, because her immediate neighbors and her villagers have suffered.

The novel is maturing for ten years.

Sometimes Tolstoy hides from his friends and relatives the fact that he is writing a novel.

He takes the manuscript with him on foreign trips; he even hides it from his brother who, nevertheless, knows that something big is maturing.

A bizarre thing—he mistakes the reality for a tale. Meanwhile, the novel is maturing, it's ridding itself of fabrications.

It's breaking free from the shells of tradition.

Originally it was an Abrek—a Russian Cossack, who escapes to the Chechens, to join Shamil's army.[29] These people existed in real life. Shamil even had cannons cast by the Russian Cossacks.

The people who usually escaped to these lands weren't just oppressed, they were morally humiliated. The Russian Abrek was a double Abrek. He had fled from his village, deserted his own people.

---

[28] Among the Caucasians an Abrek was a person banished from his clan and living the life of a wanderer or highwayman. At the time described here, the name was also applied to men who fought on their own against the Emperor and the Russian army.

[29] A legendary warrior in the classic tradition of the Caucasus, who led his guerrilla army in a twenty-year war against the Imperial Russian army in the mid-1800s. Later Shamil became primarily a literary character in the epic of Russia's battle to tame the wild frontier.

Epifan Sekhin was also a real person.[30] He crossed over to the other side. Walked side by side with the Chechens. Stole horses. Sold them back to the Chechens. There were no borders for him, just as they didn't exist for the wolf, or the deer, or the bird. The Terek Cossacks had lived along the Terek since the times of Ivan the Terrible, or the times of Tsar Aleksei Mikhailovich, an age of religious reform and correction of Biblical texts that the Cossacks resisted.

Tolstoy wrote in his diary that the Cossack's escape to the mountains didn't work. And it couldn't. Traditionally, a person who'd fled to another tribe had to fall out with his own.

To be jealous, to kill the rival and the woman—that's the nature of "The Gypsies." Or he must love. He must escape. The woman must commit suicide. As in Pushkin's "Prisoner of the Caucasus."

Tolstoy's versions kept changing one after another. There was even something like this: the Russian officer marries the Cossack girl, then the man who loved her—the Cossack—returns and kills the officer. Or kills Maryana. And then this hero, the Abrek, is hanged.

When they attack him, he doesn't fight back; when they take him to be hanged, he calmly adjusts the noose around his neck. He is fearless. And a murder takes place. And some Russian, who loved Maryana, takes the blame.

■

Aksinya, whom Tolstoy leaves for the Caucasus, is revived after many decades in a short novel called "The Devil." Here, too, the hero will attempt to kill her, to finally free himself from the temptation.[31]

30 An old Cossack with whom young Tolstoy went hunting, who later became the main character of the story "Hunting in the Caucasus" and also the character of Yeroshka in *The Cossacks*.

31 Before and even during the first years of his marriage to Sofia Andreevna, Tolstoy was passionately in love with a married peasant girl, Aksinya, who lived in Yas-

"The Devil" was written almost at the same time as "The Kreutzer Sonata."

The hero of the short novel either kills himself, or the woman whom he loves, or the author kills them both. If it is possible to visualize Tolstoy agonizing—what's to be done?—then it's here.

Ten years pass. Ten years of work on a novel that has only nine typed pages. It's a small book. And Tolstoy chooses a different denouement.

As we've already said, the Abreks cross from the other side. The Cossacks fire their arms at them. Lukashka, the man who loves Maryana, is wounded in the crossfire. Then she rejects the foreigner, the outsider, Olenin, with whom she didn't get along from the very beginning. That battle is simply a split between the Russians and the Cossacks. People stop loving, they separate.

There is no ending in *The Cossacks*, i.e., it doesn't have a traditional ending.

Olenin leaves.

Maryana and Yeroshka are standing at the gates.

They are talking.

Olenin, whom Yeroshka called "not loved," for whom Yeroshka grieved while they sat together drinking wine—Olenin is leaving. The old Cossack Yeroshka, Olenin's friend and teacher, who taught him the laws of hunting, the laws of simple life—and the woman, who after all was interested in Olenin—they are talking to each other, but not about him.

The carriage kicks up dust, the dust settles, and the memory of the man is gone. He disappeared from the life of that village.

The energy of delusion is concealed in its search for a plot. It's as if the novel was never finished. But this was a real ending. The new ending. The

---

naya Polyana, and was often employed to clean in the Tolstoy household. In his diary, Tolstoy admitted several times that his feeling for Aksinya, by whom he had a son, was like that of a husband.

endings in Tolstoyan prose were similar to Chekhov's; they weren't conventional.

Tolstoy was hiding the news of his discovery. He sold his novel as an unfinished piece. He said that he didn't want the manuscript to be cut up for sealing windows. Meanwhile, the novel was finished. Really finished.

Tolstoy left the Caucasus, but he didn't go too far. He went to fight against the well-armed French, English, Turks, and Italians, who together as a power were clipping the claws of Nicholas I, a man who slept through all the technological changes of his times. He imagined himself a lion. He was just an old bulldog.

Tolstoy went to defend Sevastopol with his hero's fate unfinished, unresolved.

And throughout all of his novels he continues searching for his real unity with that story.

Lev Nikolaevich kept track of himself, wrote diaries, made notes to himself, returned to previous ideas. It's easy to follow him when you know what to look for.

I want to get back to the road that we left off.

Tolstoy, who has already written *Boyhood*, is brooding over his genius he nevertheless believed in. On July 7, 1854, he records in his diary:

> What am I? One of the four sons of a retired lieutenant colonel, orphaned at the age of seven, taken under the guardianship of women and strangers, received neither societal nor academic education, and set loose at the age of seventeen without a big fortune or a place in society, and what's most important—without any rules; a man who has damaged his career to the last bit, who has spent the best years of his life without a goal or enjoyment, and who has finally exiled himself to the Caucasus to get away from his debts . . . From there, latching onto some connection that supposedly existed between his father and the commander of the army, he was transferred to the Danube front at twenty-six as an infantry officer, with almost no means except for his salary . . . without any practical skills—

—he is reprimanding himself; but when Tolstoy writes:

I'm not good looking, I'm clumsy, messy, and don't know how to behave in society.—I am irritating, boring to others, conceited, intolerant . . . and shy as a child. I am rather rude. Whatever little I know, I have somehow learned it on my own, in snatches, without any sense or order. I am useless in real life, in society or in business . . . I am so vain . . . that I often fear I will choose fame over virtue.

—this is a person who feels his own genius. Someone who is neglected by everyone, but who is going down his own poetic road, the road of endlessly repeating mistakes, and yet finding his way through—the only path and, therefore, the path that's almost impossible to find.

Tolstoy often made discoveries by rereading, reanalyzing his own writings—he suddenly realized that he loves the Caucasus, it is his own kind of love, but it is deep. After seeing the magnificent mountains, he goes on a different road.

"This wild country with its two opposing realities—freedom and war —is indeed beautiful." In Pushkin, he was struck by "The Gypsies," "whom, as strange as it is, he couldn't understand until this moment."

A great man, who at this point is already a writer, an unexpected one, a writer unlike anyone else, a man with his own road, he even writes his diaries not as evidence but as short stories.

Tolstoy is a huge person, and for this very reason he is a hero out of place.

He doesn't fit inside his own biography.

Even though he took part in the shootings, he didn't receive the St. George Cross for bravery, which was why he had come to the Caucasus.

He was held under arrest the day he was supposed to get it.

Neither did he get the Cross for fighting at Sevastopol; although he really wanted it.

He is unhappy because he has no road; he has no road because he is happy—he has his own road that the energy of delusion will find.

He always made mistakes in love, in arranging his life, in searching for money, in assessing a situation.

When he lies about his situation, he forgets that Gorchakov is his relative.

Tolstoy's grandmother, Princess Gorchakova, was the eldest in the Gorchakov family.

Tolstoy was Gorchakov's nephew, the commander of the Danube battalion, while his grandmother was the eldest in the Gorchakov line; this was the highest level of aristocracy.

From the Tolstoy side of the family he was a lesser aristocrat. His father was a lieutenant colonel who had gone through war, but who had spent all of his fortune, and married a fine-looking woman who was more aristocratic than himself.

At one time B. M. Eichenbaum had wanted to write a whole monograph on the Gorchakovs and the role of this family name for Tolstoy.

Arriving in Bucharest, young Tolstoy, who had just been promoted to an officer, invites other officers for supper. He is waiting for the guests.

Only one officer arrives—the "boy" Bartholomew.

All evening long Lev Nikolaevich is ill at ease with himself—he isn't sure of the character of his uneasiness; he records on July 7, 1854: "Gorchakov came to visit me tonight, and the friendship that he offered really touched my heart . . ."

But two days later: "My supper was a failure: neither Gorchakov nor the doctor were able to come. It was just Bartholomew, he ate my suckling pig and kept praising Schiller."

He writes in the diary: "Am I really not one of them?"

Yes, he was a person who didn't belong in their society.

This scene with Tolstoy is similar to the one with Charlie Chaplin, the hero of *The Gold Rush*.

Chaplin is walking in a once fine suit that's completely worn out. His shoes are too big on him. He's constantly making mistakes and is constantly in a rush.

In this powerful and bitter film he invites beautiful women to dine with him. They never come.

He is dancing alone, on the table, not with his feet, but two buns held by forks.

The unfortunate hero is amazingly stubborn and seems not to let anything upset him.

In the mountains he finds and loses a gold vein. He finds a house on the side of the mountain, it starts swaying.

The house is swaying, like fortune.

But he finally finds his gold, his fortune. Then he meets the woman whom he wants to love, he meets her as he's crawling out of a barrel in which he was hiding.

Tolstoy doesn't have a place in life.

On July 24 and 25, 1854, he writes:

> I won't hand in the report [about being transferred to the Crimean battalion—V.S.], until I'm able to breed horses and I'll use all the means for that . . . The so-called aristocrats arouse my envy. I'm so stubbornly petty and envious.

In stories, sketches, in his works Tolstoy will soon begin writing about those aristocrats, people who are constantly settling accounts among themselves. What's being born inside of Tolstoy's soul was called *mestnichestvo* in old Russia.[32]

And this will go on until he achieves the highest place of fame.

And then he'll realize that *mestnichestvo* isn't really for him.

[32] Until the seventeenth century in Russia, commissions, appointments, and other placings, such as seating at important banquets, were governed by the code of precedence, or "place" system (*mestnichestvo*), which determined an individual's position in the hierarchy of command by calculations based on his own and his clan's service record and his seniority within his clan. It was considered a great dishonor to be placed below someone who, regardless of ability, was deemed to merit a lower place. The system was finally abolished under the reign of Peter the Great.

Tolstoy keeps a diary almost daily. Reading his first work by Tolstoy, Chernyshevsky noted: this person must be keeping a diary; he knows the soul.

Yes, answers the person who has reread the unattainable Tolstoy so many times.

Tolstoy's work method, which I named perhaps without giving it much thought as I expanded on one part of his letter to Strakhov, this method is close to what he himself calls the energy of delusion.

I'll repeat.

Tolstoy said: "I don't know how to draw a circle, I draw it, then correct."

He didn't have an original plan for a book or a subsequent plan for solutions.

When Tolstoy decided to publish his *Resurrection* abroad, with the intention to transfer the royalties to the Dukhobors fund,[33] his publisher, not having the novel in front of him—it wasn't finished yet—asked for the plan.

This request was communicated through Chertkov.[34]

---

[33] The Dukhobors and Molokans of the Russian Christian movement founded in the eighteenth century, led a peaceable life in Russia's outlying districts and were sporadically persecuted for their views, which included rejection of ecclesiastical and state authority. Finally, in the 1880s they decided to emigrate to North America; more than 7,000 people wanted to leave and they needed money to pay their passage.

The money from the donated *Resurrection* was to be passed on to the Dukhobors by the English and American Quakers whose ideology was close to Tolstoy's own. However, after reading the translated novel, especially the scene of Katyusha's seduction, John Bellows wrote to Tolstoy that he could not partake in distributing the book and was abhorred by its contents.

[34] Vladimir Chertkov (1854–1936), Tolstoy's most dedicated disciple, was profoundly influenced by his religious and ethical ideas, and was responsible for publishing many of his works abroad that were banned by censors in Russia. After their meeting in 1883, Chertkov founded a publishing firm designed to produce edifying booklets for the masses at a nominal cost. After 1889 Chertkov became increasingly involved in Tolstoy's daily life as he undertook to organize and preserve all his pa-

The deal was about sending a short summary.

Tolstoy reacted to this as if he had been burglarized.

He wrote in a letter on October 15, 1898:

> Your demand to send the first chapters to the publisher for me was un-
> pleasant and, I must confess, offensive. I would have never agreed to this
> and I'm surprised that you did. And summaries for me are preposterous.
> Whether they like it or not, but I am surprised that you, knowing me,
> agreed to ask for their approval. I remember the American publishers
> wrote a few times with proposals of big payments and I assumed that it
> would be that way and that you would continue in that same spirit . . .
>
> Regarding the summary of the novel, the concept is purely theoreti-
> cal, because the first part is finished, but the second isn't typed yet, it can-
> not be considered finished and I may change it, and I would like to have
> the opportunity to make changes.
>
> Therefore, my indignation against summaries and manuscript read-
> ings is not prompted by arrogance, but by a certain awareness of my call-
> ing as a writer, which cannot subordinate its spiritual activity of writing
> to any practical considerations. There is something revolting in this,
> which offends my very soul.

A summary for Tolstoy was an insult to a person who searches for his
own road.

This wasn't something unexpected.

Tolstoy's relationship to the plan is connected with his relationship to
his diary.

On October 22, 1853, he wrote:

> I am sick of *Boyhood* . . . I hope to finish it tomorrow. Writing through
> different books is altogether a strange idea. It's much better to write every-

---

pers. Chertkov was exiled from Russia to London between 1897–1905 for his in-
volvement with sectarians and other publicist activities. He returned to Russia in
1908 and remained by Tolstoy's side until his death at the railway station in Astapovo.

thing into the diary, which ... is literary work for me, and for others, it might turn into a pleasant reading. At the end of each month ... I can select anything that is remarkable in it ... will come up with a short title for each day.

Those lines that Chernyshevsky wrote about Tolstoy after reading his first story show the unusual insight of the critic.

It's true, Lev Nikolaevich wrote primarily for himself.

But there exists one more period of Tolstoy.

This is the period before his literary career and it's in "A History of Yesterday." Almost no one knows this story. Many think that Tolstoy started with *Childhood*. Yet Tolstoy in *Childhood* is talking about something that he calls "a pre-conscious state."

"A History of Yesterday" appeared only seventy-four years later in the first volume of his Jubilee Edition, but it was a book of the future.

It hasn't been acknowledged yet as a living book.

Tolstoy is against a "unified soul" that is fixed forever, and this was the first fully mature discovery that he carried with him down the great road of his life.

He keeps his pre-conscious diary; he opens like Rousseau, his teacher, the person who doesn't believe in his own fame, in his present-day consciousness. And so, during this time, Tolstoy writes:

Do we need to write literature? Perhaps we should only write in our diary, which then people can read.

This person, it seems, never believed in himself, he always kept quiet, curbing his own ideas. He abandoned religion when he perceived his own world, alone. When he perceived his own universe.

This was the Tolstoyan way. Later he replaced Tolstoyan philosophy with ethics. This is when he told himself: one must be good.

That wasn't enough for him.

He was that same person who wrote *War and Peace*, at the beginning of which he says that he is writing about aristocracy, and he is an aristocrat himself. They are free as aristocrats. They have money and they can be consciously free.

But he didn't finish that prologue.

It was repudiated much earlier, in *The Sevastopol Sketches*.

■

One can collect several volumes of unfinished and unpublished works by Tolstoy.

Some of his works were almost forbidden by his family.

He learned about woman's jealousy.

This was almost a pre-conscious state. The first person who confessed love to Sofia Andreevna was a pharmaceutical apprentice. He kissed her hand, which she rubbed with eau-de-cologne for several days.

Time is our movement through the world. Our own time is something not very perceptible to us. It's perhaps the expectation of happiness. A woman gains a renowned husband, he is famous, he has a high social status, but they begin to quarrel and discover there had been a misunderstanding between them. Yet she is far superior to ordinary women. Tolstoy turns her into Kitty Scherbatskaya. It's Anna Karenina who finds a real place in the book, a woman whom he didn't recognize at first, he thought she would be extravagant, a beautiful Creole, relatively or completely magnificent, and at the same time she would be a complete woman, who not only wants to be greatly in love but also greatly loved.

The discovery of an artist can be the discovery of a scientist. Tolstoy teaches that events exist before they are discovered.

Anna Karenina is superior to the heroines of Boccaccio, his cheerful concubines, who are interesting, who loathe and seek out men.

Anna Karenina is not a girl.

Tatyana thought a long time before writing her letter to Onegin.

A good letter.

Vronsky is an ordinary person. A person who wears his name and uniform well. Tolstoy doesn't like Vronsky. He knows that the mother of this person has slept around. Vronsky's father wasn't a rich man, but he had worked his way into society, he knew how to spend money. He knew how to spend money as if he didn't care.

■

His son, Vronsky, is building a stable, a hospital, he has excellent French horses, he is a good rider, although he broke the back of his favorite mare, Frou-Frou.

He is an ordinary person.

A good imitator.

He is pretending to be an artist.

Perhaps he is pretending to be a liberal.

He isn't pretending to be in love.

It's a question of health.

It's because of Anna Karenina, she is magnificent.

But his heart and lungs aren't strong enough for a time-consuming love affair.

The idea of Anna Karenina was proposed by Pushkin.

He was Tatyana Larina's contemporary.

We should praise the time period that created Anna Karenina.

But I don't know how to do that.

Tolstoy does not hide the fact that a woman has the right to desire and choose just like a man, but rather fully exposes this fact in his great book. She can desire, she can love and leave the one whom she loves, go away into the unknown with the student of the great visionary Fyodorov, and then become Katyusha Maslova.

A woman capable of inspring, whom Tolstoy resurrected because she didn't die: she was pregnant with an immortal love.

This great man was a person of his own time; he was listening to Chertkov's literary advice and, fortunately, rarely following it.

As an insight into the literature of the past, a man would resurrect a woman.

A man would give the world to her.

Tolstoy spoke about this world in his own words, without hiding to whom this right of gift-giving belonged.

And so now I'd like to go back and talk once again, but with different words, about Tolstoy's journey to the Caucasus.

If you think about it, repetition can never be dull; and even the forest, the old familiar forest that you enter, becomes brand-new when light illuminates it in a new way.

The story of this man's journey, whose name was Lev Nikolaevich Tolstoy, and whom we now know as Lev Tolstoy, is a story that lies at the origins of a transformation, a passage from one name, his reputation, into a completely different time period.

■

Pushkin, exiled in his youth, left with almost no money and a stingy father, is a gambler and a womanizer, a person who doesn't know how to pay his own bills, a daring person, who appears to be a failure. Even his friends were unaware of who he was and what he knew. Vyazemsky, a person who prided himself on being Pushkin's friend, recorded that when he started examining Pushkin's papers, he was surprised that Pushkin, it turns out, "was a thinker."

Gogol, who was egocentric and easily offended, and unsuccessfully tried to become an actor, then a teacher of life, he, too, appears to be a failure.

And Dostoevsky, a convict, was already a complete failure.

I once wrote that we don't know anything about Homer. There is not a single known characteristic about him, except that he was blind. And even that we know only by how he described things. Homer's blindness, his personal concept of a world that he doesn't see, is perhaps the result of a desire to recover a lost world for himself.

Perhaps I'm talking somewhat incoherently.

But allow the old writer not to change his habits.

What was the passion for delusion that Tolstoy wrote about?

It was the desire to explore.

When Columbus, who knew as much as his contemporaries did, had examined the old flawed maps, found the money to equip his ships after incredible sufferings, searches, humiliations, and when he sailed off to the unknown world—what he was doing was driven by the energy of delusion. He was searching for India. And he was mistaken because he thought it was close by. Then he found America. He stumbled upon America. But in order to do that he had to overcome the unfathomable despair of his crew, who had left the shores and were headed into the unknown.

Inventors cannot be happy.

Neither can those people who give them the money to realize their ideas. The rich are those who invest in unsuccessful factories and continue what had been started as the flawed creation of something new.

The delusion causes a pattern of various turns, the return to old places. A repetition of experiments. And the great experimenter Rutherford, answering the question posed by his students, who looked with reverence at this successful man—what helps the work?—said: obstacles, obstacles. Whereas he was thinking—failures.

Because if everything turns out as you had intended, then you are probably on the old path, but when you have left the old paths, when you are lost, the chances that you'll succeed are only 0.0001 percent.

Lev Nikolaevich traveled to the unknown Caucasus by an unknown route that was devised by his brother, a very talented man—Nikolai Nikolaevich, who had already been promoted to the rank of an officer, had become a good hunter, and was already being published. They devised a route to the Volga by horses, then from the Volga to Astrakhan by boat, and through the steppes to the Caucasus—a new place where Nikolai Nikolaevich had already served.

This was a whim that didn't seem to justify the expectations. All his life Lev Nikolaevich dreamed about writing his adventures on a steamboat.

The steamboat drifted on. We know that there were books on board, because on it Lev Nikolaevich read *The Count of Monte Cristo*, the novel by Dumas père.

From here we know that he loved this novel.

We know that there was a samovar on the boat, because we know that he gave the samovar to someone in the Starogladkovskaya village.

We also know that there was a tarantass aboard, a strange carriage that already, in the time of Pushkin, was quite impressive. Two pairs of wheels joined by poles.

The springs were replaced with flexible beams. All this was well thought out, but it was done in haste.

At the same time, the real people are those who get deluded, they are the ones who get lost on the usual paths, the paths of inevitability. What seems to be incidental really is inevitable. But inevitability can't be grasped immediately.

It is necessary to tear yourself away from home, from the anticipation of tomorrow or the day after tomorrow, and to fly away, for yourself, urged by some inner need, not as a bird, though, they fly through old routes, but only as a working man can fly away, someone who knows the rhythm of possibilities.

It wasn't at random that Tolstoy began writing as soon as he arrived in the Starogladkovskaya village.

It was inevitability, something we wrongly call chance or fate, that led Tolstoy, a beginning writer, to the Caucasus.

Everybody was puzzled: exiled by no one, not completely ruined yet, this young man who still had a roof over his head is going to the Caucasus, the place that had already acquired a reputation in folk songs—"the fatal Caucasus." They gave him some position. He was a fourth-rank artilleryman, which is probably less than a lance corporal.

Nobody came to see him off. He forgot his hat.

Only his dog Bulka, breaking the window glass, ran after his master. Then she kept Tolstoy company and fought a boar for his sake.

Tolstoy is the true discoverer of imaginary things.

What did he actually find?

And why does this arbitrary place in the Caucasus and his failed romance with a beautiful woman have such a firm place in literature? Why is the poorly dressed old Cossack—Yeroshka, an idle man, but an amazing hunter, a man without a place, although he is a native of those lands where the Cossacks have lived for over three hundred years—why is this Yeroshka the hero of the new world?

We all have admired Tolstoy. And, naturally, I too had the right to admire him and from childhood read his *Childhood*. It's an amazing book. The author in it appears as a memoirist, but as if he is writing without having aged, without having lost a child's perception, through a child's choice of elements, his straightforward, innocent vision.

In *A Sentimental Journey* and *The Life and Opinions of Tristram Shandy* Sterne has described a boy, a child from a peculiar family. We have certain literary influences here—memoirs about Rabelais.

Speaking of his new attempt at memoir, Tolstoy wrote:

> In order not to repeat myself in the description of my childhood, I have reread my writing under that title and regretted for having written something in such an insincere literary style. It couldn't have been otherwise, first of all because my intention was to describe not my own story, but that of my childhood companions . . . and secondly because when writing it I was far from being independent in the form of expression, being under the influence of two writers, Sterne and Topfer, who at the time strongly impressed me.

Writing in this manner brought Tolstoy a lot of grief, because he spoke not only about himself but also about his friend Isleniev,[35] whom he later tried to help.

35 A close friend of Tolstoy's father, A. Islenyev, a landowner in Tula, had married S. Kozlovskaya before she was divorced from her first husband. As a result their six children were considered illegitimate, and received the name Islavin. Islenyev is portrayed in *Childhood*, *Boyhood*, and *Youth* as the father of Nikolenka.

Isleniev was born from an illegitimate union. He didn't have a passport, he didn't belong anywhere. He was a talented musician. With Tolstoy's help he would occasionally find work and appear wearing Tolstoy's frock coat, because at this time Tolstoy was already wearing his long belted blouse that we now call "tolstovka." The frock coat was abandoned.

Let me clarify—*Childhood* and *Boyhood*, I believe, were written after the Caucasian stories. At any rate, they were conceived simultaneously. They appear as a part of a big novel, which wasn't finished. This novel was *Childhood, Boyhood, Youth*.

Even though *Boyhood* and *Youth* were finished, they aren't the kind of books that get reread. In these books Tolstoy is still using old writing devices. He depends on the old literary traditions to the extent that he molds his own biography to fit in.

What happened next? The book was received with great success.

Nevertheless, it was almost impossible for Tolstoy to prove that he was Count Lev Nikolaevich. He had forgotten his documents at home. The original documents had burnt during the Moscow fire. The copies of the originals were left at home. Tolstoy had arrived without documents. And it so happened that in the same unit there was an officer, Count Nikolai Nikolaevich, and his soldier brother, Lev Nikolaevich. And the soldier couldn't prove that he was a count, although nobody argued that he wasn't his brother's brother. And only thanks to his uncle, Gorchakov, the famous general of the new front on the Danube, where Russia was fighting with Turkey to help the Christian subjects and simultaneously gain the keys to the Holy Tomb in Jerusalem, Tolstoy finally earned his rank in this chaotic, self-righteous war, he received his officer's epaulets. But it was with great difficulty that he was accepted into the society of aristocrats, where he wanted to belong so much.

I'm not going to repeat the story about the supper with the suckling pig.

Charlie Chaplin showed better than I can the feelings of a person who is "not like everyone else."

An aristocrat and a rich man, Lev Nikolaevich will always be a person without a place. At all times he is a person without traditions. And it can be said that of all his novels only *Anna Karenina* preserves the forms of a novel. Yet in his preface to *War and Peace* and his notes regarding its genre, Lev Nikolaevich disowns the "novel" as a genre and says that Russians cannot write novels and refuse to do so.

A beginner, Lev Nikolaevich roams in search of how to write about other people, how to write in a different style. Or, in novels, how to develop characters, their mysterious ways of life.

It's not easy to see life directly.

Lev Nikolaevich was telling about the old watchdog that died in the old kennel, meanwhile the clock was ticking over her—tick-tock. But what's that—tick-tock, tick-tock?

The same outcast dogs were the ones escorting that person, his coffin. They were the ones following the cart. Alone.

When Anna Karenina is headed toward death, the whole world seems strange to her. Even the signboards are strange. Life is strange and loathsome.

Both men and women become distorted. They are repulsive if we take off their clothes. They all lie. Only the drunk carried in the cab doesn't lie, and that's only because he has no consciousness.

For ten years the great writer sought a place for his hero from *The Cossacks*. He found it in one place—in oblivion.

Herein lies the story of one composition.

He searched for this story for decades.

The Cossacks is finished in the novel *Hadji Murad*.

Although Hadji Murad isn't a Cossack, he is a mountaineer. One version of *The Cossacks* was titled "The Abrek." Tolstoy brought these people closer—Lukashka, who became the Abrek, with Hadji Murad, who knew only one person above him: Shamil.

And in *Hadji Murad*, which Tolstoy was writing until his death, it wasn't Nicholas I who was right, nor Shamil, who acted like the liberator and wanted to liberate his nation driven by the same energy as Homeini.

The person in the right is Hadji Murad's mother, who didn't surrender her son, didn't become a wet-nurse even when they were threatening her with a knife.

The person in the right is Hadji Murad, who fought so that the peasants could have their own house, their own land, and could plow it themselves.

... The years pass, we forget the experiments to master the subject. These years stretch like miles. Yet we haven't achived anything.

The explorer who takes the road into the unknown goes through the same land, he passes over his own footprints, his energy of delusion.

Lev Nikolaevich Tolstoy is a great explorer, a great scout, because the path into the future has not been paved to the end.

He loves Don Quixote like his own brother.

And the writer holds on to hope, the spark of hope that the energy of delusion will be repaid by the joy of discovery.

In the conclusion of "The Kreutzer Sonata," Tolstoy says that initially we swim along the shores but then we go further, to unknown and faraway lands, perhaps toward the flickering of the lighthouses.

Old Fyodorov talked about this long road. He dreamed about a complete transformation of this world and even the resurrection of the dead, who would happily settle in far-off, rediscovered worlds: the planets.

Every book, if it's a great book, is a great journey.

To journey through a book, one must find a ship, work out the right course.

Columbus is great not simply because he was able to obtain the ships, promising to pay for them in gold from the unknown lands, but also because he journeyed into the unknown.

There and back.

And with a fair wind each time.

This Genovese knew what trade winds and monsoons were.

Tolstoy would start a book, or an attempt at a book, and then continue his endless search for progression.

He was economical, he knew the price of stamps: if someone unfamiliar included a stamp in the letter for reply, he would make note of it. He would reply to this person out of a sense of indebtedness.

But Tolstoy didn't think it was wasteful to set text in type and then to take it apart, even though he had to pay the publisher extra.

All of Tolstoy's major books were written and published at huge intervals.

He didn't know his own path. He is almost his own hero; Nekhlyudov had come to marry Katyusha Maslova, and Sofia Andreevna knew about this. Then he said that the wedding was cancelled. Sofia Andreevna was rejoicing unaware that there wouldn't be a wedding because the groom was unworthy. His attempt was yet another delusion.

Riding in the train with political prisoners, having heard what Fyodorov's student told her, Katyusha Maslova, being sentenced to exile instead of hard labor, is leaving with a person whom she doesn't love yet, but whom she respects. And the man whom she loves is departing from his resurrected feeling of love into new delusions.

You are walking toward gunshots on this road, while the steppe is asking for songs.

3

THE DECAMERON

No word, however pure, was ever wholesomely construed by a mind that was corrupt. And just as seemly language leaves no mark upon a mind that is corrupt, language that is less than seemly cannot sully a mind that is well ordered, any more than mud will contaminate the rays of the sun, or earthly filth the beauties of the heavens.
GIOVANNI BOCCACCIO, *The Decameron*, "Author's Epilogue"

The Decameron is a rare collection of plots. Composed of various stories, Boccaccio's book as a whole represents a single story.

Boccaccio begins with the plague, describing in great detail how it spread to Florence from the East; people tried, if not to save themselves from the plague, then at least to forget about it.

The plague purified the previous life.

There was no one to be ashamed of, there was no one to comfort. Things had to be built anew, from the leveled ground.

The stories come from the past, from books, anecdotes, tales of crime, from the anticipation that a totally new form of art would emerge.

The narrators shift.

Seven young women, bound by friendship or location, accidentally meet.

One of them says they must escape death.

But we can't go by ourselves. Another lady agrees, nothing can be undertaken without the guidance of men.

"By nature fickle, we are all stubborn, suspicious, cowardly and easily frightened," says the woman. "Without a man to guide us it rarely happens that any enterprise of ours is brought to a worthy conclusion."

They decide to look for men.

The three they find have been raised in the ways of the new epoch, all of them have read the modern books. They are the contemporaries of Dante and Petrarch. Together all ten leave the city.

Each day they choose a king and a queen to begin a tale.

The stories are different.

They follow, yet contradict, one another.

The young people pass by abandoned houses, down empty streets, to start a new life on their own terms.

Today we think that, even with television, cinema, and the press, we still have a common culture.

The present is instantaneous.

The past is different for everyone. Many of us think that we ought to live in the future.

Mountain slopes are less variegated than the differences among people.

Some of Bocaccio's characters move forward, others are content in the present. Yet others are concerned with the future. All or most of this is connected to the new role of women.

However, *The Decameron* represents a re-examination of almost all the stories that are told in it.

At the end of the book, Boccaccio himself explains his motivation.

Many of the denouements are parodies.

This is of great significance.

The preceding epoch was an epoch of strict family structures and lively trade.

Revival as a literary phenomenon often occurs through parody and conflicts with reality; they may last until there's a new resurrection of plot.

I will begin by talking about the first story, and then go on to the last one.

The story is constructed rather daringly on negative relations with Rome.

Note that these stories were to be published in a territory ruled by the Inquisition.

A moneylender—a godless, impudent crook—is dying. He is so vile that it's almost impossible to bury him within the city limits.

As the older generation, we know what a pawnshop is.

Those people, the previous pawnshop owners, were the moneylenders from Boccaccio's epoch.

In the house, where this man is dying, the owners say of the city's people: "They'll raise a rumpus and shout, 'We'll not put up any longer with these damned Lombard dogs—even the church refuses to receive them! We'll have the worst of it if the fellow dies.'"

It's necessary to frame his relationship within the Church.

The man, whom the story calls a scoundrel, is dying; a friar is summoned and the dying man makes a false confession.

The confession is recounted in detail.

The friar says: "You confess like a saint."

When the rogue dies, they bury him on the grounds of the monastery, and people visit the grave as if he were a saint.

The funeral, the friar's sermon from the pulpit over the rogue's dead body that people approach, their conversations—all this is shown in a detached way.

The second story also has a parodic ending.

A Jew lives in Paris.

He is considering converting to Christianity.

Before he does, the Jew wishes to visit Rome in order to examine the affairs of the church, which is new to him.

His Christian friend, who had been convincing the Jew to convert to

Christianity, knows what to expect from the Church in Rome, and tries to dissuade his friend from traveling there.

He thinks: if the Jew visits Rome, he'll surely reject our faith.

But the Jew insists.

When he returns, he says: your great faith is powerful.

Rome and the Christian Church are presented to the Jew as a hellish place.

Rome appears to him as "a mill of devilish works, not holy."

Rome, he says, does its utmost to ruin and ban the Christian faith altogether from the world; yet your religion continually grows and becomes more bright and clear, which is why I do not doubt it must be the truest and holiest of all faiths.

The story gives an accurate portrayal of the church's life.

Possible rejection turns into an affirmation.

The third story is a famous parable about three rings.

Saladin needs money: he calls for a moneylender from Alexandria, but in order to get the money he resorts to cunning.

Saladin asks the Jew which religion is the truest—the Hebrew, the Saracen, or the Christian?

The Jew then tells of a man who had three sons and a ring that would go to only one.

The one who got the ring would receive the inheritance, and the others would have to honor him as the head of the family.

The worthy man loved his three sons equally. He ordered the goldsmith to make him two other rings, and when his time came to die he gave each son one of the rings in secret. Thus the question as to which one was the true ring remains unsolved to this day.

Delusion holds truth.

As a result, Saladin's cunning fails: he really didn't care which religion is the truest, he simply wished to outsmart the Jew.

■

The last story in *The Decameron* was the first one to be translated into Russian.

A marquis, urged into matrimony, marries a peasant's daughter. Then he tells her that he has put their two children to death.

He tortures his wife even more by telling her that he has grown tired of her, that he is going to remarry and wants her gone.

After she has undergone this suffering, seeing that she was faithful despite her distress, he takes her home again, shows her their children already grown, and honors her as his wife.

These stories are ironic.

It's as if the plots help to conceal the book's motivation by portraying crime and suffering as something almost virtuous.

■

Two stories in the book repeat each other; in the one, a father kills his daughter's lover—a valet. In the other, a husband kills his wife's lover, who happens to be his friend.

The women suffer; the offenders reveal their crimes as though they are heroic deeds.

The father sends the valet's heart to his daughter on a golden tray, spiced, if I recall, with poisonous herbs.

The woman is dying; her father weeps. She asks him: what are you grieving for, you got what you desired.

In the second story, the husband kills his friend, then pulls out the heart and gives it to the cook. He puts the stew in front of his wife and asks:

—How did you like the dish?

—Very much, indeed—she answers.

—Well, of course—says the husband—it's the heart of the man whom you loved.

The woman replies:

—You are a villain. You had the right to kill me, but not my lover.

She is standing next to the window of a very tall tower during this conversation. Without looking back at her husband, and without looking down, she flings herself out.

Her body is recovered for everyone to see and then buried together with her lover's.[36]

The same kind of thing happens in the first story.

What's going on here?

A supposed union.

Then a betrayal of the husband, which is a crime; it's revealed in the embellished inscriptions on her tomb.

This is a tragic judgment of love.

■

The fourth story of the sixth day in *The Decameron* is based on a peculiar device. Boccaccio collected anecdotes; they are repeated from story to story. However, his stories revive commonplace phrases that have undergone so many repetitions we have lost the sense of their original reference.

We say "How are you?" or "Farewell" without referring to health.

The Georgian greeting—*gamarjoba*—means "be victorious," yet we're not at war.

But there can be another method of restoring the meaning of a punch line.

In the fourth story, the cook Chichibio gives his mistress a drumstick from a roasted crane, which she eats. The cook hopes that the missing part

[36] A footnote by V. Shklovsky: This is almost the true story of Guillaume de Cabestan and the Lady Sermonde. King Raymond d'Avignon ordered to take their bodies to Perpignan and bury them at the entrance of the Church, with an inscription about the way that they died. This story appears in troubadour biographies in the thirteenth century.

won't be noticed. But his master notices the missing leg and asks Chi-chibio:

—Where is the second leg?

When Chichibio replies that all cranes have only one leg, his master, Currado, is outraged.

—Yes, it is so—insists Chichibio—and if you wish, I can show you.

His master replies: Very well, let's go see the cranes.
They see the birds near the marshes.
The birds each stand on one leg.

—There! You can see for yourself—says Chichibio.

At which point his master shouts at the cranes: "Ho! Ho!"
Showing their other leg, the cranes take flight.

—There now, do you see?—says Currado—they have two legs.
—But you didn't shout Ho! Ho! to the crane that was on your table—replies Chichibio.

These anecdotes—they live on, grow old, and get revived. We can even start classifying them.
I recall a story from my own life. I was in a village in Estonia.
On an old tower I saw a bass-relief of a crane holding a stone in its claws.
I had to give a lecture. I opened with the following words: "You live in a village where your ancestors have lived for centuries, but do you know why the crane in the bass-relief is holding a stone in its raised foot?"
They didn't know.
The cranes are famous for their vigilance. But they also get tired and fall asleep. There was a legend about how the cranes left one male bird on guard; he held a stone. If he fell asleep, the stone would fall and wake up the rest of the flock.

I know this by pure coincidence, because I read old books; they are full of symbols.

We shake hands when parting, as we know. We are used to it. We don't remember why we do this. And we hardly ever think about the stone.

I like reading the Bible.

It has been printed countless times, and it's not read enough.

One of the commanders in the small army of David (he hasn't become king yet) receives an order to go to the enemy. The commander is left-handed.

He arrives, enters without taking off his cloak.

As a friendly greeting, he strokes the beard of his enemy.

This is an accepted gesture and doesn't arouse displeasure.

But the commander has a sword; he strokes with his right hand, and with the left he takes out the sword and stabs his enemy through his cloak. Then he leaves through a door behind the throne.

Aside from being interesting, this act made its way into a religious book.

We have expressions like: selling from the left hand, or selling to the left.

The left stripes, stripes crossing from the left to right on ancestral emblems, signified that there had been illegitimate heirs in the family.

Our speech and our literature overflow with dead symbols, and without context they sound strange.

I'll try to get closer to the road I left.

We don't see a great deal as we read. We overlook many things.

Today, the behavior of the characters of Dickens and Tolstoy would need footnoted explanations.

At a reception, Karenin spreads a handkerchief on his knees after he has poured himself some tea from the samovar.

We have customs the origins of which we forget.

For example, in Westerns the hero would get into a dangerous situation, he would be threatened with death but suddenly he'd be saved. He'd fall into the hands of outlaws. The outlaws would tie him with ropes, string him up, and tie a stone to the rope. They would build a fire that would accidentally burn the rope.

This was a device for *retardation*.[37]

We must wait in fear.

All of these adventures, even the cowboy himself, have become commonplace. It's hard to sell them, unless it's done from the left.

I have seen old catalogues for selling Westerns; one of them depicts a cowboy playing a children's harmonica.

The cowboy is a daredevil.

It's difficult to come up with something new.

Let's turn from this long detour and get back to our road.

Each story is based on some incident.

Most often the story and the novel lived on the roads—from an ordinary world to the world of accidents.

I am asking the reader to go over Boccaccio's two volumes and count up the number of shipwrecks.

There were so many that it's impossible to imagine how much it must have cost to insure a ship.

Yet the majority of the ships would arrive at their destination.

The Greek ships in the stories would constantly fall apart, and surprises would wait around every corner. Folkloric life would begin.

The characters would fight with Homeric weapons. In all cases, as a rule, the heroine would be threatened by violence. But tradition demanded that at the last moment she should be saved.

Of course, she would preserve her virginity for the hero.

This restraint of the enemy in regard to the woman is obvious to Tom

---

37 The device that Shklovsky calls retardation (*zamedlenie*) is based on a set of digressions that slow down the reader's perception and expectations of a certain narrative progression. By transposing parts of the novel, the author sets his own aesthetic laws, which underlie both the transposition and the slowing down of the action. A good example that Shklovsky often uses, one which makes excellent use of this device, is Sterne's *Tristram Shandy*.

Sawyer: the pirates put the women in cabins and serve them as if they were princesses.

In Boccaccio's stories, the ships undergo every possible folkloric wreck; it's quite amusing—people drown, sometimes they get saved; then there are those incidents when a person is saved on a box with treasures inside and becomes a rich man.

An old circumstance is repeated.

But then there is the seventh story of the second day. This one is a long story.

The "Sultan" of Babylon (I don't think there was such a Sultan) gives one of his daughters to be married to the King of Algarve.

She is sent off to her husband's palace. The subtitle of this story declares: within the space of four years she comes into the hands of nine different men in various places. But finally she is brought back to her father a virgin, and goes to marry the King of Algarve, as she had set out to do in the first place.

This story is full of shipwrecks and murders. The woman's name in this story is Alatiel.

In the prologue to the story, the narrator says that the lovers want to protect themselves from fate's surprises, but they have desires. Women try to enhance their fatal beauty, desire impels action.

The story is constructed in the following way.

Alatiel doesn't know any languages except for her native Babylonian, which is little known.

We know more about the Babylonian chaos of languages.

They used to speak in Semitic dialects in Babylon.

Alatiel wasn't an educated woman. She had never tasted wine.

When her vessel crashed, and more than half of her entourage drowned, Alatiel was saved and fell into the hands of a venerable man, who somehow knew that he was dealing with a lady.

Then the Sultan's daughter drinks wine, for she hasn't the slightest idea of its powers.

Then she wants to show how they dance back in her native land.

Then she invites the man with a gesture.

This does not end in a scene of rape.

The woman enjoys herself. Then she passes through many hands—and note that they all are the hands of venerable men—passes through palaces, witnessing how they kill men and throw them overboard, and the woman isn't distressed. She isn't linked to the environment in which she happens to be. These are strangers; the only thing that unites them is their desire for the same woman. But she isn't responsible for her behavior in front of these men.

The events happen through a chain of accidents. And this story that we are talking about is a delightful one.

It even charmed such a man as the great philologist Aleksandr Veselovsky.[38]

He said: "She's got character. This woman has preserved desire and eliminated repentance."

This story is different from the other stories in *The Decameron*.

■

When we read Boccaccio, we should note that what seems incredible to us was at least sometimes possible for Boccaccio and his contemporaries. This was a different time, which was, however, quickly progressing.

These were people who were involved in trade, knew Latin, wished to learn Greek, got robbed, robbed others, and recomposed street anecdotes into stories, which can be read even today and still have the power to surprise. But the most incredible thing (although it shouldn't surprise us) is the brilliance of those times, the fabric of which was being woven from various threads, including threads of the future. Literature doesn't just fol-

---

38 Aleksandr Veselovsky (1838–1906), Russia's foremost scholar on comparative literary history. A professor at St. Petersburg University, he contributed immensely to the establishment of historical poetics, which influenced the conceptualization of Formalist theory.

low the trails of the past. Sometimes it runs ahead. Perhaps that's why it never gets old, because it's woven out of human desire.

Boccaccio's collection of stories portrays a variety of morals that existed at one time.

As he was making up the list of characters from *War and Peace*, Tolstoy said about Natasha Rostova that she doesn't need to be an intellectual, she's much higher than that—she loves the bed.

In her conversation with her mother, she childishly asks: can one marry two men?

Rather unexpectedly, even for her, she wants to elope with Anatole Kuragin, although she loves Andrei Bolkonsky; Bolkonsky is an excellent match.

This proposition—whether one can love two persons—is of course disputable, but Tolstoy understood it very well. Kitty Scherbatskaya rejects Levin by saying: "That's impossible." This is a strange reply. She loves him, but she also loves Vronsky. She loves two men at the same time.

Female characters in novels were usually created without any options. The woman had no right of choice. It was the man who chose.

This situation did not reinforce a woman's virtue; it interfered with her fidelity.

In Boccaccio's story about Lady Filippa, the heroine from the small town of Prato, which is near Florence, doesn't recognize the law because the laws were made without women's consent.

This is the seventh story of the sixth day; it recounts the speech by Lady Filippa given in court.

The narrator is a man.

He says: "In the town of Prato, there used to be a law in force . . . to the effect that any woman caught by her husband in the act of adultery with a lover was to be burned alive, like any vulgar harlot who sold herself for money."

Lady Filippa was caught by her husband in the arms of a handsome and high-born youth.

band didn't kill anyone, but he brought charges against her.
ends advise her to escape, but she appears in court and says she
es that the charge was fair.

ever, she adds, "Laws should be equal for all, and should be made
he consent of those whom they affect. Such is not the case with this
cular law, which applies only to us poor women, who, after all, have it
ur power to give pleasure to many more people than men ever could. If
u insist upon enforcing it, not at the risk of my body, but of your immortal soul, you are at liberty to do so; but before you proceed to pass
judgement . . ." I will cut her speech short.

The woman addresses the judge: "That being the case, your honor, I'd like to ask him, since he has always had all he wanted of me and to his heart's content, what was I to do with all that was left over? Throw it to the dogs?"

People in the gallery burst into laughter. The law was changed.

Four hundred years ago women demanded equality with men in issues of love, and all other affairs.

They demanded that moral codes should be equal for both men and women.

Otherwise, evil things happen.

This theme, raised with comic or tragic consequences, appears variously in *The Decameron*, testing ground for new social morals.

The campaign was unsuccessful. Whatever was said in Prato was left unfinished.

Whatever was not resolved there was not resolved anywhere else.

There still exist two moral codes, as if separate.

A man's and a woman's, each with different prohibitions.

In a nutshell, the story is about men judging women by a different code.

I have already compared the two stories of the fourth day in *The Decameron*. They bring us back to the story of Anna Karenina. In both cases we are reminded not of the heart, torn from the chest, but the lovers' tragic union after death.

Anna was not forgiven by her society.

This theme about male and female fidelity was acceptable in novels because they were written for an audience that belonged to a circle of particular morals and laws, rules about what one can and cannot do.

Nevertheless, the unplanned adultery, or the possibility of adultery that has no justification, forms the basis of many novels.

In the novel of knight-errantry, the wife of the great king Arthur betrays her husband with Lancelot.

The knight tries to keep the affair hidden.

In the French novel, we often encounter men hesitant about adultery. This is the theme of Flaubert's *Madame Bovary*.

In the English novel, the woman remains faithful. In *Dombey and Son*, Dombey's wife, out of revenge, starts a rumor that she has betrayed her husband with his servant. In reality, nothing of the sort has happened. At the end of the novel, the reader is reassured as to the virtue of the heroine.

The pump was invented a long time ago. They began to use it in England for the removal of water from mines. Later on coal-fired engines were invented, in which heat from burning coals moved water through the pipe. The valve was shut and the pressure of the air forced the piston down. The piston was suspended on a rocker arm, which was connected to the plunger of the pump. Then the pipe was cooled off, and the atmospheric pressure pushed the water through the pipe. The valve was closed and the pumped water was poured out. This was the coal-fired engine. Later they invented the steam engine. Here, the engine had a separate built-in boiler, from which the pressurized steam pushed the pistons. This was the working stroke. It was the steam engine. The carriage already existed at this time. The steam engine was mounted on the carriage. The rocker arm of the engine swung, and through the crank, which we now call a crankshaft, the linear movement was transformed into a circular movement. Later on they mounted various engines on the same carriage and rode it. When the electric motor appeared it was merely a modification in the application of the problems of motion. Nothing is lost, everything is reinvented.

Women have always betrayed their husbands. Except in the age of Adam, and probably because he was the only man.

The question of adultery was judged in different ways.

Not too long ago, and at the beginning of "our era," they would stone a woman for adultery.

Infidelities by men were not judged at all.

There were two systems—male virtue and female virtue.

With different punishments for trangression.

But even in our times, adultery by a woman was considered a violation of a man's rights in regard to his property. I am not going to complicate this question by referencing the existence of polygamy, and the existence of polyandry, in, for example, Tibet. It was accepted in society that the bride had to be a virgin. The narrators of *The Decameron* didn't dispute this.

But the maidservants in *The Decameron* told how in their villages there wasn't a single case where, during a marital union, the woman was a virgin. That's how, it seems, the book is framed.

We are wrapping up the prologue to our discussion about Anna Karenina.

Tolstoy liked to insist on how little things changed for men. The only thing that changed was the sheepskin coat. Now it had two buttons on the back.

When copying from Olearius, he took pleasure in the fact that the Russian prince lived in his home like a peasant.

Tolstoy wanted to live in the past.

But he lived in the present.

Yet he was destined to live in the future.

He outlived Chekhov.

The present is only the peak of the roof.

We all live in the future—although the demands that we cautiously place on ourselves come from the past.

The sound of human existence gets out of tune, gets discordant.

Lev Nikolaevich tilled with a wooden plow. Such a tool is hardly ever used today.

But he was interested in a Japanese breed of piglets.

He wanted to create a new breed of horses.

He wanted to live in the future, for himself, renouncing human desires.

He dreamed about a life without marriage. I should add, though: he was jealous of all beautiful women.

In the first drafts of *Anna Karenina*, Tolstoy conceives a pretty woman who attracts men, but who is not a complete woman. She doesn't know how to dress, she has bad manners, but at the same time she resembles the much-adored Pushkin, or at least his daughter, whom Tolstoy had seen.

This is how Tolstoy loved the woman who had the features of the future.

4

A BRIEF NOTE ON EXPOSITIONS, THE BEGINNINGS AND ENDINGS OF WORKS— COMPOSITIONS

I.

About forty years ago I was traveling as a journalist through the steppes, passing Almaty to Semipalatinsk. It was in connection with deciding the route of the future Turksib railway.[39]

As I had expected, we were supposed to go through the desert. But we didn't see a desert. Instead it turned out to be a steppe, where we encountered high prices and workers who complained that a whole ram cost three rubles, and they didn't know what to do with its skin. I wanted to buy apples in Semipalatinsk. The apples were sold from the carts. I asked how much the apples were. They said—three rubles. As a typical journalist, I

[39] In 1930 Shklovsky wrote *Turksib*, a children's book about the successful completion of the railroad between Turkestan and Siberia during the first five-year plan.

took out a string bag from my pocket, and the whole town started laughing at me; they laughed for a few minutes. It was three rubles for the whole cart, each apple twice the size of my hand. Obviously, all couldn't fit in the bag. They were telling how in the mountains, when the wild apples would ripen and fall into the streams, the streams would overflow.

I didn't go into the mountains, but I did see the flocks of sheep, and the meat was so cheap. We kept going further, coming across not villages, but nomadic *yurt* camps.[40] The tents stood far apart from each other, so the pastures wouldn't get spoiled, and as soon as the grounds got trampled down, the encampment relocated.

The stars would light up at dusk. They would light up in the grass, because nothing hindered their view, and the mountains were too far away.

Here they told me, translating from a song, how once a man from one tribe loved a woman from another tribe. They were not allowed to marry each other, and both died from despair. Two trees grew over their graves, and when the wind blew from the west the branches of the trees entwined and sang together; when the wind changed its direction the trees lowered their branches and stood alone, parted forever.

After many decades, I am reading *Turkish Folk Tales* published in 1979; these tales, judging by the translation, are written in almost contemporary language: a man and a woman are in love, they are separated, and they die, after many miracles the two lovers are buried together, and trees grow over their grave.

They had talked through poems, and their identities were recognized only through those poems, and they conversed not only through poetry, but also riddles. The poems were like signals between two far-flung camps. Love, and poetry, and prose, and in prose the myths are all conjoined through riddles.

The riddles are so difficult that my teacher Sancho Panza used to say how he preferred to hear the answer first and then the riddle.

40 Tent dwellings in Central Asia.

Poems, novels, and stories are woven with riddles, but they have multitudes of answers, they all vary—the subject matters, the events, the people are not named; their character is not determined, it's created by way of the author's groping in the dark.

Knowledge progresses in steps, but the wind of denouement is already in the air.

The trees entwine their branches, and people recognize each other.

. . . The torment and secret of Raskolnikov. First, the riddle. It's not clear what he is up to, what he is about to commit, and the act itself—the crime—is only his experiment. A man wants to test his strength. Instead, he learns about the bitterness of his mistake. The mistake is as frightening as unrequited love.

Epics are being written. About unresolved love. Tatyana made a mistake in her timing. She fell in love before being loved; Onegin didn't fall in love with her after reading her letter because at the time he didn't know what love was.

Tatyana's letter to Onegin was translated into the Kazakh language, and girls sang this song as they milked cows. I heard this from people who knew for sure what poetry was.

They were ready to meet the true poet and, as a gesture of recognition that poetry was higher than prose, they were ready to get on their knees and wash the feet of the poet.

Similarly, in the Gospels, John the Baptist says how he wished that Jesus would immerse him in the water.

And he washed Jesus' feet at his arrival, in recognition of his superiority.

One good novelist, almost our contemporary, said that manuscripts don't burn.[41]

---

[41] "Manuscripts don't burn" was one of the quotes from Mikhail Bulgakov's (1891–1940) *The Master and Margarita* that quickly became a famous saying in the Russian underground.

This is a mistake of optimism. When Tynjanov was sick and they were carrying him out of Leningrad, he had strangers living in his apartment. It was cold there. Very cold. They had a little iron stove, which they heated with manuscripts. They didn't know that in fact they had burned the correspondence between Pushkin's and Kyukhelbeker's mothers.[42]

Two people as boys argued with each other, asking one another about answers and riddles, but in fact manuscripts do burn.

In the steppe, Khlebnikov, according to Dmitri Petrovsky, burned pages from his manuscript in order to "make the light last longer."[43] But he had them memorized.

When you burn manuscripts, take the advice of an old experienced man. Read everything that you burn. We used to do that in the House of Art. The manuscripts of the Serapion Brothers were initially read by the fire, and this isn't a bad reader for a start.[44]

[42] Vilhelm Kyukhelbeker (1797–1846), a Decembrist poet and Pushkin's friend. Leading Formalist Yuri Tynjanov (1894–1943), who was known especially for his brilliant comparative studies on Pushkin and Griboedov, wrote his novel *Kyukhlya* (1925) on Kyukhelbeker.

[43] Velemir Khlebnikov (1885–1922), leader of the Russian Futurist movement. At first influenced by the Russian symbolists and the Pan-Slavic nationalists, Khlebnikov began to experiment with neologistic poetry, exploring the ancient Slavonic roots and forms of contemporary words. But sharing few values with the symbolists, Khlebnikov gravitated toward the avant-garde.

[44] In 1920 Yevgeni Zamyatin and Viktor Shklovsky were working with a group of young writers on translations of Anglo-American literature. A year later the students from the Translators' Guild founded an official group called the Serapion Brothers, taking their name from E. T. Hoffmann's story about an individualist who vows to devote himself to a free, imaginative, and non-conformist art. Members included Lunts, Tikhonov, Kaverin, Zoschenko, Ivanov, and Fedin. The Serapion Brothers experimented and applied Formalist theories to their prose; by 1921 they had inaugurated a new era of Russian literature, which unfortunately, under the pressure of Lenin and other Soviet intellectuals, was distorted into Socialist Realism.

Osip Mandelstam[45] used to walk along dark stairways. He composed poems orally, searching for the answer in the sound of the spoken word. He used to say that the unwritten strophe is like a blind swallow that flies to "the palace of shadows" and then starts again: "I have forgotten the word I wanted to say. / A blind swallow returns to the palace of shadows."[46]

The number of so-called drafts is unusually high, especially when the drafts are drafts of thought.

Thoughts are wordless, observed Einstein, and for that reason the thinker is taken by surprise when he finds the answer to some mystery out of thin air.

The mysteries of drafts are unfathomable. It's as if mankind thinks in hypothetical ways. The answers are hidden in the already finished works, but have not yet exposed themselves.

It's as if human thought is premature. One answer replaces another. So do unaccomplished inventions. And so do revolutions. Under unexpected rainfalls, cities turn into hills. Houses, covered in the dust of centuries, become overgrown with trees. I have seen olive trees that looked like clenched muscles. When they were digging up those hills, they found rooms with writings on the walls and thought they were grottoes, not rooms, and they called the writings and drawings grotesque, because they had no answers.

A phenomenon in art never fades away.

[45] Osip Mandelstam (1891–1938), founder of Russian Acmeism along with Gumilev, Akhmatova, and Gorodetsky. In 1933 he sharply criticized Stalin in a poem titled "Stalin Epigram" for which he was arrested and exiled to northern Ural. In the coming years, at the height of the Great Terror involving the 1936–37 "show trials" and the mass arrests of "people's enemies," the literary establishment began a systematic assault on him in print, accusing him of harboring anti-Soviet views. His wife Nadezhda Mandelstam wrote about those years in her memoir *Hope Against Hope* (1970), in which she described how the Shklovskys helped them hide from the police and maintain a half-decent intellectual life. The official date and cause of Mandelstam's death in a Vladivostok labor camp was recorded as unknown.

[46] From Mandelstam's *Tristia* (1921).

Pushkin wrote about this, comparing the works of art with the achievements of science. The scientific achievements can get old, whereas the creations of art never do. This was something Marx wrote about. According to him it is comparatively easy to show how a certain foundation, certain conditions, create works of art, but it's difficult to understand why certain works of art outlive the environment that created them (Introduction to *A Critique of Political Economy*).

We all know that Homer, Shakespeare, Tolstoy, Dostoevsky never get old. I will clarify: if in certain periods of time Shakespeare, Pushkin, and Homer seem outdated and require alterations, then this period passes away and the recognition of the original text is renewed.

How can this phenomenon be explained?

I can't give a categorical answer, but here is an assumption: the work of art has various answers, and those answers, even though contradictory to each other, can all be right.

I can give a comparison; let's return to the riddles.

Riddles often are rhythmic. They are constructed in such a way that they contain a question. But a riddle's purpose is to have only one true answer, and myriads of other answers that are approximately true.

When you are given one or two clues to find the answer, you begin picking up on the implications, which you think coincide, but when they tell you the true answer, you think to yourself: "I would've never guessed that." You are pleased to find the answer.

Sancho Panza was profuse in his proverbs. These proverbs usually have nothing to do with the things that Sancho Panza alludes to, but they do renew the words in their meaning. There is some sort of a game going on, like a game of cards. What intrigues you is that you don't know the true answer.

Pushkin's *Queen of Spades* is based on this premise. Hermann was ruined because of a slip-up. He said something that he didn't intend to say. The answers attached to the riddle are constructed in this way: there is a true answer; however, it has erotic content, it's obscene. There also exists another, a proper answer. The person telling the riddle is playing on the embarrassment of his listeners. He's counting on misinterpretation.

Works of art are much broader in scope. They resolve things that were previously considered impossible to resolve.

The journeys of Odysseus are countless. The epic suggests an end to the journeys. Odysseus is carrying an oar on his shoulder. He meets a man who asks him: Why are you carrying a spade on your shoulder? The oar is mistaken for a spade. They haven't seen an oar before. Here, in these places, nobody goes on journeys. It's as if Odysseus has reached the end of his geographic riddles.

According to Dante in the *Divine Comedy*, it turns out that Odysseus dies. Behind the Pillars of Hercules he crashes against a mountain, which had emerged from Lucifer's fall as he rebelled against God. Lucifer pushed the earth at its antipode, creating a new mountain, which is Purgatory.

A pagan, Odysseus knows nothing about the mountain. It is from another myth.

■

The open-ended nature of human fate and the unpredictability of finding answers appear even in religious books, illuminating them from a different angle and somehow making them ironic. Job in the Bible loses all his wealth and children. He is afflicted with leprosy. The reason given is that God had a bet with Satan. But he gets well, recovers his flock, fathers new children. He is blessed.

Samson, blinded and powerless, regains his superhuman powers as his hair begins to grow back in prison. The secret of his strength is in his hair.

To kill the Philistines who laugh at him, he fells the stone pillars.

Yet it's true that in art happy, safe solutions don't last forever.

In Voltaire, the happy ends are ironic.

In Thackeray, they are foreshadowed by the author himself.

The happy ends in *Resurrection* and *Crime and Punishment* are based on a faith in God's goodwill.

Even though these denouements were promised by great authors, they weren't carried out. The new answer to happiness is promised only as a bribe.

Then we had tragedies. Their endings were terrible, dreadful; still, one tragedy followed another, thus establishing the well-being, if not of the individual, then of mankind. And maybe this solidified what was called the resolution of a tragedy.

Shakespeare's tragedies ended with the death of the heroes. But we need to bear in mind, here, the affects of time. According to Belinsky, Hamlet and Othello both see their own deaths as happy endings.

Pushkin dreamt of a happy ending; in the end, maybe love would be realized, maybe he would weep over his own imagination. That's a poetic resolution, but *Eugene Onegin* is not finished, neither is *War and Peace*. The latter ends with Andrei Bolkonsky's son, Nikolenka's dream. But alongside this are the arguments of Pierre and Nikolai Rostov. We observe that Nikolai, a well-to-do man, an ordinary person who has collected a huge library, who never bothered to buy a new, different book unless he finished reading the old one, this man, Nikolai Rostov, is the truest and fiercest enemy of the Decembrists.

Lev Nikolaevich died in his last attempt to justify the contradictions of his life.

There was no such man as Nikolai Rostov. He was constructed, as a matter of fact, rather remarkably, but he is that same ordinary person who would smash the Decembrists and die, counting himself a hero.

I got sidetracked from the topic.

But it was my idea to set an objective. I have yet to figure out what it is.

For the time being I'll make another correction. The great critic Vissarion Belinsky, whose greatness I found only in my old age, saw the wonderful actor Mochalov in the role of Hamlet eight times. He was trying to find out why tragedies bring pleasure through their outcome.

In the meantime, we started a conversation on expositions, the beginnings and endings of works—compositions.

About denouements, about the attempts to overcome the contradictions of life.

II.

According to Aristotle, a whole is something that has a beginning, middle, and end. But a work of art, especially a work of literature, doesn't have or doesn't always have a beginning, middle, and end. Maybe we can have a whole in music, or sculpture, or painting. These works are supposed to be a whole. But statues don't move.

Art (literature) makes a whole through movement.

The beginning is usually given through exposition.

Homer begins *The Iliad* with:

Rage—Goddess, sing the rage of Peleus' son Achilles . . .

What does it mean?

Achilles isn't fighting.

The rage of Achilles, who's lost the woman he won in the initial victory—this anger is a break in the balance between the Trojan forces and the Achaeans surrounding them.

A literary work is conceived with a view to disrupting harmony. This theme persists throughout *The Iliad*.

The scales of the gods oscillate as they jealously guard its balance. And so let's compare: the hand of fate pushes the scales of the worker, she has been harvesting for many hours and wants to weigh her cropping. She watches how the scale's arrow oscillates and thinks to herself: is this enough or not enough to compensate me for the hard labor and get a modest dinner for my children?

Disharmony is one of the laws of art.

We experience life through disharmony, through contrast.

Works, compositions, often begin with an exposition. Not always though.

It wasn't always like that. It won't always be like that.

Oedipus as a child is thrown out of the house in which he was born; breaking the harmony of his ancestry, from the very beginning Oedipus is destined for misfortune, murder, marriage with his own mother. Abruptness in the juxtaposition of contrasts—this is the nature of exposition in most Greek tragedies.

Sometimes in later, more modern works the exposition appears in the form of a document: an inheritance, a deed, a record of purchase, or a posthumous letter, as in Thackeray.

This is the traditional style of creating an exposition or a denouement.

Such an exposition exists in one of the threads in *War and Peace*: in the hall Drubetskaya is quarrelling over an inlaid portfolio with a woman from the Bezukhov family. The women aren't saying anything to each other; they are quarrelling in silence. If only their mouths opened, they would begin swearing. Meanwhile in the next room there is a dying man—Bezukhov, who is probably the historic character of Aleksandr Bezborodko, a very affluent man who owned documents about the inheritance of the throne. The portfolio contains Pierre Bezukhov's fate; he is the illegitimate son, and this is basis for an imbalance, for the arrow to oscillate on the scales.

Bezukhov gets the inheritance. This is the exposition, because the now rich Bezukhov falls victim to Helene, or rather, her father: this was the way they regained their loss. Thus begins the drama of a man who lives as an eccentric rich man and who, nevertheless, loves in a simple and passionate way another woman who is completely unaware. Later, Bezukhov's fate oscillates differently: he is one of the Masons, and they help him.

Then it turns out that the exposition could have been better if rendered more realistically. The Masons don't help Bezukhov on the road; they don't bring him any provisions. Like the rest, he goes with the prisoners.

In one of his compositions, Thackeray listed the unlikely but most commonly occurring denouements. One of them was inheritance, the discovery of a document.

In Dickens, for Little Dorrit to get married, the imbalance between her position and that of her future husband is resolved through the happy ruin of Dorrit, who left his fortune in the hands of a swindler.

The exposition for one of the storylines in *Nicholas Nickleby* arrives in the form of the will that ends up in the house of a Jewish moneylender and is saved with the help of a blow on the head from a bellows—a wonderful weapon because it knocks out a person instead of smashing his head. The balance is restored.

In Dostoevsky's *The Adolescent*, the conversation constantly revolves around an important document, which gives status to an illegitimate person in a foster family, but the will does not materialize.

Apart from the will, the exposition may contain a mystery, which is later solved; this persisted in English literature for quite a long time; like a mystical recipe, the hidden ingredients of a heavy rich dough, these novels were based on a secret.

■

Let's digress and say a few words about beginnings.
When Pushkin opens his *Eugene Onegin* with:

My uncle has most honest principles:
when he was taken gravely ill . . .

such a beginning does not foretell the denouement, but rather the way in which the textual content will unravel throughout the entire poem. It will be as unexpected as its opening.

After such an opening, one can digress in any direction.

The denouements are difficult, they are more difficult than folkloric riddles, they are difficult in their persistence.

Hegel, when talking about denouements, remembers how the pride of a young person "lunging with his horns into a wall—is blind."

Pride and love will change into something habitual—a failed happiness, "an ordinary story."

Thackeray resented the idea of denouement. He compared it with the residue of tea on the bottom of a cup; it's too sugary. It's obvious to the reader that it is a condensation of unresolved conflicts.

To humor himself, Thackeray wanted his footman to write the ending for him, after he was done cleaning his boots and dress.

So then it appears that denouements are based on the premise that they don't really exist.

This entire thread—this dying thread, is the road of a plot that has been abandoned.

■

Some expositions are disguised.

A simple carriage with middle-class landowners, priests, and somebody else arrives in an unknown city. This is from *Dead Souls*.

Two peasants are examining the carriage. They are describing the carriage, its wheels, how far they can go.

This helps show that the man who is in the carriage will go far, that he's a vagabond, that he's looking for something. There's a mystery in the description of the wheel.

But notice how this carriage appears again in Chekhov's "The Steppe."

Chekhov calls Gogol the tsar of the steppes. And he sends a britzka into the steppe, that same britzka in which Gogol's hero rode. The britzka is carrying a priest, who sells wool, i.e., he is a dealer, a novice dealer; a boy's uncle, who is also not very experienced; and a boy, who is the most important person in the carriage. He doesn't know anything, and because of that he sees everything with new eyes.

Gogol's britzka is connected to the search for dead souls. The document replaces the missing peasants; they are bought and sold, but they are non-existent.

This will be shown when the owners of the dead souls appear one by one, each reacting differently to the proposal to break the law.

It's done for money, or out of thoughtlessness, or in the case of Chichikov, the purchaser, through cunning. The author is not in a hurry to reveal the purpose of the bargain and what exactly the title of the work means; the exposition is pushed far into the novel, and so is the characterization of the main hero. Meanwhile, time is passing.

■

At the beginning of *War and Peace* there was a dispute over a document. Simultaneously we are presented with an adolescent love affair, where the girl, in order to kiss the object of her infatuation, first asks him to kiss her doll, then kisses him, standing up on a box for flowers.

In the exposition, Pierre Bezukhov's characteristics are changed, embellished. Here Tolstoy is fleshing out the witnesses of the 1812 events.

But let me show where and how this happens. At the reception of an old lady, the court's maid of honor, the conversation spins around Napoleon, how he has captured Genoa and Lucca.

So partly, the exposition is staged as in a theater, through the conversation of the characters.

But time is passing.

In *Anna Karenina*, the novel's exposition is unconventional, it's framed sideways, not through the main characters. A secondary character has an irrelevant dream. He sees women in the shape of carafes, and singing glass tables. This is the kingdom of a frivolous person. This is a false kingdom in which the king, an aristocrat who leads an easy life, is Stiva Oblonsky.

Right away we are told that even though Stiva is dreaming in his study, on the divan, where he slept because of a quarrel with his wife over his affair with the governess, all the characters in the novel are on Stiva's side. Even the children whose father committed adultery.

Even the old nurse who raised the woman who had been wronged.

The exposition reveals the clashing forces.

In this way, the second part, the adultery by a woman, is pushed far aside and even concealed.

Anna Karenina likes Kitty Scherbatskaya, but she unintentionally robs Kitty of her suitor, although Vronsky isn't really planning on marrying Kitty. His intentions are not to seduce the girl. He is merely won over by her charm without having any concrete plan in mind.

Then the story unravels through Dolly's conversation with Stiva's sister, where Anna suddenly says that she is guilty, guilty just "a little," and she says this using the tone of her brother.

Here we are given views on male and female adultery; this is a theme talked about by the philosophers so copiously and accurately quoted in Eichenbaum's book, among them Schopenhauer and someone else.

I'll make a digression here.

I think that I'm in the position of a cyclist who can't ride on the road because there are too many cars and can't ride on the sidewalk because there are too many pedestrians.

At the beginning of *Crime and Punishment*, when Raskolnikov comes to his friend Razumikhin, the latter suggests that he translate a German book, *Is Woman a Human Being?*; the book—complete rubbish—was in vogue; it re-examined the roles of women.

All right, I'll make another digression: I think I'm almost like a magician. He pulls out the rabbits: they seem to have vanished. They reappear. No, that's not it. They are still there, but concealed.

The re-examination of women's role.

This was the topic of the century. It was raised differently in France and differently in Russia; for us it emerged in another context.

In Russia, Lev Nikolaevich wrote a very good story: "Idyll."

A woman is unfaithful to her husband. She sleeps with the herdsman. The husband finds out and beats her, then lies by her side on the stove. They make peace and a child is born. The child has the features of someone else, but at the end there is almost no jealousy.

Tolstoy, like Pushkin, sees class differentiation in jealousy.

Pushkin goes to a warring region and meets with a Cossack who is returning from his long service.

They talk.

Pushkin wants to know what he would do if he discovered his wife had been unfaithful to him.

"If she hasn't stored away some hay for winter, I'll beat her."

This episode is from the drafts of "A Journey to Arzrum."

Literature emulates different things differently. But it doesn't merely emulate, it torments itself, inviting us to watch these tortures. I will reflect more than once on Tolstoy's house in Khamovniki.

A good manor house, somewhat outside the estate, which had neighboring houses that were also built specifically for wintering in the city. They were like winter *yurts*.

Lenin said that the person who lived in that house lived differently on each floor.

And so this person gave resolutions and expositions in his own way.

What can be more frightening and profound than the simple exposition of "The Death of Ivan Ilych"? A dead man lying in his coffin like any other corpse in a coffin.

His wife is a little sad—she is concerned about the pension. His life was dreadful, but his death doesn't seem so frightening. The exposition speaks about the dread of the ordinary.

∎

I'm not writing a biography, that is, I don't have to accompany the carriage full of treasures as an infantryman. And I'm not writing a manual for young fiction writers about how to open or close their prose works. Life will teach them that. Step accidentally on your untied shoelace, fall down and you'll understand a thing or two about the theory of literature. I'm a tired cyclist. There was a time, there once were the young Futurists;

—allow me to change the course of my thought.

In Paris, I don't recall on which street, there's a marble statue of Napoleon. He's nude, but he looks dignified. His nudity is reasonably covered. But one can't imagine him getting down and walking with the people.

On the Mayakovsky Square, there, on the cross section, stands Mayakovsky in bronze. He's black and huge. It's made absolutely clear that he can step down, walk on the street, argue with people, give directions.

He died too soon. And at the end of his poem he wrote a request to be resurrected. Those were his very words: "Resurrect me."[47]

To resurrect in order to see the future—the great hope that consumes solipsism.

[47] From "About That" (1922).

∎

I'll make one more digression, abrupt, but necessary.

In art there aren't absolute methods for structuring compositions.

A work has to be composed so that it turns into something unexpected and innovative. Sometimes denouements conflict with the main structure of the text. Then readers will say, or at least assume, that the denouement is in the work itself, and maybe in its ending.

The wife of the landowner in Gogol's "Old World Landowners" dies first, imagining that the return of her cat is a bad omen. Then her devoted husband dies. Their idyllic life at the beginning of the story is shown in a different, unexpected light.

We experience a new sensation from what we've just read, envious of the old couple's quiet life.

Now let's return to *The Iliad*.

The Iliad is not fantastic fiction. It's a real world, in which there are women who earn their living by harvesting bread. There are seasons and gods, but they are asleep when humans sleep, and this is why unreal things seem more powerful in *The Iliad*.

The epic is constructed on a series of battles, prophecies, and personal tragedies, which have happened or will happen.

Andromache, who is presented as a loving mother and wife, appears in the burial scene as a woman talking about her future, mourning for her own fate and the fate of her son.

Now let's talk about what could have been the ending of *The Iliad*. We know, as I mentioned, that *The Iliad* begins with the verse:

Rage—Goddess, sing the rage of Peleus' son Achilles,
murderous, doomed, that cost the Achaeans countless losses.

At the end, the mother first warns her son about his possible death as she hands him the weapons; by the end of her song we are unexpectedly forewarned of the outcome.

The armies go to save Patroclus, and Achilles is to be blamed for his fate.

But these two tragedies, the deaths of these heroes are connected.

I'll give a longer quote.

It's remarkable.

And Xanthus the horse with flashing hoofs
spoke up from under the harness, bowing his head low
so his full mane came streaming down the yoke-pads,
down along the yoke to sweep the ground . . .
The white-armed goddess Hera gave him voice:
"Yes! we will save your life—this time too—
master, mighty Achilles! But the day of death
already hovers near, and we are not to blame,
but a great god and the strong force of fate.
Not through our want of speed or any lack of care
did the Trojans strip the armor off Patroclus' back.
It was all that matchless god, sleek-haired Leto's son—
he killed him among the champions and handed Hector glory.
Our team could race with the rush of the Zephyr,
the strongest, swiftest wind on earth, men say—
still you are doomed to die by force, Achilles,
cut down by a deathless god and mortal man!"

He said no more. The Furies struck him dumb.
But the fiery runner Achilles burst out in anger,
"Why, Xanthus—why prophesy me doom?
Don't waste your breath. I know, well I know—
I am destined to die here, far from my dear father,
far from mother. But all the same I will never stop
till I drive the Trojans to their bloody fill of war!"[48]

48 From *The Iliad*, Book 19.

This excerpt talks about gallantry, i.e., the real end is foretold here and it takes place inevitably.

This is why we presume that the absence of the ending in *The Iliad* is somewhat questionable.

The entire audience is as if unified in its knowledge of this mythology. The warnings given by the horse should be enough. He is reminding them about something that everyone already knows. He is escorting a man who is going to his own death.

It seems like Achilles is preparing for his death. He swiftly gets up to pick out the sheep; chops the wood, does everything required for a sacrificial rite and last supper. He harnesses the horses.

Crowds mourn Achilles.

Hecuba mourns Hector.

Andromache mourns her husband and her future fate.

The end of *The Iliad* is about Hector's death. His father doesn't plead with the gods.

Achilles' rage is exhausted. There's a burial, a strict ritual ceremony, and thus ends the epic, the first word of which was "rage."

So, we shouldn't say that *The Iliad* doesn't have an ending. The only thing that's not described is the victors' death.

We must differentiate two things.

The end of a hero.

And the end of an epic.

■

Let's talk about something closer to us, something we are all familiar with—*Eugene Onegin*. At the very end of the poem Pushkin says that won't be an ending. It's as though he is getting excited by the fact that there is no ending.

And strangely, Tolstoy repeats this statement in his prologue to *War and Peace*. Lev Nikolaevich says that a traditional resolution takes away the meaning from the process of setting up an exposition. He regrets that compositions have to end with a death, but he points out that the death of one hero transfers our interest to other heroes.

Let's remind the reader that for our folktale performers it's clear that the heroes are dead. Achilles' death didn't hinder *The Odyssey* from appearing after *The Iliad*.

The fact that this was written by the same person was even checked, I believe, by computers.

Although computing machines arc of little use when it comes to calculating the properties of fiction, because they are specifically programmed to not make any mistakes.

It took Pushkin ten years to write his *Eugene Onegin*. His generation was gone, he was sent to exile, the echo had vanished.

Pushkin was alone, like Arion saved by a dolphin.

He was finishing his song, which was destined to last forever. He was finishing it on a lonesome boulder and drying his sodden clothes.[49]

Tolstoy was saying that denouements in old novels (that usually ended in weddings) were wrong. Because a wedding is only the set-up, and certainly not the resolution of a conflict.

Aristotle once said, and I started this discussion by quoting him, that a whole is something that has a beginning, middle and end. But poetry doesn't recognize ends. The fate of Achilles is a famous myth. Even his horses know it. But it's not enacted, not realized, only foretold. And Odysseus's journey in *The Odyssey* is not finished. We can only repeat that the death of the hero shifts our interest to another hero.

Pushkin loved his poem "The Fountain of Bakhchisaray."

The fountain didn't dry out, and now it is the "fountain of tears." The drops of water fall from one cusp onto another and then evaporate.

A sad fountain.

This is how Pushkin ends his *Eugene Onegin*:

[49] Imagery from Pushkin's "Arion" (1827).

But those to whom at amicable meetings
its first strophes I read—
"Some are no more, others are distant,"
as erstwhiles Saadi said.
Without them was Onegin's picture finished.
And she from whom was fashioned
the dear ideal of "Tatyana" . . .
Ah, much, much has fate snatched away!
Blest who left life's feast early,
not having to the bottom drained
the goblet full of wine;
who never read life's novel to the end
and all at once could part with it
as I with my Onegin.

Many people spoke and wrote: how is it possible not to have an end? Onegin was left alive. And so was Tatyana. But the poet was only able to put life aside. There were no denouements, but a reversal. His Onegin was not allowed to live in Petersburg ("harmful is the North") or anywhere else. Except for Siberia. Tatyana said, and she said it with conviction, even almost defenselessly:

I love you still (why dissimulate?)
but to another I belong:
to him I shall be faithful all my life.

But it's difficult for me to break so abruptly from a theme that's been on my mind for such a long time.

Once, when we were young, the opera *Victory over the Sun*[50] was staged

50 The first Futurist opera, *Victory over the Sun*, with sets and costumes designed by Kazimir Malevich, a prologue by Velimir Khlebnikov, music composed by Mikhail Matushin. The opera was first performed at the Lunapark Theater in

for a very short time. It was written by Mayakovsky and Khlebnikov, and presented by Kruchenykh, none of whom are alive today. At the beginning of the presentation two circus strongmen opened the curtains and announced: "All's well that starts well."—"Ends," someone would correct from the audience. And they would answer from the stage: "There won't be an end."

Russian literature, great Russian literature, doesn't have endings.

They were persuading Pushkin to finish *Eugene Onegin*.

But he knew that a work doesn't have an ending. He welcomed people who could put aside the half-finished goblet. He lauded himself for being able to make his parting bow with life as abruptly "as I with my Onegin." This turned out to be prophetic. Pushkin was foretold of his end. He didn't finish writing his life and couldn't finish writing about the structuring of the censored chapters, chapters that were encoded, where he talks about the Decembrists, with each Decembrists' name spelled out. Onegin appears in their context.

Pushkin made a sketch.

He is standing with Onegin, leaning against the heavy granites along the banks of the Neva, the Fortress of Peter and Paul in the background. The site where the Decembrists were hanged.

Eugene Onegin was destined to die with the people from his generation. This is understood by the mentioning of names with whom the epic, or the novel in verse, had begun. They no longer exist. They have ceased and not ceased at the same time because their work has not been finished.

St. Petersburg in 1913, on a double bill with Mayakovsky's play *Vladimir Mayakovsky: A Tragedy*. The plot that symbolized the human conquest of natural forces and the conquering of the old by the new revolved around a group of strongmen who capture the sun and enclose it in a square container for destructive or constructive purposes. Dissonant music and sound effects accompanied the actors' movements and speech.

Pushkin had them in mind when opening "The Fountain of Bakhchis-araay"—the fountain of tears—with the following epigraph:

> Many have visited this fountain, as I
> have done; but some are no more,
> others are distant.—Saadi

Eugene Onegin continued to exist, as though transformed, in that quote. This quote became the words of the poet himself:

> "Some are no more, others are distant,"
> as erstwhiles Saadi said.

But this quote was offered to divert the attention.

The true demise of Onegin would have interrupted Tatyana's story. It was beyond expression, incommensurable with the unfortunate love that was realized much too late.

Eugene Onegin is not finished. The epic, though, that Pushkin began was finished.

You will probably say: how is that possible?

Maybe you will even ask: which epic?

I'll answer: the pre-extant epic.

For all this had been already foreshadowed, foretold as it was being written: "Here's an epic that probably won't ever be finished."

Great Russian literature is adept at not having endings.

Happily married, experiencing happiness at home, even though a bit worried, but still happy, Anna Karenina was riding in a train during a storm from Moscow to St. Petersburg. The description of the storm is powerful; nobody succeeded in describing it so well in fiction before. Karenina is reading an English novel about some baronet who at the end of the novel achieves his "baronet" happiness, a happy life at his country estate.

But the endings of great English writers are deceitful.

Literature, great literature, does not recognize happy endings.

Once, in a humorous journal, young Chekhov listed things that were forbidden to writers. Among them he had faithful servants devoted to their masters. There were many happy endings.

But Chekhov himself never wrote any happy endings. *The Cherry Orchard* ends with everyone leaving the house around which they are cutting the cherry trees. Left alone in the house, the servant says they have forgotten a person behind. It's the faithful, happy servant who was supposed to be in an English novel.

Happy endings are for a different mankind, a happier mankind that will be able to live without wars, that will create a new kind of love that Mayakovsky dreamed about, the kind of love Blok rejected.

Blok wrote: "Really, must we swear / to ancient faithfulness forever?"

And before that he wrote: "Yes, there is a sad delight in love / that will melt away like snow."[51]

Spring arrives. The birds, those that don't fly away, feel the sun. They begin to chirp in a different way. They sit differently on the branches. The other birds return, those that know how to fly away from winter, yet faithfully return to their old nests.

Poets rarely last into their old age. And if they do stay alive and get old, they become ministers of small republics, or producers of old plays that reinvent puppet theater. I am talking about *Faust* and Goethe.

One shouldn't be afraid of death or life, but should finish writing the books in which he is unable to describe his visions of the future.

But the future does exist.

Snakes outgrow their old skin because the skin can no longer expand. They shed their coat, called *deadskin*. When Dahl said this word to Pushkin, he laughed.[52]

[51] From "On the Islands" (1909).

[52] Vladimir Dahl (1801–72), a Russian lexicographer who took great interest in the Russian language and folklore. He traveled by foot throughout Russia to collect

Some day old literature will become beautiful deadskin, beautiful as old art.

Art, in the multiplicity of its experiments, in the long search for methods, is creating paths along which all of mankind will pass in the future.

The delusion of art is the energy of search. It's not a dance, or a shamanic spell where the shaman moves with heavy iron bells hanging from his body.

Art in its endless search for perfection knows only one thing—not how to end, but how to see.

What is a happy ending?

Chekhov wrote that the writer who'd come up with a new ending for plays, besides a death or a departure, would be the greatest artist.

Chekhov advised, that as soon as the story was written, before even reading it, one should tear out the first few pages, the ones with the exposition. But Chekhov also knew how not to write expositions. He knew how to force the reader to look at things that would purify him without illusion.

The happy ending claims: life doesn't need reinvention or alteration.

—I started this chapter with Aristotle's words.

—And so.

Does this mean that we are living in a world that's incomplete?

---

popular sayings and folktales. His important work, *Explanatory Dictionary of the Live Great Russian Language*, was published in 1863–66, and later became an influential linguistic work in the study of the Slavic etymological lexicon.

5

PLOT, REVERSAL AND STORY

PARODY AND REINVENTION OF PLOT

I.

And so, there are two books.

The first one is called, let's say, "Energy of Delusion." I am basing this book mainly on *Anna Karenina*.

The second, I imagine, is called "The Death of Myth, or The Disintegration of Structure."

What we define as plot is the analysis of a certain theme and its narration in a style that has been found the most effective.

Gradually this method of writing becomes more difficult.

It's the true and accurate depiction of a century; but centuries, too, come to an end.

The second book begins from here.

... And so, we see and know that plots are repeated in fairytales, stories, novels and even newspaper articles—not so much repeated but rather changed to reflect life more accurately.

But for accuracy we must choose a certain method for arranging the material, which simultaneously gives the material form and, unfortunately, confines it.

This method compels us to use words selectively.

But there are two strands in literature:

—chronological succession—historiography

—and oats that sprout through the matting. The emergence of new material in the field of art.

I'll give an example.

Let's go back to our discussion of *The Decameron*.

We notice here that there are three kinds of plot.

First, we have direct recordings of anecdotes, clever remarks and word games; this is the first, and of all of them, the weakest element.

Second—the narration of extraordinary incidents where people emerge from difficult situations in extraordinary ways.

These are erotic tales recounting, or rather, rewriting an erotic plot so that it ends happily.

Sea voyages were very difficult in the Greek and Roman worlds. There was the threat of piracy, women got abducted, people were turned into slaves; all of which, even today, exist in children's tales in their true form, as, for example, in the dream world of Tom Sawyer.

Third is plot that becomes a parody.

And so, the pirates' abduction of a woman is a game with danger. We want her to be saved, yet we can't do anything. Then a new abduction, a new attempt to save her, and so on, until we are once again faced with danger.

On certain occasions this kind of plotting was based on the envy of gods —the woman was beautiful and famous, the gods would become envious and plunge her into adventures.

The heroes undergo a process of selection.

A hero must be helpless and have little individuality.

I'll take *Daphnis and Chloe* as an ideal example of this type of fiction.

A man and a woman are together, but they are slaves to different masters; their fate is that of a slave's—inconstant. But since we don't fear very much for what happens to the slave, there is an alteration in the device.

There are three kinds of dangers inherent to *Daphnis and Chloe*:

the woman can be abducted by pirates;

she can be married off;

or the man can become another man's lover. In those days this was a very common thing.

But the games must eventually come to an end. Daphnis and Chloe, whom we saw in the garbs of slaves, turn out to be the children of noblemen and rejoice that they've finally found their happiness.

Which means.

A diagram has been formed with plotted characters based on raw material.

This comes through in a novel such as *Aethiopica*. The novel gets complicated through its portrayal of incredible fates set up in incredible and exotic circumstances. A high-ranked Greek fighter, for example, wins a battle with a savage because he knows the weak spots on the human body.

I can give another example.

Let's take the subject of female infidelity, her cunning, but in the following episode there is a shift in the subject, it is sort of reversed. I am vulgarizing everything.

In one of Boccaccio's stories there is an old man who can't satisfy his pretty young wife. He decides to explain his weakness through abstinence and tells her about the inappropriateness of sexual union during feasts and holidays, which happen to be almost every day.

His wife falls into the hands of a pirate and becomes his mistress. Her husband, a traditional sort of man, a judge and an affluent man, collects money to pay ransom for his wife.

But the wife doesn't want to be ransomed. She tells him that she scorns him. If you were to be squeezed from head to toe, she says, there wouldn't be a thimbleful of sauce to show for it. Her husband promises to try harder. He warns her of losing her honor, of making a mistake. But the wife replies:

if you must speak of honor, you should have done so earlier—I am staying with the one who proves to be a real husband.

It seems the plot has been reversed.

But it must be concluded somehow, at least in a decent manner.

The story proceeds to tell about the death of the first husband.

The lovers then get engaged and officially become husband and wife. Meaning, the wolves are fed and the sheep is still alive.[53]

■

There is another well-known example of theme reversal.

I'll have to repeat Boccaccio's story of Alatiel.

In this story, which was Veselovsky's favorite by the way, the Sultan of Babylon, (implying the ruler of Alexandria), sends off his daughter escorted by her entourage to another king, her future husband. During a storm the ship is wrecked, her servants drown and she is saved by a handsome man, who politely entertains her. Knowing nothing about wine and not knowing the language, she cannot respond to love, which she perceives through a smile. But she becomes tipsy and wants to show how women dance in Alexandria.

Then she ends up in bed and, completely drunk—or, let's say, in a state of drunkenness—invites the man, who is very handsome, to her bed.

Since she doesn't know his language or religion, she feels no guilt.

But then there are eight other incidents where she passes from hand to hand.

She's kidnapped, carried away, she's supposed to keep the bed warm for her lovers.

Very simple and realistic motifs.

As a result, somewhat worn out, she sees the Sultan's servant, who promises to take her back to her father and teaches her how to explain her long absence.

[53] A Russian saying, meaning both sides are satisfied and no one is harmed.

Back at home, she tells about the shipwreck, how she was saved by women from a Christian monastery, who were the devout worshippers of St. Stiffen-in-the-Hollows, and how she was really honored there as a woman who performed the truest rites.

Everyone believes her story.

The story, by the way, is farcical, because it's told in a Christian country about a Christian monastery.

She finally is united with her destined husband and learns that lips don't lose their freshness, but are renewed by kisses.

This story is a parody of Rome.

But let's take such a qualified expert in literature as Veselovsky. He describes the story of Alatiel and says that it breaks away from the ordinary folklore.

How so? This fable reveals a new relation to something that was considered sinful and brought misfortune.

Or, in misfortune pleasure is found.

These sorts of changes occur very often. There is an element of parody in *The Golden Ass*. An enterprising and curious young man is magically transformed into an ass and passes through adventures that become very erotic at the end.

■

In the book by Dickens eventually titled *The Posthumous Papers of the Pickwick Club*, Mr. Pickwick is characterized at his first appearance in the following way:

A casual observer [. . .] might possibly have remarked nothing extraordinary in the bald head, and circular spectacles [. . .]: to those who knew that the gigantic brain of Pickwick was working beneath that forehead, and that the beaming eyes of Pickwick were twinkling behind those glasses, the sight was indeed an interesting one. There sat the man who had traced to their source the mighty ponds of Hampstead, and agitated the scientific world with his Theory of Tittlebats, as calm and unmoved as the deep waters of the one on a frosty day, or as a solitary specimen of the other in the inmost recesses of an earthen jar.

The hero is presented as a parody. The ponds mentioned in this passage are in the city. The tittlebat, I'd say, is the worst of all the fish. The hero himself, his frock coat and his gestures—everything is a parody. The hero talks of his future deeds:

Traveling was in a troubled state, and the minds of coachmen were unsettled. Let them look abroad and contemplate the scenes which were enacting around them. Stage-coaches were upsetting in all directions, horses were bolting, boats were overturning, and boilers were bursting.

These are the accounts from an ordinary trip around the city and its outskirts.

The audience is relieved to know that the expedition of Mr. Pickwick will be funded out of his own pocket.

This is a caricature of travels in Africa, the "arduous expedition" to explore the basin of the Nile, a caricature of things that some decades later would become material for Jules Verne.

But the novel begins, the heroes are presented, every single one—a parody. Their deeds are unsuccessful. A parody adventure begins, and all of England is watching it.

Travel is the simplest method for showing not just the localities, but also the hero.

Since the hero somehow reflects us or our neighbors, his actions are unpredictable, but it is necessary for us to learn about them.

Pushkin said that a hero lives in hypothetical circumstances. He is given an assignment, a map for his future travels, but they turn into something unpredictable.

Surprising are not only Khlestakov's behavior, but also all of Chichikov's travels.

But we'll talk about this some other time.

■

So, plot is almost always based on a real conflict that has been resolved in different ways at different times.

This is why plot is constructed on the emotional, as in the early novel of knight-errantry *The Song of Roland*, or on parody, as in *Don Quixote*, or on the poetic, as it is, again, in *Don Quixote*, because—for Dostoevsky— Don Quixote, who cannot change the world, represents a tragic theme.

Don Quixote is the long journey of an old man who learns and evolves along the way.

So, let's note: a traditional plot from a certain time period gets reinvented and resurfaces in another time period.

Every construction lives alongside the existing world in which it is created. Occasionally it outlives its epoch. This occurs when the work, while remaining unchanged in its main points of construction, becomes renewed through reinvention.

And we have seen instances where the parody of old form transforms into something new.

The knight-errantry novel was being enriched for a long time, and it went on to parody itself for an equally long time.

Ariosto's epic, one of Pushkin's favorites, was an ironic parody on the knight-errantry novel:

—on the concept of faithfulness to woman,

—on the concept of the all-conquering man,

and this novel, not having evolved into its final new form, was abandoned.

The new development of the knight-errantry novel coincided with the emergence of printing presses.

The knight-errantry novel gained a new reader.

In *Don Quixote*, one of the owners of the inn tells how he kept a box full of knight-errantry novels, both in print and manuscript form, and how he liked to read them to the harvesters, and we are meant to understand that this is a means of payment.

Don Quixote initially was a parody on the knight-errantry novel, whereas it was made clear which things were being imitated in the parody sections.

Even Don Quixote's armor was a parody.

Had Achilles taken his time to examine his new weapons, and had this taken the biggest portion of *The Iliad*, this segment would have been retained or further developed in the knight-errantry novel.

Don Quixote was originally conceived only as a comedic work.

Originally, Don Quixote is a poor gentleman, not a don, but a hidalgo, a man from an impoverished family, whose household consisted of a few sheep, a servant, a housekeeper, a niece, and a dovecote that supplied a meal for Sundays and manure for fertilizing the lands.

In the first chapters of the novel Don Quixote's speech is imitative and the author even points out which novel he is imitating from. Don Quixote is not a very clever man. In his description of Don Quixote's departure, Cervantes writes: "the sun advanced so fast, and with such intense heat, that it was sufficient to have melted his brains, if he had had any."

His attempted departure ends with the knight's conflict with a muleteer of the merchants from Toledo. Beaten and stretched on the ground, in his delirium Don Quixote continues reciting verses from the romance.

What am I trying to say?

The author of the novel was an old man who previously had published close to nothing. The novel was written in prison, which is clearly stated in the author's preface, and it was conceived directly as a parody of the knight-errantry novel, i.e., the parody was based on something that everyone knew very well.

Work changes a person. There is a Russian saying, "The eyes are afraid, whilst the hands create." The hands are capable of doing what the eyes haven't seen yet. The hands teach the head.

A person writing a novel learns how to write if he is indeed a writer. And in the process of writing he masters the subject, creating something completely new.

The examination of Don Quixote's library is an interesting bridge between the parody of the old form and the emergence of the new one—the new possibilities in expression of the new content. It's like a device for retaining the old heritage, analyzing it, a rather authoritative selection of what is important, which in its turn expels the elements of parody.

But what if the hero himself is a parody, dressed in parodied garments, repeating the great tradition of receiving magical or super weapons?

His pasteboard helmet is the death of the old epic weapons.

This parody lasted until the emergence of new kinds of weapons—firearms.

Don Quixote began to commit real heroic deeds.

The parody is replaced with new evaluations of the old culture.

The second part of *Don Quixote*, to which we refer less often, is set ten years after the first part. The hero lives among the people who have "read" him.

By doing so he becomes a person of his own times, a contemporary.

It's the same Don Quixote, whom, according to the preface, everyone knows, all the lackeys who can read, the children and the old.

It's the reanimation of the old expended hero.

And the parody form transmutes into the new form of the psychological novel.

I don't have enough knowledge, the exact knowledge, to prove that the choice of Catalonia, instead of Saragosa, the choice of Barcelona, the city of revolution, and Don Quixote's meeting with the robbers and his association with them is the beginning of the social novel.

The robbers of Schiller, already unified by centuries, were the friends and the imitators of Cervantes's robbers.

■

In this manner parody creates new forms.

Let's try to see what gets discarded from the old form.

Prefaces in verse;

theoretical prefaces;

dedications;

and the speech in verse addressed to the heroes in the knight-errantry novel are transformed into parody.

People write romance songs and use this form to address Rosinante.

Now let's try, with a certain authority, explainable by the fact that my life is not eternal and this is my attempt to leave behind at least some notes as a keepsake—let's try to see what happens when a new form is created.

The unnecessary elements disappear.

Plot, the method of sustaining a structure, the organization of the narrative becomes simpler.

The most tattered elements of the old plot fall out.

I know that I'm making a big leap here, but let's look at *War and Peace*.

The instance where Andrei Bolkonsky's father considers his son dead and orders a memorial for him, as a gesture to put an end to his hopes, could have happened in the Greek epic.

These prearranged tombs had a specific name in Greek literature, which I won't mention here.

The sudden appearance of the person who was thought to be dead, the wise speeches, all of this is retained in the belletristic novel.

The novel, as Cervantes states at the end of the first part in defense of the knight-errantry genre, leaves behind something that he thought, consciously thought, was right, the new novel leaves behind the travels—

—the depiction of new lands, the elements of philosophy, the discussions.

Later we will quote Cervantes's argument with his imaginary adversary, who in this case is dressed as a clergyman.

■

Likewise, Tolstoy's stylistic novel restores certain elements from the ancient novel. I am referring, of course, not only to the opening of *Anna Karenina*. The restoration occurs not because Tolstoy is a new writer, but because this is a carefully selected form, which for this reason can be invented twice.

A second application for a patent at the patent office is a common thing.

There were two equally serious claims for the invention of the telephone, one later than the other by a few hours.

Mankind is capable of uniting and recognizing previous experience.

Cervantes purposefully attributes parts of the novel to a fictional author, who supposedly co-wrote the book.

When inventing something new, mankind is hooked up to the cybernetic machine of universal thought.

What's supposed to survive, survives.

And the old elements, belonging to the traditional school of literature that have had a very long life, drop out.

In novels, just as in fairytales, incidental encounters are common.

The hero runs into a magician, does him a favor, and the latter fights for him.

The hero accidentally finds a portrait of a woman and falls in love with her.

Then these incidents recur, they repeat, thus establishing themselves, their validation.

Occasionally, repeated sayings, such as "you can have this only after you wear out the iron boots," become part of the fairytale narrative.[54]

A person is given iron boots, or accepts iron bread, because this prosaic impotence helps show the persistent efforts of the hero.

People encounter friends and supposedly by chance find the right documents.

---

[54] A hyperbole used in Russian folktales where the hero is granted his wish only after having fulfilled a number of difficult tasks such as walking in iron boots for a certain period of time.

Regarding this, Thackeray said that he didn't want to take advantage of a testament being found in a broken-down carriage.

This was almost a natural coincidence.

When the Tsar's censorship demanded that Ostrovsky, in his play *A Family Affair*, punish the antagonist, so that someone would appear and win, Ostrovsky repeated what Molière was forced to do at the end of his *Tartuffe*—arrest the antagonist by the king's orders.

You, too, once rejoiced when reading a book in which your favorite hero was saved.

Just as in Jules Verne's *Children of Captain Grant*, the heroes, saved from the savages, are afraid of their ship's arrival. The ship was supposedly taken over by pirates, but it turns out that their plot was revealed and they were on the ship under arrest.

But I have started repeating what I had said earlier.

The old elements of the strictly literary work disintegrate and die out.

We have had enough of such examples. And before we go on with our discussion of parody, the reinvention and creation of plot, I should say something about plot, reversal (peripeteia), and storyline.

II.

In the eleventh chapter of his *Poetics*, Aristotle wrote, "Reversal of the situation is a change by which the action turns toward its opposite, subject always to our rule of probability or necessity."

What is the significance of reversal in fiction?

Reversals are important because they slow down time and provide an opportunity to grasp the reality anew.

A reversal is a return to a past that's not the same anymore, or better yet, it's a multiple examination of the story from various points of view.

Rather than being just a way for keeping the reader interested, a novel's reversal is a device for making him participate in the unraveling of a specific event.

In *The Iliad,* Achilles' rage has its own reversals too.

His anger is complex, it changes after the death of Patroclus; still, its nature is transformed after Achilles' conversation with the father of his friend's assassin.

Readers will ask, how is this possible? You speak of Achilles' rage as "something" that possesses "its own" nature, "its own" behavior. But if you look at *King Lear,* the king of France speaks of his feelings for Cordelia —after she has been denounced by her father, rejected by the duke, and silently betrayed by her sisters:

> Gods, gods! 'tis strange that from their cold'st neglect
> My love should kindle to inflamed respect.

The king of France is talking about his love and desire as if it were something that had its "own" behavior.

It's necessary to mention here the words of Heraclitus the Obscure.

He was called Obscure because he knew how to reconcile contradictions.

"The universe, unified of all, was created neither by gods nor by men, but it ever was and is and will be an eternal fire, burning in a natural way and fading in a natural way."

Lenin quoted these words in his *Philosophical Notes.*

■

The reversals in Khlestakov's character are important to us because he makes so many blunders.

It's as if he has taken on a different persona, a different character, the character of a guilty person—a guest who hasn't paid for his lodging.

These reversals, though, consistently support the main idea behind his character—this person's unconventional frivolity of thought and the ease with which he keeps switching back and forth, his almost childish eccentricity.

Exposing the transformation in Pugachev's character in *The Captain's*

Daughter is an excellent example of reversal—the various qualities, various properties of this man whom we encounter at first accidentally, but who turns out to be a man possessed with great soul, influence, and possibly even ingenuity.

One might even say that in *The Captain's Daughter* the reversals switch the hierarchical structure of the heroes.

First, we have Grinev and his servant.

Then it's the men of the fortress; and finally, it's Pugachev, who reappears in the scenes, different each time.

The title *The Captain's Daughter* also functions as an intentional reversal created in order to divert from the purpose of the composition.

The woman who succeeds in getting forgiveness for the man she loves is an old theme, but to employ these reversals in the Russian reality of Pushkin's time—this was almost an impossible task.

As a result, Masha and Grinev, as well as his father, are pushed into the background.

And, as I hope to demonstrate through my analyses of the epigraphs, the foreground is reserved for the Pugachevian uprising.

In an expurgated chapter (due to censorship), Grinev accidentally comes across a raft with Pugachev's men executed on it, hung from a gallows—one of them is an old Chuvash peasant, Grinev's servant, who was not mentioned before this passage.

Pushkin's analysis of the people in the uprising is exhaustive.

As I wrote in 1922 in *Notes on Pushkin's Prose*, his trivial characterization of Catherine, a description of the famous official engraving showing the Empress strolling through Tsarskoe Selo, its abruptness, lack of detail, gives import and articulation to the other, unnamed event.

The fact that Masha is leaving without having seen St. Petersburg intensifies the portrayal of the Pugachevian uprising.

Here the sudden omission centers on the woman who has saved her future husband. She hurries to inform his relatives. The reversal directs you to the principal moments in the plot—St. Petersburg is irrelevant here in relation to the storyline, i.e., the means for developing the plot, the means for guiding the audience's attention through the development of the plot.

The traditional storyline has its advantages.

It requires no groundwork, especially in theater.

These are the storylines against which A. P. Chekhov warns his brother in a letter.

The storyline as a device for guiding the reader's attention can be quite varied.

Some storylines, mostly those that occur in theater, are used to make perception easier.

Before we go on, however, let's mention how Tolstoy very accurately described the conventionalities of the theater in *War and Peace*. He compares the opera Natasha is watching with the conventionality of morals.

She likes Kuragin. She likes Bolkonsky.

This world is conventional.

The conventionality of life—Tolstoy saw it well and pointed it out, rather blatantly, in the theater.

This conventionality is strangely connected to the distinction between the fairytale and the novel.

Great literature tries to move away from storyline to plot.

This is a new phenomenon.

Because fairytales are not "plotted."

Great literature has always talked of the present, while breaking away from the fairytale.

In art, the storyline creates an unusual diversion of the reader's interest to specific situations.

The same is true in theater performance.

The storyline of a ballet or an opera, rather conventional forms of art, requires that there be only one hero.

Let me remind you that the word "plot" once meant the main actor on stage—the actor in the spotlight, the performer of specific dances, a solo performance, an aria by Chaliapin, for example.

To explain this in a simpler way and strike up a lively discussion, as I'm usually inclined to, I'll tell a story that I heard from Chaliapin, whom I met only once, in Berlin, at Gorky's.

After his fame in Soviet Russia, after he'd been applauded by the whole world as a man who had advanced himself and whose name had revolutionized history, in London, at any rate, Chaliapin appeared on stage in the opera *The Mermaid*.

He had a small part.

So Chaliapin comes out, expecting applause. The hall is silent: the orchestra has played its bit and come to a pause.

Chaliapin remains standing.

"It's hard to stand on a stage in silence."

"But I know *how* to stand on a stage."

Chaliapin says.

"Later I was told that I stood there for three whole minutes."

An infinitely long time.

Someone started applauding, which then turned into an ovation.

"I had convinced the audience."

"And the audience had agreed with me."

"Then I sang very well."

"It's hard to do it right each time."

Here, Chaliapin made an unexpected reversal, he reconceived the part of a famous lead singer who was supposed to perform a specific passage and tie the storyline of the whole piece.

As far as I can remember, he sang the aria of the miller, the father of the drowned girl.[55]

[55] The opera is based on a romantic story between a prince and a miller's daughter, Natasha. The prince leaves the young girl to marry a princess. Natasha, who is pregnant with his child, hurls herself into the Dnepr. Years later and after an unhappy marriage, the prince returns to the banks of the Dnepr, where Natasha lives as a mermaid. The grief stricken miller pushes him into the river and the mermaids carry him off.

Through the use of his own experience, Chaliapin diverted the audience's interest to an issue relating to a specific historic event.

The unusual example with Chaliapin touches upon the complex question of what plot really is.

Different epochs have interpreted plot differently; does this mean that the author is interpreting plot in different ways?

■

Storyline and plot are closely related to the beginning and ending of works.

Today literature is experiencing a weakening of beginnings and endings, which seem to have been deteriorating.

Quite often in great writers, such as Tolstoy and Dostoevsky, we observe how the ending is a search for the hero's final fate.

This is true of *Crime and Punishment*.

It's also true of *Resurrection*.

But the endings seem unclear, sort of distorted.

The Song of Igor's Campaign has a distinct ending, it's well known to the audience.

The Song of Roland also has a distinct finale familiar to everyone.

Still, we know there have been attempts in the folklore to defamiliarize, to oppose the ending.

The perception of these transitions coincides with the end of a civilization, with the end of a specific era.

Under such circumstances, folklore becomes parody.

Take for instance the parodies of Rabelais, who often, with a precision unusual for his era, imitates the Bible, things like the birth of Jesus or the story of Cain.

For now, however, we'll content ourselves with a few remarks, without going into too much detail.

The strangeness, as well as the magnitude, of the writer's task today has increased.

But it turns out that the writer is plotting something and executing it at the same time. We have shown with individual examples that a work is born through the consecutive replacement of the so-called drafts, or versions.

At this point, we have to remember that in the past a great many works went into print and got published even before they were finished.

So this creative process can go on for years, maybe even decades.

It was like that with the epigraph to *Anna Karenina*.

This was a mysterious beginning, and it remains a mystery to this day.

Labyrinths of linkages reemerge in the same old place again, after the disintegration of old ways of life.

Therefore it's hopeless to try to explain the peculiarities of a literary work through grammar.

Art has a life of its own; it exists through its own internal conflicts.

It somehow reconstructs life, crystallizing it.

There are traces of a storyline in *Anna Karenina*—in the beginning.

The train, the journey—this is a "storied" beginning.

Especially before the invention of the railroad system; and even after the spread of the railroads, it was left as it was.

This novelty only highlights the tradition of the "storied" beginning.

Anna's death also seems to be part of the storyline; however, the plot of *Anna Karenina* does not coincide with its storyline.

Here is the storyline in a nutshell.

A woman makes a mistake.

And she dies.

The scenario: a woman seeks the celebration of love in an unusual situation, which society allows but doesn't approve of.

This separates her from her surroundings.

She knows that "society does not punish for delusions, but it demands secrecy."

The plot of *Anna Karenina* is the exposure of this secret.

In *The Decameron,* nearly everything is story-based, and most of the stories develop through narrative progression.

But there is also the rare instance where the storyline is disrupted—I mention for the fifth time the tale of the Babylonian Sultan's daughter.

The linear progression is seemingly preserved, i.e., the multiple attempts to possess the woman; the plot, however, is that she is actually well satisfied with her lovers.

The plot's motivation is based on the fact that she is beyond moral codes, religion, and language, she is outside the realms of her suitors that are always different, always changing.

The storyline requires a clear-cut presentation of the hero when he appears.

A clock is shown on the town square—and everything begins.

Next scene—who is doing what, and where.

Aristotle wrote a great deal about the process of "familiarization."

This is inherent to the storyline.

In a way, Tolstoy also resorts to story: two parallel fates—two marriages —an orthodox marriage and a marriage of chance.

The plot, however, lies in the fact that both of these threads are disrupted and reexamined.

At what point does plot become storyline?

The storyline, according to Tolstoy and Chekhov, consists of the hero's death or his marriage.

In reality, "the death of the hero deflects our interest onto others."

Hence, Chekhov expurgates his storylines—takes out their beginnings and endings.

That's almost the exact content of his letter to his brother.

The storyline is a matrix, the determination of type; a shipwreck in the Greek epic is a "storied" shipwreck.

The shipwreck in *Robinson Crusoe* is also a "storied" shipwreck.

But Robinson's life on the island is plotted.

And so, here we cite the words of Chekhov.

"The plot must be new, while the storyline can be omitted."

III.

I have no intention of writing a book about the process of creating a plot. For Pushkin, plot was a character, a staged character that existed only in proposed circumstances.

I'm too old to write a long book.

We see how difficult the work of a prose writer is.

I'd like to emphasize here that I am going to discuss prose, because unfortunately I have not worked on verse. I know all that's been done by the Structuralists, and I see a lot of terminology—probably successful, or precise, in any case—but I don't know how to use this terminology as stepping-stones to the essence of a work.

Structuralism got carried away by, if you will, the cover of a book.

I need to restate this.

The Structuralists are not interested in the object itself, but its "packaging."

A somewhat older and fairly erudite Pushkin, in speaking of the future, of what he was living and hoping for, said: "At a moving tale my eyes will fill." [56]

There is undoubtedly a national—which is to say, emotional—aspect to a literary work. After hearing the story of the star-crossed lovers who were doomed to endless flight over the circle of hell, Dante faints.

I think Gogol the satirist treats even Nozdrev emotionally. Not that he likes him. As he studies Nozdrev, he comes to admire the complexities of a lie and its meanings. I have no clue how one might approach this by using terminology, or nothing but terminology. Hence, I'm staying within the borders of "unpretentious prose" as I try to understand how artistic creativity exists at the moment of its creation. And how this moment, a period of transition, the instant of draft replacing draft, helps us understand the necessity of artistic creation.

[56] From "An Elegy" (1830).

It's fairly easy to understand how a certain construction, a certain way of life, can create literature for itself alone.

It's much harder to understand why or how a work can become necessary after many years, centuries, and even millennia.

Among the properties of an artistic work I note—perhaps mistakenly, but I'm obliged to note it out of necessity—is the multiplicity of ways of how to interpret it.

The plot's riddle can be solved in various ways at various periods of time.

To repeat my old friend Sancho Panza's words, he would have preferred if they told him the answer first and then the riddle. Sancho Panza was wrong. If you know the answer to a riddle, there's no point in listening to it. Meanwhile, some make up riddles and others try to find answers to them, and those who were unable to give the correct answer have paid with their lives.

The ambiguity of a literary work does not end with its riddle, of course. For centuries we've been trying to figure out Shakespeare, Cervantes, or Pushkin. I knew Mayakovsky well enough, but I was never able to figure him out.

In a work of art, the hero grows and changes. The fate of a work in the process of its creation is complex and never the same.

Dostoevsky said—not as an author though, but through his underground hero, the embittered man—that it's true, two times two *is* four. But "two times two is five can at times be a precious little thing."[57] This multiplicity of meaning, which, of course, has nothing to do with the simple mathematical improbability, turns out to be one of the properties that ensures the work's permanence.

∎

---

[57] From *Notes from Underground.*

"In the beginning was the word"—thus opens the Gospel of John. It goes on to say: "And the word was with God, and the word was God." It is said weightily, but if there *was* a beginning, and if it's said that it meant something, does this then suggest that there was nothing but the word and its meaning?

There were poets who were saying that poetry was the word. Later, there were theorists who were saying that the theory of poetry was equivalent to linguistics.

Even if you believe in the Malevich square, the idea that geometry itself is art, you will then believe that the Malevich square is simply the entrance into another form of art, which perhaps may be very old.

An ornament.

The question of "what and how" has still not been answered. You can't always judge a whole by its parts. Meanwhile, the complications in terminology are intensifying. The number of parts seems to increase without a determination of the question—is it part of the whole, or is it the whole?

But we'll always continue—as long as we are alive—the analysis of parts as an analysis of the whole. Taking a breath isn't just the stretching of the muscles that expand the lungs. It's the return to the air, to the atmosphere, to the whole. We'll rejoice when the number of terms is reduced, when it's apparent that they can be replaced.

In film, montage isn't so much about the superimposition of two frames. Eisenstein used to say that any two frames could be put together on the basis of the movement, or contrast, or meaning, or outline of the framed object.

We have to remember the purpose of montage when montaging.

One of the key concepts is *far montage*.[58]

---

[58] The term *far montage* originates from Eisenstein's theory that any two pieces of film juxtaposed to each other inevitably create a new concept. However, Shklovsky takes this rather arbitrary concept and complicates it in literature, establishing that a

An unexpected reinvention.

The most important contrast in the *Divine Comedy* is the new meaning overlaying the old notion of history, the notion of love and moral codification. The circles of *The Inferno* vary not by their grade of sin but by the revelation of meaning. Dante's journey is difficult because this is his reinvention of life.

To show his encounters with medieval people, his indignation at them, pity for them, and powerlessness to change their fate, Dante uses rhyme and meter. The life and events in Florence are superimposed onto the life of the world, the old tangible world, and in the quarrel with Beatrice one foresees intimations of the tragedy of love in the centuries to come, although Beatrice, dressed in a cloak like the ones in iconography, affectionately says to the poet not "lift up your head," but "lift up your beard" when he finds her in the other world.

This is the deliberately prosaic tone of the poem.

I will single out two things here.

First—we can't have a simple montage; we need *far montage* because it leads to an unexpected reinvention.

Second—reinvention, like any movement, requires meter—no, it doesn't require meter, that's not accurate.

Meter arises as a consequence of the striving for harmony.

Meter—and that implies rhyme—is the only way to move while maintaining balance.

Or, in other words, the way to maintain balance while moving.

---

literary work arises from extra-literary phenomena, which can be grasped best when the process of their origin (hence, *far* montage) is understood. The texts that are juxtaposed to a certain literary work then can't be arbitrary, but must be carefully chosen to illuminate the work in a new unexpected light. History, in this sense, becomes a particular method for studying and reinventing the present through the facts of the past.

Pushkin's rhymes in *Eugene Onegin* are impossible to understand without analyzing the Onegin stanza and meter—the last two lines of the stanza; rhyme not only draws them together, not only plays with words, but also reinvents the entire stanza.[59]

Rhyme is a device for returning to what has been said, a "promissory note" that is repaid not only with a following line but also through a new conceptualization.

Here is Vladimir Mayakovsky, contemplating how to fully regain his own voice, how to restore voice to the word—a meaning to speech, the meaning that people gave to a voice, hence maybe getting closer to Socrates and Joan of Arc, both of whom were killed.

■

Let's get back to our previous discussion.

When you look at the sea during stormy weather, the whole sea seems to be moving, all the way from the horizon to the shore.

It's the boat that rocks.

The words are not final in elegiac and ironic verse.

The matter does not end with them.

When the scales oscillate, they waver while weighing—while comparing the new to the old.

Old weights are the measure of the new, but they don't determine the new.

What we're calling plot isn't an occurrence in and of itself, or a series of events weighed by words. Words are necessary; through them we touch life, which we haven't fully grasped.

At the entrance to the writers' house, on a quiet street—and, to avoid

---

59 The Onegin stanza as a distinct form contains 118 syllables and consists of fourteen lines, in iambic tetrameter, with a regular scheme of feminine and masculine rhymes: ababeeccididff.

needless mystery, opposite the Tretyakov Gallery—stood a short, broad-chested, broad-shouldered man in a summer hat with its brim covered with snow.

I'm talking about Yuri Karlovich Olesha.

Past this fine man—with calm blue eyes, passed another man, dressed appropriately for the weather.

Yuri Karlovich asked the passerby:

—I've read you. You're good at writing. But what are you going to do now? What are you weighing with your words, why are the scales of perception oscillating?

I'll repeat what's important for me: Lev Nikolaevich Tolstoy said that he didn't know how to draw a circle; he had to close the line and then correct it.

He knew how to think by juxtaposing words, by awakening them, in a way.

When he wrote his major novels, he would begin with something plotted, i.e., something that was happening or had already happened, and sought the relationship between the incidental and inevitable.

He studied the thoughts of a child and how cunning emerged at its first stages.

The so-called draft version is not an adaptation of a text to the norms, not sorting through gems, like jewelers do when making necklaces and crowns.

Drafts weigh the essence of events. The scenarios, which the hero of the work goes through, they should be called "hypothetical circumstances."

This is the analysis of how man was created, i.e., his sensation of the world, and how through the movements of scenarios, experimented and tested hundreds of times in fiction, the truth becomes clearer.

This work is like that of a captain who navigates by the stars and moon, using his chronometer to verify and make sure of their hypothetical place in the sky. The captain is testing the ship's course.

The book I'm writing is still moving in front of me, swaying on the waves. I'm cutting away at my subject with words—the way a stonecutter or sculptor works. I'm searching for meaning.

The purpose of my search is art.

The world moved in front of Tolstoy. He was near-sighted and never wore glasses, so as not to introduce yet another convention into his vision. His books move; they show mankind's way of thinking in those times.

The fates of heroes—I'm not going to list any works—change from draft to draft.

Don't think that the writer is free. According to rumors, even geniuses, more than others, depend on the very traditions they're violating, they depend on the choice of words, the choice of denouements.

Tolstoy argued with Turgenev and wrote him many rude letters.

The matter went as far as discussions about a duel. But there is a reason that he dedicated one of his early sketches to Turgenev. He understood the structure of *Notes of a Hunter* better than anyone else.

We have no visual description of the narrator's face or his dress, but he defines our perception—in an inconspicuous sort of way, without the author's intervention.

This is how *The Sevastopol Sketches* are written. My friends have often analyzed imitated forms and points of similarity; however, true imitation uses an existing work as a whole and completely reinvents it.

Centuries don't disappear. They don't decay. They're resurrected in newly proposed circumstances.

We are going to study the movements of the scale inside the creators' minds.

There is a street with the fine name Metrostroevskaya, which shakes when trains pass under the ground.

But the street has a heart of steel, next door, in the museum. Tolstoy's drafts are kept here.

If the movement of thought, the renewal of circumstance in these draft versions was conveyed through kinetics, then the street would ripple as if it were reflected in water, and the earth would shake underneath the water.

■

Proposed circumstances.

This phrase has emerged along the way, as this book is being written.

We have to differentiate the circumstances proposed to the author, proposed by life and chosen by the author, from the circumstances proposed to the hero—chosen, created, and hypothesized by the author.

In other words, there are real linkages of circumstance; the author experiences them and then proposes to his hero.

The journey of our perception of plot is getting longer.

■

The poetics Aristotle created were based on an analysis of tragedies that employed myths.

The myth, like the epic, was based on conflicts that kept recurring. Aristotle believed that the subject of the enemy killing his enemy was not tragic. The tragedy was in the unexpectedness of who the enemy turns out to be. A mother who turns out to be the enemy of her son. A wife who kills her husband.

In the most common situation the invincible hero is humiliated by his master.

Achilles is the son of a goddess, albeit a minor one. He is majestic, but he has been humiliated by Agamemnon, the king of kings.

A new ring in a newly forming society.

Agamemnon feels guilt towards Achilles because he has stolen a share of the gains that originally belonged to Achilles. He has wronged Achilles because what he stole was a woman.

Achilles may have already begun to love her.

■

In his essay on drama, Pushkin wrote: "Tragedy predominantly depicted serious villainy, supernatural and even physical suffering (for instance, Philoctetes, Oedipus, Lear)." Pushkin talks about how "habit dulls sensation." We might say that Oedipus in the various tragedies from the same trilogy belongs to eras with different moralities.

Even today we call this kind of polemic—tragic. The fate of Gregor Melekhov, the hero, is tragic.[60] He has old scores to settle with the system itself, with other relationships.

■

In classical drama, the plot didn't have to be new. The plot was usually suggested by myths, but the chosen myths were of a kind that would ensure and confirm the truth and probability of a complex storyline. Traditional plots included the element of surprise that had been previously used. These reversals could come about in keeping with probability or inevitability. So said Aristotle.

I'm not going to say that this has been refuted.

I'll say that it has been supplemented.

Pushkin says: ". . . habit dulls sensation; the imagination inures us to murders and executions, it regards them indifferently, the portrayal of passions and outpourings of the human soul is always new to it, always engaging, magnificent, and edifying. Drama took charge of man's passions and soul."

We have already demonstrated that the origin of the psychological novel is connected, above all, with the name Cervantes.

The drama of Orestes is repeated. Hamlet is the son of a murdered father, and he has to take vengeance on the murderer's wife—but the murderer's wife is his own mother. She has married the slain man's brother. Moreover, there is also the matter of the stolen crown. Hamlet hesitates in a different way than Orestes. Orestes was pursued by the Furies, the spirits of old values.

A mother is closer than a father. But everything is resolved through

---

[60] The hero from Mikhail Sholokhov's (1905–84) great epic novel, *And Quiet Flows the Don* (1965), a Cossack's son who goes from the Reds to the Whites and is forced against his will to continue the civil war to its hopeless conclusion.

human relations, and when Hamlet hears his mother's exclamation that she pities him, he rejoices bitterly.

The clashing elements are real. In drama, which is closer to us in time, we understand the scenes that take place in it, but these proposed scenes are selected. They are either gory or comic.

Like Pushkin, young Grinev belongs to a clan humiliated by Catherine's coup. She murdered Peter III; she was an imposter. She has no right to the throne. In this respect she, too, is an enemy, albeit an enemy accepted by the new society she has created. Catherine and Pugachev are linked by the fact that they are both imposters.

Thus, the proposed circumstances that the author selects are different from the circumstances the author proposes to the hero.

The first is as if a labyrinth of linkages; the second is closer to reversals.

The circumstances of drama are "proposed," as well as selected. In tragedies, they had myths in which the hero was unfortunate not as a result of his depravity but as a result of a tragic accident: guilt for a crime committed in his clan, and what's more, they had to hypothesize the investigation of a crime stipulated as tragic.

So, Aristotle says: ". . . the most outstanding tragedies portray the fate of a very few clans."

What is new about tragedy is that the heroes of Aeschylus, the heroes of Sophocles, and the heroes of Euripides treat the events predicted by the myths in different ways.

New people placed in old situations. The newness of these people, and their way of reacting and overcoming the ordinary, marks a new interpretation of the phenomena of morality in human consciousness.

■　■　■

There are as many morals as stars in the sky.

Each house has its own set of values, and naturally morals in the city are different from those in the province.

Plot is like a ship that touches the shores with its side; it transports something from one continent to another.

The multitude of morals is basically the core of the multi-interpretation and reinvention of plot.

Let's turn to Tolstoy.

In his drafts, in the process of work, when struggling for reinvention, Tolstoy is struggling against the incidental.

In a certain hunting scene, when noblemen from various ranks meet, their behavior is unusual, the strong are defeated by the weak. In the scene with a chase, "Uncle" Rostov's hound attacking the wolf is what appears to be the multiple use of fates of the same hero.

In the drafts, "Uncle" appears on the field of Borodino with other heroes.

This is possible.

But this is more likely to happen in a novel. Besides, the officers who were supposed to accompany "Uncle" weren't present in the actual battle. All of this was taken out.

Getting rid of the incidental was one of Tolstoy's main features. Pierre Bezukhov saves a French officer from a madman who was trying to shoot him.

Initially this Frenchman was introduced as an Italian marquis who was a belated admirer of Napoleon; he's a Mason and communicates with Pierre through coded language. Then this person helps Pierre while he is in prison, he follows him and provides him with food using his Masonic privileges.

Later this high-ranking young man becomes instrumental in Pierre's marriage to Natasha, i.e., through this chance meeting, through the opportunistic resolution of something that's irresolvable—the novel laid bare the hand of the novelist.

But then Tolstoy changed this high-ranking character to a simple-minded, almost uncultured, typical officer. And then he abandoned the character altogether, mentioning in passing that he was captured and held in prison.

Tolstoy knew very well the obstacle that all writers find themselves confronted with—one cannot keep introducing new characters.

But he was rather good at introducing new, probable and memorable characters.

I'm talking about Platon Karataev.

Of course, Platon Karataev isn't just a peasant and a soldier from the old army who may have met Suvorov.

He represents a longing, the poetic desire of the author.

It's as if he is pulling a net of possibilities.

Without the people who really understood him, Pierre Bezukhov wouldn't have made much sense.

Tolstoy kept narrowing the scheme of his plot.

He took out the scenes that had to do with chance.

Coincidence in Tolstoy was turned into inevitability. He tried to substantiate inevitability.

Hopeless, embittered and in despair, Anna Karenina goes to Dolly and there meets Kitty, from whom she has, crudely speaking, "stolen" Vronsky.

This chance meeting becomes inevitable, Anna has no one else to go to.

She is forced to go to the people whom she considers her enemies.

She is lonely.

She turns to something familiar, to people who lived a conventional life of questionable morals and weren't punished for anything.

The scene where she is looking for help, the meetings with some of the previously described characters, becomes clichéd, they refuse to help her, for they are Karenina's enemies, and she challenges them by mentioning her attraction to Levin.

Tolstoy conceals the quantity of characters behind a set of unusual decisions. When Katyusha Maslova is sent to exile and hard labor, the man who was the cause of her fall is trying to save her, he is looking for justice. These questionable advocates for justice, this world of evil men, the government officials who are awfully clever, they are not even evil but blinded like a horse—if you remember, a horse has blinders so that it doesn't get frightened.

People in blinders; their narrow-mindedness is part of the artistic intent. In search of help, in his attempt to help Katyusha, Nekhlyudov is taken away to prison, where he is an uncomfortable but a respected guest. He goes in the same coach as the prisoners, he sees the revolutionaries, meets a fanatical sectarian, who says that he is answerable only to himself— he is the tsar, his own king.

The novel became simple and complex.

It became a social novel.

Tolstoy not only tore off the masks from people's faces, but he also tore off their blinders.

It's as if he forced them to see the true world, and this was the novelty of the novel's design.

■

The battalion square of the Turkish army that Vronsky wants to fight, where he hopes to find his death, is a convention, because war, as Dostoevsky already mentioned, had gone into the trenches.

People don't move in a battalion square.

Despair and the ways of freeing oneself from despair are conventional.

The world into which Nekhlyudov falls seems to be arbitrary, but this world is necessary to the search for a lost conscience. Pushkin formulated this into poetry in the following passage where he is talking about the Neva, which is calming down after a storm:

As suitors beat in supplication
Unheeded at a judge's door.[61]

The search is for historic justice because the place where the city stands also represents something heroic, yet it can be seen as something guilt-ridden.

The threads of the novel are once again twisted together, unified, and this heroic act, just as in Dostoevsky, cannot be repeated.

[61] From "The Bronze Horseman" (1833).

Shatter the world into pieces.

The meaninglessness of this world is a reality too.

It's shown in Kafka.

There exist folkloric sayings, riddles, delirious tales; these are the attempts to break free from the net in which the mentality of mankind has been trapped.

Tolstoy wanted to tear the nets of the Tsar and simultaneously build a new system; he wanted to do this alone.

In Shakespeare, who didn't create his own plots, there is a reinvention of plot, revisualization and reclassification of methods for evaluating the action.

The adventures that Shakespeare adopts from the Italian novella are weakened, they show a different kind of reality—things that were conventional or made into parody become tragic.

Shakespeare didn't "imitate" the novellas.

He would break them into pieces.

Romeo and Juliet is an exact rendition of an Italian story with exactly the same characters.

So is the Moor who kills his white wife.

But in Shakespeare he is different.

Here he is shown as a hero who bears torments, repents and is eventually acquitted.

In the original story he was a cunning man who never repents the murder of his wife and, to disguise it, stages a tragic death by knocking down the beams in her room.

In both stories, the man commits the same act, but the motivation is different in each case.

He is perceived differently.

Hamlet is not only the descendent of Orestes, who seeks revenge for his father's death, he is also someone who ponders his act: a reflective generation that evaluates the past—this becomes the essence of the work.

I need to remind you that as a part of world literature, Russian Realism reinvents literature as a whole.

The smart, graceful femme fatale becomes, as it were, the hero of the realistic story.

Tolstoy tells about her "heroic" deeds: she is unfaithful to her husband, she has left her son.

But while analyzing her actions, Tolstoy exalts her, turning from critic to admirer.

He analyzes the origin of her sin; Aleksei Karenin turns out to be his wife's senior by twenty years.

The old theme of the bad husband recurs; the woman's act is explained, but in this version the husband isn't a last figure. He is human, mourning the loss of someone he loved.

The plot of *Anna Karenina*, this simple or maybe much-too-simple plot, is complicated.

This is a judgement about time, about its moral laws.

The creation of a different kind of morality appears, as it were, the cause for the work's reinvention.

The woman betrays her husband after she reads a love story with another young man.

I recall a phrase from memory: "That day we read from it no more."[62]

Which means both the woman and the reason were condemned, but Dante, the judge, can't save the woman from hell and he faints on the stones of hell out of sympathy for her.

The attempt to correct a sin will not bring justice.

I am trying to show in passing that Tolstoy's work, the work of the greatest preacher of new morality, is not preaching about Biblical moralities, rather it's the reinvention of all the moral laws . . .

One of Tolstoy's late stories, "The Death of Ivan Ilych," begins with words on how the dead man was lying, as dead men always lie, "his yellow waxen brow exposed."

His death was ordinary, his life was frightening. Here the analysis shifts

[62] The passage refers to Francesca and Paolo da Rimini in Dante's *Inferno*, from the end of Canto V.

from the unusual part of the events to the evaluation of the ordinary and universal.

The stories written by Tolstoy in the small and almost demonstratively modest house standing on a far-off street in Moscow are very simple when it comes to their eventfulness.

They are powerful not in their moral views but in the method of exposing the imperfections, the shortcomings of the old norms of life.

The life of the murderer of his wife is shown so that we perceive the murder as the killer's sorrow.

The moral norms have been dropped out.

Two stories are about murder prompted by jealousy; we are confronted with the question of what is jealousy.

It's as if the woman is the property of the jealous man.

The hero from "The Devil" isn't sure whether to kill himself, or the woman who seduced him, or kill both himself and her.

The old notion of Hell has been destroyed.

These stories, even the one about a horse, "Strider," were the subject of Tolstoy's quarrels with his wife, not just because of the royalties, but also because of who was guilty in the story.

The story discussed the old morals.

In "Strider" everyone is guilty, except for the old horse. He is guilty only in one thing: his skin color is different from the rest of the herd.

He is gelded for this.

They use him even after his death, they eat his meat.

He has a successful master who could have turned into the hero of a novel about high-society, someone like Vronsky:

dead among the dead.

■

The world in which Tolstoy lives is actually a world enclosed in other worlds, each existing with its own set of morals.

He lives in a displaced world. When he is writing about not fitting in, he is talking about his own world.

Dostoevsky said about *Don Quixote* that, when Judgement Day arrives, mankind will put the book by Cervantes in front of God and say: this was man.

He was kind and pure, but wasn't able to change anything.

Dostoevsky said that Don Quixote was guilty of one thing only—he was alone. He alone tried to reconstruct mankind through separate heroic acts, and he remained alone.

This, of course, can be said about Tolstoy.

It's strange to talk about Tolstoyan philosophy now, but in 1905, when it was possible to create a society when necessary to do so, one needed to have at least twenty-five people on his side, and Tolstoy, who was rather admired in his estate, still couldn't find even twenty-five people to agree with him.

Those people whom he called to heroic deeds—at a time when there were hundreds of them and they all believed in him—they couldn't do anything because he told them that everything had to be done from the inside, through self-reformation.

So, one can write a very sad book: "Don Quixote and Lev Tolstoy."

Famous, rich, well known, able to touch people's hearts and see human sorrow, he was guilty of one thing—he was alone.

True, there was Chertkov, but he was more like an unreliable long, black shadow.

Anna Karenina throws herself under a train.

Not an evil, but a rather conventional, person, Countess Lydia Ivanovna sees this merely as something distressful for poor "Saint" Karenin.

Anna's son, Seryozha, doesn't say anything, and is perhaps right when his uncle Stepan Arkadyevich comes for a visit.

He keeps a straight face, trying not to cry.

There are boys around him—they could see.

Vronsky notices something only when he looks at the train's wheels.

He has the impression that it was the fault of the iron wagon.

Both Anna and Aleksei Vronsky had dreams about iron.

It's as if no one is guilty.

Therefore, nothing can be fixed.

A world of blinders.

A world of rustling paper.

The world of Tolstoy wasn't disrupted, although he told people more than the truth: he told each of them about their faults.

And now we can finally turn to *Anna Karenina* and *Resurrection*, two books that are remarkably similar and yet very different from one another.

We still have time.

■

I remember it was a freezing cold day. We met in Komarovo, near the seashore of the Finland Gulf.

It was pure accident. I knew him from before. We used to argue, reconcile, write together, and then we went our separate ways. His name was Viktor Maksimovich Zhirmunsky. It was when Akhmatova had died. Her manuscripts had disappeared.[63] It was the fault of some people who thought that her papers belonged to them.

Anna Andreevna Akhmatova, whom I remember as a young woman, had died that day or perhaps the day before. The house across from the Letni Sad, behind Nevsky Prospect, felt very empty. She used to call it the Fountain House.

There used to be many fountains there.

This, indeed, was highly ironic.

Or, it was parody.

A parody of, say, the ice frozen along the bordering granite columns of the Fontanka. The Fontanka always felt to me like a wound that turned into granite scars.

[63] Anna Akhmatova's (1880–1966) poetry was banned from 1922 and to keep her quiet, Stalin had her son imprisoned. In 1949, when her son Lev was arrested for the third time, Akhmatova committed her poems to memory and burned all the manuscripts; among them, her famous anti-Stalin "Poem without a Hero" which she began in St. Petersburg in 1940 and continued to revise until her death.

When a person dies we remember or try to remember the person as a whole; the art of seeing a person is a rare thing. We were friends with Zhirmunsky through Opoyaz. We never worked together, we didn't even think alike, but we thought about the same thing, differently. We met as very close friends. All this time Viktor Maksimovich, aside from his usual literary work, was trying to collect Anna Akhmatova's manuscripts. He had to find her signature. We were both grieving and when we met, we forgot all about our arguments.

The truth is, we never agreed. I remember him, as well as Boris Eichenbaum, Yuri Tynjanov and Yevgeni Polivanov. These names stayed in the heart, it its very depths, not as wounds but as a journey.

We were walking on the quiet snow, wondering how only yesterday we argued.

—What were we arguing about?

—I disagreed with you. And still do.

—But you never read me.

—That's true. But we used to talk. We used to think out loud. You listened.

—In a different way—said the man walking next to me, a close friend.

We argued, widening and narrowing down the subject. The way people look into the sky through the magnifying lenses that are arranged inside a shiny copper tube. I thought, if you want to see clearly, you probably shouldn't widen the field of vision. A compressed field of vision. The sky is brought closer at the expense of the margins, at the expense of the neighboring parts.

It clarifies the subject.

This was a conversation, which was recorded after many years, and I can't put anything in quote marks, citing in a footnote an exact name of a book or its page numbers.

We were walking side by side, remembering what made us close and what would make us close.

—But you—my interlocutor and friend said—don't want to write in the strictly academic style, listing all the results as first, second, third, fourth . . .

And my friend mentioned the subjects of our arguments. I could have answered, I hadn't forgotten anything, but I remained silent.

The cold air clears the sky. The telescope pierces the sky; the stars are more lucid in the context of constellations. We were talking about this as we were approaching his house, a two-story summer cabin. It was very quiet, quiet as the cold air. He and I never drank—either on our own or separately. He dug out a bottle of vodka from under a snowdrift, and I think there was a glass, too. We drank without getting drunk.

It was hard for us, we saw the work of this other person, the work of a woman who lived there, in the Fountain House on the river, which was still like a granite wound, surrounded by cast iron. Then we were talking about the whole.

To talk about constellations without knowing the stars is misleading. To talk about the stars without knowing what a star is—is wrong. But the starry sky is an ordinary subject of a search, the goal of observation. Yes, I confess, I don't know how to write so that you have the first answer, then the second, and third. I'm not familiar with the devices. I'm a writer.

A poet without rhyme, without rhythm, but with a thick distinctive drone of the heart.

Who observes the discoveries of art, its methods that bring one closer to art.

At least that's how I felt in the quiet of the cold night.

The stars get dispersed when the telescope is taken down, people get dispersed when their names are enveloped in black frames. But the subject matter is still there—the sky. I'm going to write erratically and at the same time I'll try to be precise. I'll write without being content with my own little experience, but by relying on the pronouncements of other writers, their experience, their contradictory words, trying to find a definition of the subject by intersecting the readings.

My dear friends, you have dispersed. But your books remain. Some of you crossed shores. I'm not going to elaborate. But even in dreams I try to connect thoughts, to juxtapose them.

The doctors have told me that what I thought was insomnia until three in the morning was my first dream, its first layer. It's so easy to think in a sleepless night. It's as if I'm alone, without the reader, without myself—without arguing with what I've said before, with what I'll say after, having reached the quiet shore of the endnotes, convenient for the bibliographers and people who write annotations on the works of others.

What is a poetic mentality?—I don't know.

What is getting closer to truth?—I don't know.

But even in dreams one searches for the truth through comparison, and dreams crackle like a river when the ice, not yet frozen to the shores, floats along, turning the broken pieces into a path.

Why do we go to the theater? Why do we watch the same character re-enacted by various actors? I have found a comparison. Lev Nikolaevich started to remember his own life and then wasn't able to remember, his life was affixed to the lawful currents not in the frozen parts but in the openings of rivers, memories crackled, wanting to speak of the future. And there was no comparison.

Lev Nikolaevich said that the most beautiful thing is the precision of mistakes, the energy of delusion, the energy of comprehending ocean currents, the realization that they have multiple levels. They float along, agreeing and arguing and creating what we'll later call by one word.

The infant has no memory. The infant, Tolstoy said, "is used to the eternity." He doesn't know anything about the sun, the grass, or the sky, but this pre-conscious state of the infant is immeasurable.

However, even in that state, comparisons exist. With the first word or the first sound, the first demand, the infant is startled at the separation and happy that this independence will discover the first condition, the first knowledge.

All children are loud, they are always discontented with something, because all the rivers wash away the banks under shifting currents. In Yasnaya Polyana when the children falling asleep in their little cribs, next to each other, would make noise, the old nanny, her head covered in a scarf, would come and say in a frightening voice: "And who's not asleep? At this hour when everyone is supposed to be sleeping." And the children would recognize her voice.

They had heard this voice a thousand times, but they would almost believe Yerofeevna, they played with fear, drifting in and then out of it, like the spectators in theater who can't believe and at the same time believe that Othello is killing Desdemona.

Young, handsome Blok was in Shakhmatovo, performing for the peasants. A beautiful girl was playing Desdemona; she was Mendeleev's daughter. The people who were in front of the balcony were quiet at first, then there were occasional laughs.

They weren't laughing at the gentry or the idea that people were preoccupied with absolute nonsense, they were laughing to justify their inability to intervene and save the woman.

Art palpitates. It hums like an electric wire. You have probably never heard or perhaps forgotten that blue humming of tall electric poles, the electric illumination in the streets of Petersburg. When the plays would blare on the stage with characters flying like clouds, and the conflicts of the scenes would turn tragedy to excitement for the audience.

Belinsky said, for an actor his torments are sweet, and we understand how his soul rejoices at the idea that the spark that erupted in his soul will scatter among the crowds with a thousand sparks and burst into flames. We convert both torment and joy into experience.

■

Now we need to make a big digression.

In order to move forward.

We must return to the preface.

According to the preface there are two books, unified in a third.

It also mentions reconstructed streets, how while reconstructing them, the builder lays the road in the old landscape, or let's say, old topography. The topography is old—the landscape will be new.

The preface says that like everywhere else there are gates here.

Here is a narrow turn.

And so, there are a few consistencies—threads; they intertwine and form the weave.

There is a path that originated with *The Cossacks*; it was laid by Tolstoy, or it's better to say that it was continued with Tolstoy's life.

There is a difficult path that's known only to us: it has a beginning, an exposition, but what about its end?

And then there is a path where a sketch meets the novella.

A sketch that evolves into a literary work.

This is a big subject.

We have discussed it in LEF and in Opoyaz.

I think I'll begin by talking about the "Tolstoyan sketch."

Tolstoy's sketches on the Caucasus later transformed into a system of sketches—I'm talking about *The Sevastopol Sketches*.

His best sketch is "The Snowstorm."

But it's not just a simple snowstorm.

It was begun by Aksakov.

Then continued by Pushkin.

In a snowstorm, one needs to keep both eyes on the road.

One may run into a "guide" on the road in a snowstorm.

It might turn out to be Pugachev.

6

DIFFERENCES BETWEEN NOVELLA AND SKETCH

THE SEVASTOPOL SKETCHES*THE SEVASTOPOL SKETCHES*

The writer must remove himself from and overcome his own past.

Lev Nikolaevich passed through the heights of the analytical sketch—we'll call it a *sketch* starting from the times of Turgenev.

"A Journey to Arzrum" was also a sketch but with fictional characters; the man who is recounting the great battle is not a military man, he doesn't know any military terms.

Pushkin's descriptions are amazing in "A Journey to Arzrum."

The depictions are perfect even in the plainest passages.

Black clouds don't pass over the Caucasus, they tumble in.

The sketches end with an encounter with Griboedov's murdered body —as if a link to the world of literature.

I'll list some of Tolstoy's Caucasian sketches—

"The Trip to Mamakai-Yurt."

"The Raid."

"The Wood-Felling."

Tolstoy's sketches give meticulous instructions of what should be used as material from real life.

Some of them are reminiscent of geographic reports.

This style of writing can also be seen in *Youth*.

Although the latter can't be put into any specific genre.

Tolstoy wasn't too fond of *Youth*. When they asked him what ages the book should be recommended to, he replied: "No age at all."

He was dissatisfied because in the book, which was still his favorite, real life was fused if not with fiction, then at least with parts of other people's histories. It showed that children don't separate those two circumstances, closely relating themselves to their grandmothers, their father and mother, and even their father and the maid who spends their mother's money on herself.

By carefully fusing the realistic and the selected material, Tolstoy is illuminating his own biography through the life of his contemporary, Isleniev, who was to become a very close friend, a very gifted, interesting, but also irritating person.

But not yet crystallized, Isleniev was much more traditional in literature than Lev Nikolaevich Tolstoy; his name was recorded in the church registry along with the names of his older brothers and sisters.

The Sevastopol Sketches transcend what at the time was called a sketch, because they are direct and critical. The conventional or traditional sketch assumed an air of indifference. The hero of *Notes of a Hunter*, the hunter, seems to be neutral, he's as if invisible, not a participant in the realities of the other characters.

Sergei Eisenstein was planning to film *Notes of a Hunter*,[84] and he wanted to keep the location of the camera obscure, i.e., not showing who the narrator was.

But before we go on, I must explain the differences between a novella and a sketch.

The novella usually contains a question that demands an answer.

[84] A footnote by V. Shklovsky—This should not be confused with another story connected to the filming of *Bezhin Meadow*.

Something like this: The gold has been stolen. We must find out—who stole it?

A wise man gathers everyone around and tells a story about three brothers who created a woman.

One cut her figure out of a tree.

The other dressed and adorned her in gold.

Another breathed life into her.

Now here is the question.

Who gets her as a wife?

One of the listeners says: the brother who adorned her in gold.

The wise man then replies: you stole the gold—it's the most important thing for you.

These types of stories are common and rich in variety.

Here is a story from the Gospels.

They ask Christ about the case of a woman whose husband dies, followed by the death of his brothers.

According to the law, if the dead man was childless, the widow must become the wife of the second brother, so that the family line doesn't end. This custom was called *lévirat*.

But in this case all the men die.

In one of the Hindu stories the question is the following: they cut off the heads of two men, and then put the heads back on the wrong bodies.

Then a magician resurrects them.

One of the dead men was some woman's husband.

Whose wife is she now? Does she belong to the head or the body of her husband?

The Gospels give the following answer: There is no marriage or desire in the other world, so the question is irrelevant.

The bottom line of the question is that the Bible doesn't know how to "resurrect from the dead."

The epoch of Jesus knew how to.

The woman's difficult situation was supposed to show the absurdity of the idea of resurrection.

■

A sketch doesn't contain a question.

It often resembles a pencil drawing, sometimes rendering only a part of the object.

A novella usually asks a question. A hidden question.

Who is right and who is guilty?

Who does the reader side with?

Tolstoy's sketches from the Caucasian period such as "The Wood-Felling," "The Raid" and others don't carry a question.

"The Demoted" also seems not to contain a question.

A demoted person is someone who has fallen, someone who before becoming a soldier was an experienced debater, who had his own following.

Here the person is made into a laughing stock, like a soldier who is afraid of the war, and in the soldiers' stories, he is treated as less than a human.

According to Tolstoy, *Notes of a Hunter* was the best of what Turgenev had ever written.

"The Wood-Felling" was dedicated to Turgenev.

Let's quote Nekrasov in connection to this.

We need his words in order to show how the relatively astute contemporaries of Turgenev and Tolstoy saw cultural continuity; and also to look at how they perceived that continuity.

Nekrasov wrote to Turgenev:

We are going to publish a story by a cadet called "The Wood-Felling" in the ninth issue of *Sovremennik*, it's dedicated to you. Have you seen it? It's a sketch on various types of soldiers (and some officers), which is something that has never been done in Russian literature before. And it's done so well! The form is completely yours, there are even expressions and comparisons reminiscent of *Notes of a Hunter*, and one officer is quite your Hamlet of the Schigri province dressed in uniform. But all this is far from imitation—it seems so only at first glance.

To Tolstoy, Nekrasov wrote:

"The Wood-Felling" was accepted without a problem, although they did take out a few precious features. My opinion on this piece is the following: in its form it reminds me of Turgenev, but that's where the resemblance ends; everything else belongs to you, and it couldn't have been written by anyone else but you.

"The Wood-Felling" first appeared in the ninth issue of *Sovremennik* in 1855 under the slightly changed title: "The Wood-Felling: A Story of A Cadet (dedicated to I. S. Turgenev)."

Later Tolstoy said that he didn't understand what exactly a "dedication" meant. His question, of course, was rhetorical and didn't require an answer.

In *Notes of a Hunter*, a man goes hunting along with his dog and a serf of another man; the dog and the serf both chase the game.

They see many different things. But nothing in it requires an answer.

This was partially due to censorship.

The first sketch appeared in *Smes*.

There was a conversation in it between two peasants, one was a hard worker, the other—not a complete loafer—was a poet.

They were good friends.

This story was the first in the series.

There are no direct questions in the *Notes of a Hunter*.

The author abstains from giving any opinions.

The sketch seems to have been written by a child or a person who stands outside of political or social questions.

It doesn't assert anything. The author states: this is what I saw, this whole thing was beyond me—figure it out yourselves.

In reality, *Notes of a Hunter* contains an encoded message.

Without any strain, in a matter-of-fact way, as if he were an inattentive passer-by, the narrator is telling about incidents that occur under the generally accepted serfdom laws.

This is a question that doesn't exist in the series of the Caucasian sketches.

Men are at war, and the best ones fear only what should be feared.

The soldiers are fearless.

Tolstoy was vulnerable when it came to the question of his family name.

He couldn't get a position as an officer for a long time because he didn't have the documents of his birth with him, he couldn't show his ancestral history; the certificate was either in the Heralds' College or it had been burnt.

He felt mistreated.

He received neither a St. George Cross nor a place in society.

He was constantly the younger brother—essentially demoted.

The matter was resolved when, as I already mentioned, the commander-in-chief turned out to be Gorchakov, a very close relative of Tolstoy through his matrilineal side. His grandmother was much higher in birth than the general—she was a superior to the person who was in charge of the front.

Without any difficulty Gorchakov signed the papers establishing Count Tolstoy.

Whatever happened in the Heralds' College—did they ever figure things out?—we don't know. In any case, Tolstoy's brothers used "Count" when signing their names.

Many of the Tolstoys never used this title with their names.

For instance, Fyodor Petrovich Tolstoy, the president of the Academy of Arts, usually signed with his name and surname only, without the title.

I've gotten somewhat carried away from my subject.

But this is an important matter.

And I'll repeat the story with the suckling pig.

I think this is called a leitmotif.

Tolstoy invited some guests over, officers (the commander-in-chief could have been among them), everyone, even the regimental doctor, and ordered a suckling pig prepared.

No one came.

Tolstoy found himself in the same situation as Charlie Chaplin, who had organized an evening and invited women.

No one came.

He ate very little, but he danced, imagining himself and the woman as two buns on forks.

The forks made the buns dance.

It's as if Charlie Chaplin doesn't feel his own poverty, his déclassé position. He sees himself as a person and people love him for that; they go to the cheapest movie theaters to see him.

A person who doesn't stand in his own place may be right if the place is unworthy of his humaneness, if it contradicts humanism in general.

Tolstoy's search was not a search in literature, he hated that word; it was a search of humanism—in everything.

He destroyed any and all kinds of falsehoods.

And he was not content with himself; he saw his own mistakes—due to his untiring search for honesty, truthfulness.

Tolstoy examined the contemporary person, someone from his own class, someone who is false and unhappy, and at the same time, if you will, someone who mustn't be blamed.

He even placed the coffin of Ivan Ilych in his own room, describing the exact same curtains that he hung up himself.

Shakespeare, Pushkin, and Tolstoy seem to have transcended their own times.

They were already in the future, but they weren't disconnected from their reality.

The changes in literary form are similar to the changes in an inaccurately defined reality, the world, or the facts of existence.

This is important for us because Tolstoy creates a chain of connected pictures from Sevastopol.

The characters under the siege live like blind people, they have few interests.

The quartermasters steal.

The officers drink, and at some level are involved in robbery.

For example, the artillerymen can take loads of hay that hasn't yet been taken by the soldiers.

The horses aren't going to complain.

Tolstoy said that if an author really had talent, no matter what his initial thoughts were, he would get down to the truth.

Because he knows his path.

He knows where the truth is.

In *The Sevastopol Sketches*, the war is not fair.

This is clear to the young officer who has just arrived from military school to join his brother and will be killed in the next couple of days.

His brother doesn't realize this, or maybe he just doesn't want to think about it.

The sailors and soldiers of Sevastopol, who were barely surviving in the barracks, were nevertheless able to resist the English troops.

One can clearly feel the general idea in *The Sevastopol Sketches*, the unified theme that connects all episodes.

I must comment on Tolstoy's *Childhood*. The boy sees both truth and falsehood.

But somehow he sees things, as Eichenbaum once said, from an adult's perspective.

His childhood has been cut short.

The nanny in *Childhood* is unhappy, she isn't allowed to marry the man she loves.

Before departure, according to a Russian custom, people sit next to each other on a bench—people belonging to different classes sit on the same bench.

The boy sees this and it seems awkward to him.

Things like this in Tolstoy happen very often.

In *Anna Karenina*, the main issue isn't that the woman has betrayed her husband, or that her brother has used up his wife's dowry, it's that he is systematically unfaithful to her and is still respected by everyone.

The main issue is truth.

The issue is that we constantly need to evaluate other people's situations: as if we are invited to a trial.

And we have a final say over the verdict.

So the sketch can be compared to a witness at a trial.

The novella, like the novel, is a legal proceeding, usually with an unexpected verdict.

Andrei Bolkonsky's function is slightly more than the function of a sketch, but only to the extent that through him we are given a true depiction of the events.

This grand idea wasn't realized. Andrei Bolkonsky tragically dies. His destined role is eased by the fact that Tolstoy casts him in a love story, he is used for the descriptions of the landscape that he sees, the war; but even the secondary characters in military sketches or stories, whose likeness can be found in Denis Davydov,[65] are portrayed in light of hunting scenes, with a sensibility of a hunter, i.e., a person who knows exactly when to let the dogs on a wolf, and this perception is shifted to the hunting scene with Nikolai Rostov, for the description of military conflict that follows must begin from his hunter's hunch.

But at the end of the novel, the main hero is dissolved in Tolstoy's new realism.

[65] Denis Davydov (1784–1839), a hussar poet in the Napoleonic Wars, a Russian hero and the inspiration for the character Denisov in *War and Peace*.

First he was replaced with Platon Karataev, then with the grand character of Kutuzov who in theory is well prepared and is picturesque. But Kutuzov the warrior is different from the old soldier; he sees everything during the battles, yet he doesn't change anything in the events, the outcome of which depends on him.

The shifts of perception in Tolstoy single out his novel from all other novels, even from Stendhal's description of the dead at Waterloo.

The Russian soldiers march through Austria. They are dressed up, they look smart in their uniforms, and next to them is their commander. Through comparison Tolstoy wanted to show what unified troops looked like.

They must look uncompromising.

They have no shoes, they have no provisions, and at the same time the singer, dressed in heavy uniforms, beats out time with his spoons and sings: "Akh vy, seni, moi seni!"[66]

This song is overlaid on the conversation of the demoted Dolokhov with a former friend. Kutuzov looks at Dolokhov and says a few words. But Dolokhov is different now; he has forgotten what it's like being an officer. And the whole dialogue, a very difficult conversation, moves with the rhythm of a high-spirited song, as if under the beat of the soldier's wooden spoons.

This "choir" scene is directed by Sergei Bondarchuk, the talented film director of *War and Peace*. But this episode in the film was shot separately. The two worlds do not intensify the perception of the shift from one life to another.

The song is there.

But there is no conversation to the beat of the song.

They make fire and fill the pot that's hanging over the flames with ingredients that aren't supposed to be mixed.

[66] A Russian folk song.

The same happens in the hunting scene with the Rostovs and their neighbors, the rich landowners and the poor "Uncle" who has nothing but a dog.

This isn't just a description of the hunt, but also the description of existing hierarchies in high society. And this is variously described in the novel.

In the meantime, the impolite reception of Andrei Bolkonsky's bride by his father, when the prince receives her in his robe, at some level explains Natasha's attempt to run away with Anatole Kuragin.

War and Peace is multilayered.

The construction of the novel is linked and each link has its own evaluation, its own logic of the character's behavior.

The place that *Anna Karenina* took in the writer's life was intended for Peter I, meaning, the history had to be changed.

Peter I couldn't hold up under Tolstoy's analysis, and this character was apparently supposed to portray the image of a criminal and false leader.

Tolstoy wanted to "correct" the story of Paul; but Paul's difficult story wasn't appropriate, it couldn't decide the fate of a great country.

■

This is how *Anna Karenina* entered the fields plowed by a sketch of a historical novel, a sketch with precise descriptions; this was preparation for a deeper plowing.

I'll repeat once more.

A writer's handwriting reflects past experiences.

The poems of Pushkin, and his descriptions, those experiences become part of *Anna Karenina*; but the story of *Anna Karenina* is somehow closer to journalistic prose, it even belongs in a newspaper. We can decide and we must decide to express our opinion on the actions of the heroine, recalling each day or at least each week of her life. At first, life appears as though through newspaper fragments.

The novel incorporates both the history of the Borodino battles and the war games. Italy is still treated with some dignity. And the military life of the aristocratic regiment violates the life of some unimportant official, who is somewhat protected by the law, and yet unprotected.

It's not the dresses that are fashionable, but their models; what they eat, what's on their menu, the new railroads, the atmosphere surrounding the tables, the temptation to switch the desire for the marvelous with the desire for something petty—all of these compose the daily events of *Anna Karenina*.

The names and surnames show from whose perspective the views on life and the footage of life are made. Everything is overturned in the novel and it's impossible to fit into it.

7

THE CAPTAIN'S DAUGHTER

The search in literature is the search for new meaning in life; old interpretations recede, a new one comes forth that seems will last forever.

The foremost prerequisite for this search—disenchantment with old forms—is basic to the progress of art. It's the clash of different needs.

All that Pushkin lived through and all that Tolstoy experienced were like premonitions before an earthquake, a feeling of being doomed.

Just as animals, which have no consciousness, no need to formulate things, torment themselves before an approaching catastrophe.

Aleksandr Herzen wrote about nature:

Nature! Surrounded and captivated by her, we can neither free ourselves nor go any deeper inside of her. Uninvited, unexpected, she seizes us into the whirlwind of her dance and carries us along.

. . . She loves herself with innumerable hearts and gazes at herself with innumerable eyes. She has divided into parts in order to take delight in herself.

Eagerly rushing to transmit, to fulfill herself, she keeps creating newer and newer forms.

This is the process that occasionally goes through delusions, but it doesn't allow for the decay of elements that aren't necessary anymore, things that once were beautiful, extraordinary, and essential.

In his speech on the anniversary of Pushkin's death, there, in the suburbs of the city, Aleksandr Blok spoke of the poet's death with a distinct sadness, insisting that his name was joyful.

He lived in debt; he was beloved by his friends; understood by his readers, if we take them as a whole; partly understood by his wife—during the Revolution someone stole Natalya Goncharova's letters to Pushkin from the Rumyantsev Museum. The letters from the poet to his wife were written and sent to a very clever person. The poet was, as if playfully, trying to get even. The notion of getting even was perhaps a difficult one.

But let's not try to change the lives of the great ones; they have a right to their own happiness and unhappiness, and we shouldn't take it upon ourselves to correct anything.

We have their inheritance—their novels and poems.

Tolstoy reproached Renan for writing too realistically. He says that there is gold in the sand, but one shouldn't think that the most important thing is the fact of its being in the sand. The writer pans out the sand; one mustn't turn art's attention only to its origins and former life, i.e., sand.

The torments of the writer, the ever-changing drafts that nevertheless seem alike, occasionally permit one a glimpse into the writer's vision—the vision of the future, not the past.

To see him fearless before the future.

■

Pushkin wrote under difficult circumstances. The censors kept an eye on him and only a few people had a rough understanding of his work.

Pushkin wrote to the hussar poet Denis Davydov, who had earned his respect, that he was sending *The History of Pugachev's Revolt* and described Pugachev[67] with the famous lines:

[67] Yemelyan Pugachev (1740–75), a Don Cossack who organized an uprising against Catherine II during 1773–4. The uprising was crushed in 1774, Pugachev was captured and placed in a metal cage and sent to Moscow for a public execution.

He would've been a dashing warrior
in the first ranks of your battalion.[68]

He juxtaposes Pugachev, the warrior, with great events.

But how to write about this?

The censors expurgated the title.

Pushkin's original title, *The History of Pugachev*, was changed to *The History of Pugachev's Revolt*.

He wasn't allowed to write openly about Pugachev. He was able only to compose memoirs about an old woman who had wished to call Yemelyan Pugachev by the name of Peter Fyodorovich, the Emperor, not the impostor.

Pushkin saw villages that were burnt down to capture Pugachev, he saw people who were mutilated and he saw the gallows.

But how does one write this?

How does one unravel the true story behind the revolt?

Pushkin spoke about the poetics of Pugachevian proclamations.

When beginning his work on Pugachev, Pushkin had made several drafts.

Grinev, the accidental witness to the revolt, is the son of a gentleman who keeps a den of thieves on his own country estate, but this is something petty, it reminds one of the story about Dubrovsky, it doesn't bring Pugachev closer to the important facts of history.

In his drafts, Pushkin places epigraphs at the beginning of each chapter.

This was strange: an epigraph was like the formal dress of the text to follow; it preceded the birth of the chapter's content.

In the final version, all epigraphs referring to Pugachev were taken from poems that contained the phrase "Tsar of Russia," a phrase that Pushkin

[68] From "To D. V. Davydov" (1836).

had left out. For example in Chapter X, "The Siege of the Town," the epigraph reads:

He pitched his camp upon the hills and meadows
And, eagle-like, he gazed upon the city;
He had a mound made beyond the camp
Concealing fire, which at night he brought to city walls.

In Kheraskov's *Russiad*, this excerpt in its full context reads:

The Tsar of Russia pitched his camp upon the hills and meadows
And, eagle-like, gazed upon the city . . .

This is Kheraskov's description of Ivan the Terrible's conquest of Kazan in 1552.

The epigraph to Chapter VI reads:

Listen now, young men, listen,
To what we old men shall tell you.
—*A folk song*

This song was included in Chulkov's *Collection of Songs*:

Listen now, young men, listen,
To what we old men shall tell you
About Ivan the Terrible, about Vasilevich,
How our Master, our Tsar, warred under Kazan.

In the fairytale told to Grinev, Pugachev calls himself an eagle who wants freedom, not blood. Grinev argues, he objects—the revolt has only produced dead bodies. But in the epigraph to Chapter XI, supposedly from Sumarokov, Pugachev is likened to a lion:

The lion has just had a meal;
Ferocious as he is, he asked me kindly,
"What brings you to my lair?"

The epigraph states that this was quoted from Sumarokov. But there never was such a poem. It was composed by Pushkin. Ten years ago they found the drafts of this epigraph, from which I will quote:

THE REBEL'S CAMP

(Then the lion)
    (the lion asked with no anger)
    (without a frightening roar)
Lion (what brings you to my lair?)
At the time (was) just had a meal
    although he
The lion said in kindly spirit (and) ferociously
The Lion has just had a meal,
    ferocious as he is,
"What brings you
    To my lair?"

Four inscriptions that attempt to clarify something.

Why are we interested in these epigraphs?

The epigraph somehow prepares one, guides one on the path to great events and presents the great people who live in these epigraphs; and only here—in these epigraphs—will you find a close-up shot, if you will, of the Pugachevian revolt. They amplify things that would have slipped past our eyes as something ordinary.

What we are about to say now was Pushkin's own discovery.

The epigraphs were excerpted from different works, as if from different sides, different perspectives, and they illuminate the main event in different ways.

There weren't many books in Russia; only a few people kept books on their shelves. But the foretaste of the sound, intended through the epigraphs, covertly aimed at preparing the reader for a lofty reading experience.

Marina Tsvetaeva wrote an essay called "Pushkin and Pugachev," on the first page of which the word "guide" stands out, pointing to the fact that in *The Captain's Daughter* Pugachev guides one through the plot. And I'm glad that I met Tsvetaeva, that this great writer and I met on the same road.

In 1937, in my small book on Pushkin's prose, I said the same thing, perhaps in words that were less clear.[69]

The Orenburg snowstorm, described by Aksakov, was later adopted by Zagoskin.[70] In *Yuri Miloslavsky*, Zagoskin portrays a Cossack who, during the snowstorm, saves a prince.

The descriptions of the snowstorm in *The Captain's Daughter* and in Aksakov match in the practical nature of their pathos.

Pugachev, with his secret coded language, replaced Zagoskin's best character, Kirsha, the servant of Yuri Miloslavsky. A gentleman offers Pugachev his own hare-skin jacket during a blinding snowstorm, rescuing him from the cold; in turn Pugachev saves the gentleman for this small, but kindly gesture.

The choice of the hare-skin jacket isn't random at all.

Pushkin took it from *The Impostor Tsar Peter III*. In the second volume of this book, among the documents that listed lost property, a gentleman wrote a complaint about the loss of his hare-skin jacket.

But after this accidental meeting, Pugachev helps Grinev when he is in trouble.

He frees Grinev, prompted by one of his confidants, a big fellow with cutoff nostrils.

From the scaffold, Pugachev recognizes Grinev in the crowd and nods to him a minute before his execution.

He is fearless.

[69] *Zametki o proze Pushkina* [Notes on Pushkin's Prose].

[70] Lavrenti Zagoskin (1808–90), a lieutenant in the Russian navy who led an expedition to Alaska, author of *Lieutenant Zagoskin's Travels in Russian America, 1842–1844*.

Pushkin treats Grinev affectionately, putting him through misfortunes that are endearing, but the story ends with how Grinev's descendants are among the ten "benefactors" of his estate: ten owners in one village; there was a phrase in those years, *desiatipanovka*, that was used ironically, it meant almost poverty. That was the fate of Grinevka village.

■

Poetry, prose, and music are not beyond history, beyond their complete dependence on history.

Art passes down its accomplishments from generation to generation. These treasures are usually not readily recognizable; they lay in wait at the bottom of the sea, like statues found by the sponge harvesters, the descendents of the ancient Greeks.

Young Tolstoy, whose story I want to tell, was a few years older than Grinev when he almost died somewhere in the steppes near Novocherkassk.

The story is simply called "The Snowstorm."

A caravan of lost sleds is overtaken by a snowstorm. One of the sleds is carrying a gentleman accompanied by coachmen; they are telling each other tales; they aren't afraid. But Tolstoy is frightened, he falls asleep and dreams about a peasant and a servant who is ordering him to kiss the peasant's hand.

This is a repetition of the scene at the Belagorsky fortress where Grinev, pardoned by Pugachev and deaf to the entreaties of his servant Savelyitch, refuses to kiss his savior's (Pugachev's) hand.

Poetry has its periods of death and immortality.

Lev Nikolaevich's memory fished up treasures from the bottom of the literary sea.

Pushkin worked on *The Captain's Daughter* from 1831 to 1836. The story appeared in *Sovremennik* without the author's name.

There were six drafts of the work.

Marya's name appears only in the sixth one.

In the first two drafts, written probably after *Dubrovsky* was finished, the hero's name is Shvanvich, a gentleman who voluntarily sides with Pugachev. This character is based on Basharin, a real person whom Pugachev took prisoner, and who later escaped to the side of those who suppress the rebellion.

In the state report regarding Pugachev's punishment, Grinev's name is mentioned among those who were arrested but were eventually proven to be innocent. Two gentlemen rivals, Grinev and Shvanvich; the creation of these two characters can perhaps be explained as an attempt to get around censorship. One of the heroes is supposed to be good.

During the snowstorm, Basharin saves a Bashkir man; then the Bashkir saves him in turn during the taking of the fortress.

In the third draft, the character of Shvanvich is developed further. He is shown as an unusual gentleman hero, a Russian musketeer.

Shvanvich's father is on friendly terms with the Orlovs. Shvanvich wounded one of the Orlovs and they signed an agreement: if two Orlovs were in a tavern, Shvanvich refrained from entering it; if there was only one member from the Orlovs, Shvanvich could enter the tavern. Shvanvich is sent off to the garrison for misconduct. He hands over the fortress to Pugachev. He also partakes in the plundering of some estates, but saves his father's neighbor.

When Shvanvich is charged as a traitor who sided with Pugachev, his father arrives in St. Petersburg and begs Orlov, his old acquaintance, to pardon his son.

The drafts also introduce a man named Perfilev, a merchant, a first-class fistfighter, he is almost as good as an Olympic fighter.

Pushkin mentions several times that Grinev's father was made to retire the same year when Catherine became Empress.

Grinev the son would have been born in 1755, which meant he could not have been an officer during the rebellion. Which is why it was presumed that the coup forced Grinev's father to retire when Elizabeth I came to the throne.[71]

For Grinev, born into a family of insurrectionists,[72] Pugachev somehow resembles Catherine the Great; this peasant is one of the claimants to the throne, he has no more nor less right to the throne than the German who has become an Empress. Two impostors with parallel fates.

Pushkin's attitude toward Pugachev, as we saw in the epigraphs, is positive; in his conversation with Grinev, Pugachev says that he's not a vulture scavenging for carrion, but an eagle consenting to live a short life.

This declaration is tempered by Grinev, he condemns Pugachev for his murders.

But it would have been impossible to publish a novel in which a gentleman befriends an insurgent serf, therefore the plot had to be weakened in its construction.

The Bashkir man, prompted by Zagoskin, whom Grinev saves in the first drafts, is replaced with Pugachev in the final work. A traditional link is created between Pugachev and Grinev, the origins of which can be seen in the novels of Walter Scott: an accidental event where the hero offers help to a weaker character becomes vital to him when he finds himself in a difficult situation.

This kind of "storied" construction was used for a very long time.

"The History of Pugachev" had complications with the censors. Pushkin had to cut the scope of the events. Young Grinev has no significance in St. Petersburg. He's just a young lad. His father was a banished aristocrat,

---

71 Empress Elizabeth Petrovna (1709–62), the youngest daughter of Peter the Great and Catherine I. She became Empress in 1741 by staging a palace revolution that deposed the infant Emperor Ivan VI and his mother Anna Leopoldovna, who acted as regent.

72 Grinev's father rebelled against the German aristocrats who wanted to reign over Russia, but he is faithful to the Russian throne, and is appalled by his son who has betrayed his oath of allegiance to his own class and joined runaway serfs.

who nevertheless is faithful to the throne. Grinev saves Pugachev during the snowstorm. The chapter has a short title, "The Guide." In the Russian thesaurus the word "guide" means "an escort, someone who leads, someone who shows the way."

So the word "guide" is almost synonymous to the word "leader" and Tsvetaeva was right to call her essay on Pugachev "The Guide," pointing to Pushkin's evaluation of his own hero based on the chapter's title.

However, I realized this twenty years earlier.

Grinev uses Pugachev's accidental act of goodwill to save his bride; the reason is a romantic one, it's not political. The girl, who is rescued, saves her future husband by going to St. Petersburg. The short novel acquires a new title, *The Captain's Daughter*. And I'll remind you once again that the name Marya only appears in the sixth draft. The title of the novel may have been prompted by a line from a song that was included in one of the chapters:

Captain's daughter, I warn you,
Don't you go on midnight walks.

The captain's daughter is extolled as the heroine, but this type of heroism is beyond classification.

The girl meets with Catherine. Catherine is shown very briefly. The traditional portraits of the Empress were published all over the state and were easily recognized by everyone. Pushkin is using the tradition. The dress in which Catherine strolls in the gardens of Tsarskoe Selo is strictly presented according to the famous portrait—every detail, right down to the little dog at her feet, is borrowed from someone else's picture—without any political overtones.

The girl intercedes for her future husband.

Since she is the daughter of the captain who got killed while protecting the state, the Empress helps her because of political motivation.

This is unrealistic.

Krylov's family was destroyed when he was a boy, his father was killed, but no one helped the mother of the future fabulist.

But the humanitarian gesture of the Empress softens the controversial plot, for the subject here is evolving around an uprising, a widespread revolt. The censors, however, expurgated the chapter with the raft and the hanged men. These rafts were often left drifting down the river by the servants of the Empress.

Mironova, on the other hand, who governs as the mistress in the Belagorsky fortress, is depicted realistically: the fortress commandants, living among various nationalities of the steppes, were like the heroes of Cooper living among the Indians. In the character of Mironova, Pushkin reproduces some of the characteristics of Prostakova, such as her disdainful attitude toward her husband and strictness toward the locals: someone had let a horse into her garden and was "rewarded"—he was to give up his quarters to the officer.

The fact that Pushkin didn't put his name on the novel also tones down its intent; it appears as an old anecdote told by some old fellow, who appears to have been acquainted with Sumarokov and wrote poems himself.

The scale of the work is trivialized.

Despite Vyazemsky's objections that Grinev couldn't go into the army if his documents stated he was to serve as an officer of the Guards, which was a rather convincing argument, it was quite possible that Grinev, the owner of the Simbirsk estate, was interested in the Bashkir steppes. For Aksakov's grandfather, for example, or even for Lev Tolstoy, this interest in the steppes was a matter of business.

The methods of suppressing of the rebellion in the story are juxtaposed and softened by the portrayal of Catherine's palace with its treacherous lifestyle.

Catherine's palace was a place of great careers and great dangers. During the times of Grinev, a very handsome gentleman was said to have arrived in the palace, striking everyone with his good looks; he was killed in a duel in that very palace not too long after his arrival. This incident was the end of a promising career for this gentleman who could have become one of the men in Catherine's harem.[73]

■

When we look into the sky through a telescope, it seems as though we are piercing the sky; we limit our field of vision to enhance the light of a single star.

The historic novels of the Pushkin era, and maybe even from the times of young Turgenev, seemed to reverse the telescope. They showed our life from the planet's perspective; making everything more concise, more elegant, if you will, and even somewhat less realistic. This was a sky without constellations.

At the same time, the realism in both Pushkin and Tolstoy is based on the substitution of a wide-angle shot with a number of close-ups. In order for this to make more sense, I'll bring in the example of Tolstoy's "The Snowstorm."

The story is a result of interpreting a single calamity from different angles, i.e., seeing with different eyes.

We notice that the man witnessing the storm, someone who might perish, is constantly changing the sleds in which he is traveling, and he is changing the order of the horses harnessed in the troika.

This variety of perspectives, this search for different viewpoints comes from traveling with various coachmen. They are glad that the gentleman is getting off, God be with him, let him take his belongings along with the responsibility for his life.

People with different experiences interpret the calamity differently: the old coachmen are shown smoking as the wind becomes fiercer—

which gradually becomes more and more realistic—

since the traveler is constantly shown from different sides of the snowstorm; these movements are real, so are the horses in the carriage, and the

73 A reference to Pushkin, who died in a duel to protect his wife's honor.

bells that ring in different tones; even the way each man tires is different, the way each horse bears his weight. The narrator is young, he is strong, he wants to take off his boots during the storm, this is a heroic act for him; for the coachmen—this is life.

The story teaches the reader to see the world, to enlarge the world. This was a portrayal of something seen at its most terrible moment.

"The Snowstorm" teaches calmness; this is a Tolstoyan discovery. From this simple recording of scenes, an almost ethnographic recording, he came to a new construction of plot. The plot is given not as a search for something interesting, unusual, but it becomes a way of seeing: seeing the structure of the universe, its terrible nature.

In this way, maybe even unexpectedly, the epigraphs to *The Captain's Daughter*, through the description of the snowstorm, the storm in the steppe and the meeting with the guide, pass on to "The Snowstorm," because they are the search for a vision in a variety of perspectives, the search for a unified vision. It changes as it goes through the constantly evolving world.

After the Caucasian sketches and stories, written by a very young person, and after the creation of a style inherent to *The Sevastopol Sketches*, Tolstoy will be able to show the War of 1812.

8

EVERYTHING IN LIFE CAN BE MONTAGED— YOU JUST NEED TO FIND THE RIGHT WAY

I. TOLSTOY'S "DIARY"

I've always started writing my books in the spring; this is probably irrelevant to other people but it's good for me.

This spring however seems a bit unpredictable; you pick a subject and then the weather keeps changing. It's either snowing or melting or the snow keeps piling on the pine trees, impossible to say whether it's April or Christmas.

But life is wonderful in the sense that it continues to change—it's always different.

Most of what I have written in this book will seem repetitive to you, it'll seem unnecessary.

People today get carried away with terminology; there are so many terms that it's impossible to learn them all, even if you're a young person on vacation.

I want to return to the old writer, the eldest by birth—Chernyshevsky.[74]

Tolstoy once wrote about him: ". . . Chernyshevsky came to see me, he is clever and hot-tempered." An idea becomes clear in real life only after it's fully carried out.

In the meantime, Chernyshevsky frantically wrote one article after another on Pushkin. This was a frantic state of inventiveness, or discovery, if you will.

The phrase that I have been discussing—*energy of delusion*—means a search for truth in its multiplicity. This is truth that must not be the only one, it must not be simple. Truth that changes; it recreates itself through a repetitive pattern. But the flowers, too, repeat one and the same pattern, so do the birds. When you hold a bird in your hands, you see that it's different. Even the ichthyosaurs, the prehistoric crocodiles, are strange to our eyes if we look at them closely. This is the construction of the new, it evolves by way of new combinations.

Talking about Tolstoy, Chernyshevsky said that his observations become clear when you realize that they are the result of self-analysis, when you find out that they come from old diaries, analytical and self-evaluative diaries of a person who is looking inside himself, even though he knows that he has already been formed.

I'm quoting Chernyshevsky from his article "Tolstoy's *Childhood, Boyhood*, and Military Stories."

Count Tolstoy's attention is mostly aimed at how certain feelings and thoughts develop from others; he likes to observe how a feeling, coming

---

74 Nikolai Chernyshevsky (1828–89), radical writer, literary critic and socialist theorist, best known for his revolutionary novel *What Is To Be Done?* (1863). Chernyshevsky and Tolstoy first met in Europe and Tolstoy was influenced by many of his socialist theories, which resurfaced in his *What Then Must We Do?* (1886). Here Shklovsky is referring to the one-month difference between Tolstoy's and Chernyshevsky's birthdates, Chernyshevsky was born a month before Tolstoy, however Shklovsky is also challenging the idea of "influence."

directly from a certain situation or impression, obeying the influence of memories and the power of combinations, presented by the imagination, is transformed into other feelings, then how it returns to the original source and then again travels on, while changing throughout this chain of memories. Like a thought, born from a first experience, leads to other thoughts, getting carried away, further and further, mixing daydreams with real sensations, visions of the future with reflections of the present.

Today, we often discuss and try to analyze separate words; perhaps I'm not following very carefully, but people have become too fixated on the analysis of a poem.

I'll repeat—

I'm familiar with all that has been done by the Structuralists, and I see too much terminology floating around, which may be effective, but I'm not sure how to approach the essence of a composition with all this terminology.

I have the impression that Structuralism began its study of the poem on an ice floe; the ice floe was close to the shore, then the wind carried it away into the open sea and people don't know if they should cry or shout for help, or be happy that they chose this course, that they are on their way.

Tolstoy spoke about linkages, a labyrinth of linkages—words don't stand on their own, they exist within the context of a phrase; a word juxtaposed to another word isn't an arbitrary word, it shifts the meaning into another dimension. It's a labyrinth of linkages that has a purpose.

■

That's why Tolstoy is a "programmed" writer; he returns to the same intentions in different novels, sketches, and most importantly, in his diaries.

These diaries contain various observations, portraits of people.

These frequent entries offer various outlines, which act not so much as a framework, but rather as a means to select material from the diary. Tolstoy's *Diaries* is a work of art in its own right.

We write mostly about the published works of the great writer, but the volume of his entries and drafts in his diaries exceeds the amount of his separate works.

After all, Tolstoy and Dostoevsky didn't go down the same road.

At the end of his life, Dostoevsky started publishing the *Diary of a Writer* in separate pamphlet installments.

And in his *Diary of a Writer* he often walks alongside Tolstoy.

II. THE WORLD CAN BE MONTAGED

The world can be montaged. We discovered this when we started piecing together a filmstrip.

The discovery was made by outsiders (people who came from the side)—doctors, sculptors, painters, actors; they saw that different feelings could be expressed through identical but differently arranged images.

Lev Kuleshov[75] came up with his own theory; he showed how one shot, fixing a facial expression, could become something that reveals sorrow, hunger, or happiness. The world is montagable, it's linked. Ideas don't exist in isolation.

We will, therefore, frequently return to the analysis of the same thing, because human existence is unified at its core.

Spring will soon be here, it will finally arrive. The flocks of birds are preparing, they are already lining up, gathering their strength to fly back. The strong ones will fly in the front because they are stronger; the younger

---

[75] Lev Kuleshov (1899–1970), filmmaker, one of the first great experimentalists in the art of montage who adopted a similar position to Pudovkin, viewing montage not in terms of collision and conflict, as later Eisenstein would use montage in his films, but functioning as a device for linking and uniting the disjointed fragments. One of the best comparative analyses of how montage is used in the works of Kuleshov, Vertov and Eisenstein can be seen in Shklovsky's *Ikh nastoyaschee* (1927).

ones will fall behind and try to stay in the middle, they will fly flapping their wings in the air, which will already be full of commotion.

The flight of birds is a structure; it's not the flapping of just one wing.

The world exists only through a montage; so does unplotted art.

It's impossible to write anything without montaging, without juxtaposing; at the very least—it's impossible to write well.

■

I love Goncharov.[76]

He describes a ship, a frigate, going somewhere far off, heading toward Japan.

The pious admiral takes a vessel that has an altar on it.

But the altar is very old.

The ship sets sail.

It turns out that the ship needs some repairs.

It can be repaired in England.

The bottom part of the ship is old and has rotted out.

Then there is battle on the horizon, we see the same war that Tolstoy described in *The Sevastopol Sketches*.

There is a battle between the steamships and sailboats.

And the frigate keeps moving through the unknown waters.

But how does Goncharov describe this?

He likens it to a Russian village, a common Russian village; it has torn itself from the shore and sailed away—the village has taken off, it's going on a far journey.

It will pull into the harbor of an uninhabited island. It will change its masts—this village that turned into a frigate—it will change masts, over

---

76 Ivan Goncharov (1812–91), a Russian novelist best known for his *Oblomov* (1859). Between 1852 and 1855 Goncharov voyaged to England, Africa, Japan, and back to Russia via Siberia as the secretary of Admiral Putyatin, and published a chronicle of the trip as a travelogue, *The Frigate Pallas* (1858).

the masts of Robinson Crusoe, and it will sail onward, checking whether the emerging island is Sakhalin or a piece of land stuck to the mainland.

This dual sensation—of a calm life and a far-off journey—is fused into one, and the incredible things, described as reality, make things more perceivable.

■

Chekhov continued Tolstoy's path.

The simplest thing is the most incredible thing, and the most incredible thing is the most remarkable thing, which requires examination.

One must see the heart in a suspended moment, as it beats, as though it's transparent; one must see a living heart, a suffering heart, and then tell about it.

"The Darling" is a story about a woman who doesn't know much, she is unreligious, perhaps even unromantic. She is presented without any beautification, she is neither Dulcinea del Toboso nor Tatyana Larina, she is not a lady, but a simple woman living in a neat little house, which she cleans, and also has a cook with whom she often has conversations.

Even the neighbors don't argue with her.

Life goes by.

She gets married—several times.

Her first husband is a manager of an amusement park, a world of fake arts, but it's presented through her eyes.

She loves her manager husband. She talks to the actors, always saying "Me and Vanechka," while they laugh at her, they laugh and take her money.

But when he dies, she—and we along with her—feel sad.

Another man comes to live with her in the house, the second husband, a timber merchant; he has a storehouse, logs and boards of different shapes.

The woman drifts into his world.

And we along with her.

He leaves.

Then comes the veterinarian.

It turns out that the work of a veterinarian is very interesting; again, life is dedicated to simple relations, diseases of cattle; it's an easy life; it's not a frightening life at all, it's even exciting. The Darling lives the life of her husband.

The highest point in her life is the young schoolboy, from whom it's very difficult to part. He learns at school that "an island is a piece of land which is entirely surrounded by water." This is a discovery for the Darling, she has just found out about it.

To grasp the world through eloquent or ineloquent love; to become interested in life and its re-montage; to see its different facets from various angles.

Already financially secure, Chekhov brings the son of one of his acquaintances to his small Moscow house made of two stone barns, and observes how this boy, a student in the second or third grade, leads the typical life of a schoolboy—

the great writer, through his work, showed the intricacies of a simple life; this is a writer who is "stepping" up. Tolstoy said about Chekhov that he predicted "my ideas," which Tolstoy later employed in *Hadji Murad*.

The book I'm writing is not inconsistent. The person writing this book is also in love with the world just as Chekhov's Darling is. He is searching for comparisons—no, he's not even searching—and he's finding something new in his book every morning.

The man who wore the name of a Formalist, just as in his youth he wore the uniform from his school, grew up and moved to a different class. But at the same time, he is just like the Darling—well, at least to himself he is.

Don't analyze the word, analyze the system of words; don't search for the roots, you are ripping them away from truth.

Don't think that Shakespeare would have existed without Aristophanes.

The truth is—yesterday and tomorrow will never be the same—everything in life is montagable, you just need to find the right way to do it.

A new search for a new life. First, you must strive for a sensation of life, then—for its evaluation.

The path to Pushkin—Tolstoy—Chekhov is the path of changing evaluations of life. But be careful not to lose the sensation of life.

■

This book is probably about Tolstoy—no, this book *is* about Tolstoy, because for sixty years I have been moving alongside this man who never ages, admiring how he gets off his horse on occasional stops, then gets back on, how his felt cloak doesn't get in his way, how he doesn't let his horse get exhausted.

But I'd like to talk about not just the development of one world of art but also its simultaneous existence with the different art worlds of various movements and times.

■

How mesmerizing was the flight of birds; I was fourteen then. Or, I might have been twelve.

They were flying over St. Petersburg, along the birds' road, it passes over rivers and creeks, you can even see it; they had a certain order to their flight, there were various flocks, and when they'd float on the waters of the sea—I'll try to describe it—they looked like a proof-reader's sheet.

They sat in lines.

III. THE TOLSTOYAN DETAIL

Detail. This is a subject that can be started from any place, since all the important connections in the linkages of circumstance must pass through detail, and none of them are less important than others.

Detail is primarily connected to the strangeness of life and the author's relation to it.

We already talked about beginnings and endings.

But one can start from the middle.

That's a relatively common thing.

Let's take *Dead Souls*, for example.

Or the beginning of *Taras Bulba*.

Bulba understood his children in his own way, he even quarrelled with one of them.

Tolstoy kept Gogol in mind, and also adopted Pushkin's way of making a sudden entrance.

The novel begins with the conflict of the great love between Anna Karenina and Vronsky and the people in the theater, who are talking after attending a play.

The very beginning opens with a conflict of misunderstanding.

At the same time, this is like a strangeness of life.

And a necessity.

Let's take a look at the following correlation—

Kitty is looking at Levin.

He notices her gaze.

— . . . What were you thinking?

—I was thinking about Moscow, about the back of your head.

This strange answer doesn't surprise Levin a bit.

—How did I deserve such kindness? . . . You are too good—he says, kissing her hand.

Tolstoy often observes his heroes in unexpected moments, in a sudden close-up, in an unanticipated situation; it's a simple test—is it good or bad?

When Anna is on the train, going to see Vronsky with whom she had an argument, she doesn't know where he is, she is waiting for a letter from him, she sees—as in a montage—small, fragmented, seemingly unrelated shots, it's as if they are pieced together without any transitions.

A drunken man, signboards, girls. But these images are connected through the idea that all must be rejected.

A coiffeur, who calls himself Tyutkin.

Everything is not right—everything is a falsehood.

It seems the world is broken into pieces and has not been glued back together.

Anna says to herself that she'll tell Vronsky about this, she is trying to put the pieces back together—he'll laugh when he hears about it—then she remembers that he won't laugh, she can't tell Vronsky because they had a quarrel.

This segment in its abruptness is montaging the "road" to her death.

However, these shots aren't really connected to each other; they become linked only from the moment of their entrance into a person's life.

Pushkin's life, the construction of his works, which at first seemed to Tolstoy a bit dated in their literary style, perhaps in their construction, they'll someday be new and unexpected—more heightened in their sensitivity.

One cannot predict life.

And the moment when Anna "must" throw the red bag hanging from her arm under the train wheels—this dishevelled life exists in the world of poetry, in the world that has already been structured in a rhythm of words, the world of Pushkin.

The clock arms must show the time, but they are broken, they are showing the wrong time.

This can be seen in Blok's poems, especially in his lyric verses:

... A street. A lamp. A drugstore—[77]

The same ordinary landscape is repeated. It's as if it is eternally recurring and destroying life through its ordinariness.

A shifted perception, a sensation divorced from the person's emotional state.

It becomes almost satirical.

[77] The first line from an untitled poem written in 1912.

■

The highly exaggerated portrayal of the governor's ball in *Dead Souls* is given through the metaphor of black flies moving on cubes of white sugar.

It's the black frocks and the white dresses.

But also, it's the purposelessness of this movement.

The restlessness of Chichikov who drives around the world *comme un voyageur*—as we'd call him today—this movement is given through the assessment of his britzka's wheel.

How far can it go?

The wheel breaks off from the calm landscape and roams on its own.

It can go anywhere.

In the old novel, when the clock struck so many times, when it struck in this way in this tower or that church, it was a very banal beginning.

Although here, too, we seem to have things that are interconnected; the peasants, who are evaluating the sturdiness of the wheel, are unrelated, and Chichikov himself makes his entrance into the novel without any explanation, he doesn't make clear why he is traveling on those ordinary wheels.

And so, very abruptly and through the detail about a wheel, the actual opening—what is Chichikov really up to?—is moved almost to the middle of the work. His formal biography appears only here, in the middle of the novel, where we find out the purpose of his visit.

For instance, in one of Tolstoy's novels a person is preparing for something festive, he is nervous, and all the while, the elegant shirt he's wearing is crumpled.

The shirt was lost, everyone was looking for it, the stores were closed, his friend's shirt wouldn't fit.

This relatively small incident is torn from the general festivities of a ritual and, at the same time, very mundane wedding ceremony.

But this detail brings the wedding into another context, another world; this world is simultaneously mundane and realistic and also something else, something that is present only in what I would call a Tolstoyan detail.

Tolstoy is squinting his eyes; we are seeing through his squinted eyes.

In one of his diary entries there is a conversation of Sofia Andreevna, then a young lady, with her maid who is also preparing for the celebration, she knows and feels it, but the words that they use, the "little hairs" instead of "hair," puts everything into an unexpected context, and that context is nothing but ordinary.

In the meantime, Tolstoy is struggling against excessive details.

The ordinary, somewhat even awkward dialogue between Gogol's heroes in *The Marriage*, their differences in style, their connection through a certain idea, all this is suddenly disrupted when one of the bridegrooms jumps out of the window.

I remember a production by Kozintsev,[78] I believe, where both characters are afraid of the mysteries of marriage. This was done very well and it could've been a theme taken from Gogol.

The incident is trivial, but it's very unexpected—a jump from the window—this is emphasized through the matchmaker.

The bridegroom flies out, not through the door, but through the window.

Life is shown in a completely different light, Mayakovsky would say, and something important is perceived through nonsense.

But Tolstoy doesn't want to startle the reader with something strange.

He wants to show the strangeness of the mundane—through detail.

Everyone is happy at the death of Ivan Ilych.

They think: Thank God he's dead, not me.

And Ivan Ilych lies in the coffin as dead men always lie.

His life was one of the most monotonous and most terrible lives ever.

---

[78] Grigori Kozintsev (1905–73), film director best known for his productions of such classics as *Don Quixote* (1957), *Hamlet* (1963), and *King Lear* (1969).

Tolstoy was afraid of not only death but also life if it was always to be the same.

The description of life doesn't have to be "same as always," but as it's supposed to be.

And even that isn't true.

The description must be different, coming from a different relation.

Hence, Tolstoy's relation to detail.

One may even say that details come with directions—"necessary" or "unnecessary."

When Bagration, who is wounded, mounts his horse—Tolstoy writes without rejecting the ordinary—his cloak slips off, he adjusts it—he is doing ordinary things, things that people usually do.

But he is doing these things in a way that's not usually done before a battle.

He gets off his horse and marches as a cavalryman—he doesn't know how to walk in any other way.

The descriptions by Tolstoy are descriptions done as they should be.

They are present in his earliest works.

Tolstoy writes that all his life Karl Ivanovich (the teacher in *Childhood*) read very simple books.

Books about cultivating soil under rows of cabbage,

or the history of the Seven Years War,

or a full course on hydrostatics.

It's as if Tolstoy is using the rights of a child—he's got a child's way of rejecting life.

He is doing what's supposed to be done.

He describes death, his mother in the coffin.

He is looking at her in speechless fascination.

And that's the way he grieves.

■

As always—Tolstoy is against platitudes.

He always fought against them.

And when he is describing Sevastopol, in the morning, when they are taking the horses to the water as usual, here he is showing the most ordinary thing, the habitual, nothing amazing.

In his act of ripping off masks, which Lenin mentioned, he is ripping off the mask of all that is mundane.

He describes Kitty, who is going to the ball; her maid brings her a dress and her face expresses a full understanding of the dress's fluffiness.

They are bathing Kitty.

They wash behind her ears.

She is washing in a bathtub, but it seems that this is important.

They live like everyone else, but like one isn't supposed to live.

That's what a detail in Tolstoy can do.

One must live without pretensions.

One must live the way peasants reap their hay.

He detests people talking about precision as if it were realism.

He shows a battle in the way that a person actually perceives it, and not in the way that it appears in reality.

Raevsky is standing at the very front and behind him are his two sons.

Tolstoy says that this is irrational.

Nobody will pay attention to this—they're at war.

Actually, it might be noticed.

Look how he describes Levin's wedding.

Everyone is asking for help.

Levin himself is asking for help.

Then he looks at Kitty, thinking that she's also preoccupied with the same thoughts.

But she isn't.

This is written without a hint of scorn.

It's done very casually.

Then in his diary he will write that his wife is crying, talking about her "little hairs"—"she talks like my aunt."

His marriage turns out to be a very mundane thing.

■

Reality is not the depiction of the mundane.

It's the signification of real sensations that the mundane fights against.

Even the deceased are presented like everyone else.

In his description of the "Arzamas horror," Tolstoy tells how a suddenly awakened man—in a very realistic and well-described room, where he even gives the type of wood of the furniture—hears the words whispered in his ear and knows that this is death speaking to him.[79]

These are the same voices that spoke to the Maid of Orleans; they prompted her to heroic deeds. And when the English judge asks: in what language were these words spoken to you?—the girl answers: in French, a much purer language than yours (apparently, meaning English, or maybe even Russian).

In Tolstoy's fiction, details are written as if in a different handwriting; the willful intrusion of the wide-frame shot into the main theme is intentionally emphasized.

The intensities of the text in fiction are made different beforehand.

■

Further in the book, when we talk about *Anna Karenina*, we'll return again to Tolstoy's detail.

For the writer-realist Lev Tolstoy, the behavior of people is different at different moments of their lives.

[79] In 1869, during a trip to Arzamas to purchase lands, depleted after completing *War and Peace*, Tolstoy is seized with depression and a groundless fear of death, which later became material for "The Death of Ivan Ilych" and *Anna Karenina*.

IV. TIME IN TOLSTOY'S NOVELS

We select manuscripts by their notations, the handwriting, the paper, the relationship of text with random letters, but the time of a literary process does not equate to the time shown on city clocks. It returns and resets the time. When one needs to stop this time or slow it down, then is it possible to say that time has stopped from progressing?

Or one may do it as in Shakespeare's tragedies, throw cues that have no relation to what's happening, two or three people conversing with each other, and time passes by.

But Tolstoy, like Dostoevsky, uses a specific device for fighting against dead time, it's rather conventional.

At the beginning of each chapter, Fielding noted the time span of that particular chapter.

In his novels, Fielding draws an outline of time. The author compares the time in his novel with a stagecoach that follows a schedule. And he also notes how many actual or non-fictional days have passed in a given chapter.

In these circumstances Fielding's novel either speeds up or slows down.

Both in Tolstoy and Dostoevsky there is an unusual accuracy in detail.

The dresses, conversations about "conditioned reflexes,"[80] and spiritualistic séances.

Consequently, the time in Tolstoy can be guessed by the day of the week or even by browsing through newspapers.

The same with Dostoevsky.

It's as if the magazines popularized the crime of this student, everyone judged him.

The case is unexpectedly reversed when the painters take the blame.

Someone later said that there was no need for Dostoevsky to continue

---

[80] A theory developed by famous Russian psychologist Ivan Pavlov (1849–1936) at the turn of the century.

printing the novel, since only the names of the characters had been changed.

This element of so-called documented time—this is a device for fighting against fictional time.

Women don't age after you leave them.

Pushkin turned this peculiarity into parody in his *Ruslan and Lyudmila*. Voltaire did this before him in his *Candide*.

After many adventures, a man meets the woman whom he loved and discovers that she has an awful character.

In the meantime there had been an earthquake in Lisbon.[81]

The time in Tolstoy is precise.

The great author of the great novel begins with description that reminds one of a document in its structure and material. It's reminiscent of an early sketch before sketches ever existed.

And even though Tolstoy dedicated only "The Wood-Felling" to Turgenev, all of his military sketches have a similar rhythm.

Later, the paths of Turgenev and Tolstoy separated, sometimes the writers didn't even want to understand each other.

The military stories of Tolstoy are very specific and real; for example, the things that happen to the character in "The Wood-Felling." The construction of roads on the Caucasian front; clearing the shoulders of the forest that grows on each side; this is a huge and difficult military undertaking.

The first chapters with the anticipatory descriptions of the Cossacks were written with almost geographic precision. The long digressions show where the action takes place. Certain actions taking place in certain ways.

The sketches could have been published with inserted maps, along with the conventional or unconventional pictures of the characters.

Tolstoy's realism stands next to scientific realism and argues with it.

War and Peace has many pages of theoretical and military discussions.

81 The 1755 Lisbon earthquake mentioned in *Candide*.

Questions like, what is war?, what is the front?, what is a partisan war?, or a war dispatch?, what does war feel like when you are standing in a row with other soldiers?

The novel was supposed to have a leading character, Andrei Bolkonsky, a theoretician by his own design. Initially he was supposed to argue with the novelist, but Tolstoy's novel was examining military science. And it ended up that both Tolstoy and Bolkonsky almost didn't have a place in the novel. Bolkonsky didn't die but he was severely wounded and his actions as a hero end when he meets Natasha Rostova, the woman whom he loved.

■

War and Peace has two patterns of movements in time—movements in times of peace and movements in times of war.

War separates people and then unites them again.

During peacetime people are more comprehensible to us. They are conscious of the time in which they live.

Natasha Rostova is a girl who tracks the time as she becomes an adolescent (or a maiden, if you like) and then—a woman.

In her conversation with Boris Drubetskoy, she is counting the years before their wedding. And she is doing this while standing on a box. She is still very young.

But when one of the women from the Volkonsky family commented on the relationship that the characters of *War and Peace* have with her, Tolstoy replied with indignation that he never imitates real life, but creates all of his characters in the process of description.

The novel's characters are either fixed in history or are history's neighbors. When Boris Drubetskoy appears in the book, his old mother is described as an independent landowner. She comes from an impoverished aristocratic family, the name of which is one of the best in the country, Trubetskoy. But in the novel she becomes Drubetskoy.

The Volkonskys are known as Bolkonsky.

But the forest near Tarusy is called Bolkonsky Forest. The peasants living by Yasnaya Polyana used to say that their master was Count Bolkonsky.

This was explained in a book called something like *Adventures to the South*—but I have forgotten the exact title.

I gave that book to the Tolstoy Museum; it's the only book that documents the old Prince Bolkonsky, and his real character—a man who could stand up for his peasants.

This strong landlord resembles the hero of the novel.

Sometimes a character enters the novel with his real name. That's how Bagration and Kutuzov appear.

Initially Kutuzov is presented as someone not belonging to his times, then he is shown as someone who is reinventing his own character. In the novel, Kutuzov is more historical than he was in his own times, in real life. We can say this about the other characters, too.

When enlisting in the army, Andrei Bolkonsky, also known as Volkonsky, was originally supposed to go to Bessarabia, I think. His father wrote a letter to Kutuzov. They were friends.

The young man goes to meet the historical figure. He is embarrassed. In the ballroom, the commander-in-chief, this historical figure to whom they have almost erected a monument—he is already three-quarters bronze—this man is tying the dancing shoe of a Moldavian girl.[82]

But we are moving along.

In Borodino, Kutuzov wasn't giving any orders during the battle, it was simply impossible. There were no telephones or telegraphs back then. Sending an *aide-de-camp* was not so easy, it was dangerous, there were too many shootings, he might not have reached his destination.

With time, historical hours are more intensified than fictional hours.

[82] Before the battle of Borodino, Kutuzov was the commander of the Moldavian army fighting against the Turks on the Danube. Kutuzov, who was more ambitious, wasn't happy about this post.

The army regiments are let go, some names are announced, which later will become historical names.

Andrei Bolkonsky meets with Kutuzov again. But this time their author has changed. It's still Tolstoy, but this is a Tolstoy who is at a different stage of his literary work.

Kutuzov is met with icons and great hope. He will stay in the house of the priest and his wife, a very beautiful woman; Kutuzov gives her a few gold coins, he talks to her.[83]

Tolstoy writes that Kutuzov leaves the house after half an hour.

We see a very ordinary military love affair. It's irrelevant to the novel's events and characters. The time in Borodino is fictional; it's not by the clock.

This strange romance involving Kutuzov is inserted for a reason: almost everyone criticized Kutuzov for his behavior on such occasions, and so did Tolstoy too through his text. But at the same time, this strange commonplace trait does not disgrace Kutuzov, but elevates him. This is his natural state, which is perhaps highlighted a bit more in a moment of great military strain.

The scene in the priest's house shows the difference between Kutuzov and the tinselly pretentiousness of Napoleon—he had ordered that his son's portrait be displayed before the battle—a detail, marvellous in its own right, showing a moment from the life of the opposite camp.

Napoleon is portrayed in a dogmatically satiric light.

The French are so close that they can see the church next to the priest's house.

But Kutuzov is calm. He is reading a French novel. Then he passes some time with the priest's wife.

[83] The affair between Kutuzov and the priest's wife is implied in the following scene: "Well, my dear, and how are we getting on?"—he asked, moving to the door of the room assigned to him. The priest's wife smiled, and with dimples in her rosy cheeks followed him into the room.

The women that appear in Borodino, the relationship between the men and women during war in contrast to the relationship between the men and women in the ballroom—in art—is different, they are on a different time zone.

At their meeting in the ballroom, Bolkonsky sees a man, who, burdened with a great responsibility, is busying himself with trivial things, which is weakly justified by the fact that those things are happening at the ball and not at the front lines of the battle.

For a short time Kutuzov is tuning out Napoleon, with whom he is at war but not actually fighting.

Napoleon is treated almost with contempt.

This is the same Kutuzov who, not too long ago, during a retreat scene in a battle with the Turks, pretends to be defeated; his army is across the river, he doesn't even attempt to repair the fortifications, his soldiers walk idly around the camp. When the Turkish pasha crosses the river, Kutuzov welcomes him with a battle and then, without finishing it, crosses the river, occupies the Turkish camp, and takes their cannons.

Then, to unburden himself, and almost without any permission, he signs a pact with Turkey.

He knows that soon there will be a war with France.

He knows the future.

Kutuzov is historical, but so is Tolstoy's novel, which controls the time.

Kutuzov plans ahead for the winter; he wants to postpone the war at least till autumn. In the meantime he orders the Tula Armaments Factory, which was almost adjacent to Tolstoy's estate, to shorten the gun barrels, and make winter horseshoes and lances, and he gathers around young untrained Cossacks from the Don.

He is not a battlefield hero, he is a hero in the field of war.

He is planning strategies against the retreating Napoleonic armies; he puts his cavalrymen in a passage through which the French will have to escape.

The passage turns out to be rather wide, and lances are bad weapons.

Lances were still being used in the army and a wound from a lance was hardly ever deadly. The lance was a weapon from the times of Boccaccio.

It was living its last days here, in Russia.

During the battle of Malo-Yaroslavets, as Napoleon is trying to flee through the passage and escape the Russian troops that are hounding the French army, Kutuzov admits that the enemy might be able to break through. But with a single resolve he changes the situation.

—What am I afraid of?—he thinks—I have already lost Austerlitz. I am going to assume that he won't break through.

The enemy doesn't break through.

The time in Tolstoy's novel is the truest time; it's truer than the time shown on a clock.

This time preserves the tension, and while waiting in Tarutino, Kutuzov above all is trying not to show the enemy his anticipated victory over them.

■

Time goes by.

Kutuzov escorts Napoleon almost festively. He doesn't need to take this hero as prisoner. He wants to let him escape from the Russian borders. Because Napoleon is the enemy of England, he is almost an ally; and Kutuzov doesn't hinder his flight from Russia.

Why does a novel live on? It resolves old questions of high theoretical art, questions which are remarkable because they don't contain any axiomatic truisms; there are no axioms in this equation:

2×2 does not equal 4, but something else.

Tolstoy saw that it's as if time doesn't exist—it's "stopped."

He liked to say that time changed the sheepskin only by adding two buttons on the back—it then became a frock coat.

He saw the present as illusory.

He was very hostile toward industrialization.

At the same time, maybe because of this, he saw the superfluity of the time very well, he saw its density, its movement; he knew the future.

Tolstoy wrote a letter to Nicholas II (which he didn't send).

He wrote to the Emperor that if he didn't make fundamental changes, he would suffer the same fate as his unfortunate grandfather, Alexander II.

■

And so.

The time in *Anna Karenina* is real. It is determined by the daily routine, the work of an apprentice. The time of a certain dress code, women's fashion, manner of greeting.

The ladies of Tolstoy don't bow anymore, they make a curtsey; that's how Kitty's friend, Madame Stahl's adoptive daughter, curtseys, at the German resort, where there is an emphatic unwillingness to adopt new customs.

But time is more tragic. It places the burden of war and guilt on everyone, because people live different lives but within the same borders.

Nikolai Tolstoy, his favorite brother, replaced Lev's father in his early youth. As if unintentionally, he advised Lev to go to the Caucasus.

And this is how it happened: Lev, an artillery officer, Nikolai and Sergei Tolstoy met after the Crimean War in Yasnaya Polyana. There were no sheets or blankets in the house. The three counts slept on the hay. But the price for land was rising and because of what we call "the agrarian riots," and the relations between the landlords and the peasants, the line between them was becoming more rigid. It's as if the road between them was getting wider.

They were like vast ice fields that crack in spring and separate. They will still collide during storms.

V. INNER MONOLOGUE

Continuity can be arranged from any place.

Chronological continuity.

Antique theater.

The Decameron.

Tolstoy.

Chekhov.

But there exists an inner continuity.

Folklore.

Antique construction.

Antique construction on already existing subjects (myths)—this is the inner continuity.

I'll repeat that Pushkin showed the meaning of change from antique tragedy to drama.

The "truth of passions and true reproduction of feelings" came to replace the numbing sensations of those gory spectacles.

The second circumstance of this change is the existence of a "multitude" of characters from Shakespeare's plays and Tolstoy's novels. It is, first of all, the shift in conflicts during their transformation.

In the novels of Tolstoy, the hero does what he is supposed to do, what the circumstances lead him to do.

The hero changes. Chernyshevsky noticed this in the early works of this ingenious writer.

In new circumstances, the hero, in his essence, becomes a new person.

When a certain composition is analyzed in the right way and the analysis is structured as an architect would do—an architect who has a ground floor, a foundation, on which his structure will rise, who has time to build his frames—then the work becomes multi-layered:

—this can be visualized, this is—as Vinogradov showed—an inner monologue of the main character.

There are vast fields, and perhaps they are separated from each other or we separate them from each other. We separate them and must somehow give them names; as the hieroglyph gives a name to an anonymous and mysterious life.

But in essence, the inner monologue was spoken to the public.

It's as if the person broke off the masquerade.

The inner monologue is preserved in theater as well.

Ostrovsky used this device, and so did Gogol.

But this whole concept of an "inner monologue" is not so simple.

The monologue in Rousseau's *Les Confessions* is not merely an "inner monologue."

It's written as a speech, it's a sermon; a sermon with examples from life—from his own experience.

The lyric poem as a whole can be defined as an inner monologue.

When I pick up *War and Peace*, it seems to me that at the bottom of the book there lies an examination of military science, as it were—its psychology, the analysis of whether it is possible to have a science about battles, or what willpower of a strategist means during war.

Interestingly, in a quote that I came across, which was actually pointed out to me, Napoleon played his role in history, in the battles, almost just as Kutuzov played his role (Las Cases wrote about this in his *Mémorial de Sainte-Hélène*, 1823). We can even say that this is very likely.

In other words, it's crucial to analyze a person's willpower, the willpower of your rival.

Then you must reorganize his power.

You must analyze your own potential.

The map of the battle.

You must think of the state of the people, the determination of your soldiers.

Then witness how this changes during the war.

I got sidetracked again. Let's return to the monologue.

And Lev Nikolaevich, who changed the paths of his work many times, was attracted to the idea that folklore has no particular face.

A person sings a song, remembers it, and as if unconsciously creates something new.

But any kind of examination, travel, love story or book never submits; they argue with us. A book is sometimes capable of surprising its own author.

It was Einstein who spoke about the author's surprise in regard to his own invention.

But here we are not talking only about the fact that a person thinks beyond the realm of words.

He thinks through reinvention.

My experience is relatively little but I can see how one's intention can be at odds with what one is actually writing.

Pushkin didn't know from the beginning how Tatyana would act.

He was never able to figure out what Onegin would do.

One thing was certain: Onegin's affairs would have to go wrong.

Like that Pushkin drawing. He is standing with Onegin on the Neva Embankment, with the Fortress of Peter and Paul in the background.

This is where all sorts of reversals can occur and change the course of the Empire.

Life, social reality "reinvents" Tolstoy's consciousness.

Let's return to the previous question.

There are several characters in a play or a novel, and each one of them is thinking for himself and not for the author.

Tolstoy notes that the person dying on the battlefield of Borodino probably wasn't thinking about history or Napoleon; he was probably thinking about himself and his family.

I am thinking about Tolstoy's characters.

After a short remark about the differences of families and their fates, Tolstoy as an author falls captive to Stiva Oblonsky.

He starts thinking through his proposed character.

Through his subjects, the correlation of those subjects with real people.

We all remember the dream of Oblonsky—the female decanters, the glass tables singing something very pleasant.

These things are in the dream of a character, whose way of thinking is best known above all to Tolstoy.

Oblonsky's dream is simultaneously his inner monologue, which is made to sound rather dramatic, and his "special way" of self-justification.

He is guilty, he has been unfaithful to his wife, but the female decanters are charming and have the charming distinction of not having souls, they are just someone's property.

All the characters in *Anna Karenina* have their own world, they all have their own inner monologues.

The most tragic of all monologues is Anna Karenina's.

Because she blames everyone and doesn't try to justify even herself.

The inner monologues of Aleksei Karenin are different.

He justifies himself as an institution would.

He writes formal letters and gives formal answers.

And only when Anna is near her death he takes off his mask, he starts talking and behaving differently.

He is a person who could have been good, but he is confined in his own bureaucratic chancellery.

The greatness of Tolstoy, which is difficult to describe in words, is that he is warming up this man with his own hands, with his own breath, this man who is hiding behind the walls of his own shell.

The author doesn't make an appearance throughout the entire novel.

This is true only if we don't count Levin, if we believe that Levin isn't Lev Nikolaevich at all, and try to understand why Tolstoy has chosen a character who has his own household, work and problems.

Anna Karenina is a different person.

Her thoughts surface through "inner monologues."

This is apparent especially in the final scenes, when Anna quarrels with her lover for whom she has changed her entire life.

She sees the world, but it appears to her estranged, as if disconnected from her past and the present moment.

She sees herself from the outside.

She sees how the passing servant girls look at her laces. How people show off in front of her, trying to pretend they are aristocrats, trying to speak French. All these things (even the signboards are repulsive) strike her with their sudden meaninglessness. The drunken men, the coachman who brings her the note from Vronsky, they are all reinvented through an inner monologue.

Tolstoy projects his views through different people. It's as though he's the one who is dying from fever. He pities and almost feels love for old Karenin, meanwhile Karenin thinks for himself, and so does Vronsky.

I'm trying to make a point.

Anna Karenina, the entire novel, is constructed on inner monologues, based, as it were, on a misunderstanding among the characters.

This perhaps comes as a surprise, but when I was rereading the book, I was stunned even more than when reading Dostoevsky. There, all the characters think alike, as if since childhood they have all been reading the same author—Dostoevsky.

9

THE PATH OF TOLSTOY

It's difficult to write about Tolstoy because his works build upon one another, the doubts of the writer are revealed in the evolution of not just one book.

He keeps searching. He has several ways of formulating the things that he sees.

The life of a young count in a village was still the life of an aristocrat, and he saw his own serfs.

He was quite accustomed to them—yet they were eternally different.

The writer had hoped that these relations would become somehow humanized.

He wrote *A Novel of a Russian Landowner*[84] for several years.

This was a man who had already created *Childhood* and *Boyhood*.

He was able to show the interrelation of people through the sensibility of a child who cannot make any real decisions.

And he offered no social decisions.

Tolstoy thought that serfdom was "a good evil." Only Tolstoy could have expressed himself in such a way—in his diary—about how he relates to his surroundings.

[84] An unfinished novel discussing the improvement of his serfs' condition.

At war, first in the Caucasus, then in Sevastopol, Tolstoy met a peasant who was a soldier—just like himself.

This happened when he was writing *The Sevastopol Sketches*.

And before that, he was writing a sketch called "How Russian Soldiers Die."

Then he was drawn to the idea of starting a school.

He wanted to bring up and educate his serfs, who respected him, and who seemed to be his equals when the article "Who Is to Learn to Write from Whom: The Peasant Children from Us, or We from the Peasant Children?" was being written.

This was at the same period when a great book, *The Cossacks*, was being composed and was never finished, because it simply couldn't be finished.

What was happening in Sevastopol?

Historians estimated that the Russian army lost more than 500 thousand men. Russia spent around 500 million rubles. Almost half of the reinforcements were killed before reaching their destination.

The English compared the Siege of Sevastopol to grinding something in a mortar.

And during this time Tolstoy was having some very difficult debates with himself. Difficult, yet simple.

Every single person in that war would rather not be there.

There are some papers preserved in the Tolstoy archive called "The Beginning of a Fantastic Story." Here one can read about an evening in Sevastopol with songbooks. The evening was a failure. The young officer who had come to Sevastopol of his own will, a man of good education, someone who is fluent in German and Italian, is disillusioned and goes for a ride.

The red-hot shells arch over his head. This is Sevastopol being ground in the mortar.

The town square is big; it's raining.

The ride is unpleasant because it's wet. And then suddenly the officer feels that it's becoming somewhat easier to ride, the rain stops pouring, and some dogs start to bark. He hears their "familiar voices." The officer rides into his own estate. He opens the door and finds himself eight years in the future.

His wife appears.

She is pregnant. Then his brother. He is grown up. His wife consults with him about whether she should stop breastfeeding the child. It is his child. And he doesn't know what to do, because he is a person from his own time, and also a person from a different time, a time of war; there had been neither a child nor a pregnant wife, nor any of the other things before he left.

What was Tolstoy experiencing? First of all, a great disappointment not just in the Russian military power, but also in the whole structure of the empire.

He saw robberies and marauding. The troops were fighting on territories that weren't carefully examined on the map. There were too many mistakes.

Tolstoy returned to Russia in a state of disillusionment. There had once been a great country which he remembered from childhood stories told by his father, fathers' friends and the peasants—Russia had crushed Napoleon. The army from all over Europe was sent away reduced to a shameful number of survivors; this wasn't the case in the Sevastopol campaign.

The second disillusionment came with the consequences of the war. He thought that things would change, that people would wake up, come to their senses; he imagined this "change" would be the return of the good old days, but this didn't happened.

Tolstoy sets out to write "Two Hussars." It's a story about Kokorev, a merchant in the vodka trade.[85] He was the most influential person among the Russian traders. Kokorev said about the glories of Russia:

[85] Vasili Kokorev (1817–89), one of the richest industrialists of his times, who also tried his hand in writing, best known for *The Economic Failures*. After the war, Kokorev set up soup kitchens for the Sevastopol heroes, and during the Russian-Turkish war he contributed large amounts of money.

And the terrible committees galloped from St. Petersburg to the South to capture, expose and hang the commissariat criminals; meanwhile, in every city, the war heroes were treated to honorable speeches and dinners. These men who'd lost an arm or a leg were given a trynka[86] on the old country roads.

Old Russia had become defamed in the eyes of Tolstoy, and it wasn't just a coincidence that he appeared in a magazine that published Belinsky and Chernyshevsky. At that time Tolstoy wrote about Chernyshevsky that he was "clever and hot-tempered."

But the idea of moral revenge, the rehabilitation of Russia, was for Tolstoy connected with 1812. And that's when he conceived *War and Peace*. Or better yet, he conceived a book, as he always did, an epic depicting a victory over a crisis. That's how he conceived *Childhood*, *Boyhood* and *Youth*. That's how he conceived his novel about the landowner. And that's how he conceived the novel about 1805 and 1812. He wanted to show the passage of Russia, and the passage of the Russian man, on his own, from failure to success.

In his first draft, Tolstoy began *War and Peace* with the return of the future hero, Pierre, an old Decembrist, an aristocrat who has lived through exile, and his wife Natasha, "a Decembrist's wife."[87] Nekrasov had already explored this theme and made it quite popular.

---

[86] A trynka was equivalent to three kopecks.

[87] In a show of loyalty to their husbands, nearly all the wives of Decembrists followed the men into exile. Among them numbered eight prominent members of the aristocracy, the most famous of these were Yekaterina Trubetskaya and Maria Volkonskaya. In order to strike the Decembrists totally out of their lives, the Church and State passed a law whereby the Decembrists' wives were considered widows and allowed to remarry within their husbands' lifetime without an official divorce. However, Trubetskaya along with the others turned down this offer. When they departed for Siberia, they left behind their privileges as nobles and were reduced to the status of exiles, with restricted rights of travel, correspondence and property ownership. They were not allowed to take their children with them, or return to the European part of Russia even after their husbands' death.

War and Peace was started during the sobering experience of Sevastopol, after the period of Russian *arakcheevshina*,[88] after the defeats suffered by Pierre Bezukhov, Davydov and the others whom he knew. Then there was also Arakcheev, and the good gentleman Nikolai Rostov who didn't think too much and was conscientious in his own right.

So, let's say that Tolstoy started his description of the Russian victory over Napoleon with a story of what happened after the victory.

This was a sad beginning.

Art is very complex. It's always open to multiple interpretations, even while retaining its uniqueness.

During a war, it's very important to have *rocades*, communication roads running parallel to the front, before the enemy lines. These are still used in contemporary wars. And so the writer approaches the real frontline, the place of action, by building a *rocade*.

The draft of *War and Peace* has over 5,000 pages and the handwriting is very small. But apart from that, Tolstoy was constantly rewriting—he would go so far as to destroy parts that had already been set in type and start all over again, from the very beginning. When we talk about "a field of influence" regarding a work, we mean the trails of a search—it's not just the refinement of style, not the reworking of characters, it's an examination of the actual times, the purpose of which is to see the world as if anew.

The discoveries made by great writers are in some sense unexpected, and they often negate themselves.

Lev Nikolaevich wanted to create a hero in the character of Andrei Bolkonsky, who would be a smart person, an aristocrat who in his own way and rather accurately would understand and reinterpret the war. But during

[88] General Aleksei Arakcheev (1769–1834) occupied the unofficial position of prime minister during the second part of Alexander's reign. The "military colonies," which Arakcheev oversaw at the behest of the Emperor, were intended to lessen the costs of maintaining a standing army by allowing soldiers to farm, have a family, and practice drills at the same time. The rules for the regimented lifestyle were partially based on the order at Arakcheev's own estate, where women were required to bear children annually. The colonies bred constant revolts and were eventually abolished.

the course of his work, it turned out that the true heroes were the soldiers, the rank-and-file officers like Tushin, or old Timokhin, who took part in the assault of Izmail, who it seems was never able to fit in with society, but whose war experience was crucial and who plays a key role in the success of the bloody battle at Shengraben.

The heroes are understood and materialize during the work, in the process of writing.

Tolstoy is trying to unravel the image of Kutuzov, step by step. He is trying to understand the nature of war, the nature of history. He is like a person, a great person, who is entering the structure of a new building, discovering new lands, he doesn't know what they are, he doesn't even know the significance of his own experiment.

Tolstoy works on his novel for a long time. He writes, stops, then abandons it. Abandons it when he has already found what is most important, when he has already seen his own times through new eyes.

He needs to get deluded in order to rediscover the novel and restructure it.

It turns out that the book isn't about war or peace.

It's about the people—Russian consciousness—and why it's impossible to conquer something that never resigned in its spirit, that never recognized its own defeat. People who refused money or silver to bring hay for the conquerors' horses by simply neglecting the conqueror. And that was their victory.

War and Peace was written over a very long time.

"A very long time" means ten years.

Not too long after that Tolstoy finished "A Prisoner in the Caucasus."

In this simply crafted work he shows something other than a romantic affair between an officer and a girl from the mountains, as Pushkin had it.

Zhilin and the girl are friends and equals.

She helps him escape from the pit.

She is interested in his art. Primitive dolls made of clay.

Tolstoy thought that this story was flawless.

War and Peace was created by a person who knew the army well, who had seen defeats and understood the soldiers.

The novel is like an appeal of the verdict that Tolstoy imposed on the Russian society—the dereliction of duty, the marauding of the soldiers, the bad tactics and lack of knowledge of the battlefield terrain.

Everything is described accurately, but Dickens also described the Sevastopol war, as a journalist. He wrote with respect to the Bear, that's what he called Russia, and England was the Bull.

The Bear didn't let the Bull pass beyond the shore.

War and Peace begins with a family story and, in its course, encompasses the grandiose battles of that period.

It's like a study of the causes of defeat and an attempt to understand how to attain victory.

The range of the work is very wide, even including research. It contains Andrei Bolkonsky, a positive protagonist who nevertheless could not have been the main hero in a description of war.

Kutuzov is understood only toward the end of the book.

It's the people's opinion that raises Kutuzov to his pedestal.

He thought in unison with the army.

He didn't believe in theories of war from the book, he fought against all the rules, which is why he didn't lose.

The great epic is built on the analysis of a mass movement.

The baker leaving Moscow, and the princess riding off to the Volga because she doesn't want to serve Bonaparte—they have both made the same decision.

The book was successful with all its characters except for Andrei Bolkonsky, who, it seems, isn't necessary to the war: he could have been the hero of another novel, but then the novel would have been flawed.

Bolkonsky, who is trying to resolve his personal issues, the question of his love for Natasha Rostova, her betrayal, all of this is done very seriously; the question of a woman's faithfulness is already raised and the man's wound is so deadly that even though Andrei Bolkonsky, the hero of the epic, forgives his bride, he accidentally dies from an old shell on the battlefield.

But Natasha Rostova was simultaneously analyzed and conceived as a woman returning with her older husband, the exiled Decembrist.

She nurses her husband. For him, she is almost even his senior.

This is the same Natasha who in a previous draft was said to love the bed. This is the same girl who asked her mother if she could marry two men. She was attracted to both Andrei Bolkonsky and Anatole Kuragin.

This question was taken up by another woman, another Anna with a surname Karenina, as Aseev called her in his poems.

Anna didn't solve the question.

In the meantime, the wives of the Decembrists in the minds of the people had become equal to their husbands, but times had changed.

Everything changed with time and nothing made sense anymore.

The woman, who could have been the granddaughter of Natasha Rostova, experienced a very difficult love affair.

She learned about the tortures of conscience.

The new morals didn't exist yet.

In the novel, of course, Anna Karenina is right.

■

It's important that after the epic, where the heroes change, where the fate of Europe, and perhaps the whole world, is at stake, Tolstoy, after an attempt to write a novel about Peter I or Paul, or about something grandiose like the victory of the individual—

—turned to the family novel.

The reason I'm using the word "family" is because all the characters in the novel are presented within the circle of their personal interests.

Not only do they talk through inner monologues, but they see the world through their own window.

I can't include my analysis of *War and Peace* in this book because it would be too long and I am too old.

Children with big heads are born with great difficulty.

When everything was turned upside down and nothing would make sense anymore, the personal story evolved and became the most important thing, but it was still left unresolved.

And for a long time Tolstoy wanted to solve this question together with the question of religion.

Perhaps even start a new religion.

Maybe—a new kind of asceticism.

Turn the peasant psychology into the psychology of mankind.

The great work, which was both a family and a social novel, turned out successfully.

The purpose of Anna Karenina's life was less successful than the life of Natasha Rostova.

Except that Natasha Rostova saw the labor camps, which, as we'll see later, was experienced in a more severe form by another woman—Katyusha Maslova.

The woman who was exalted among the crowds.

■

The world of Anna Karenina's first life is very narrow. The young woman treats the affairs of her husband, Aleksei Karenin, a high-ranking minister, with near veneration, or as Tolstoy says, by covering her irony.

This is a man who is known even abroad.

The nihilists, the theorists of modern times, people who could have in their own way understood if not Andrei Bolkonsky, then at least Pierre Bezukhov, they are constantly present in *Anna Karenina*.

But they seem to be behind the stage.

They are shaking the so-called decorative walls.

They are mentioned in all the drafts.

Bazarov, the nihilist, in a short description rendered very realistically, became, spiritually, the model for great people; someone like Pirogov understood him very well.[89] This was a man who knew how to live and die.

The brother of Konstantin Levin, Nikolai, is also a nihilist.

He is trying to set up a peasants' cooperative.

He is stronger than Konstantin in one thing, but he can't really argue with his brother because he really doesn't have much room in the novel.

When Konstantin tells his brother Nikolai about his plan to run the household—getting the workers interested in profit—his nihilist brother says: you are repeating old ideas (that's communism), but you have taken out the most important factor (the question of property).

Tolstoy admires Kitty, she knows how not to insult the former prostitute who is now practically Nikolai's wife.

Tolstoy sees that Kitty isn't afraid of death because she is religious.

But the nihilist gentleman who ruined his life, who argued with his brothers about the inheritance, he also knows how to die.

When the priest says: "He is gone," the man on his deathbed answers: "Not quite . . . Soon."

He knows how to die just as well as the Russian soldier who was dying in front of Tolstoy's eyes.

That's how Pavlov was dying.

■

When Lenin spoke about the contradictions of Tolstoy, he connected them to the most important thing—the history of the country.

The country was changing very quickly and with paradoxical contradictions. It was changing in such a way that its various parts, the layers of its life, had found themselves in direct opposition.

Art moves along the *rocades*, along the frontlines of life.

---

[89] Nikolai Pirogov (1810–81), Russian surgeon, author of many scientific treatises, who worked as field surgeon during the Crimean War in Sevastopol.

10

THE WRITING OF
ANNA KARENINA

"Thoughts are getting mixed up"—what does this clichéd expression mean?

It means that we don't know the order of our thoughts.

We don't know the points of intersection where we can or cannot trust our own thoughts.

Tracing the path of thought of the person who wrote *Anna Karenina* is almost inconceivable. We can only see the struggle to make decisions—the reexamination of his decisions.

Which is why choosing the method of interpretation is, I'd say, quite simple. We are going to provide excerpts from letters written during the composition of *Anna Karenina*.

That's why we propose the next few pages that, like a sieve, separate the real facts from unclear statements.

Tolstoy; no, I'll paraphrase this—Tolstoy's light britzka; no that's not good enough, Tolstoy, it seems, wrote almost with the lightness of Mozart. The magical carriage rolled in its lightness and ease.

It rolled effortlessly, it plunged into the great and impassable dough of life. This man almost at once got to kneading and arranging, he got straight to work; he started plotting and cleaning the world with his plot, a world that seems to be getting mixed up all the time.

The story of writing *Anna Karenina* is long, complex and, yet, simple.

The term itself, "energy of delusion," was created in the process of this story, a story that flows alongside the story of the novel's publication.

The first person who took note of Tolstoy's words about delusion was Boris Mikhailovich Eichenbaum.

Quoting is necessary. I have said and will say again that we are walking holding on to the quotes, as we would hold on to a wall.

And, also, there is nothing truer than a quote, and the harder the work is, the harder is the task of quoting; and Tolstoy, whose work, whose soul, is continuously alive and continuously grows, is one of the most difficult examples.

Anna Akhmatova, as she was going over Pushkin's epigraphs, said they were inexact quotes, they were redirected by the flow of great thought.

Obviously, so were Mayakovsky's quotes.

Because they were "redirected."

When people would point this out to him, he would reply: "I finished the line in my mind."

Besides, the idea of quoting, the transporting of a thought into a new context, changes the original meaning of the phrase.

The Genesis is still preserved and checked by those who quote from it, but the idea has evolved, or to be more precise, the feeling is continuously alive, it is being reconstructed.

One may encounter various quotes in the history of religion, they ordinarily confirm Genesis, but the inevitability of evolution makes them the basis for debate and seemingly a deliberate lie.

And Lev Nikolaevich, after reading the sacred scriptures and seeking justification for the mysteries, says to the commentator, i.e., the quoter: "Go to your father—the Devil."

And so, after these words, let's reread the story of *Anna Karenina*'s composition through the letters of Tolstoy.

The windings of his soul, the turning points of his work, the energy of his undertaking, his imagination—everything can be traced through these letters.

It's exactly like traces on the sand; it's not a rhythm, but only the traces of a rhythm.

The novel *Anna Karenina* was begun in 1873 and finished in 1877.
—from *A Bibliography of Works by Lev Tolstoy*

MARCH 25, 1873
An unsent letter to N. N. Strakhov

I'm going to tell you about myself, but please, keep it a secret, because it may be that nothing will come of what I'm going to tell you ... After work, I happened to pick up ... a book by Pushkin[90] and as always (for the seventh time, I think), reread it all, unable to tear myself away from it, as though reading it for the first time. And what's more, it seems as if it resolved all my doubts ... And there is a line, "The guests were getting ready to leave for the country house." Involuntarily and quite unintentionally, without knowing why and how, I began thinking up people and events, went on doing so, then, of course, changed them, and suddenly everything tied in so beautifully and unexpectedly, that the result was a novel, which is almost finished in its draft form. A very lively, passionate and complete novel with which I am pleased; it will be ready, if God grants me good health, in two weeks, and it has nothing in common with the piece I have been struggling to write in the past year. If I finish it, I'll publish it as a separate book, but I'd like you to read it first. Would you take on the proofreading, with the idea of publishing it in St. Petersburg? ...

Please do not scold me for such an incoherent letter—I have been working happily all morning. I'm excited that it's finished, and now, in the evening, I have a hangover.

90 Footnote by V. Shklovsky—*The Tales of Belkin*.

MARCH 30, 1873

to P. D. Golokhvastov

You won't believe it, but I recently read with a joy, such as I have not experienced for a long time, *The Tales of Belkin* for the seventh time in my life. No writer should ever give up studying this treasure. The new reading had a profound effect on me.

APRIL 6 OR 7, 1873

to N. N. Strakhov

. . . I answered you straight away, but didn't send off the letter and two weeks have passed in the meantime. I didn't send the letter because I was writing something about myself that was premature, and it turned out to be exactly so. I will send you the letter or show it to you someday.

MAY 11, 1873

to N. N. Strakhov[91]

. . . I am writing a novel that has nothing to do with Peter I. I've been working on it for over a month and have finished a rough draft. The novel —and it *is* a novel—the first in my life—has truly got a hold on me; I'm completely carried away by it, although, I've been giving much thought to philosophical problems this spring. In the letter, which I didn't send you, I wrote about this novel and how it came to me involuntarily and thanks to the divine Pushkin, whose work I picked up purely by chance and reread in full with fresh delight.

MAY 17, 1873

A letter from N. N. Strakhov in response to
a letter from L. N. Tolstoy that was not preserved

For some reason I kept thinking that you were writing, but to hear such good news that you already have drafted a whole novel—*that* I didn't expect.

[91] Footnote by V. Shklovsky—The letters from Strakhov are quoted from *A Correspondence between L. N. Tolstoy and N. N. Strakhov, 1870–1894* (1914).

MAY 31, 1873

Again to N. N. Strakhov

My novel is resting, too, and I'm already losing hope that I will finish it by this fall.

AUGUST 24, 1873

To N. N. Strakhov

... And I must confess, shamefully, that I am now correcting and trimming the novel about which I told you in my letter, giving it a more frivolous and less formal style. I wanted to be mischievous and now I can't even finish it and I'm afraid that it won't turn out well, i.e., you won't like it.

... I am as healthy as an ox, and like a locked-up mill, I've collected water ...

From N. N. Strakhov

... The contradiction which I found in your letters consists in the fact that at first you wrote that you gave your soul to this novel, and then—that it's rather frivolous ...

SEPTEMBER 23, 1873

To A. A. Fet

... I am beginning to write, that is, rather I'm finishing a novel that I had already begun.

SEPTEMBER 23 OR 24, 1873

To N. N. Strakhov

I have moved far ahead with my work, but I'll hardly finish it before winter—maybe December or somewhere around that time. Like the painter needs light for his final touch-ups, I, too, need to have an inner light, which usually begins to fade in the fall.

NOVEMBER 17, 1873

To N. N. Strakhov

... The work before this was coming along pretty well. I can say that seven sheets are ready to go to print,[92] and the rest is being kneaded into dough, so the end is only a matter of time. I have already begun to think about publication, and all my hopes are on you.

FEBRUARY 11, 1874

A letter from N. N. Strakhov in response to
a letter from L. N. Tolstoy that was not preserved

... You write that everything is ready; save the manuscript, for God's sake, and take it to the press.

FEBRUARY 13, 1874

To N. N. Strakhov

You are right to assume that I'm very busy and have been working a lot. I'm glad that I didn't start publishing anything, as I wrote in one of the previous letters. I don't know how else to draw a circle but to close it first and then begin correcting the original flaws. And now I have just come to the closure, and the corrections are endless ... It never happened to me in the past that I wrote so much without showing it to someone or even telling about it ...

But so much has already been written and reworked, and the circle has almost been closed and I'm so weary of the changes that I've decided to go to Moscow around the 20th and hand it to Katkov.[93]

---

[92] A printer's sheet was equivalent to 40,000 print characters or 700 lines in verse.

[93] Mikhail Katkov (1818–87), the editor of the *Russian Herald,* who serialized *Anna Karenina* from 1874 through 1877, receiving new and reworked installments from Tolstoy throughout this time.

MARCH 6, 1874

To N. N. Strakhov

I returned from Moscow yesterday and handed in the first part, around seven printer's sheets of the manuscript, for publication. The whole novel should be forty sheets. I hope to finish everything by May.

I read several chapters to Tyutchev's daughter and Y. Samarin . . . and it seemed this didn't make much of an impression: but not only did this not diminish my passion, I have begun refining and perfecting with even more vigor.

MARCH 6, 1874

To A. A. Tolstaya

. . . I am writing and have begun to print a novel that I like, but it will hardly please others, because it's much too simple.

MAY 10, 1874

To N. N. Strakhov

My novel lies idly. Katkov is publishing it slowly—one printer's sheet per month; still, I'm glad. It would be very interesting to show you a segment from the novel and hear your opinion. To be honest with you, I don't like it anymore.

MAY 25–BEGINNING OF JUNE, 1874

To N. N. Strakhov

I am sending you the letter from Bunyakovsky. I am also sending a letter to the printer—to stop the publication . . . You have no idea with what joy I await your arrival, and absolutely not because I want to show it to you.

JUNE 20, 1874

From N. N. Strakhov

I read with horror that you have stopped the publication—you are torturing us with anticipation.

JUNE 23, 1874

To A. A. Tolstaya

I find myself in my summer frame of mind—i.e., not occupied with poetry and have stopped printing my novel. I dislike it so much that I'm about to drop it . . .

JUNE 27, 1874

To N. N. Strakhov

But all the parts that have been printed and set to type were so repulsive to me that I made a final decision to destroy the printed sheets and rewrite the entire beginning, all that pertains to Levin and Vronsky. They will be the same, but even better. I hope to start working in the fall and finish soon.

JULY 29, 1874

To P. D. Golokhvastov

Strakhov was here a few days ago; he tried to revive my interest in the novel, but I just dropped it. It's terribly distasteful and revolting.

AUGUST 15, 1874

To P. D. Golokhvastov

My corrections, as hateful as they are to me, are now in your hands.

AUGUST 30, 1874

To N. N. Strakhov

The novel isn't moving along, but thanks to you I have resolved to finish it, and hope to do so by the end of this year.

NOVEMBER 3 OR 4, 1874

To N. N. Strakhov

I am going to Moscow tomorrow . . . And besides I want to offer my novel to the *Russian Herald* at the rate of 500 rubles per sheet, and I want ten thousand in advance, which I need for purchasing some land. I think that by tying myself thus, I will be obligated to finish the book.

NOVEMBER 8, 1874

To N. A. Nekrasov

My need for ten thousand rubles has forced me to retreat from my intention of publishing the novel as a separate book. I considered myself bound by a casual promise to the *Russian Herald* . . .

They began negotiating and I was very glad that by doing so they freed me of my promise. I am now making the same offer to you . . . realizing that the terms offered by me are difficult for a magazine, and I won't be surprised if you refuse to accept them.

NOVEMBER 23–25, 1874

To P. M. Leontev

I had offered you my conditions . . . 20 sheets at 500 rubles per sheet for the last part of the novel and wanted that in advance. But I have already borrowed that amount . . . I am busy now . . . with my work at the school.

DECEMBER 10, 1874

S. A. Tolstaya to T. A. Kuzminskaya[94]

The novel is not coming along, and we get all sorts of letters from publishing houses: offering 10,000 in advance and 500 rubles per sheet. Levochka won't even talk about it, and acts as if he has nothing to do with it.

MARCH 16, 1875

To N. M. Nagornov

I get wires from Katkov every day—they are pressing me to finish up with Karenina, I'm sick of her . . .

MARCH 1 . . . 20, 1875

To M. N. Katkov

Dear Mikhail Nikiforovich, I will never give promises ahead of time in regard to my writing. The chapters seemed ready, but as soon as I was go-

---

[94] Footnote by V. Shklovsky—This is an excerpt from the correspondence of Sofia Tolstaya to her sister.

ing to send them, I realized I had to correct a few things, and everything got delayed.

AUGUST 25, 1875

To N. N. Strakhov

I haven't touched a pen in two months and I'm very pleased with my summer.[95] I am now going back to the boring and tasteless *Anna Karenina*, with the sole desire to finish and free up some time —I really need it.

AUGUST 25, 1875

To A. A. Fet

I haven't stained my hands with ink or my heart with any thoughts in the past two months and now I must return to the boring and tasteless *Anna Karenina* with just one goal—to finish it and free up some time for other tasks . . .

SEPTEMBER 6 . . . 7, 1875

To N. N. Strakhov

. . . I try to work on my novel in the mornings, but *nothing works*—and so I go hunting.

NOVEMBER 8, 9, 1875

To N. N. Strakhov

All this time—for two weeks—I have been nursing my sick wife who gave birth to a stillborn and was near death herself. But—a strange thing —I have never been able to focus as much on the issues that occupy my mind as during this time. I have read and reread Wundt[96] carefully and

---

[95] Footnote by V. Shklovsky—Tolstoy spent his summer in the backwoods of Samara.

[96] Wilhelm Wundt (1832–1920), a German psychologist and Marxist at the University of Leipzig, proclaimed that man's soul—if indeed he had one—was irrelevant, as man could only be understood in terms of physically observable phenomena. A search for the spiritual nature of man, he reasoned, was a waste of time as there was no psyche. Thus psychology was the study of the spirit in order to deny the spirit.

for the first time understand the power of the materialistic outlook, and I even turned into a materialist for two days, but for the first and last time in my life . . .

My God, if only someone could finish *Anna Karenina* for me! It's unbearable.

NOVEMBER 8 . . . 9, 1875
To A. A. Fet

I received your letter at a terribly difficult time, my wife was near death . . . she gave birth prematurely to a dead child. Fear, horror, death, cheerfulness of the children, food, commotion, doctors, falsity, death, horror . . .

NOVEMBER 30, 1875
To N. N. Strakhov

. . . I am thinking of the path that I've trodden and looking at the present, trying to fathom from this trodden path and observations of my surroundings the mystery of what the life I've led means, and the even greater mystery of what awaits me there, in that place where I'm involuntarily headed. This state I would call old age . . .

JANUARY 1 . . . 2, 1876
To N. N. Strakhov

I'm not writing anything about *Anna Karenina* in the letter, and won't from now on. If it comes together, be sure that you'll read it.

JANUARY 17, 1876
To A. M. and T. A. Kuzminsky

Farewell, good-bye. Sonya will describe everything, and I have written it all in *Anna Karenina*, and nothing is left.

JANUARY 24 . . . 25, 1876
To N. N. Strakhov

Anna Karenina is making progress.

FEBRUARY 14 ... 15, 1876

To N. N. Strakhov

I am very busy with *Anna Karenina*. The first book is dry, and, anyway, it's no good, but right now I'm sending the corrections of the second book, and this, I know for sure, is good.

FEBRUARY 29 ... MARCH 1, 1876

To A. A. Fet

And I must finish the novel that has become a nuisance to me.

MARCH 8 ... 12, 1876

To A. A. Tolstaya[97]

I am fed up with my Anna, sick and tired; I am dealing with her as with a pupil who has turned out to be unmanageable; but don't say bad things about her, or if you must, at least do so *ménagement*; after all, she has been adopted.

MARCH 12 ... 15, 1876

To A. A. Fet

I still dream of finishing the novel before summer, but I'm beginning to have my doubts.

APRIL 8, 9, 1876

To N. N. Strakhov

... Everything is ... vile, and all must be reworked and rewritten: everything that has been printed needs to be crossed out, dropped and disavowed, and I have to say: I'm guilty, I won't make promises ahead of time, and I'll try to write something new ... This is the state that I'm coming to and it is very pleasant.

[97] This letter to Aleksandra Tolstaya was mistakenly put in an envelope addressed to S. S. Urusov, and Aleksandra received Urusov's letter, which has not been preserved.

APRIL 23 AND 26, 1876

To N. N. Strakhov

In everything, almost everything that I wrote, I was driven by the need to collect my thoughts that were all linked together, to express myself, but each thought, especially those expressed through words, loses its meaning and is terribly degraded when taken away from its linkage. The linkage in itself doesn't consist of thoughts (I don't think), but something else, and to express the origin of that linkage directly through words is completely impossible; it is only possible through an intermediary—through words that describe the forms, actions, situations.

JULY 31, 1876

To N. N. Strakhov

Instead of reading *Anna Karenina*, you should finish writing it for me and save me from this sword of Damocles.

DECEMBER 9, 1876

S. A. Tolstaya to T. A. Kuzminskaya

We are finally writing *Anna Karenina* in earnest, i.e., without any intermissions. Levochka is animated and very focused, he is adding a new chapter each day . . .

JANUARY 11, 12, 1877

To N. N. Strakhov

If nothing gets in the way, I hope to finish in one sitting and free up some time for new work.

SECOND HALF OF JANUARY, 1877

S. A. Tolstaya to T. A. Kuzminskaya

. . . Levochka has stumbled across something and says: "Don't grumble at me that I'm not writing, I have a heavy head," and goes off to shoot rabbits.

MARCH 22, 23, 1877

To A. A. Fet

March and the beginning of April are the most productive months for me, and I just can't free myself from this delusional state. What I'm writing is very important, although I know that in a month I'll be ashamed to even remember this.

DECEMBER 10, 1877

To V. A. Islavin

I am offering him [Bistry] the following: I buy the land without installments, per 10 rubles, i.e., 40,000 on the deed (or in two payments, I can make this concession), but with one condition, a very important one, that I don't have to buy the buildings that are already on that land.

JANUARY 27, 1878

To S. A. Rachinsky[98]

Your judgment about *Anna Karenina* seems wrong to me.[99]

On the contrary, I am proud of its architecture—the arches are drawn so that one can't even notice where the castle is. And I've worked on that very hard. The structure is unified not through the plot or the relations of the characters, but through an inner unity.

■

The term "energy of delusion" appeared only in April of 1878.

[98] Sergei Rachinsky (1833–1902), a university professor and literary critic from Moscow.
[99] Footnote by V. Shklovsky—Rachinsky criticized that the book was lacking in architecture.

11

ANNA KARENINA

One is an artist because he sees things not as he wants to see them, but as they really are.
        LEV TOLSTOY, from his Introduction to the works of Guy de Maupassant

Among the works of Tolstoy, *Anna Karenina* is one of the best known. It's considered his most successful work and his most widely read book. I heard that after reading *Anna Karenina*, the wife of Count N. A. Tolstoy, who was a powerful aristocrat in the Samara province, left her husband, breaking up the family, abandoning the children, and went to live with A. A. Bostromoy, a small landowner, the step-father of Aleksei Tolstoy.

Anna Karenina is an imposing book. In *Tolstoy in the Seventies*,[100] Boris Eichenbaum, a prolific Tolstoy scholar, explained why the novel had to be published. His strong arguments were perhaps my own fault (because I consider this a fault).

Old literature inhabits new literature as if without permission. It exists

[100] Eichenbaum wrote profusely on Tolstoy and his art, his most in depth study being the project *Lev Tolstoy*. The first volume (1928) of this massive work is devoted mainly to the 1850s, the second volume (1931) covers the 1960s. *Tolstoy in the Seventies* was completed in the late 1930s and was scheduled for publication when the type was destroyed during the bombardment of Leningrad. The partially completed manuscript and materials for a fourth volume, on the 1880s, were lost in 1942 when the ailing Eichenbaum was being evacuated from Leningrad. *Tolstoy in the Seventies* did not appear until 1960, when the climate had become more favorable for those who had been branded as Formalists some three decades ago.

like a magnetic field that has undergone changes after a catastrophe above ground.

This terrestrial catastrophe is a new phenomenon on the earth.

The arrows showing the course of human acts keep changing their directions.

The words of a particular language can be found in a dictionary, but good writers write in different languages, although they probably think in words of one and the same language. Old literature makes its entrance into new literature in various ways, but it can only stay there altered.

On the Polynesian Islands they didn't use bows and arrows. There was no need to hunt on those islands. People there were more interested in the sea. But the bow was still used in children's games. That's how travelers found out about the bow. It happened as if by accident.

The tragedy of *Anna Karenina*, the existence and roots of such a tragedy, worried Lev Nikolaevich for a long time. I think that he must have heard about that even back then, when they used to call him Lyova.

This game has always been around; the elders play with the young as if they were dolls. And Lyova was once put to bed as if he were a child, a small boy. And he fell asleep because he *was* little. But the intention with which the game was played was wrong because that's not how it was supposed to be played.

I think that little Lyova already back then probably felt—even if he didn't think it—that something was "not right."

■

The French novel began to develop in Tolstoy's times; it came from the country of the classical romance novel.

French novels were popular, but very few people could read French, which is why the books usually appeared in translation; and apparently, they say, Lev Nikolaevich dreamt in French.

Lev Nikolaevich, who was like a magnetic storm for his contemporary Strakhov, wrote a philosophical sketch that was published in the Jubilee edition of his complete works. It was titled "About Marriage and the Woman's Calling."

Tolstoy wrote in response to Turgenev:

> The unsolvable complexity of the cryptic question about marriage, which according to Mr. Turgenev was developed by Mr. Auerbach and other European and Russian intellectuals, is founded on the same difficulty of the question of human appetite, where one wants to eat two or ten meals at once ... He who wants to marry two or three women, won't have a family ... The children ... need the influence of both the mother and the father, who live in the unity of family harmony.

I've seen children ask: "What was there before me?" It seems the question carries a hint of suspicion: maybe when I didn't exist, you didn't exist, either?

You probably hear the dissonance here.

Tolstoy thought that family and family influence have always been one and the same thing. There were children and a family, but the families were different, and the hands of the clock were pointing in different directions. I think it was in ancient Sparta, a country where women were very independent because their warrior-men would leave home; anyway, it was here that the newborn child was presented to the father and would become a member of the family only through his approval. Apparently, otherwise, the child would get cast off.

Stories similar to Oedipus' birth are very old, and this was even before the times of Sparta. Back then it was possible to reject a child.

Or, the child belonged to the clan rather than his parents.

Polygamy instigated a different kind of consciousness.

In Central Asia I've seen a happy family with many children; there were several wives; the oldest wife didn't have any children; she was an honorable wife and was exempt from giving birth. One of the younger women gave birth to a son. The first wife took the child and brought him up, and somehow it turned out that the real mother of the boy saw this as an honor. She would visit her child joyfully and with respect.

The relationships between children and parents in the Bible differ, and the cold relationship between the Arabs and the Jews, despite the fact that they are so close in blood, was expressed consciously or subconsciously through the fact that they all had the same father, but different mothers. The oldest child along with his mother was cast out or rejected from his father's tent.

The angel, however, consoled the mother by prophesizing that her son's offspring would be plentiful and strong.

There were many kinds of women during the times of Tolstoy, just as today; there were nursemaids, family helpers and there were many prostitutes, and Tolstoy believed that the eighty thousand prostitutes in London were legitimate, otherwise the family could not exist.

He wrote to Strakhov (on March 19, 1870), what would happen to the families, was it possible to keep the wives and daughters pure, what would happen to the morals that people liked to guard so much—and then Tolstoy referred to Michelet: "The woman's calling—the bearing, upbringing and suckling of children—is after all the most important one. Michelet puts it excellently that there is only womankind, and that man is *le mâle de la femme* (the woman's male type)."

This is from a letter included in Volume 61.

The letter is appearing for the first time. Tolstoy wrote many resolute letters, but he never sent them. And even though he was a powerful man and writer, he wrote curt letters to many people but never mailed them.

We are relatively insignificant, compared to Tolstoy, and even if we tried to collect a large archive of our letters and lectures, it would inevitably turn into mutterings.

Tolstoy read and admired Schopenhauer, and Eichenbaum thought that Tolstoy's words quoted from his letter to Strakhov were written under the influence of Schopenhauer. Matrimonial fidelity has always been an artificial trait in men, natural in women.

Hence, adultery in women, both as an objective and subjective idea, is far more unpardonable than adultery in men.

Tolstoy in his *Resurrection* period is as though apologizing to himself in that letter.

Nekhlyudov was supposed to be Katyusha Maslova's only husband. But at the same time Tolstoy was very fond of "The Darling," as I mentioned before, considering that even the neighbors didn't blame the woman who kept changing her husbands, which she did for rather natural reasons— their deaths.

Schopenhauer claimed that the view supporting man's commitment to fidelity was an unnatural one.

In that same letter, Tolstoy said that a person's duty was family procreation, and the inevitability of the appearance of the so-called "magdalenes" was not connected to any of the moral values in monogamy, but to the complications of life.

Lev Nikolaevich was a very capable man, and not just in literature; he could do things that we could never do.

All the students at the gymnasium were supposed to know Greek, which according to Tolstoy was as absurd as demanding that all students learn ballet, but Lev Nikolaevich learned Greek and then read *The Iliad*.

When Lev Nikolaevich decided to translate the Bible, he began studying Hebrew.

As a young man, when Tolstoy was in the northern Caucasus, he would talk to women in the gypsy language by mistake.

It's simple. To him, that was the language of love. He saw the woman and switched to her language.

So we can't really judge Lev Tolstoy because he could do things that we could have never done; he would constantly renounce and at the same time create what we call cultural history. Perhaps I'm not being clear. He was history itself. He lived in different countries and in different languages at the same time.

His view of matrimony was negative; he mourned his daughter's marriage. He used to say that one should cry at weddings. A person was free, and then suddenly they would hang two hundred pounds on his back.

■

The great philosopher Heraclitus, who was known as the Obscure, once said that there must be other existences in order to have a whole. This idea can also be found in Lenin's *Philosophical Notes.*

Heraclitus cites an example, which I've used as a title for one of my books.[101]

The bow is made of a stick and a string. And they make a whole.

That's how the lyre or the wind is, and everything else that we call life.

Again, I have accidentally wandered off from the quote.

Let's turn to a subject that seems to have nothing in common with what I've said so far.

These are superfluous words.

Subjects don't change, they exist in their contradictions, but sometimes people choose the wrong contradictions, and then it's better to keep silent.

I have been citing Eichenbaum's thoughts with great pleasure and even envy, but in his diverse life Lev Nikolaevich didn't read just philosophical or classical books.

He read, very carefully, the small volumes of Dmitri Nikolaevich Begichev's newly released book, *The Kholmsky Family: Morals and Way of Life of the Russian Gentry.*

From this book Tolstoy acquired a habit of keeping a diary and giving himself a grade, as he would to a pupil, indicating each time he rejected temptations.

Among all his descriptions that we could give, there is another one— he was an archaist.

Begichev's book came out in 1832, then many years later Belinsky, somewhat ironically, would express his amazement about this volume, and

---

101 *Bowstring: About the Dissimilarity of the Similar* (1970).

many years later it turned up in my own library. During a difficult period in my life, the library was sold in entirety to the Writers' Union, and unfortunately the bookcases have not been opened until this day. It's a good library, a collection of Russian prose.

One must learn how to open a bookcase.

Inside this little-known book live the characters of Griboedov. The Begichevs knew Griboedov, and according to an old rumor, Griboedov had insulted Begichev.

Begichev's book incorporated Famusov, Chatsky, Molchalin and many other characters who were perceived differently as contemporaries than they are perceived now.

Famusov, once a government official, is now a shrewd dealer who is robbing Chatsky little by little.

Chatsky—this is in the sixth chapter—is shown through the words of a writer, the aristocrat Pronsky: "Pronsky met with Chatsky a few more times. He would often look at Chatsky with amazement and think to himself: was it really that brave and fearless Chatsky with whom he had served in several campaigns, whom he had seen in the heat of battle . . . always a hero . . . ahead of everyone else. Was it really the same darling officer whom everyone called the 'knight Bayard'[102]—thought Pronsky.

—Was it possible to change in every aspect and to such a degree . . . Chatsky didn't talk about anything else but illnesses, medicine and doctors, telling about the kinds of illnesses he's had and who cured him, how and when . . . Finally Pronsky couldn't restrain himself: 'For heaven's sake, Aleksandr Andreevich, I can't even recognize you! What happened to you?'—'What else is there to say, brother! The past is the past,'—replied Chatsky."

■

102 Seigneur de Bayard (1474–1524), French military hero, called *le chevalier sans peur et sans reproche* [the knight without fear or reproach]. He exhibited bravery and genius as a commander in all the important battles of the Italian Wars.

We are finally getting closer to our subject. *The Kholmsky Family* depicts the life of the aristocracy and their families; it shows the sisters in their misfortunes and empathy with each other, and all of this is evaluated by the shrewd Madame Sviazhskaya.

Here is the young Tolstoy, not having yet written the two novels—for which they would criticize him—the novel of Vronsky and the novel of Levin; but if we take Begichev, an unpretentious writer, in the sixth volume he is saying good-bye to at least twenty families with business connections to each other, which are, by the way, not very honest.

Although Begichev is irritated by Beaumarchais and talks with delight about his devotion to the Tsar, the homeland and all the rules of the Russian Domostroi,[103] these are only excuses. So, even though the author is not that talented, it's interesting to read him even today. The question that he raises is quite interesting.

People in those days lived a life full of petty enjoyments, taking cheap pleasures, arranging marriages, conversing; of course, Schopenhauer didn't write about this, but this is what the great man of the future, the great archaist, Count Lev Nikolaevich Tolstoy was reading and writing, and who ran the most archaic household in the village, which at the same time abounded in machines and new breeds of animals, because that's how Tolstoy understood life.

■

Like any truly great writer, Tolstoy was out of place. I think that such characters as King Lear, Hamlet, Anna Karenina, are also people who are out of place.

Before Tolstoy there were a few novels about the life of the aristocracy; they were written at a satisfactory level, and it's as if the authors in those

[103] The Domostroi was the official code of household management rules in sixteenth century Russia.

novels were licking their lips from delight at their own depiction of reality. At the appearance of *Anna Karenina* there were critics, some even published, who said it was worse than other high-society novels, but nobody doubted that it was indeed a high-society novel.

It was and it wasn't. It was unsuccessful in terms of the old genre.

In *Anna Karenina*, the person who comes closest to the author's conscience, Konstantin Levin, is perceived by the others, mostly by Kitty's mother, Princess Scherbatskaya, whose daughter Levin is in love with, as a failure. Even though he has a large estate, still he isn't a kammerjunker, and surely not a colonel. He is a person without a title, without a proper place that corresponds to his birth. This, by the way, gets in the way of his proposal. Kitty's mother thinks that Vronsky, in contrast to Levin who owns a large estate, is the one who has his own distinct place, is rich, has a title and is even charming—in other words, he is the typical hero of the novel.

But novels are born out of different perceptions. Tolstoy knew that aristocracy was in vogue, that there was a desire to belong in this group of high-borns. The characters who have names in *The Sevastopol Sketches* all flock around the aristocracy. Everyone wants to be with people who seem to be higher than themselves.

People of excellent military reputation are happy to promenade with a good-for-nothing, vain person if they think he's an aristocrat. Tolstoy says that this fashion for aristocracy is borrowed; it comes from abroad, probably from the English novel.

Let me clarify.

This is why in *The Sevastopol Sketches* Tolstoy says that there is not just one hero; he is referring to the old literary tradition.

Tolstoy considered that the hero of his stories was the truth, and he was right.

Tolstoy's hero is the process of revealing a person's essence.

But Tolstoy also wrote that he was the son of a lieutenant colonel, who was raised by women—i.e., women brought him up—and that he was still a failure who squandered half of his fortune. After giving such a description of himself, Tolstoy rode off to the Caucasus.

The Caucasus wasn't just a place for romantics.

The Caucasus was a place for failures.

In the unpublished preface to *War and Peace*, Tolstoy says that all of his heroes are of aristocratic origin because he doesn't know any other society and he can't possibly write about the seminary student who had been punished with a rod twice. I once, somehow, noticed that they exercised the punishment with a rod more often in the cadet academies than in the seminaries. They even had special rods for flogging. There was a man at the Naval Academy who would flog with a certain picture in mind, carving it on the victim's body.

Tolstoy was both proud and uneasy about belonging to the aristocracy. He would break this term down, as if it were in quotation marks, describing the soldier with great precision and the officer—with slight condescension. But they orient themselves with respect to each other. He analyzes the different types of aristocrats. One doesn't want to consort with the others. And although they are braver than others, it seems they are equal according to their epaulettes.

We were talking about the Kholmsky family and the marriages of their daughters. The Kholmskys had the title of counts, but theirs was not a pure aristocratic family.

I must mention that the reason why I'm talking about the Kholmsky family is to show how people of that generation generally viewed themselves.

■

The Scherbatskys were once very rich, but the old Prince spent almost all of this fortune.

The father of Natasha Rostova, Count Prostov, which we realize is a very strange name for such an aristocratic family,[104] didn't squander, but ate away his fortune entertaining his guests. The members of the gentry compared their own fame and high birth just as the officers of *The Sevastopol Sketches* competed with each other in ranks.

The Scherbatskys were ruined. They struggled while living in Moscow, spending more than they could afford; they were finishing off the last bits of their fortune. They had no other choice but to live in Moscow, because this is where the market for brides was, which Pushkin commented on with sadness but with no resentment.

Tatyana Larina was on that market, too. The people who brought her there were happy when she became a general's wife.

It was the mother who reined in the Scherbatsky family. She made sure that the children learned French and English. That her daughters were in society. And in order for them not to show their pretty legs before the right time came, the girls were expected to wear long dresses. Kitty, the youngest one, had very pretty legs that the skirt wouldn't cover.

This is what Tolstoy wrote (we are getting a little ahead in regard to Kitty's age):

> The panics that had been lived through, the thoughts that had been brooded over, the money that had been wasted, and the disputes with her husband over marrying the two elder girls, Darya and Natalie! Now, since the youngest had come out, she was going through the same terrors, the same doubts, and quarrels with her husband still more violent than those over the older girls.

Stiva Oblonsky seemed to be a good suitor.

He squandered his fortune; he was apparently the descendent of the famous Rurik dynasty, he had a job where he didn't do anything; but he suc-

---

[104] The Russian word *prostoi*, which is the root in Prostov's name, means "common."

cessfully imitated a busy man, at first as a government official, then, when things got worse, at the railroad construction agency of the Jew, Poliakov.

The oldest daughter was married to Stepan Arkadyevich Oblonsky.

The second of the Scherbatsky sisters became a Lvova, and this family is almost not mentioned in the novel, except that there had been scarlet fever.

It was time to marry off the third daughter. Kitty had a much better success than her older sisters.

She had good suitors.

Once Vronsky unintentionally mentioned to Kitty that he was expecting his mother from Petersburg. But Kitty's mother had assumed that Countess Vronskaya was coming to look at the bride.

Kitty's character, the situation she found herself in, made her sick, she was doubting the moral purity of that house. She thought badly of herself in her own thoughts.

■

Anna Karenina, the subject we have finally reached, was Stiva Oblonsky's sister, a countess who'd married a successful minister, the best suitor in the province.

The only shortcoming of this marriage, which took place under the best of omens, was the fact that the groom was twenty years the senior of the bride.

It was accepted and approved in ancient Greece that the husband should be fifteen years older than his wife.

The wife was an object of respect and value—you can take these words any way you like.

But Anna Karenina entered the social circle of her husband.

This was a group of famous and high ranking aristocrats, and at the beginning Anna was extremely proud of her husband's surroundings.

Then there was the gentry of their province. She became the grand dame of St. Petersburg. She was acquainted with members of aristocracy

with ringing names. They all lived a free life. But it was done very dis-
cretely so that nobody would notice. When society turned away from Anna
Karenina, she felt as if she were on an uninhabited island, but she didn't
know how to shield herself, she wasn't able to create a counter-position so
as to despise her old connections.

Anna Karenina was raised so high that when she arrives to see Dolly,
who is in despair from her grief over her husband's infidelity, who is crying and has lost weight, this woman is gratified that her famous sister-in-
law, the wife of a man who reports directly to the Tsar, has come to console
her.

The ministry was only a stepping-stone for Karenin; they said about
this man that he had an intellect rarely encountered in Europe.

■

The beginning of each book, each drama, must draw us in immediately
and unexpectedly; certainly if there is no special announcement of what's
what, who's the hero and what's the situation.

In *War and Peace*, for instance, those who are discussing Russia's state
of affairs, Napoleon's campaign and Pierre, are people who accept and respect Andrei Bolkonsky; Tolstoy says this openly.

In *Anna Karenina*, however, the author almost never interjects himself.
The world of the heroes exists only within the limits of the book's world.
It's depicted and exists within its own laws, which we don't question when
reading the novel. When they ask what was the beginning of all this, what
was he thinking when he started to write about a woman who lost herself,
when they say that this story is almost connected to the story of a common
woman who lived with a gentleman outside of marriage and who threw
herself under a train because he left her, then I think that it probably was
this story that fascinated Tolstoy. But this can't be right because in the first
drafts of the novel, Anna Karenina throws herself into the Neva after the
conversation with her husband. The train appears much later. It wasn't the
train that urged him to write the novel.

And it was hardly the sentence from Pushkin's draft: "The guests were assembling at the country house." It has been written about so often, and, as we know, people like to discover things anew. They want to find the realistic origins of the work, "something like that happened in real life." And indeed, a few sketches of the beginning tell how the guests arrive at the country house of a certain princess, how they gossip, how the hostess behaves. In his later drafts Tolstoy says that Anna was sitting and talking to Vronsky, who at the time had a different last name.

Everyone in the room was listening and the table where Anna sat with Vronsky—he had a different name—was like a drum beating in full motion.

When Pushkin wrote in a different excerpt about the carriage, this was a shock, a surprise, because the carriage was out of place.

The beginning of the novel is unexpected and this sense of unexpectedness is carried on throughout the novel.

■

I already had the opportunity to say this and I'll repeat once more that with his plot the writer is wiping off the world, which has grown tainted and dusty.

And so the different writers, who live in different times, come across the same pattern, the same chain of circumstances, which reveal themselves in different ways each time.

This is how plot travels through time.

■

Pushkin wrote prose simultaneously with *Eugene Onegin*. He was writing the beginning of some major novel. One of the installments from this novel gets printed under the subtitle "The guests were assembling at the country house," and the other under "At the corner of a little square."

The heroine of the first excerpt is Volskaya. She was married at a very young age to a simple—not a tragic, not a villainous, not even a poetic—person.

One summer, at some social party, Zinaida Volskaya meets an officer and they talk on the terrace for a long time.

The heroine from the "At the corner of a little square" excerpt continues the story started in the first excerpt.

This second heroine falls in love with Volodsky as "she becomes repulsed by her own husband, a feeling known only to women and perceived by them only."

Entering her husband's room she declares that she is in love with someone else, she doesn't want to lie anymore and wants a divorce; this is as unexpected for the husband as it is for Volodsky. "He never intended to tie himself with such bonds."

The heroine of these excerpts is shown with great love, although her conduct is completely contradictory to Tatyana's.

It turns out that then, too, there had been another possible outcome. But it was similarly tragic. Although the names of the heroines were almost identical, we didn't notice that the two excerpts were based on the fate of a single woman.

But Lev Nikolaevich Tolstoy did. Leafing through Pushkin, he saw this excerpt, and perhaps the second one, and began writing *Anna Karenina*. He was hoping to finish the novel in a few months. He was rejoicing that he had finally found the right subject. He stopped the work that he'd begun on a novel about Tsar Peter I, removing the scaffolding that held up the historic novel before this.

The material was ready and in Sofia Andreevna's words: "The characters were already dressed, they just needed breath."

The novel about Peter I opened with: "Everything was in confusion in the Tsar's household." This opening was supposed to be followed by the sorting of material seen from a new angle—a novel about tragic conflicts; this was very clear and it stood at Lev Tolstoy's door, like an invited guest would stand in front of the yet unopened door.

But he wasn't able to solve the fate of the woman from Pushkin's fragments. He only realized that this fate was as important and as honorable, and even as amazing, as the fate of Tatyana.

A literary work changes with time. It's the same, and it's simultaneously different. It was Pushkin who said that one could find all the words in a dictionary. The themes repeat. It's through plot that literary constructions pass from one epoch into another.

Now let's go back and discuss the unexpectedness of the opening and how it's sustained.

The novel opens with the words about how happy families are all alike and every unhappy family is unhappy in its own way.

This opening with a moral evaluation of what is happening, an evaluation of the unexpected, didn't appear at the beginning of the book, but it was moved here because it was something nobody expected; this was a new beginning.

And so was the opening of *Eugene Onegin*: "My uncle has most honest principles . . ."

The quote from the Bible and the remark about unhappy families create something unexpected when juxtaposed next to each other.

Moreover, this opening about unhappy families was in fact a comparison—from the very start the reader is told that this is not a novel, but two novels in one.

Here is one subject, and here is the other; this was plotted from the very beginning.

The novel is about search.

The other, more ordinary, and somewhat conventional opening with the hero Ordyntsev, the future Levin, shown at a farmer's fair, was also unexpected: gentlemen hardly ever went to such places.

And they hardly ever went to the skating rink.

Levin meets Kitty Scherbatskaya on the skating rink and he is overjoyed when she suggests to him that they "skate together." He knows how to skate, he is a master at skating.

He can dash down the wooden steps in his skates, balance himself and skate off. He surprises us with his enthusiasm, how unlike others he appears.

Levin's unhappiness is that Kitty, whom he has known almost since childhood, gives him a strange answer to his proposal, his proposal of love. She says: that cannot be. That is, she points out directly that her fate is already decided.

The heroine of the novel, the woman whose name appears on the cover of the book, after the quote from the Bible, after the opening lines, and after the dream of Stepan Arkadyevich—Anna Karenina is somehow like and, at the same time, unlike her brother.

She is a complete and healthy woman, but due to her intellect she appears in a different category. She has a different destiny in life.

The rest that follows is a long engagement with Anna Karenina. As we said, she was headed from St. Petersburg to Moscow; she is arriving like fate. Her brother comes to meet her, there is a passage describing him, and then suddenly she becomes the rival of another woman. Her character is changed.

Anna appears from the train—Anna who is about to begin a romance. She appears as a god; something that will change everyone's fate.

Let's talk about Anna Karenina's appearance. In the first drafts she is a full-figured woman with very beautiful eyes; she is attractive to men and unattractive to women; she is dressed provocatively. She is kind, yet she isn't *comme il faut*.

In the actual writing of the novel Anna becomes a magnificent, self-possessed, well-mannered, strong young woman who knows her superiority; she is slightly condescending toward her husband. Especially toward him.

Her inner potential, her youth is hidden. She is shown in conversation with an old lady, Vronsky's mother, who is an older and similarly renowned version of her. She could have become the heroine of a high-society novel and could have made the man she is in love with famous.

At first, in the drafts, Karenin was an old wrinkled man, with red marks on his face and strange manners; without respect he would have been ridiculous.

He is ostracized from society. Tolstoy says, though, that he is above society.

He drinks tea with loud sips. His appearance is observed with condescending remarks. One should have betrayed this man long ago. A woman like Anna must have a shadow, a man who follows her everywhere.

But later Karenin appears in a new light, and both Karenin and Anna Karenina are elevated to higher beings, they are created for great conflicts.

Vronsky respects Karenin.

The clash between Karenin and Vronsky is the collision of two giants who have just unexpectedly discovered one another.

Anna Karenina clashes with Kitty, too, but this is the conflict between the great beauty and the charming young girl who is not yet spoiled from the success that will evolve over the years.

The novel begins with the transformation of the heroes. Anna Karenina learns to lie to and despise her husband, she pities him, yet despises him nonetheless. She is excited about her future betrayal. And when her husband finally falls asleep after a difficult conversation and begins to snore, she rejoices: "It's too late, it's too late," they can't do anything about it. She is pleased with her future decision.

She appears as a woman who has the right not only to social respect, but also to happiness.

Tolstoy does not hide the fact that her love is carnal. Anna is almost cynical because she feels she is being "starved" and is, therefore, right. During the awkward conversations about love, when they start to talk about having another kind of relations, she suddenly sets the date:

"Tomorrow at four."

This is not cynicism. This is the resolve of despair.

Much later in the novel we see Anna's dejection.

Love comforts her in her misery as if naturally. To Vronsky's question of whether "she is happy," she answers: she is as happy as the hungry person who has been given something to eat.

It's all right to laugh at someone, but the reader mustn't question whether the hungry person has the right to be hungry. And although Karenin is a clever man, he says that the bond between him and his wife is illuminated by God, and this sounds more like an excuse.

An older minister marries a young countess.

She is seduced by a young colonel.

He is smart, handsome and of good family.

God has nothing to do with this.

He created Adam and Eve. This is not a matter of "society."

The novel is not judgmental, but tragic.

In this novel the happiness of a woman is shown as the happiness of a man.

■

At the beginning of *Don Quixote*, Cervantes is consulting with his friend; the matter is about the entrance of a man into the literary world. Cervantes had already written many things but with no success, and essentially he talks about imitation and how it creates an impression.

Cervantes is smart, worldly, wise, and here gives us a conversation that reexamines the style of writing.

Yes, it's a customary thing to make references, cite other books and draw comparative conclusions at the end. However, the fellow friend says ceremoniously—and Cervantes agrees—nobody really reads the cited paragraphs.

More often it's the writer who reads them, but they are the traces of his thought.

The citation has its proper place, it reinforces its context. It's necessary to base things on a concrete structure of thoughts, it's important to not just toss words around, but also give their coordinates. That's a good principle. Because our publishing houses don't have libraries or even a collection of bibliographies, so they can't really check the references, which is why I've made notes according to which it's possible to track down the quote; it's an unconventional record, if you will, that validates my book.

It seems like we are walking around like blind people, constantly holding on to the wall of quotation. I have so many books on my desk right now that even if I were an acrobat, I would not be able to jump over the desk.

The books would be in my way.

But they are necessary and it's good that I have so many of them.

And among them is a volume on *Anna Karenina* that came out during the novel's centennial.

It's a book by E. Babaev called *The Novel and its Times*, published in 1975.

It's a good book. There are many references in it and I'm convinced that all of them are accurate.

But the novel is not analyzed as a whole. It's taken apart and discussed separately.

Each part, each thread of the novel is examined very intelligently, but at the same time the action of the novel is depicted as if in isolation.

Tolstoy said, the novel is a "labyrinth of linkages"; the links exist, there is a labyrinth. It's the unity of linkages. The work of art is unified, it consists of multitudes that generate semantic contradictions.

The squirrels eat pinecones in the forest and it seems that without looking they know where the hard membranes are, the tissue between the seeds.

But for the squirrels the crux of the matter is the search for the seeds. The squirrel drops the empty pinecone on the ground without thinking twice (neither do I) about the republication of this already analyzed work.

Anna Karenina is a unified work, it's a unity constructed on contradictions. It's a unity of multitudes.

Which is why Tolstoy spoke of its architecture with a feeling of pride.

The architecture of the novel is connected to the architecture of his times.

Princess Scherbatskaya, coming from the old traditions of her ancestry, is a mother who in the present times doesn't know how to marry off her daughters.

She knows that in France women take care of their own fate.

In England, it's the parents who arrange the marriages.

But how does one proceed about such matters in Moscow in the present times, how do these things happen now that she is here and thinking about it—this she doesn't know.

As a matter of fact, everything in Russia was changing, turning upside down, and nothing made sense anymore.

Konstantin Levin, with his philosophical views, who is proud of his ancestry and is the owner of a fine estate, sees that everything has turned upside down. He doesn't know how it will all make sense. The system where the essence of life lies, life's movement, about which his brother Nikolai talks when addressing his favorite youngest brother: "You've borrowed an old idea, distorted it, and think that it's your idea."

Levin loses his temper, or better yet, he's irritated because his brother is right, and he understands that he doesn't know what's right.

At the end of the book Levin says that there is an entire order of links, an order of concepts; he knows that the sun doesn't set and it doesn't rise.

He knows that the stars don't move as they seem to be moving when seen from the earth.

He sees the elements of ancient life without even squinting.

The sun rises each morning.

In the evening it goes down.

Once this was not only visible but also understood. It was the beginning of astronomy.

Levin wants to see the world as it has always been, but he knows that in order to do so one needs to squint.

The world moves by laws that are unfamiliar to him.

The architecture of Tolstoy's novel is based on the search for the moral laws of the world.

The world is changing.

But he wants to see it unchanged. At the very end of the novel we see Levin as a married older person.

He says that he will go on living in the same way.

These are the words of an owner.

He confirms the immobility of the world.

This was attempted in the Bible by Jesus Navin who said: "The sun must stop, and the moon must not move."

The attempt was successful in the Bible.

A landowner, Levin wants to make his peasants his shareholders, yet at the same time he says that he must pay them as little as possible.

In such a system it's difficult to come to terms with workers.

The peasants have very little land.

Levin has eight thousand acres of land. The land is fertilized.

These are excellent meadows.

The peasants work on terms negotiated with Levin that the mowers get a third of the grass from his land, but he doesn't believe that they are taking a third and checks the carts. The peasants try to reason with him saying that the hay is dry.

Levin demands his two-thirds. He accuses them of theft. This is a long conversation. But at the same time this talk touches upon Levin's personal matters, his relationship with his wife.

Tolstoy was writing *Anna Karenina*.

Art is a path that can't be discovered right away.

The symphony is composed of different measures, and each has its own laws of existence. Even though these measures coexist, they have their own different laws.

There is an energy of delusion in art—an energy of movement—and this movement in art depends upon the energy of changes in life.

■

Anna Karenina is a work in the novelistic genre. In this novel Karenina squints her eyes; she gained this habit after she left her husband and her son; but Levin, too, a family man, a strong fellow, a philosopher, he too squints, striving to understand how the laws of sensation are associated with the laws of universal existence.

However strange it may be, when the Tsar comes to the races, the same races where Vronsky falls and breaks the back of his favorite mare Frou-Frou, the Tsar is also squinting his eyes.

That's the world. And no one is directly at fault.

Tolstoy asserts with all the force of his talent that a woman—her desire—is right.

Through his character, whose name is Konstantin Levin, the root of which remains "lev," Lev Nikolaevich considers that a wife must be responsible for domestic work. Tolstoy even insisted that the name should be spelled Lëvin.[105]

When Levin found the wife he wanted, she took care of the housework. She made jam; she was free to make it any way she wanted to. The world in some aspect submitted itself to her. And the preparation of jam in the Levin family was perhaps something like a liturgical service.

The old nurse and other servants of Levin also take part in this. They have a different method of making jam. It's as if they are Old Believers. They think that Scherbatskaya, the mother-in-law, overcooks the jam; but even so they do what all women must do—sew, cook, and most importantly, give birth to children and nurse them—and that's the way it should be. But there is something that can be imagined only through squinting the eyes—that Anna Karenina, who apparently also can make jam, has a son who loves her very much.

She also reads books, she has written a novel for children and it has a publisher. She understands art. She wants to change the world for herself.

For Vronsky, Anna Karenina constitutes a great part of his world, but Vronsky owns the whole world, and in this love he might jeopardize his honor.

■

[105] Pronounced Lyovin, (ë = yo). Tolstoy was called Lëva as a boy.

The creator of this novel constructed a grand character that attracts every reader, they all fall in love with Anna Karenina. But at the same time the novelist married Sofia Andreevna. She strongly resembled Kitty. She oversaw the preparation of jam, took care of the huge household, managed the business of publishing, sold butter, sold the apples that grew at Yasnaya Polyana, rented out the rooms to students, and all of this despite their affluence.

She sold books in the barn. They would sell the *Primer* in bulk.

But when Levin, not Lev Nikolaevich but his created hero, began looking for a wife and chose Kitty, then saw Anna Karenina, she seemed brilliant to him and Kitty rather plain.

There is nothing to argue about here. Lev Nikolaevich won't be able to leave this subject, and neither can we, we'll never be able to and there is no need to even try.

For the concepts of man and woman are never separate, together they form a whole.

Just as there is the night and the day, the right side and the left side, and the notion of guilty and not guilty. And after his brilliant Anna, Lev Nikolaevich wrote:

—I'll draw up a short list:

"The Kreutzer Sonata," a story about jealousy; he wrote an afterword to this work in which he offers a new wide path, a life in a lighthouse in the ocean where one doesn't have to look at the shore because there are other lighthouses. And this wasn't supposed to be the question of man and woman.

"The Death of Ivan Ilych." Death that refuted the life of Ivan Ilych.

And Ivan Ilych lived in a house very much like the one in Khamovniki.

Lev Nikolaevich bought that house and rebuilt it. He created a big office for himself with a separate entrance, an office that had a very low ceiling. He wrote there, sitting by the small table and on a chair with shortened legs.

He was near-sighted and never wore glasses; he wrote with his head bent.

This is where he wrote "Strider," the story of a great horse, a super-trotter. The horse was not of the same color as the horses of his kind. For this—he was gelded.

Strider had a bitter life.

Tolstoy was fascinated with his bitter and profound conversation with the other horses.

■

When Lev Tolstoy began writing *Anna Karenina*, his household was going through a period of success. His garden was getting bigger, his family was growing. Quarrels were being patched up with a soft putty of love. And even though there were deaths, Count Lev Nikolaevich, powerful as an ocean, thought that he would achieve happiness.

He was as happy as Job before his temptations.

Lev Nikolaevich was in need of money for purchasing land. He wanted to increase his property and he had every right to do so. He knew how to plow the land and was a good landowner.

He wanted to borrow money from Fet. He needed ten thousand rubles. Fet refused him. He had to look elsewhere. There was an agreement on a novel; the advance for the novel was supposed to be the exact amount of the advance that he had to pay for the land—ten thousand rubles.

Then he had to actually purchase the land.

This great man was indeed a great figure of his times. He wanted to escape the present, yet at the same time he wanted to finish the novel for himself, and he found a way out.

He went to search an estate. It was necessary to purchase an estate with a forest so that the person selling it had no idea about the value of the forest; once the forest was resold, it would be as if he had got the land for free.

Ryabinin was the merchant who bought the forest from Stepan Arkadyevich Oblonsky. He counts the trees as he buys the forest because he knows that it's going to be his forest. The person who purchases the land, the new owner, is a man of his own times, he can purchase land where the peasants are advised not to own land.

The business of peasant emancipation was a business of robbery.

There used to be a saying: "We belong to you, and the land belongs to us."

So they were freed but not completely. They were supposed to plow and mow on someone else's land; there was no way around it.

This was evident to Levin and the creator of *Anna Karenina*.

A man comes to purchase a large estate from a merchant in Arzamas; the contract is almost finalized; he retires to his room to sleep, next to his room sleeps his servant, and suddenly the man, this new landowner, experiences nightmares in his sleep.

He thinks: if we divide up the forest, the entire forest of Zaseki, if I become more famous than anyone has ever been—then what, and why am I so afraid?

And death whispers in his ear: "You are afraid of me."

Tolstoy called this nightmare "Arzamas horror," and the most frightening thing in this horror was the candle, which the new landowner saw after awakening. The candle was on the table made of Karelia birch, it was burning out and the paper wrapped at the bottom of the candle was about to catch on fire.

Prosperity and death—that was the "Arzamas horror."

The horror that was described in *Anna Karenina* was the fear of being cleansed.

Scholars think that this was a segment from Fet's poetry. No, it was a chapter from a great person's biography.

The river flows, it goes down the hillsides, it overflows, then it narrows and finally grows shallow.

A person lives his life but he also has a conscience, how does one free himself from it?

It was difficult. He was afraid of his own conscience, the boredom of a mundane life and the usual hoarding.

And then Lev Nikolaevich tried to resolve his own fate through Anna Karenina, and her fate was terrible, just as terrible as the "Arzamas horror," the horror of injustice.

Mankind stands before its own conscience and is plagued with injustice. King Lear makes a mistake when dividing his kingdom, he is deceived, and his jester reminds him with his jokes about the royal guilt that destroys Cordelia.

Anna Karenina enters the novel like a train's wheel that rolls along the old rails undisturbed.

Anna's death, her suicide under the wheels, the terrible wheels of the new, strange times, after which a person becomes like a hollow pinecone, a skeleton, this death brought an end to Anna.

Later Tolstoy kept adding new chapters to *Anna Karenina*. It was terrifying to end a novel where suicide was described in such precise detail.

■

Anna Karenina was supposed to die.

This was given at the beginning of every single draft. She had to die, and he even had the form in which she was to die. Tolstoy's old aunt, the *fraulein* of the courts, knew of the outcome, but the form of suicide seemed to her just as vulgar as the act of suicide itself. Initially Anna Karenina wore the marks of a doomed person. She was attractive, yet extravagant and dressed unlike everyone else. She stood out among the herd. But the more Tolstoy wrote the more he liked the woman whom he neither painted nor created, but came across, as it were, on the paths of history.

Then he'd write that he had "adopted" her.

He was creating not only a novel but also the image of a woman with whom he was falling deeply in love.

Anna's crime had to be punished by God. This is how Dante loved the woman who was once seduced by a book she read with a man. The last phrase is marvelous: "That day we read from it no more." The beautiful love was realized. It was realized for Dante as well.

Dante passes in the company of Virgil, the great writer who created the principles of art, and faints when he hears a woman's speech.

He envisions a whirlwind of lovers, doomed to eternal flight.

They are all guilty.

Anna was supposed to be guilty, but she isn't and the more Tolstoy describes her, the more she becomes exalted.

I remember when the young Gorky—back then he seemed old to me, he was fifty—explained "why Karenina was unhappy. In *Madame Bovary* Flaubert creates a temple of love, but Karenina and Vronsky haven't even seen Rome. There is not a line about how they lived there."

Were they unhappy? Was Tolstoy happy? I don't know. I don't know what happiness means to birds, but when a flock of geese or quails fly over the ocean to their dear old nests, the nests on each side are probably identical.

They are each just as precious.

Is the goose happy after his flight from Egypt to the Arctic Sea? He is probably made for such a flight, and his stroking wing coincides with the movement of the air that carries the flock.

While searching for a path of life through the life of his novels, Tolstoy was perhaps occasionally happy.

But it's impossible to create a complete novel and sometimes it's impossible to finish even a song.

■

Tolstoy judged life with his novel.

When Anna is dying in postpartum fever, death seems inevitable. And during this time the guilty woman in her delirium speaks to her husband as someone higher than him, as someone who forgives him.

In the same room another Aleksei is crying.

There are two of them—Aleksei Vronsky and Aleksei Karenin. They have one thing in common, they both are old rails along which will pass the old wheel, the cast-iron wheel: "she is guilty, she must die."

Both Alekseis are crying.

It's a long scene, you will read it. Maybe you'll cry, too.

Karenin didn't simply forgive his wife, he decided there was no fault at all.

Far away from Tolstoy, Dostoevsky found this scene remarkable. He wrote in his journal that no one was at fault.

Indeed, in the drafts Karenin made the bed for Vronsky because Vronsky lived in his house, and it was impossible to order others to make the bed—*such* a bed.

Vronsky was grieved when he found out that the person betrayed wasn't the worthless one, but the one who'd made all three of them suffer so much. Deceived husbands were not the only ridiculous ones, although they had to mourn not less than a thousand years.

Vronsky is a healthy man, so healthy that he thinks he can sleep at night even after the horrors of life.

Then he says "Of course," recognizing that he is humiliated in front of his beloved woman who sees him cry; he says "Of course," trying to shoot himself, to find a commonplace way out.

Almost guessing what it means to really love.

But "of course" great Dostoevsky would be delighted. He finally got to read a love scene in which nobody is at fault. This scene doesn't burn from the gunshot of the person who is committing suicide, but becomes illuminated by the gunshot; by some chance he stays alive and everything begins all over again. Before Vronsky didn't have anything to compare to; he's like someone who's playing a broken record on a gramophone.

It's a good record.

Of course—of course. Looking at the child that's not his, Aleksei Karenin doesn't think about what has to be done.

He looks at the little creature, which isn't even described, and smiles.

Tolstoy writes that Karenin smiles in such a way that even the hair on his head moves.

And he doesn't feel any despair or fear, there is only the feeling of being freed from something.

Karenin is not guilty. And neither is his young son, Seryozha. His eyes resemble his father's eyes. Anna Karenina saw this.

No one is guilty.

Then things get back on track. Vronsky recovers.

Vronsky and Karenina leave for Rome and at the beginning they are quite happy. Levin, who was jealous of Vronsky because of Kitty, realizes at the same time that Karenina is superior to him. Levin marries Kitty, they have a child together, Vronsky leaves for Serbia hoping to die at war. Levin becomes a large landowner, he wants to create a new theory of life, rethink life anew, but in such a way that he doesn't lose anything. In the meantime he's hiding the gun and rope so as not to shoot or hang himself.

Nobody is happy.

Karenina dies after she finishes reading her own book.

The candle of life is extinguished. This isn't poetry, it isn't a reproach.

But the candle didn't get extinguished by itself; it was blown out. Due to the difference in morals for men and women, a woman lost her place in society.

What happened to Tolstoy and his characters could have happened earlier with the characters of Pushkin in the excerpt "At the corner of a little square."

■

Anna Karenina is a judgment on life.

It's a judgment on judgment. I began the story of Anna Karenina with the stories of two Venetian women, one was not so famous and the other was the daughter of a prince. In fact, I think there were three of them.

There also was Lady Filippa, who was being judged in the small town of Prato for infidelity.

She was threatened with being burned at stake according to the new law, but Lady Filippa challenged and refuted it by saying that this law was unfounded, since it was adopted without the participation of women. They didn't vote for it.

All the stories with dramatic endings talk about the different attitudes toward male and female infidelity. One of the women demands that her story be at least written on her tombstone along with the name of her lover.

Many parts in *Anna Karenina* had been moved around during its writing.

The expression "writing" is not correct in terms of novels. Novels aren't written, although in response to a question about how to write a novel, Mark Twain said: "By sitting down." Novels are constructed. The chapters get moved around, the characters get reinvented. The novel isn't like a lake, it's like a river, and one could take the following words from *The Song of Igor's Campaign* as an epigraph to every novel:

O Dnepr, famed one!
You have pierced stone hills . . .

. . . When citing Tolstoy and, say, his sources, we must always remember that the word "source" in its original meaning is the beginning of a river, its origins.

And rivers never stay close to their source.

We often use the word "source" incorrectly—a source is taken to be the indication of the cause of a phenomenon.

The place of birth is replaced by the concept of birth itself.

Tolstoy always departs from his sources. His books are like journeys that start from a source of observation fortified by a stream flowing from a book source, or more accurately, the book source augments (it doesn't engender) the attention to an observed phenomenon; then he begins the study of the subject, i.e., in this case, the novel.

Tolstoy's novels are his studies.

Where he arrives at the idea, which at times may not be directly expressed, that first impressions are always erroneous.

My personal opinion about the source of many of Tolstoy's ideas, the source that passes through layers of doubt, through heaps of variants, this source is something that in those times was called nihilism, and what's more—this source always existed along with its contrary.

This sort of drama reveals itself in such scenes as the conversation of Levin with his brother Nikolai. I already mentioned it.

In real life Nikolai is Tolstoy's brother Dmitri, who once read Gogol's *Selected Passages from a Correspondence*[106] and withdrew to a village to realize his ideal of a landowner.

It didn't work out, and he became a nihilist.

So when Levin tells his brother about his plan, the plan to get the peasants interested again in their work, his brother, the nihilist, says: "You've borrowed an old idea, and distorted it"—he is talking about the question of property.

Levin has nothing to retort.

Tolstoy can't help him either.

This is an important issue for Tolstoy himself: the question about property, and particularly the question about landowning.

---

106 This work, which purports to be a collection of letters from Gogol's correspondents together with his replies, is in fact entirely the work of Gogol. It reads like a lengthy and discursive catechism, where the main point of the world view is that a creator, God, has made everything in a certain way, assigned all beings to a certain station, and that the creation of God is just and good. Any attempt by an individual to leave the station into which he or she was born, then, is tantamount to opposing God's will. Such rebellion carries with it its own punishment in the form of personal and social misfortune.

The most important thing, which is ignored, and which turns people to nihilism, is the question about landowning.

The question about property—I know I'm sounding naïve—has always been the most disputed question, but I'll add this: just like the question about a woman's faithfulness.

■

Tolstoy had many children.

In her diary, Sofia Andreevna called her family beautiful.

She loved her family, according to her own words, "to the point of madness."

But this family was at the same time a family of heirs.

The family emphasized the question of property.

And in exactly the same way this question about land inheritance constantly surfaces in the mind of Nekhlyudov in *Resurrection*.

I'll remind you of a thought recorded in Vyazemsky's notes, which have been long forgotten by many. I will mention this thought because his words are incredible, especially because they were written only for himself.

Vyazemsky, Pushkin's friend and a talented person in his own right, wrote that a woman can't have a lover because this introduces a new heir, it changes the idea of birth.

But if she is already pregnant and can't get pregnant a second time from somebody else, then this changes the situation.

This, perhaps, is the only direct place that I know where the question of infidelity converges with the question of inheritance.

■

The origins of Volga are over here—look it up in the encyclopedia.

Then the river flows endlessly far away from its origins.

And at some point, near Samara (look on a map), it bends. Here are the Zhiguli Mountains, the cliff of Stepan Razin.

Here they drilled the ground, took samples of earth, and discovered a cavity with a certain geological type—there had been a rupture: the rock under the soil had cracked long ago and slid down.

Immediately after this comes the short bend of Samara.

This is only a comparison.

But we can compare this to the changes in the way a writer thinks; it's one of the causes of the so-called delusions—or, in any case, contradictions.

Let's not turn Tolstoy into a political activist, but let's look at him through his relation to Russian history, the revolution that he lived through, the people he described. Let's say that these disruptions, these sharp bends of thought brought about by sharp turns of situations, these bends ruptured Tolstoy's heart.

I don't know if I have ever written this down, but after spending half of my life reading Tolstoy, I know it by heart.

He didn't just see the revolution. He evaluated it from the point of view of a young gentleman from the Krapivensky district, Count Lev Nikolaevich, an officer of the Russian army, a person who later preached, when seeing evil, not to resist it with violence.

■　■　■

For the realist Tolstoy, the behavior of people is different at different moments of their lives.

These different relations, the repeating words that mean different things when pronounced at different times, all of these are elements of plot.

Plot is constructed not only on the basis that a person experiences various events, but that when meeting new people, the person is utterly changed.

Apart from this, there are devices like hooks that link the episodes to each other unexpectedly and tightly.

When Anna Karenina meets the guests at Vronsky's house, she, the hostess, has a different name. She isn't Vronskaya. This awkwardness with

names will first of all wound Anna. It continues threading from one segment to the other. It's constructing Anna's real fate. Dolly, who comes to
visit her, is Oblonsky's wife. Dolly has several children. Anna explains
to an amazed Dolly that there are contraceptive methods. Dolly listens
"opening her eyes wide . . . For her this was one of those discoveries the
consequences and deductions of which are so immense that all that one
feels for the first instant is that it is impossible to take it all in, and that one
will have to reflect a great, great deal upon it."

Now Dolly understands why the families that she has been visiting have
fewer children. The conversation between the women is omitted but they
ask one another questions. Anna justifies herself by saying that the child
that she'd give birth to would bear an illegitimate name, "for the very fact
of their birth they will be forced to be ashamed of their mother, their father, their birth." Anna continues: "What is reason given me for if I am not
to use it to avoid bringing unhappy beings into the world . . ." Anna already
has a daughter from Vronsky. Only with great difficulty will it be possible
to legitimize this child.

The question raised is very profound, but it will persist and grow. Anna
goes to have a talk with Vronsky, she knows that the explanations are going
to be useless, but she must talk to him. The people surrounding her are
changed because of her situation. Everything that Anna hears is rooted in
misunderstanding and quarrels, although Anna knows for sure that Vronsky loves her. But she simultaneously understands the situation of a divorced woman.

She imagines a fictional conversation:

"I'm not holding you," he might have said. "You can go where you like.
You were unwilling to be divorced from your husband, no doubt so that
you might go back to him. Go back to him. If you want money, I'll give it
to you. How many rubles do you want?"

This is an imagined conversation with a prostitute.

In the quarrel, the actual quarrel, Vronsky says: "This is getting unbearable." She sees that Vronsky is leaving and it's the scene of a man's calm departure. He is putting on his glove, leaving in an open carriage, not a coach, but it's as though this scene repeats the subject raised by Pushkin, when the man is departing from his lover, at the corner of a little square.

Let's make a big digression and return again to Pushkin.

The traveling plot.

The excerpts from Pushkin coincide with *Anna Karenina* not only through the relationship of Anna to Vronsky, but also such details as the tugging on the glove that's already on the hand.

Tolstoy was delighted when he began the novel. It seemed to him that the story or the novel would be finished very soon. In his letters Lev Nikolaevich praised the speed with which Pushkin inspired but he didn't send the letters because he knew they were too revealing.

This excerpt is very much like the scene between Tatyana Larina and Onegin if she left her husband, the general, telling him frankly and without hiding that she loves Onegin.

But of course there lays an abyss between the excerpt and the unfinished ending of *Eugene Onegin*.

Now let's return to Tolstoy.

He understands that chance is something that one inexplicably cannot avoid. A whole chain of events takes place: Vronsky's conversation with someone, a conversation with a woman through the window, and a slipped note. As Anna is walking through the Obiralovka Station, everyone is hateful and false. Suddenly a woman who was in the same compartment with Anna repeats the phrase that Anna had said to Dolly:

> "That's what reason is given man for, to escape from what worries him," said the lady in French, lisping affectedly, and obviously pleased with her phrase.

The lady seems vile to Anna, she ridicules her forced pronunciation, but the lady is only repeating Anna's ideas.

Anna had said that one mustn't give birth so there wouldn't be any unhappy children. In Tolstoy's mind, abstention from childbirth now had become equivalent to murder, a strange way to avoid something unnecessary.

Tolstoy continues: "The words seemed to answer Anna's thoughts."

To escape from what worries one, repeats Anna.

It's as though she knows the story of this woman, all the bends of her soul. A number of confirmations come after this. The coachman Mikhail, red-faced and cheerful in his smart clothes, proud of having so successfully performed his commission, gives her a letter.

"I am very sorry your note did not reach me. I will be home at ten," Vronsky had written in a careless hand.

The accidental becomes inevitable. Everything is ready. In Vronsky's house Anna Karenina dressed very well, perhaps even better than in Karenin's house, but there she never appreciated her own attire, she considered it a part of her life. A strange association by Tolstoy. This is how the gentry felt, that honor and money was supposed to accompany them like feathers on a bird. But the world in which Anna finds herself begins to fall apart. Two servant girls walking along the platform turn their heads, staring at her and making some remarks about her dress. "Real," they say of the lace she is wearing.

Anna Karenina feels as if she is wearing someone else's dress.

In Vronsky's house Dolly Oblonskaya feels ashamed to undress in front of the maidservant because she is wearing a patched-up blouse. She sees the smartly designed house, but it belongs to someone else.

Here the old gentleman Tolstoy, who never really liked the expensive dinner parties, the dresses and hats of his daughter, sees his own possessions as though they belonged to someone else, although Vronsky is juxtaposed with Levin, the peasant-like gentleman.

But if the extravagant laces of a woman who is headed toward death are real, this is a rejection of a false reality.

Anna's world is falling apart. Tolstoy notes that she "takes a little red bag on her arm." She walks past the train cars, and it's repeated in passing how the platform begins to sway and she imagines that she is in the train again. She recalls other memories connected to the railroad. The memory of the man crushed by the train returns to her mind.

All these accidental events become apparent. The first meeting with Vronsky, the exaggerated first impression.

In order to experience the fate of a person, it's necessary to perceive it as your own experience.

Before the boy Petya Rostov was killed in the accidental attack, we see his dream. He hears the voices of those who are surrounding him but he perceives everything as a musician, the neighing of the horses turn into music. It's as though he is conducting an orchestra.

We begin admiring this person, we single him out and after a few seconds we find out about his accidental death. He doesn't even notice how he got mortally wounded.

Anna Karenina is a woman of her own time. Together with Tolstoy she once illumined and quenched the light in his consciousness.

For her, darkness is not the same as it is for us. Her light was so much brighter. But people knew very well what darkness meant.

The red bag on Anna's hand makes her stand out in the crowd. Anna stands close to the rails and the wheels pass by her. She wants to fall under the wheels but for some reason wants to take off the red bag, because she is alive and the bag for her is something real, something habitual.

After she takes off the bag, she crosses herself, a gesture that reminds her of her childhood, then falls under the wheels. Nothing more is said, except for the impossibility of struggle, the power of death and then—death itself.

The wheels roll over the beautiful woman.

In order to kill her at the end of the novel it was necessary to create her, make her into the light that was surrounded by darkness.

The old world becomes the world of guilt and Tolstoy remembers his Arzamas horror, the horror amid everyday life.

This is how the novel is made, of which he tried to retell only a millionth part, as part of the novel's links and those are the links of something fully understood, something that was experienced anew.

Life—the life presented by a woman—ends.

In a letter to his aunt Tolstoy wrote that he had adopted Anna, that he didn't want anybody to reprimand her. The tragedy of Anna is not the tragedy of one minister's wife from a far-off country, in a different time. This tragedy, in the most banal language, is the tragedy of woman.

Then there is Dolly, Kitty gives her part of the inheritance.

There is also Kitty, who successfully gives birth, she is with a man to whom she is married, she is getting used to her child, teaches her husband to love his child, but there is no trace of the woman whose name appears on the great novel, and it's not our business who will judge and who will take revenge.

It's none of our business that Levin, the person who speaks for the author, continues living in his usual way, squints his eyes, and through his narrowed lids, sees the world ready for its destruction, but at the same time is at peace.

■

Crossing the sea that is Lev Tolstoy is an experience that cannot be explained in brief.

But there are solitary people who go around the world alone in sailboats or at least across the ocean.

Let's talk briefly about Anna Karenina.

What's happening in the novel?

Anna Karenina begins with a scene where a pleasant man has a pleasant dream. He sees singing female decanters. They are decanters but they are also *chansonettes*. The person having this pleasant dream drops his feet from the sofa and suddenly realizes that he is not sleeping in his wife's bedroom, but in his own study.

He feels some guilt and this makes him ill at ease.

He had a quarrel with his wife because he had been unfaithful to her and caught in the act. But Tolstoy says that everyone in the house, the servants, relatives and children, they all stand on the husband's side, the side of Stiva Oblonsky.

As a result, his sister, Anna Karenina, also Oblonskaya, the famous countess from the Rurik dynasty, comes for a visit.

Here is a woman who has come to bring peace between her brother and his wife, and she does succeed to a degree.

But on her way she travels with Vronsky's mother and they talk. Later she reads an English novel. And suddenly she feels ashamed.

Ashamed that in Moscow she felt an attraction for Vronsky. And besides, she is ashamed of the novel—it doesn't please her.

Tolstoy at this time was reading Schopenhauer. Schopenhauer thought that there is a difference between the morals of a man and a woman, that to demand the same faithfulness from a man as demanded from a woman is illogical and leads to a tragedy.

These relations between the two kinds of morals within the same family, within the same society, are the points of collision in *Anna Karenina*.

The argument is still going on till this day, and the world is still being re-examined.

Dostoevsky wrote in his article about *Anna Karenina* that this work isn't an ordinary one. He said that everyone was guilty and then it turned out that nobody was at fault.

The two lives that were falsely mended try to carry on after the death-bed scene. Karenin, who continues living his false life, turns stiff again and begins to rustle. In a séance he raises the question of whether he should give his wife a divorce or not, and is glad when someone in an imagined or real dream tells him that he need not give her a divorce.

Anna begins to live in Vronsky's society. She socializes with a few people. Travels abroad where no one cares with whom this foreign woman lives. Then she lives at Vronsky's estate.

But Karenin still has her son, Sergei. Anna Karenina returns home. The porter, the servant and her son's tutor let her in. They all know that she is not supposed to be in that house, yet at the same time they can't refuse her. To them it's a kind of a moral crime to not let a mother see her son. But it turns out that the son already understands that his father is her enemy and says that "he won't come." Everyone is guilty.

In the meantime, in a rather strange way, or an ingenious way, the novel unites the love life of various ordinary and unordinary families in the question of landowning, the question of whether one should own land and how to pay the worker and what is a moral value.

Dostoevsky's *Crime and Punishment* is a novel about what constitutes a crime.

Anna Karenina questions what constitutes a crime against love.

Levin wanted to marry a girl from high society.

At first she refuses him because she thinks that Vronsky is in love with her, she refuses him because it appears to her that Vronsky is more brilliant.

Yet Tolstoy has something in the novel that no one has noticed yet.

When Anna Karenina arrives to see Kitty who has a guest—Levin—Kitty receives her with confusion, and at the same time Tolstoy writes a sentence that hardly anyone understands: he writes that only Kitty and Anna Karenina know that Vronsky and Levin are very similar to each other.

To be sure—both men resemble the same person who created them, Lev Nikolaevich Tolstoy, who wrote the novel and used the following epigraph translated from German: "Vengeance is mine, and I will repay." It was Eichenbaum who pointed this out to me.

In other words—I am someone who knows the degree and nature of guilt.

This is an old story, which first appeared in the Gospels as a parable about morals.

They bring a woman before Jesus, she had been unfaithful to her husband and she was told that they were going to stone her. This was a test for

Jesus, the heretic. If he said that she wasn't guilty, he would have broken the law of Moses. But Jesus said: "Let him among you who is without sin cast the first stone." And the men disbanded.

What happens at the end of *Anna Karenina*?

Vronsky goes to the front in order to hack his way into a battalion square. He creates a regiment at his own expense. He is seeking an honorable death.

Anna throws herself under the wheels of a freight train.

Levin is hiding a gun and a rope in order not to shoot or hang himself.

Kitty, who is raising her child, is at peace. There is no need for vengeance here.

■

But Tolstoy's attempt to solve the question of guilt didn't succeed. He wasn't able to find the formula to let go of the guilty ones.

Nobody was able to, neither Schopenhauer, nor Princess Betsy, nor Countess Lydia, nor any woman who knew how to sin honorably, nor Vronsky, nor wise Karenin, nor the nihilists whom Tolstoy kept writing about and erasing from the drafts, erasing several times. And the matter is transferred to the next trial, which becomes *Resurrection*.

12

THE EPIGRAPH TO
ANNA KARENINA

I.

"Vengeance is mine, and I will repay."—The epigraph puzzles everyone.

There have been many arguments around it, various interpretations; Tolstoy never gave his final interpretation.

An epigraph is often born not only to affect the reader's emotions with the author's, but also to leave him in the land of the energy of delusion.

Tolstoy didn't know what he would write.

The novel started getting printed even before it was finished.

The novel was alive and evolving. Anna Karenina was changing; the relationship between the author and his creation was transforming.

At the beginning she wasn't very striking. She was beautiful but it was an ordinary beauty. There was the landowner who was searching for paths in life, but the breadth of the future novel was still not there. At first, the work was intended to be a leisure pastime for Tolstoy. He wanted to write about something ordinary and express it in ordinary words. This is exactly what he wasn't able to do. He came to the novel after the success of *War and Peace*, but *War and Peace* had emerged from a failed attempt, *The Decembrists*.

However, as we know, things worked out.

The novel was a huge success. But that was a different work with a different title and different characters.

There is a Central Asian legend about how a great poet, living in poverty, wrote an epic (I forget the title); when he died, as the funeral procession was coming out from one of the gates, another one, a majestic one, was entering, with praise and presents from the Shah.

This would seem to be a story about belated fame.

It's remarkable, but not true; or let's say it's true, but there is another, equally true version: the poet leaves through the gates, already past his fame. He leaves in order to find refuge from what is called fame, fame that's recorded in, let's say, a newspaper; but there were no papers in Homer's times, and neither was there fame.

■

The name "Anna Karenina" appears along with a note stating that the novel is made of separate appendices. It's like a postscript to the novel. It appears in four versions.

Then the title and the epigraph appear.

"Vengeance is mine, and I will repay."

This is not an accurate quote.[107] You can't find it in the Bible.

But there is a similar line.

The passage where Anna Karenina dies, on the platform, next to the rails, is a deliberate exaggeration of death.

The old Countess Vronskaya, who in the novel is presented as a corrupt woman, someone who knows no boundaries in her silent corruption, says about Anna: ". . . She had no mercy for him, but deliberately made his ruin

---

[107] The last part of the epigraph in Russian is "az vozdam" (in the Bible it's "ya vozdam") where "az" is the name of the first Russian letter (A) in the alphabet. It was also used as the personal pronoun "I" in Old Russian. So Tolstoy introduces a Russian subjectivity to the biblical quote.

complete . . . her very death was the death of a vile woman of no religious feeling."

Anna Karenina ruined her son's career, made him quarrel with his own mother, and died on purpose, as if to spite her.

Step by step, Tolstoy's novel releases the woman whom he had considered the guiltiest party in the Scherbatsky family. It's as if Tolstoy was in love—he never loved anyone—he was choosing a bride from the Behrs family—out of loyalty, it was Lisa first, then out of flattery it was Sonya—he considered himself too old for her.

In the family novel, Tolstoy loves Anna Karenina.

Thus a man who had abandoned religion at an early age finds his own "red corner" that has nothing to do with religion.[108]

Exhaustion frees him.

He creates Anna Karenina with great difficulty; at first he thinks that she has something in common with Stiva Oblonsky, that she is *comme il faut*, that her ability to "forget" is in vain.

In his novel, the writer wanted to fall in love with Kitty, the youngest daughter of Senator Scherbatsky. In his choice between Anna Karenina and Kitty, Tolstoy chose Kitty in life, not in his dreams, and he seems to agree with Vronsky on this subject.

Although Vronsky was merely amusing himself. He gambled with love and it consumed him completely.

Tolstoy chose Kitty, but he loved Anna Karenina.

He justifies the woman.

He broadens her world.

Or, perhaps, he may have wanted to isolate himself from the world with this woman.

And we should repeat: Aleksei Maksimovich Gorky said, how indeed strange it was, she was still beautiful in her death, she traveled through

---

[108] Traditionally, the Red Corner was a place in a house for religious icons.

Rome, yet she never experienced it. He doesn't have a single line about Rome, as if she never saw it.

Kitty is a good mother; she'll have many children; she is happy to make a nest for the future; she makes jam in Levin's house, but in her own way, the way her mother taught her.

In order not to depress her husband with such thoughts, Kitty wasn't thinking at all during the wedding, she let her husband think for her; but instead she was beaming with smiles.

Sofia Andreevna was happy for the novel and its success. The heroes of "The Kreutzer Sonata" and perhaps even "The Death of Ivan Ilych" were sad because the curtains that Ivan Ilych hung in his apartment were the exact same kind and hung in the same way as they were hung by Tolstoy in his own house that he'd built; like the staircase that he had built; he built everything for Kitty, a very good house. It was a comfortable house, but Tolstoy could have built a better one.

And in this house he found a low, wide room, where he wrote on a very small table fenced with a railing to keep the sheets of paper from falling down. He wrote a book about disappointments.

Mikhoels said that even though Tolstoy rejected Shakespeare, he repeated the story of King Lear.

The family was large and the boys wanted to live separately, on their own, and the girls wanted to get married; and the people who were sharing the fruits of his great work, they felt shy and even sorry for their father. But everything was so simple.

Sofia Andreevna, a smart woman, guided her six sons through the narrow corridor of a simple life. She was convinced that there could be no other way of life—but she was kind.

She gave coffee to Aleksei Maksimovich, who came to her door almost a beggar, not having yet written anything.

She was life's inertia.

She was a vengeance that belonged to the old world. It took its revenge because one tried to conquer it by himself, alone.

Putting on his armor, taking his horse, the person wants his adversary to punish him, just as he has punished others.

■ ■ ■

He was able to resurrect Katyusha Maslova.

He studied more than a dozen books about the gentry, searching for the names of those who had left their homes, who were lost.

Aleksei, a devout person, had left his paternal home and then returned to his family unrecognizable.

And lived under the staircase.

He lived as a beggar in his own father's house, and he dreamt about how his mother cried, thinking that he was lost.

Nobody could have done anything greater than what he had done.

But all of these things weren't enough for Tolstoy.

And he showed a world, a new kind of light that can't be shown by re-telling; he was an experienced hunter, a laborer, he created characters (some of us erroneously call them "types"), and sent them out into the world so that in their multitudes they could see the world and tell him about it.

He never tried to change the world. He perceived the world in its dis-order and it seems that this was his task; he populated the world with his own children, not born of him but of his creations, and this is not supposed to contradict what I said a minute ago.

We'll say that he was unhappy; but any unhappy or successful poet, I think, would have exchanged places with him and would have taken his sorrow just in order to have his vision.

He taught how to see the world in a new light. He moved people away from the ordinary: religion, war, greed, the city; he didn't make them happy but he enabled them to see.

"I will repay."

This was his revenge for their resistance.

But while turning the world around, he was unable to get out of its rut.

Well, in a sense he did.

But then he died.

II.

The contradictions between ordinary morality and the morality of desire are already present in *The Iliad*.

When Paris escapes from Menelaus, Helen's husband, and returns to his wife, she meets him with indignation.

But Venus was protecting Paris because he had given her the golden apple.

In turn, she had given him the belt of passionate love, and Paris goes into their bedroom with his wife.

Here the collision of these two moralities provides the form of the plot.

Whereas the problem is solved in two different ways.

In the Catholic church, a priest can't have a wife.

But Paul in the Epistles says that a bishop must be "the husband of one wife."

A pastor can't remarry.

We should mention, in passing, the Pharisees.

They have been misunderstood.

They are perceived only as liars and thieves.

In reality they are the transition from an old culture to a new one.

They gave—they had to give—another, softer interpretation of the ancient laws that were already contradicting the new codes.

It's called the "pharisaic" interpretation of laws.

In Pushkin, when the husband is contemplating what to do with his wife, who has declared her betrayal—whether to act upon it or not—he is acting like a Pharisee.

The epigraph to *Anna Karenina* and its inaccuracy is connected with the fact that the Bible lives through slip-ups, it lives through various readings.

Tolstoy is a person who moves through the different epochs of moral values, he has changed the meaning of the law that's declared in that epigraph.

But he kept it, the epigraph, so as not to declare—as in a slogan—this emergence of new morals.

There is a certain connection, according to Eichenbaum, between the broken spine of Frou-Frou and Anna's death.

The connection is Tolstoy's own tragedy.

Tolstoy didn't claim that the earth spins, that the sun goes around it —or the other way around—but that workers will always be hired. He claimed his position as an upright landowner.

The analysis of Tolstoy's actions begins with the analysis of the actions of Natasha Rostova; she wants to run away from one lover to another.

He also wanted to run away to another woman, and he probably even wrote about it; her name was the Devil.

This is one of the conversations that strengthens the book.

■

We see the "energy of delusion" in love affairs, in the contradictions of Mayakovsky's, Pushkin's, Yesenin's love. No, I'm not saying this correctly. We only feel that there are contradictions, or there should be.

Only now can we understand the power of the plot in one famous painting—Jesus Christ delivering a woman.

The issue is that the epochs of moral changes don't manifest the change of moral codes in general.

Like great ice floes they collide into each other, cutting a path for Nekhlyudov, and Katyusha Maslova, who leaves with Simonson.

These ice floes can be compared to the pieces of a single broken morality.

The ice floes recur in Tolstoy's vision even earlier, that spring day when Nekhlyudov leaves Maslova at the very beginning of the novel.

This is a plot solution.

But even Tolstoy later changes this solution with the many historically unravelled testimonies of the evangelists.

And we have already quoted or will quote the words of Chekhov; he said that people still need to prove their historic accuracy—from one epoch to another.

This muddled, multi-epochal (forgive me for this word, but it's accurate, you can't put it more accurately) person, a man who earned recognition several times, recognition through the fame he was trying to achieve, who accepted being born to a high family, who accepted the new system of morals—this was Tolstoyism,[109] and it was as imprecise as dreams usually are, dreams in which the conflicting solutions of the day are unified without being coordinated.

Yeast ferments the must, turning it into wine, and during this process tears "the old wine-skin, into which one shouldn't pour the new wine," according to the Bible.

[109] Tolstoy wrote in regard to Tolstoyism in his diary in 1897: "I was glad to have had an opportunity of expressing myself and making it clear to myself that it is a great and gross mistake to talk of Tolstoyism, to seek my guidance, to ask for my solution of questions. There never has been such a thing as my teaching; there is the one eternal, universal teaching of the truth, which for me, for us, is expressed in the Gospels with particular clearness. . . . It is like rowing on a river which spreads beyond the current. So long as a man is not in the middle current, but in the calm, he has to row himself, and here he may be guided by the direction of other men's rowing. There I, too, myself rowing toward the current, was able to guide people; but the moment we have entered the current, there is no guide, and there can be none. We are all borne down by the power of the current, all of us in one direction, and those who were behind us may be ahead of us. If a man asks whither he should row, this proves that he has not yet entered the current, and that he whom he asks is a poor guide, if he was not able to bring him to the current, that is, to that condition where it is impossible to ask, because there is no sense in asking. How can I ask whither I should row, when the current bears me with irresistible force in the direction which gives me joy? People who submit to one guide, and believe and obey him, are certainly wandering in the dark, together with their guide."

■

We know that among the mammals the male inseminates the female, but among the fish the female lays the eggs and the male fertilizes the offspring that's already born.

In order to do this, the male and the female leave the ocean and scale the steep river, overcoming not only rapids, but also small waterfalls.

Then they go about their business, and when they finish spawning, they die.

That's exactly how literary schools replace one another.

I'll return to my point. The epigraph was written before the novel was ever finished or to be more accurate, even before it was conceived and written down.

One of the main themes in *The Sevastopol Sketches* is how the officers divide themselves into aristocrats and non-aristocrats. Each group is a closed circle. The bravest, most famous officers are proud when they get into the circle of the aristocrats, who consider themselves higher than the other group of officers.

The divided world is frightening because its division is false.

That's why they defend themselves so desperately.

This is the theme of Tolstoy, Thackeray, Dickens.

It's not God, it's class society that executes Anna Karenina through expulsion.

Or, let's say, the circles of hell.

The epigraph, "Vengeance is mine, and I will repay," is taken from the Bible, but it's repeated there several times and each time it's different.

The Christianity of the first centuries resulted from the social disorder of the time.

This disorder would change with the appearance of titles and names in the church hierarchy.

■

Tolstoy was a genius, but he wasn't free from the age in which he lived.

In the last chapters, Levin, who is trying to understand his rank, his place in life, understands that "... it was necessary not to lease the land, but to farm it himself."

"A hired peasant who went home during the working season because his father had died couldn't be forgiven." He knew that "workers had to be hired as cheaply as possible, but they couldn't be put into bondage for less than they were worth by advancing them money, even though this would have been very profitable. He could sell straw to the peasants during a shortage, even though he felt sorry for them ..."

And generally: "now that since his marriage he had begun confining himself more and more to living for himself he felt certain that his work was vital, even though he no longer felt any joy at the *thought* of his own activity; he saw that it was advancing much better than before, and that it kept growing more and more."

He kept cutting "into the soil more and more deeply, like a plow, so that he could no longer extricate himself without turning over the sod."

The sod of the world—the farm—conquered the dissenter.

For some time Tolstoy was able to affirm Levin, but he wasn't able to affirm himself, Lev Nikolaevich, and by plowing too deeply he ruined the sod.

Anna Karenina ends not only with Anna's death, but also with a compromise.

I'll say this once more, in different words.

Stiva Oblonsky's betrayal was pardoned. Everyone tried to understand —his children, servants, Anna Karenina. But Dolly wasn't happy; she had nowhere to go.

Anna's unfaithfulness to her husband, who was twenty years older than her, was tragic.

Anna fell under the train.

She wasn't pardoned.

In some strange way, the epigraph reinforces the difference of these two cases.

The biblical quote, "Vengeance is mine, and I will repay," was, let's say, a kind of communal justice, stoning the guilty person.

If read in its original context, the epigraph is an appeal, the assignment of the case to a new trial.

The novel contradicts its epigraph, which is why the epigraph can never be interpreted.

13

THE SHARE

It's difficult to talk about great people because they speak for themselves, as did Tolstoy.

His diary is the most coherent, lucid and truest trail of his life.

I don't think there is a single book, especially a diary, where the writer is completely objective.

But Tolstoy's life from the *Anna Karenina* period can be studied through actual documents.

The documents can be found in that room with the Sistine Madonna print, across from which are the volumes of the Brockhaus and Efron Encyclopedia from 1891.

The third volume contains the following story: we'll call it the story of plundering the Bashkir lands.

■

When Lev Nikolaevich finished *Anna Karenina*, he was happy.

He was expanding his property; he purchased a young forest for his daughters' future dowry.

The daughters would grow up and the forest would be theirs.

It was also possible to buy lands from the Bashkirs.[110]

110 Bashkir people belong to a Turkic ethnic group that settled in the lands between the north Caucasus and south Himalayas. Russian colonization led to several Bashkir uprisings in the eighteenth century.

The story, though, was complicated.

The new borders of the Bashkir free lands were drawn by natural borders. It would be as if you were standing on a mound and saying: Do you see that hill over there on the horizon? Now look to the right, do you see the mountains? Even further right there is a little creek. You can have the land in the middle.

In a short period of time, between 1876 and 1880, the Bashkir lands were all misappropriated without exception.

Lev Nikolaevich avoided buying lands directly from the Bashkirs. The robbing of Bashkir lands had begun earlier, and it's recorded as a matter of record in the notes of such an objective person as Aksakov.

Lev Nikolaevich bought lands from people who had gotten them earlier from the Bashkirs and were now reselling them.

After a while, Lev Nikolaevich rode to those lands that previously seemed to him a happy place.

But this time he was miserable.

The forty acres of land that was allotted to each Bashkir according to the new law, as it was generally understood, was excellent for farming, but too small for cattle-breeding.

Anna Karenina is a book of confession; everything in it is truer than what you'll find in newspapers and maybe even in an encyclopedia.

So the great writer, a person who is not poor, buys some Bashkir lands, but not directly from the Bashkirs; he consults with his wife about this unusually profitable deal.

His wife hesitates; she can't imagine how they would live in the steppes, without any trees.

But she eventually consents.

Lev Nikolaevich becomes a considerably big landowner.

In the novel, Anna Karenina's husband, Aleksei Aleksandrovich, is a powerful official who investigates land abuse.

This is described in the novel in such a way that even without direct references we recognize the story concerning the Bashkir lands.

Countess Lydia explains how one should talk during an important interview, she receives the minister, or perhaps he is a civil servant specially appointed by the State Council.

The thoughtful countess knows how to teach the art of debate so that the reputation of those who are close to the Ministry won't get damaged, and so that nothing really comes out of it.

Time doesn't go backwards. The tragedy of farmlands and the tragedy of sheep-grazing lands is the tragedy of mankind. It's a tragedy of land, of life in which everything has been turned upside down and nothing fits.

Lev Nikolaevich enters this history, this chain of contradictory circumstances, as a gentleman from the Tula province, as the father of a large family, a huge household, someone who has more than twenty people at his table.

■

The river flows down the hill—sometimes overflowing its banks, at other times narrowing, turning shallow.

But in fact there were two rivers, and at first it was as if they were flowing separately; then there came the time for them to unite, to mix into each other, the living soul was overfilled and then—the "Arzamas horror"—it was the tragedy of wealth, of greed, and of the conscience.

The tragedy of Lev Nikolaevich was yet to come, and meanwhile he was thinking about acquiring land for himself and the members of his family. He thought—rather paradoxically—about creating a small island of truth in the midst of the ocean of lies and violence. At the same time he wished to show the importance of peasant settlements and ownership in the borderlands.

This was supposed to be "an Iliad."

In that island of justice, the land would be rented out to the peasants for incredibly low prices, based on the model of the purchase of the Bashkir lands by Russian landowners.

But he wasn't able to realize the creation of this kind of household. He assigned it to his friend Alekseev, an honest man, but Sofia Andreevna, urged by the law of prosperity, the law of her children's preservation, about whom she used to say that she loved them "to the point of madness," ordered the lands to be rented out at the regular price.

And so Lev Nikolaevich Tolstoy became linked with evil.

The conflict that ensued was rather unexpected, but it was incomprehensible to the outside world.

What happened next?

At the time when Lev Nikolaevich had already determined to renounce his property, when he disowned the works that he'd written, there was a legislative order, but there was no actual law.

In *Dead Souls*, in the chapter about Plyushkin, Gogol wrote about how a squandering person lived, how the trees shimmered in the light that reached their roots.

That's how a squanderer would feast.

But there was a restraining order against squanderers. All the governor had to do was declare a ban against the squanderer and assign a guardian over him.

The assigned guardian was usually his wife.

Besides, there was a town mentioned by Saltykov-Schedrin—Suzdal, which today is renowned for its tourist sites.

There was a prison in that town for incorrigible schismatics and, according to popular belief, for those who squandered. Golovleva, the housekeeper, used to threaten the disobedient children with that prison in Suzdal.

These are not tales, it really happened; it was up to the governor to decide who should be the guardian and who should be the ward, whereas the squanderer had no rights whatsoever.

He had no rights, including the decision of how his inheritance should be divided.

There is a line in the Bible: "A man's enemy will be a member of his own household."

A person negotiates peace with his family against his will or through weakness, and this doesn't come easily.

■

The newspapers wrote about Lev Nikolaevich's life in their usual liberally tolerant fashion, but once there was an article that, according to his older sons, Lev Nikolaevich was helping the peasants with his own manual labor. In legal language this meant that Tolstoy was not a squanderer. He was simply helping the poor peasants to prop up the collapsing wall of a hut. A person taking part in this is not a squanderer.

And the children of this great man gathered to divide the cattle, carriages and land.

They divided everything equally among themselves.

While this was going on, the great dreamer and author of great books was probably sitting in his study, the room in which he wrote, the one in the basement with the high window and nothing on the walls.

As a result, Tolstoy used to say that he felt sorry and ashamed for ruining the lives of his children by turning them into his heirs.

Yes, they gambled, they played cards and wildly caroused.

Instead of a simple troika, one of his youngest sons, Mikhail, would harness his sled with several pairs of horses.

And he would parade—flying over those roads covered with snow.

■

This style of living off your father's inheritance, this unheroic path, wasn't something new.

In Russia there existed a sect of runaways. A person, usually a merchant, knowing his own sins, gave shelter to these people who ran away from either their own wealth or their importunate heirs. A man of a unique order leaves everything to have the right to enter God's kingdom, the gates of which are as narrow for the rich as the eye of a needle.

He returns as an old man, taking refuge in the cellar of his own house or somewhere under the staircase.

The family reports to the police that their father is lost. After about three years they come of age for their inheritance. But how does their father, who is thought to be dead, live?—Nobody knows.

By the way, among the saints who were revered long before the times of the Byzantine Empire, Aleksei was known as a devout person. He left home, then returned as a beggar, unrecognized, and lived there, underneath the staircase, until he died.

His parents mourned him.

The church believed him.

■

Anna Karenina was coming to an end, but nothing really ended.

Everything in the house of the Romanovs was going in its usual way.

Safeguarding the household became a priority.

Let's refer, one more time, to the conversation between the Levin brothers.

Nikolai's words to Konstantin:

—you missed the most important part.

The conversation is about property.

The question that was raised by Tolstoy himself

—in the room with a candle—

—the Arzamas horror—

—by death itself—

—but it wasn't death, it was life.

Lev Nikolaevich chose not to resist.[111]

And so.

Property became a type of evil.

Everyone used to say, including Tolstoy: "my land."

But it turns out one ought to say:

[111] In one of his letters from 1890, Tolstoy deliberates on non-resistance to evil: "All these apparently complicated propositions about non-resistance to evil and the objections to it reduce themselves to this, that instead of understanding, as it is written, 'Do not resist evil or violence with evil or violence,' instead they understand it to say (I even think intentionally), 'Do not resist evil, that is, be indulgent to evil, be indifferent to it.'"

—"we are of the land."

It was as if the division of property was like the spread of evil, a disregard of those who were still alive.

By their own children.

Tolstoy was deeply repenting that he had made his children wealthy, prosperous people; as if he gave birth to them improperly—the second time. Incorrectly guiding them into life for the second time.

They drew lots. All in all, there were nine lots. The land was evaluated at 550,000 rubles, a very low price.

Sergei Lvovich got just over 2,000 acres of land in the Nikolsko-Vyazemsky village, on condition that in the course of the year he would pay his sister Tatyana Lvovna a sum of 28,000 rubles, and within fifteen years a sum of 55,000 rubles to his mother plus an annual interest of four percent.

Tatyana Lvovna got Ovsyannikovo for 38,000 rubles.

Ilya Lvovich got Grinevka and about 1,000 acres in the Nikolsko-Vyazemsky village.

Lev Lvovich got the house in Moscow, a little over 1,000 acres of the Samara estate and 5,000 rubles payable over the course of five years.

Mikhail, who was still a student, got 5,700 acres in the Samara estate, but was to pay 5,000 rubles to his brother Lev.

Andrei and Aleksandra got 11,000 acres of the Samara estate, and they were also supposed to pay Tatyana Lvovna for their portion.

Ivan got 1,000 acres of Yasnaya Polyana.

Sofia Andreevna got the rest of Yasnaya Polyana, and they were supposed to pay up the remainder.

This took place on April 16, 1891.

Lev Nikolaevich renounced the royalties from his works.

He had written his favorite story, "A Prisoner in the Caucasus," that was unlike Pushkin's romanticized Caucasus.

"A Prisoner in the Caucasus" was a transition to *Hadji Murad*.

It was the result of all his doubts from *The Sevastopol Sketches*.

And also, from the not-yet-written *Hadji Murad*.

But let's move on to the woman.

The question of guilt.

Tolstoy began to analyze his youth.

He gave it different meanings.

To Biryukov's[112] rhetorical question whether it was a careless life, Tolstoy replied—"No."

He wanted to write about how a man saves a woman, instead he wrote about how she refuses that and in turn saves him.

And how she leaves for the great road, the end of which he understood very well.

But he couldn't understand the cause of the workers' discontent.

He couldn't understand why they had come to the Winter Palace even though they had boots and drank tea every day.

It seemed as though they lived better than the peasants.

■

One had to notice how people changed, how they got ruined as they passed through Yasnaya Polyana.

How the situation never got better, it only got worse.

This was a man of great conscience and great courage.

He knew what typhus was from living in the barracks in Sevastopol.

He resolved to fight the famine, to stand up to the great poverty and suffering.

During this period, the famine in Russia had spread all across the country. Crop failure came at the time when the family was dividing the inheritance of a man who was still alive.

[112] Pavel Biryukov (1860–1931), known as "Posha," was introduced to Tolstoy in 1884 by Chertkov, and soon became one of Tolstoy's faithful followers. He helped organize the exodus of the Dukhobors, and later, in collaboration with Tolstoy, wrote memoirs about the great writer and his life.

Lev Nikolaevich records in his diary: "I don't sleep well, and I'm utterly repulsive to myself."

The subsistence of a person who will be driven away from the system, who will be beaten, he will be beaten with a thousand rods—this is not a blessing.

A blessing would be the destruction of this kind of life.

Lev Nikolaevich consulted with his friend, Raevsky.

Raevsky was a man of legendary strength. He could lift up a wagon fully loaded with bread.

The friends were talking about bread.

Lev Nikolaevich gave the following instructions: "Choose a place in the midst of the most famished villages, and store in these places flour, bran, potatoes, cabbage, beets. Put them in the middle of the village. Be prepared."

Lev Nikolaevich also gave a detailed proposal in the newspaper: how to prepare forage for the cattle, because if they let the horses die, they would have another wave of famine. That's when Chekhov said that Lev Nikolaevich could have been the minister of provisions, for he thought in such a straightforward and simple way.

Lev Nikolaevich, his daughter Tatyana, Raevsky and many others went around, checked, made arrangements and organized soup kitchens. This was a difficult task.

Raevsky died from a cold: there was no firewood in the famished villages.

Lev Nikolaevich survived.

But that is another story.

14

RESURRECTION

If Sancho Panza isn't Tolstoy's favorite hero, then at least he represents the absence of the main hero.

When Chekhov wrote "The Darling," Tolstoy read this fascinating non-moralizing story and said that the Darling had to become as popular a character as Sancho Panza.

Why am I referring to the story's non-moralizing quality?

One could have written on the lock of her door of her small house:

—Vengeance is mine, and I will repay—her union with the veterinarian was not blessed by the church.

But she loved the little schoolboy the most, that same boy whom Chekhov loved, too.

Chekhov didn't have children.

And in his house on Sadovaya Street he kept this boy as a guest, who raved, made mistakes of the simplest things—but he was remarkable because he represented life.

Anna Karenina had children, and so did almost all of Tolstoy's characters.

But it's only in "The Death of Ivan Ilych" that the boy appears. He is still young, with circles around his eyes, the origins of which Tolstoy knew very well because he also had the same kind of circles of childhood vice in his boyhood. Because he wasn't born an angel and he didn't have the bravado of Rousseau's frankness at that time, before the revolution that hadn't happened yet, but that gnawed at the roots of what was allowed and what wasn't.

The boy cries for his father who is dying, and the latter feels that this is some kind of forgiveness.

But let's return to Sancho Panza with whom, it seems, I accidentally but appropriately started this chapter.

Sancho Panza said that he would have liked to have the answer first and then the riddle.

He has no interest in searching, he doesn't want to know the excitement of making a mistake.

He doesn't realize that he has already undergone this effort many times before: the effort of incorporating both truth and falsehood into his life. In the meantime, Sancho Panza's whole existence is rooted in the fact that he believes and doesn't believe in Don Quixote.

This is the nature of his poetics.

He knows that his master gets beaten, he sees that miracles don't happen, he even sees that when he is tossed in a blanket for not paying the bill at the inn, Don Quixote, the great Don Quixote, stands behind the fence and doesn't help his servant.

But the excitement of life is in making mistakes and then correcting them.

A child throws objects from the table on the ground, some of which break and others don't.

This is how knowledge is gained.

And how sacred to me is the memory of a two-year old boy who ran back to me from the street, terribly upset (they didn't even have the time to take off his little hat), and said:

—Papa, it turns out that the horses don't have horns—

he had discovered something.

That's the quintessence of art—it's a multitude of discoveries, a multitude of wanderings—it has numerous steps.

And what we call a reversal is something like a staircase that goes up and down.

Tolstoy wasn't able to completely figure out the source of Anna Karenina's unhappiness.

He simply followed the woman, who was an aristocrat, and had been unfaithful to her husband. This was the reversal of her life:

—they didn't stone her (this was the ancient biblical method of fighting against female infidelity; nobody stoned men for polygamy).

According to rumors, I think there was a place near the Temple of Solomon where women consoled the pilgrim men.

But then again, that was insinuated by Rozanov, and he wasn't a scholar.[113]

There is a part in *Anna Karenina* that I'd like to bring to your attention.

The woman is the wife of a man who is twenty years older than she; he is preoccupied with state affairs, bureaucratic battles with ministries, and he is less occupied with the woman, which is really not his fault.

In other words, she had nothing to talk about with him in bed.

And so his faithful wife, who was afraid of the "shadows" that followed her, was beautiful, and at the very beginning of the novel it is made clear that women who are followed by "shadows" end badly.

But it was also said in the same novel that the woman must be proud when someone makes a proposal to her.

■

The woman has fallen and nobody is saying anything bad about her, yet she feels tormented.

Her lover asks her: Are you unhappy? And she replies—no, I am not unhappy, I'm like a person, a hungry person who is given something to eat.

[113] Vasili Rozanov (1856–1919) was one of the most controversial Russian writers and philosophers of the pre-revolutionary epoch. Shklovsky wrote an excellent analysis of Rozanov's work (*Solitaria* and *Fallen Leaves*) in his *Theory of Prose* under the title "Literature without a Plot."

She is ashamed, perhaps she even knows that it's the end, but nevertheless she eats—this desire, a woman's desire, is not described directly, but it has been talked about profusely in novels about men.

Her feelings are described with a frankness that doesn't exist in any of the most explicit romance novels.

Tolstoy explored the notion of marriage—one of its notions—to the core.

Chekhov used to say that a woman gained an entrance into life—the method of relating to life—from a man.

. . . We know that the children of nomads were shepherds.

And only a few of them, like Joseph in the Bible, were their fathers' favorites.

This is a simple truth, and it seems, there is no need to stone anyone.

It's the truth about a person who is hungry.

It's a bitter truth because it was never really expressed completely.

In his book, Boccaccio includes a story about an educated judge, an old man who had married a young woman. Nothing good could come out of this, and I already mentioned how things ended.

Tolstoy said that Anna married Karenin under the best of omens.

The best husband in the whole province.

And it's impossible to forget her son, Anna loves him more than her daughter from Vronsky.

When the novel begins, Seryozha has already been her replacement for happiness for eight years.

In her son she loves the man whom she hates, and then she pushes her deceived and ridiculed husband aside; she pushes him aside as one would push aside a plate after dinner.

That's how in Boccaccio, a pirate takes the disappointed woman prisoner and turns her into his wife, I'm talking about the wife of the judge; the husband wants to buy her back, but she refuses to return.

The husband tells her about shame, and she replies that he should have thought about that before; she says that she's not interested in his holidays but is now occupied with the joyful work of what Boccaccio calls "threshing wool" with her new husband.

As a person of his times, a realistic person, Boccaccio says that the husband dies, the lovers get married and everything ends well.

But let's return to the main theme of many peoples' lives, which is also the theme of this book. It feels easy to write and I'll finish it soon—yet it has always seemed so.

It has taken me ten years, and now two more.

But art lives through impediments, through the concentration of multiple interpretations, and what we call a reversal is the movement toward an unknown truth.

■

The plays of Aeschylus, I mean *Orestes*, and the drama of Hamlet, and the drama of another young poet from Russia—Treplev, the dramas of other poets whom we've known and seen die in real life, the dramas of various generations—it all comes from experience gained from life, and originality of designing a novel. It's the art of creating a perception of life.

And a riddle is the seed of a work of art that has been sewn and sprouted in the wrong place.

■

This is how we've finally gotten back to the road that we left in order to look at some of the surroundings, the road that none of us can leave—we can never leave it.

And no one can disagree that this is a difficult and often winding road, but only in the sense that it's very easy to get lost on it.

Anna Karenina, like Katyusha Maslova, is a heroine on thorny paths.

It's the path of fate and its dangers.

It has unique and colossal railroad stations with countless tracks.

But Katyusha Maslova, as we shall see in the following pages, creates a different kind of life, a different kind of love and—had this word not been ruined to its core, I'd say—a model of life. Katyusha is as fascinating as the future, she moves, with ease and at the same time with difficulty, like an airplane moving on its wheels on the ground, trembling, and she rises in her flight to a new level of morality.

II.

Time erases us, like the teacher in an elementary school erases an incorrectly solved problem on the blackboard with his chalk; that's exactly how time erases generations.

I became acquainted, rather accidentally, with the old retired senator— Anatoli Fyodorovich Koni.

A certain publisher who tried to restore the former Russian empire used to buy manuscripts from writers and signed contracts for exclusive rights. The contracts were printed according to the Soviet formatting, but they were stamped with the old imperial emblem.

These were hefty contracts.

The contract stated that if there occurred any disagreements, the matter would be resolved through a court of honor.

And so once there was a dispute and they invited Koni to preside over the court.

On another occasion, Koni had presided over the court where Vera Zasulich[114] was being tried; she had shot Trepov for beating a political prisoner.

The Tsar's court, the court of jurors presided over by the already-not-

---

[114] Vera Zasulich (1851–1919), a socialist revolutionary, who in 1878 shot and wounded General Fyodor Trepov, the military governor of St. Petersburg, after he had ordered the flogging of the revolutionary Arkhip Yemelyanov. At her trial a sympathetic jury found her not guilty. Fleeing before she could be rearrested and retried, she became a hero to the Russian Radical Populists.

so-young-but-famous defense lawyer Koni, decided that Vera Zasulich was not guilty.

This court proceeding left a very powerful impression on Tolstoy. He corresponded with his aunt on this subject and said that it was a sign that the times were changing.

Now in front of old Koni lay a minor complicated case.

His appointment as chairman of the court had ended his career, to which he reacted very calmly, by becoming a littérateur.

He wrote excellent memoirs and a famous article on Friedrich Joseph Haass, "the holy doctor of Moscow," who worked to improve the conditions of prisoners, and who wore their chains and walked in them in his room to feel what it meant to be in shackles.

Koni examined the case and asked the publisher:

—Your agreement says that the matter will be taken up by the court of honor. But the problem is that your documents are addressed simultaneously to two governments—the Soviet and the Tsar's. You have a Soviet form and an imperial emblem. I suggest that you appeal to either one of these governments to which your documents are inadvertently addressed —either the Tsar's, or the Soviet—and submit your carefully drafted agreements.

I remember this man very well, how he walked along the Nevsky Prospect without slouching, just merely leaning on his stick; he knew that times were changing, that the written or printed word was being reinforced by a new concept—*film*.

He saw the times changing.

In the meantime, Koni was founding the Institute of the Live Word.

As far as I remember the institute was on the Nevsky Prospect, but I can't remember the building's number.

Many people remembered and respected Koni.

Tolstoy knew Koni very well and often asked for his help to intercede on behalf of someone, to help prove that the case was illegitimate for its times—or all times, I should add.

Once Koni was visiting Tolstoy in Yasnaya Polyana.

This was in June 1887.

He told Tolstoy about a peculiar case.

When he was a prosecutor in St. Petersburg, a young Finn came to him asking for help.

His father owned a big estate in Finland, a part of which was being leased. One of the leaseholders died and left a daughter. The old landlord took the girl under his roof and raised her. First she lived in the nursery, then in the local convent.

Later she became a chambermaid.

But she didn't lose her charm, her knowledge of French, and the son who had returned from the university into his father's estate somehow, accidentally, thinking "everybody does it," seduced the girl.

Her name was Rosalie.

Some time passed.

The student, who had become a respected man, was appointed as a juror.

They were trying a prostitute who had stolen a hundred rubles from a client.

The juror, who was much older, recognized Rosalie. This was a worn, trampled woman.

He had his own particular views on morals.

He recalled his love for this girl, remembered his own father and hers.

And the Finn decided to marry this woman to relieve his guilt.

He approached the prosecutor asking for a way to set her free.

Koni, a prominent and honest person in his own way, warned him:

—You are right, of course.

—But your life and hers have gone in two different directions.

—It is possible that she has children.

—I think that you may have rushed in your decision.

—Maybe it's better to help her with money.

The young man replied in his calm Finnish manner:

—I gave presents not only to the head of the prison, but also to all the convicts, and, of course, first—to her. She was crying. They were congratulating her. I gave her my word. Asked for her forgiveness.

Koni went on with his story.

There was a bad case of typhus in the prison.

And Rosalie died.

He was telling this story to Tolstoy who had once seduced a chambermaid in his brother's house.

Back then Tolstoy was publishing not only his novels but also, with the help of Sytin, printing a series of small moralizing books—they were stories about great people.

Chertkov was in charge of the printing.

He was hard-pressed financially.

So he would only take free manuscripts.

—You should write a story about this young man, Anatoli Fyodorovich —Tolstoy told Koni.—You are an excellent rhetorician, everyone respects you, you know how to prove what's good and what's evil.

Koni tried.

It didn't work out.

Then Tolstoy asked if he could have the story and started writing himself.

He made many attempts.

Trying to find ways comprehensible for the reader.

He always referred to the novel as "Koni's story."

The work went on until December 1899.

Tolstoy was not satisfied with the work. He used to say:

—This isn't my story, it was given to me.

What exactly wasn't working?

The good-natured, sensible Koni, heroic in his own way, thought that everything was as it was supposed to be.

The woman experienced happiness, she saw the man whom she once loved, fell in love with him again, forgave him.

He expiated his offense.

She died.

He avoided the bitter consequences of the act that he was about to commit.

Koni's story portrayed a strange kind of happiness.

How instead of happiness, it is death that comes to certain people, wiping them from the blackboard of memory with a wet cloth.

Lev Nikolaevich was writing a novel in which he kept getting lost in his solutions, in the search for a solution that would be reasonable to him.

. . . The writing of the book took ten years, the subject kept getting more complicated.

The figure of the calm Finn—he was calmly headed toward his heroic deed—was replaced by another figure, a favorite of Chertkov, a composed aristocrat who had to endure his mother's opposition, then do something about the woman, adopt a "simple lifestyle," go to England to escape persecution and there write books about landownership.

He was supposed to prove that Henry George's theory—the introduction of a single-tax system that would force the landowner to renounce his land—was a worthwhile idea.

Lev Nikolaevich had his own solution—industry, ships, trains, the cars that at the time were already passing by Yasnaya Polyana, all of this seemed to him a mistake that would soon be rejected by mankind for moral reasons.

These had no relation to the way of life that the great Tolstoy had envisaged.

He kept writing; he was writing a good book. Little by little he cleared the student's guilt; he said how he was in love, how good it was for both of them to be in love.

How they played hide-and-seek.

How they weren't guilty in front of anyone.

He wrote remarkably about the purification of a person who in the act of love felt the sanctifying power of truth.

He imagined how the river flowed underneath the ice.

The river cracked the ice.

The moon hung above the drifting ice, promising either the end of the world or the beginning of spring.

He wrote how in the man's arms the girl said: No, no. Meanwhile her body said: Yes.

Sofia Andreevna, a shrewd woman and someone who understood the vast world of her husband, wrote in her diary how it pained her to see Lev Nikolaevich describing this affair with a particular relish, as though an epicure savoring food. The main character had already been turned into an officer. Most of all, she was upset by the fact that this hero was marrying a prostitute.

The novel's design kept changing as it was being written.

There is a Russian saying: to get lost amid three pine trees.

This ingenious man roamed in vast forests where wide rivers flow.

The little stream over which the moon hung, the stream that was covered with crackling ice, in the novel grew into a great Siberian river, along which the ice moved scraping the banks.

The girl from the novel falls in love with a man with an immortal kind of love, she doesn't want to ruin his life.

Her love is so strong that she changes everything, changes all her previous decisions made before the romance.

In the book, she leaves the man. She already has a part of Tolstoy's experience—she has experienced pre-revolutionary Russia.

Under Nekhlyudov's protection, the ex-prostitute leaves in a train compartment with political prisoners.

With her half-peasant insight she realizes that the people had been badly hurt and were paying for someone else's mistakes.

In order to show this in the novel, it was necessary to introduce a fictional time-frame.

"The sun must stop, and the moon must not move," Jesus Navin had once said during an unfinished battle.

It had worked in the Bible.

But had this happened in reality, there would have been a universal catastrophe.

In literature, however, it's necessary to change time, to slow it down or speed it up.

Time was necessary in order to test Nekhlyudov's decision.

Tolstoy created a construction equal to his own strength.

He devised an impeded time-frame, chaos in a process of punishing someone.

The members of the jury felt sorry for the woman, but somehow made a mistake in their sentence.

They did a bad job of formulating an answer to the question about the woman's guilt, how was she guilty and how was she not guilty.

They wanted to help the woman.

She still had that same attractiveness for which one can't blame a person. She preserved the same look of Katyusha Maslova that Tolstoy remembered vividly and Sofia Andreevna hated so much, even though she never saw it.

The case was transferred to a court of new hearing. The Senate.

Now it was necessary to pass through various court hearings; the novel had to be expanded.

The romance novel obtained not embellishments but paths for walking on the court steps.

It roamed and searched for the truth.

Like the Neva in Pushkin—at the foot of the prison doors of the Fortress of Peter and Paul:

As suitors beat in supplication
Unheeded at a judge's door.

The search for a simple truth, the search for true topographies of life, the search for true justice.

After all, the Neva wasn't guilty before Peter, just as Peter wasn't guilty of anything before the Neva.

Time revises, time re-examines everything.

And Tolstoy himself passed along the paths of possibility—this is the clearest, most pure energy of delusion, because this is the energy of the search for truth.

Natasha Rostova could have been happy even without Pierre Bezukhov.

She lived in the land of the happy.

Katyusha Maslova could barely exist.

Tolstoy was searching for her path.

■

Lev Nikolaevich Tolstoy's school was located in the left wing, as if cut off from other constructions; this stone wing was separated from the other wing—today, the trees have grown much taller than the buildings.

There were many different teachers there.

Some of them were students who had organized "revolts."[115]

They were detained, though not for long.

Then released on one of the Tsar's holidays, since they were "not posing a serious threat."

Among them was a student of the great Fyodorov, the man who wrote *The Philosophy of a Common Task*.

People live and then die.

How does one repay those for what they have suffered?

Heaven, as Mark Twain had already guessed, was a boring place. It was overcrowded.

[115] The Russian government had introduced tuition fees and compulsory matriculation cards in the 1850s, which resulted in revolts and disturbances in St. Petersburg and Moscow. Police arrested some of the mutinous students, others were expelled from the university and Tolstoy offered teaching jobs at his school to several Moscow students.

In *The Brothers Karamazov*, Dostoevsky or the Grand Inquisitor says that only a few people will be saved, but what about the ones who are guilty only by having been born?

The Grand Inquisitor was hinting at the hypocrisy in the Church.

Bartering for the grace that's held in the priest's hand could be absolved either with a heroic deed or money.

The Church took on the responsibility of the cleansing sins like a teacher washes away the wrongly solved problem from the blackboard.

But this was not a solution.

Fyodorov suggested that the dead should be resurrected.

And they should be given a new kind of life, immortality.

This immortality was new.

The Bible didn't recognize the immortality of the soul.

It only recognized the immortality of a race.

But in order to make all of mankind happy, since the earth was too crowded—it was necessary to create settlements at least on the closest planets.

Fyodorov was a librarian in an old marvelous library, which became the foundation for the present library named after Lenin—he was a librarian, a bibliophile, a monk of the new order, who used to say that the earth was too crowded for mankind.

This man's student taught in Tolstoy's school, where the little pupils behaved as though they were Cossacks from the Terek.

And so this man—Simonson (Petersen, in Tolstoy's school)—who had a Finnish name because he, the literary prototype (as they say in bad books), was a Finn on whose estate a love story had developed and then the girl was forsaken—so this Simonson who believed that the whole world was alive, that the world could be resettled, falls in love with Katyusha Maslova in front of the astonished prisoners.

She was already changing in the company of a woman who despite her mistakes in the perception of history, nevertheless, loved mankind.

When Lev Nikolaevich realized that he had gotten deluded in the draft of his novel, that the woman was the light itself, and the rest were her shadows;

when he told his wife:

—I changed my mind, Nekhlyudov won't marry Katyusha. His wife rejoiced—of course he won't marry her.

But she didn't know that the right to Resurrection had been passed from the gentleman to the prostitute; and she also didn't notice how Katyusha is resurrected with a wide halo of people who loved her unconditionally.

The tragedy had been acquitted.

It was as if it had been corrected.

This was a new kind of truth.

On the great judgement day in *Resurrection*, where the clergy was not invited, where no one swore to tell the truth, on this day grief was acquitted, and what brought people out of their grief was not a poet or even a writer, but truth itself.

At this time, Katyusha Maslova had already refused Nekhlyudov.

He didn't understand this immediately, but the woman prisoner, Marya Pavlovna, told him that had Katyusha gone with him, her fall would have been worse than what she had experienced in the houses of suffering.

Katyusha Maslova became unsociable.

She became arrogant.

Meanwhile Nekhlyudov at this time was in the houses of people from his own circle, they understood him, because they saw that this eccentric man wasn't a mere gentleman, but he also belonged to the aristocracy and was very wealthy.

They forgave him his eccentricities—his visits to the train compartments for political prisoners.

Simonson really loved Katyusha Maslova. He wasn't seeking forgiveness.

He resurrected the kind of love that everyone believed in.

The immense depth of the novel became more or less understandable.

■

But in order to take the halo off Nekhlyudov, it was necessary to show another guilty person juxtaposed with him.

Some peasant named Taras, whose family needed another worker, married a very young girl. She was yet incapable of falling in love. Taras's love seemed offensive to her.

The girl then poisoned him.

The case reached the court.

Life with Taras went on.

She fell in love with him.

I forgot to mention, she poisoned him slowly.

This tragedy was real, something of which great Dante didn't know and couldn't possibly conceive.

Taras was able to protect the woman from the inmates by force, pushing them with his wide chest.

He went with her to the labor camps.

His heroic deed overshadows or half-overshadows Nekhlyudov's somewhat eccentric deed.

■

In *Hadji Murad*, in the Caucasus, the Chechen says: the rope should be long, the speech—short.

I should keep my speech short.

Katyusha Maslova refused Nekhlyudov.

He went back, they took him across the river back into the country where he had an estate, a house and shirts with golden cuff links, and a bride who treated him well.

The ominous Siberian ice floats between him and Katyusha Maslova, the ice floes pass one after another from the far mountains into the ocean, an indestructible line.

The heroic deed is not assigned to you, Nekhlyudov, and it's not you who will be resurrected.

The rope should be long, the speech—short.

My old friend and linguist Yevgeni Polivanov, who died a long time ago, had once lived in Japan. He was studying the Japanese language.

He lived an extraordinary life.

He was the student of the great philologist Baudouin de Courtenay. And himself was a great linguist.

Only two of his books were published, posthumously.

But what he wrote will remain—in stone, engraved with stone letters, you can even touch them.

And he told me that in Japan, of course, there existed many kinds of love:

—love that's one of a kind

—love that's like a game

—love that grows dull

—love like ours

—or, perhaps, different.

And we do not love with the same kind of love that Homer's characters once did.

Someone wrote an opera, and Polivanov sang me an aria from it:

Ra-ra-a-a . . . Oh, sweet Katyusha, the sun will set . . .

And this opera had reached the distant shores of Japan—the fishermen would sing it.

Among the various books in Japan and among the various words in the lives of the Japanese there emerged a Russian word—*lyubov*—love.

And it was defined as the feeling that Katyusha Maslova had for Nekhlyudov.

Now I have finally finished talking about Katyusha Maslova and her resurrection.

. . . Let's remember Mayakovsky.

He died when he was still very young.

But how many times has he been resurrected in his own poems, experiencing hundreds of regenerations in the old world. He walked along the pathways of a zoo and thought how the woman whom he loved would come, they would meet again, even if he wouldn't beckon her back.

Mayakovsky dreamed about resurrection.

He had so many poems that he tried to empty his pockets, burn the drafts.

That was a mistake.

Pushkin kept some fragments from his drafts, as if knowing that seeds are almost immortal; anyway, they are tougher than us.

Of course, there is another end to *Resurrection*; it's conventional, like the old habit of crossing yourself when passing by a church.

The evangelical ending.

Resurrection begins and ends with passages from the Gospels. The quotes are there as if to fill in every description, as if to foretell the resurrection as a religious resurrection.

Chekhov who understood literature, said that Tolstoy, by citing passages from the Gospels instead of writing an ending, must have been convinced beforehand about the idea of the complete truthfulness of the Gospels.

To our grief, we should mention that *Crime and Punishment* ends in a similar way, thus covering up the true suffering of crime.

Raskolnikov goes to prison. And together with his companion, Sonya, who once was a prostitute and who is somehow identical to or seems to have an identical life with Katyusha Maslova, they read from the Gospels, and Dostoevsky promises to write about them in another book.

But this book, like the book about Nekhlyudov's life, was never written.

Had it been written, it would have disappointed us.

We shouldn't forget Chertkov.

Tolstoy had devised a plan.

At some level, Nekhlyudov was Chertkov's student; meanwhile the main similarity of Nekhlyudov with Chertkov was that he, too, had a skeleton, without which no one can move.

In his uncertainty regarding the end, in his attempt to create an ending, Tolstoy thought: Nekhlyudov, like Chertkov, will become a publisher in England. He knows English. He will work on the land and take care of the household based on the teachings of Henry George.

And Katyusha will take care of the garden.

This was like a sketch for a sketch.

■

What was Tolstoy's discovery in *Anna Karenina*?

He doesn't hide in his great book the fact that a woman has the right to desire just as a man does.

She may desire, love, and out of love leave the one whom she loves, go away from him into the middle of nowhere with the student of the great fantasist Fyodorov, and then become Katyusha Maslova.

A woman of grand inspiration, whom Tolstoy didn't resurrect because she hadn't died; she was always filled with love.

Tolstoy belonged to his own times; he listened to Chertkov's literary advice and fortunately never followed it.

In ancient literature, the man would rescue the woman. He would give her "the world" and his life.

Tolstoy told about this world—and to whom the right of giving belongs—in a different manner.

What is it that I'm trying to say in my short analysis of *Resurrection*?

I want to point out a moral turning point in art, a change in representation that is expressed through many divergences.

It's as if mankind searches for a new moral path by groping.

. . . This love is what Katyusha feels toward Nekhlyudov . . .

I'd like to state that the concept of love naturally wasn't created by literature, but it was perceived through literature.

Mejnun, the Arab madman, followed the girl he loved.

He followed her when in the whole world he had nothing else but a dog from the same street where the woman he loved lived, and that was his best companion.

He was one of the first selfless lovers. Krachkovsky[116] wrote about this. He was searching for Mejnun's predecessor in various corners of Arab culture and was never able to find anything.

He didn't find anything because Mejnun had introduced a new kind of moral construction.

But the madman Mejnun is the equal of Romeo, who proudly declared that none of the world's philosophies could ever replace his Juliet.

Now I will return again to Boccaccio's stories. Let's take a new look at the story of the fourth day. When the husband found out that his wife had a lover, he killed him and tore his heart from his chest.

He then ordered that the heart be prepared for dinner and served the dish to his wife on an ordinary plate.

After the wife had eaten the heart of her lover, the husband asked whether she enjoyed the meal.

—Very delicious—she replied.

Then the husband revealed the truth.

The woman was standing by the tower window.

Without turning around, she said to her husband:

—God forbid that any other food should pass my lips now that I have partaken of such an excellent meal—and she jumped out of the window.

This is an attempt to change one's place on the map of morals.

Mankind gropes its way in the search for a new moral path.

---

[116] Ignati Krachkovsky (1883–1951), philologist and scholar of Russian-Arabic comparative literature.

15

"STRIDER"

Talking horses already existed in Homer.

So Strider belongs to a very long literary history.

The great book by Jonathan Swift, *Gulliver's Travels*, is based on a sharp and exact description of the differences between the people the traveler sees.

He sees the Lilliputians and transfers to them the morals and desires of the Englishmen from Swift's times, and those desires turn into something insignificant.

He sees the giants and tells them about the government plans of the English nobility and they treat the idea of war with firearms with great contempt and indignation.

Then he sees horses.

The horses have their own morals, their own way of life that excludes ownership and hypocrisy.

This excellent book is, nonetheless, restricted to its times, the topics of the day.

Strider clearly belongs to and has inherited the philosophy of Swift's horses.

We should add here that according to Swift, the name of this country, Houyhnhnms, means *horse*; etymologically it means *nature's perfection*.

But Strider is much grander in his meaning compared to all of Swift's heroes, including all the heroes in the land of the horses.

But let's think in terms of people.

Count Vronsky originally had a different last name in *Anna Karenina* and he looked different.

He was a Cossack officer, young and strong, his grandeur was in the way he wore a ring on his left ear. Apparently according to the Cossack custom. This is only an attempt to show Vronsky's background, a man of Anna Karenina's circle, but at the same time slightly different, a Cossack.

Then Vronsky appears at the station, near the train that arrived in Moscow from St. Petersburg. He is a young, handsome, distinguished officer.

Vronsky is good-looking and he is rich.

His wealth is newly acquired. The origins of that wealth are perhaps connected to the person whom we see as a dry, hunched, but well-mannered old woman.

Her son treats her conventionally with great politeness.

He grew up almost without a family.

He was brought up in the Pazhesky army corps. Then in an aristocratic regiment where they loved him.

He had devised a concrete plan on how to live.

He mustn't lie to men.

He could lie to women.

Debts had to be paid.

But it was all right to pay the tailor later.

Lev Nikolaevich paid the tailor who made his suit for the trip to the Caucasus after ten years.

For Vronsky—everything is the way it's supposed to be.

Vronsky has a friend, Serpukhovskoy.

A general who was promoted to a higher military rank.

He patronizes Vronsky and tries to save him from Anna Karenina.

Yes, he must love and have a high-society liaison; Vronsky's mother agrees with this.

But he mustn't complicate his life.

Vronsky in his development is just as we see him—we see him as a friend, as the lover of Anna Karenina—he knows how to negotiate, knows how not to give in, and how to stick to a price when selling bread.

The whole world is charted for him.

He knows his proper place.

A good place in a game of chess. And on the board of conventional life he knows exactly what moves he is allowed to make.

Vronsky is a good rider; one can say that he is very attached to his horse.

Serpukhovskoy is a different kind of person, he has already been to war, he knows what military work entails, and even though he is very good friends with Vronsky, and perhaps even values their friendship, he is a person with a much wider connection to life.

He offers Vronsky a career.

Serpukhovskoy and the friendship with him—this is what Vronsky sacrifices when he announces his liaison with the wife of a very high dignitary of that time.

Let's leave Vronsky and move on to other things.

■

In a later version of "Strider," Serpukhovskoy, or his actual name, resurfaces in a different form.

Serpukhovskoy is resurrected at a different age.

Here, he is forty years old, fat, bald-headed, with heavy mustache and whiskers.

Apparently he was good-looking before.

Now he has sunk physically and morally.

At any rate, the name Serpukhovskoy, the name of a well-known young military officer, who was also a connoisseur of horses, and Vronsky's friend higher in rank, is resurrected in "Strider."

"Strider" is a difficult work that was written over a long period of time.

It was written between 1861–63.

And then, resurrected, it reappeared on Tolstoy's writing desk in 1885.

This manuscript had its own family history in Tolstoy's home.

Lev Nikolaevich renounced his rights to his own works, written during the epoch of his literary fame, even before what later became known as Tolstoyism.

First introduced in 1861, "Strider" and its royalties belonged to Sofia Andreevna.[117]

The "Strider" of 1885 belonged to everyone.

The book originated from the stable, from the story of a horse.

This satirical story written in the manner of Swift is about human ignorance.

Strider is a horse of the best breed, but it's as if he is illegitimate.

All the other horses like his colorful coat very much, Tolstoy says, but it has the wrong colors and disrupts the genealogy.

According to his coat, he is a piebald.

Strider sees the world in his own way; he has experienced a lot on his own and has become kinder.

Old Serpukhovskoy arrives at the house, the stable where old Strider lives.

Life has been wasted away.

Every single day of it, all that has gone by has been wasted according to Serpukhovskoy, who had squandered two million and was now a hundred and twenty thousand in debt.

He was a wasted man, a person who couldn't finish his own story the way he would have liked to.

The gelding Strider had become laughable.

[117] Tolstoy renounced the rights to all his works written after 1881. When Sofia Andreevna was transcribing the first draft of the story, she subtitled it "An Experience of the Fantastic Kind. 1861." The year was mentioned intentionally so as to claim its copyright. However Tolstoy changed the title to "Strider: The Story of a Horse" and it appeared in print only in 1885.

When he returned to his herd, he was encircled by the beautiful, majestic and well-fed figures of other horses.

And he neighed.

But gelded horses never neigh. They don't call the mares.

It was sad, shameful, and ridiculous to look at him.

But Strider had kept his strength, his trot.

Serpukhovskoy, on the other hand, had lost his good looks and strength,
he had squandered everything with his own hands, which were useless for
anything else.

He had lost in a love triangle, a long time ago, in someone else's house
to which he had galloped on the beaten-down Strider, the former glory of
Russian horse breeding.

We know already that the horses didn't recognize Strider immediately.

Then they accepted him because of his story of equine misery.

The master was showing horses of a mediocre breed to a visitor. As he
went past the groom, Nester, who sat on the piebald waiting for orders, the
visitor slapped the piebald's crupper with his big fat hand.

The piebald recognized his master, his former master Serpukhovskoy.
He neighed with an old and feeble voice.

Next, Strider got sick.

They led him away.

He wanted to drink, they didn't let him.

Two dogs were looking at him as though he never really was a celebrated
horse.

They were waiting for his meat.

The men were sharpening knives.

Then he felt something being done to his throat.

His blood streamed down.

He felt much better.

They chopped his body into pieces.

An old wolf found the horseflesh.

She fed her cubs with the pieces of meat.

She went up to the smallest.

The cubs sat in a semi-circle.

They were howling joyfully.

The wolf went up to the smallest, and bending her knee and holding her muzzle down, made some convulsive movements, and opening her large sharp-toothed jaws disgorged a large piece of horseflesh.

The bigger cubs rushed toward it.

But she moved threateningly at them.

The little male cub took the meat and went off to the side.

Serpukhovskoy died much later.

His body walked about the earth eating and drinking.

But when he, a great burden for everyone, died, they dressed him in a good uniform.

They cleaned his boots and put him into a nice coffin with tassels at its four corners.

Then they put that coffin in another coffin made of lead.

This is how the dead bury their dead.

But all this is described in such great detail that it would have probably been much more difficult for a person who had fought on the battlefield to describe a village cemetery.

It was difficult for Lev Tolstoy to write about this.

Tolstoy was writing about a healthy, ruthless herd and about one horse.

■

Tolstoy's Strider talked about people with sadness.

They spoke of him as "*my* horse."

And he was astonished—how could he be someone else's when he was his own?

Tolstoy was telling the sad story of Yasnaya Polyana.

He wrote as a liberated person.

There are people who call the land theirs, though they have never seen that land and never walked on it.

I was thrice unfortunate, says Strider.

I was a piebald.

I was a gelding.

And people considered that I did not belong to God and to myself, as is natural to all living creatures, but that I belonged to the stud groom.

This is how Tolstoy, who already wasn't his own person, judged his property, his old hopes.

He was great.

He had become the country's glory.

And he didn't belong to himself anymore.

They followed him.

Restricted his actions.

And sold everything that he wrote.

The final murder of Strider occurred when he sewed the scandalized manuscript—who does it belong to?—under the lining of his armchair.

He wanted everyone to be himself and his own person.

Anna wasn't her own person.

She was Karenin's.

Then she was Vronsky's.

If everything worked out she could have been Anna Vronskaya, but all the same she would have been surrounded by people who weren't their own persons, they didn't belong to themselves.

In a search of oneself, people release an unnecessary energy, they trample on their own lives, at times they neigh in a weak voice so that someone will answer them back.

Just now I crossed several famous fields of old literature.

And you followed me.

What should I wish for you?

You don't need youth.

You'll have children.

I wish that you were your own person.

■

The paths from home to the nearby market, from home to the temple, from home to the oldest person of this village, all these paths have been walked.

But the great paths of literature and the energy of delusion are sacred.

And this path is for yourself, for yourself only and so that a person, as it were, does not exploit another person. So that they can be their own person.

I didn't embellish this book with too many quotes from other books.

With remarkable and colorful quotes.

But quotes get weathered.

When extricated from an artwork's labyrinth of linkages, a quote can easily die.

Tolstoy wasn't afraid of portraying death.

The death of a horse.

Wolves eating the meat of an old slaughtered animal.

This is grander and more sacred than the Crusades.

Tolstoy wasn't afraid of the death of the strong.

Horses aren't literate.

Strider told his story orally, with the full attention of his audience. They believed him.

Tolstoy thought that at least a horse could speak the truth.

The horse had to be forced to speak the truth.

Of all evils of mankind Strider spoke about one thing only in his calm sardonic tone—property.

Strider escaped the Arzamas horror that struck the landowner as he was looking for profitable purchases to enlarge his property for himself and his children.

Naturally, thoughts must have precise and coherent links.

This is just as important as the linking of train compartments.

Talking horses were common in fairytales.

And they usually said kind things.

According to a fairytale: there were three brothers—two were smart, and the third was a fool.

But foolishness here means simplicity and the treatment of one's life with a sense of duty.

Duty to one's love.

Only the fools achieve everything in fairytales.

Hence those who are wise should examine them more closely.

Only those heroes who sacrifice everything acquire character.

The eccentric ones, who are not afraid of being different from the others.

The heroes who don't listen to the warnings of a horse.

As it is in Homer.

■

Talking animals aren't anything new in art.

There even exists an entire volume of Hindu stories in which the characters are animals representing different human occupations, various social values. And you forget that these aren't human beings as you read along.

In these stories animals transport fire from one place to another.

The world of animals knew a man who was transformed into an ass due to his curiosity in magic.

It was the golden ass of Apuleius.

In Cervantes, dogs represent creatures that resent the world of the rich.

In the world of the declassified, they represent the Spanish people in a calm, respectful manner.

The dogs are realists that remove the veil of romanticism.

In Gogol, dogs appear in *The Diary of a Madman*.

They find out that the woman with whom Poprischin falls in love despises him and loves someone else. They say that he has hay on his head instead of hair.

Swift's world is a world of horses where an emigrant from the human world arrives, a traveler who has been in various countries, where he was a giant and a dwarf, and even where he was able to fly.

This world is not real, because the horses here can work as if with their hands; it's as though it wasn't thoroughly thought out by the fantasy writer who preserves the relation of big and small in everything.

■

But the greatest of all beings who grieves for human suffering is Strider.

Strider is an innocent horse who has been castrated.

A horse of excellent blood, excellent qualities; he unites all the horses and acts remarkably as their teacher.

The coat of the noble-blooded piebald trotter contains the characteristics of a brilliant gentleman living among philistine gentlemen.

People—only God knows of what stature—refuse to share a table with him.

The world of horses is better.

At first everyone in the herd detests the old gelding.

Then they get to know him and listen to him as if he were a teacher of life.

At one time Tolstoy had wanted to breed a new kind of horse. He wanted to do that in the steppes along the Volga, he wanted to present Bashkiria with a new breed of horse.

In the context of world literature, Strider is placed in King Lear's shoes.

He is a king, but he has lost everything.

It can be said with sadness that he has lost his family of horses.

But on the other hand, he knows the family of men. And he teaches people not to trust those who are dressed well.

The *comme il faut* people.

Dressed in suits from the best tailors.

Strider is humanized in such a way that one doesn't ask: but how could he have hands, or how could he talk?

He was the friend of a groom who was flogged and who cried on Strider's shoulder—the horse who learns that human tears have the taste of salt.

Strider was in the highest society.

Now he has become a detestable creature serving only the needs of the groom. He gets ahead of every trotter in the races, he is present in the life and adventures of the rich youth, and he sees wealthy people and recounts with contempt how man calls everything his own.

Strider's story is a long conversation.

It's a long sermon about how property is not only theft but a concept that doesn't include the fulfillment of personal dreams.

He may not own anything good, even though he is rich.

When telling his story, Strider turns to ideas that may have been read in the books of Charles Fourier or Proudhon, the books that Herzen read and wrote.

Books that Tolstoy had read and for which he had wanted to find a different solution.

Knowing that Herzen was banned and unread.

In Tolstoy's opinion, Herzen's books encompassed forty percent of Russian literature.

Tolstoy himself, though, didn't fit within Russian literature.

He turned out to be much bigger.

■

Tolstoy was proud of "Strider."

If a famous person wants to get a monument, then this structure is ironic with regard to the very concept of posthumous fame.

Strider is essential even after his death.

After they had killed him and cut him into pieces, the wolf stole some of the meat to feed her cubs, and this is appealing to us.

Meanwhile the man, whose name I forgot again, is buried in a smart uniform that corresponds to the coat of the horse, according to which one can tell his breed.

They take him somewhere, dig up the bones of other unnecessary people, and bury the impoverished aristocrat there, with the new tassels at the corners of his coffin.

In "Strider," Tolstoy bids farewell to the gentry's notions about breed, rank and attire.

"Strider"—I'm going to say something else now—and "The Devil" are the saddest works of an aged man.

A person, meaning a person who is isolated from human society, is unhappy.

It's very unpleasant for a wife to read that she has castrated her own husband. She is not his *khótia*—his sweetheart. They use this term in southern Russia.

And he has no right to love.

If he loves, millions of people crush him with the help of a train, or they criticize him because the object of his love is socially inadequate, in other words, she's not his equal.

That's what their whole existence was based upon, and not on just wanting to be happy.

And that was Tolstoy's point.

He lived in their world.

They stole his love life, just as they did with Anna Karenina.

Tolstoy himself had a rather undistinguished horse, and every summer he went riding through the forest; they criticized him because he owned a horse, he gave her up, they unshod her, he got her back, unable to give her up.

According to the decision made by Lev Nikolaevich's former pupils, the horse was buried at the feet of Tolstoy.

This was the custom of the Russian *bogatyrs*: the horse had to stay with his owner.[118]

Tolstoy had planted one of Europe's largest apple orchards.

There was a terrible frost. The trees froze.

He had planted the Antonovka type. This is the most hardy, prehistoric rootstock.

The trees stood in their blackness—it was the Black Death.

They were cut down. Some of them were left standing; they stood in their blackness for one, two, ten years.

And one day they bloomed.

They are still standing until this day.

I told you about the nature of human culture.

It's reborn, a witness to its own resurrection.

The most vital quality in Tolstoy is that he is above what we call human culture.

It's not his artistic achievements, but his ability.

■ ■ ■

But everything is not so simple.

I can't leave "Strider" like this.

Swift's text about the country of the horses is mixed with contempt toward people.

"Strider" is written as an attempt at scorn.

It didn't work out.

Tolstoy's horses pity humans.

Strider, as Tolstoy explains in the text, has the sweeping trot of the Russian Orlov trotter.

---

118 A hero of the Russian folk epics or *byliny*. The duty of the *bogatyrs* was to protect the Russian land against foreign invaders, especially the Tartars. The most prominent of the *bogatyrs* was Ilya of Murom, to whom Nikolai Karamzin dedicated the poem "Ilya Muromets" (1795).

This is an outcast aristocrat, but he is of very high blood and capabilities.

But in response to Strider's statement, that he is the creator of a new equine breed, the horses say that it's impossible. He is a gelding.

I'll repeat one more time that when the Levin brothers were arguing about inheritance, Levin's brother told him: your plan regarding the labor commune is good, but you forgot the most important question (the question of property). Strider would say the same thing as the nihilist brother; the most important thing in life is not mentioned—the question of property.

Tolstoy understood this.

He bought land and made a note to himself: here, I bought this land, and the nightingales are singing just as they did before and don't even realize that they belong to me now.

Strider was saying that human happiness isn't the same as equine happiness; for humans, happiness is the attempt to own as much as possible.

Strider was talking about the necessity of changing human psychology. Swift didn't touch upon that subject.

But at the same time, the question here was about sexuality, because being a "gelding" according to people is an improper condition.

But this condition gives birth to something completely different.

Gradually, the story about a highborn creature that makes his breed famous turns into a story about what the trotter really sees among humans.

Strider was already mixed up in their messy lives of drinking-bouts, and carried people who were concerned about silly things: this is my lover, my estate, mine. Then, after becoming a work horse in the stable where they saddled him badly, he understood everything; he was in much pain, although, as Tolstoy notes, he liked it—the pain from a wrong kind of life.

Tolstoy, who not only lived wrongly but also knew it, was experiencing an unusual Strider-like pleasure—pain.

"Strider" is a story about the failures of romantic socialism, based on what we call "pity."

Moreover, Strider here is contrasted with what Gogol called a "gray gelding."

Apparently, in the vernacular, "gray gelding" was used for swearing.

Tolstoy justifies the gray gelding; he is surrounded by human stupidity, they don't have a special funeral for him and the wolves feast on his flesh. Whereas the depiction of the wolf pack is almost idyllic.

The ritual semi-circle of the cubs doesn't take away the piece from the little one.

And the horse on which Vronsky galloped was one of those horses that don't talk because their mouths aren't intended for conversations.

Strider is, so to speak, Tolstoy's vision before his own death: nothing can be done—alone.

Tolstoy's ordinary family was occupied with an ordinary activity—the dividing of property, which is usually divided among the brothers. But the division didn't change anything, it didn't bring about any good.

The division of the gray gelding's flesh is juxtaposed with both this family affair and the death of Serpukhovskoy—the ordinary human burial in coffins with tassels.

Tolstoy's mare was buried at the feet of the man whom she loved.

It was Ferapontov, Tolstoy's pupil, who took care of that, and Fedin tells in his long interesting book about how his children were interested in this burial; they thought it was fair.

Chekhov in his "Heartache" tells about a failure, a coachman, who is hardly able to earn food for his only horse.

He can't find a person who will understand his heartache.

And he tells it to his horse, a half-starving nag.

He tells her in detail about his grief, and thus, in Chekhov, the case of the human-equine story reemerges in another form.

16

HADJI MURAD

I'll repeat—continuity can be started from any place.

Childhood was the beginning of a certain path.

The Cossacks was the beginning of another path.

"A History of Yesterday" started yet another path.

There was a path begun by *Anna Karenina*; a path that was envisioned by Pushkin and re-envisioned by Tolstoy.

The path of "Strider" was a journey of trial.

Then, there was Tolstoyism—the non-resistance to evil.

There was Christianity, and there was something truer—there were undisjointed ideas about a unified soul or unity of souls.

But like a river, ideas flow under the ice, boiling, the troubled water is hot and steaming, forcing its way through, and the water's temperature is the same everywhere. Try to measure it, any place in the water, and you'll see that it bursts unrestrained in its heat.

Spring is like that, too.

. . . Tolstoy was writing *Hadji Murad*.

As though a continuation to his analysis of *The Cossacks*.

When the arches of such a writer as Tolstoy finally join, many unused pieces are left strewn on the ground.

And this is just the same as if man was fashioning a horse on the third day of creation, the horse that was created by God, and now being re-created by man; here stands man, and around him on the ground lies what seems like extraneous material, what man, unlike God, wasn't able to unify the way God would have.

He can only see the uniqueness of God's creation, which never repeats itself.

Because we don't have Tolstoy's strength and ability to construct the temple of the human soul.

■   ■   ■

Among property crimes there was the crime of lusting after state property.

The Cossacks and the young Tolstoy, who has come to their village, are all Russian.

But they love the world.

The hero, Olenin, and his guide, Yeroshka—first Yeroshka, then Olenin—realize the truth for which the people of the Caucasus are fighting.

Here is another beginning, the beginning of the *Hadji Murad* path.

. . . Aleksandr Sergeevich Pushkin was very critical of his own works. He probably related to them as a traveler would relate to his home that he's left. The subject of the love of a woman who stands outside the borders of our civilization was for the European one of the main subjects of early modern literature.

Voltaire took pleasure in describing the love of an American Indian; the way details of tradition were uncovered, baring the essence of the matter. The Huron Indian is sincere and full of strength, it's as if he tries to rectify European customs.

The reproduction of life at home is almost always reinforced through journeys among people living in new surroundings.

Pushkin's "A Journey to Arzrum" is ironic in a different way. He sees the essence of things and human desires among the people he has fallen in with, registering himself in their environment in some way. Love was usually mentioned in works as the pigment least open to misinterpretation; love has very few colorblind people who distort what they see.

In the mind of young Olenin, the "beautiful blue-eyed Circassian girls" were directly associated with the beautiful mountains; it's as if they helped interpret a new kind of beauty.

In *The Cossacks*, Maryana was conceived differently; she is tall and strong, almost colossal.

She is like an antique statue that has come alive, an embodiment of antique female beauty.

Maryana is right, of course, to love the Cossack who is her equal, even though Olenin is ready to convert to the Old Faith, i.e., leave his own society in order to become her lawful husband; to end their relationship, Maryana tells him: "Get away, I'm sick of you!"

After a quick glance at Pushkin's "Prisoner of the Caucasus," Tolstoy was stunned by the details.

Here love is rendered in its purest form, it's elating; a few marvelous lines were specifically edited out because they were too explicit for the censors, who among other shortcomings were also known for their senile punctiliousness. But the girl in the poem is beautiful and so is her lover as they come to the bank of the Caucasian river, as if it were a cathedral, to vow their love to each other. This scene was replaced with another where the woman throws herself into the river after her European guest leaves.

Once, when I was young and could easily cross a mountain pass without even noticing it—and the ice arches left from winter are good bridges over the river—during one of my journeys into the far lands I had been talking to a woman and when I was leaving, she said: "Are you leaving? I'm in love with you."

My guide, a stern man from another Georgian tribe, consoled me: "Forget her and don't remember her with a sigh. She was being polite to you, she knows she'll never see you again."

And then I learned by heart that it's difficult to drown in the Caucasian river; it's so powerful that it swirls the stones and creates nests at the bottom. The river breaks you, it doesn't drown you. It can kill you and fling you out.

There are no mermaids in that river.

Tolstoy, arranging the huge halls that were filled with memories written a long time ago or a short time ago, spoke about a peasant girl's love; but this was also his general conception of *the* peasant girl—a Tula peasant girl from no specific time. Her mysterious relations with a strange well-lit house, where she went to wash the floors, perhaps, and nothing more.

Tolstoy wrote "A Prisoner in the Caucasus" for children—as a beginner's book. And he considered it, or at least he said that he considered it, to be his only book that was written correctly, that was clear and free from lies.

A story that lied unintentionally.

Ahead of him, Tolstoy still had *Anna Karenina*, *Resurrection* and *Hadji Murad*.

But he had declared the mountain village in "A Prisoner in the Caucasus" as his capital city.

In this story, he explains coolly and accurately why people of different tribes do not always come to love each other. We meet with an older Russian officer, a person who has become accustomed to a silent need—he now has a girl who loves art, and this girl, who is not a woman yet, boldly and unexpectedly accepts the European-looking clay women from another tribe, another mentality. The mountaineers relate differently to the Slav, Zhilin. They have different lives, different conflicts with the Russian and a different lifestyle.

Zhilin, with his craftsmanship, his ability to mend a watch, or make toys —without any particular enthusiasm or interest—is accepted as a technically advanced person.

It's not love, but friendship that connects Zhilin with Dina, the poor girl from a village whose inhabitants have been expelled from the valleys.

Zhilin has his own Russian friend who is wealthy, spoiled, and cowardly;

he doesn't even help his own fellow tribesman when he could have saved him from prison. We are given a specific portrait of this person.

The escape is described in great detail. Zhilin tames the dogs. Then he befriends a young boy, gives him a bow and arrows, so that they can go up the hill and look around.

Where is the Russian fort?

The escape takes place not with the help of a ladder, but a pole that Dina pushes into the pit. The Russian prisoners are in the pit for their first attempt to escape. It's obvious where the pole is taken from, whose roof; and the girl, Dina, who has arranged everything for their escape, is crying—her friend is leaving; it's described with a strange clarity—a friend in art, she loves art the way children love sculpting. Like people—brothers, who have learned about their fatherland.

Tolstoy, like King Lear, gave up his kingdom.

He learned about a different life.

In the name of "A Prisoner in the Caucasus," he renounced his novels, stories and sketches in various articles; this world was known only to Tolstoy; but this is a text for writers, too. Learn how to write. Learn not how to invent, but how to think, how to separate ideas; how to separate a phenomenon from a horde of ideas.

Like a Robinson Crusoe, Tolstoy journeyed through the Caucasian mountains, he knew North Caucasus very well and all its rivers flowing to the Caspian. Here he fought for good prose against bad literature.

Occasionally he would make mistakes: he would get mixed up in the regions of the Caucasus, then—he would confuse the various nationalities. He would say that the trees in the Caucasus aren't fascinating, that the *chinara* there is the same as the beech.

That's not right. The *chinara* is a plane tree. A big tree with its own crown and its own leaves.

A royal tree, it wasn't famous in that part of the Caucasus where young Tolstoy had gone.

Tolstoy described nature not as a traveler but as a hunter.

He described war not as the aide-de-camp of some big commander, not even as an officer of the light or heavy cavalry. His plans were broader, more general and realistic. He thought through phenomena, not through words, and he didn't retreat from knowledge, he didn't think it was sufficient.

He composed a great story, *The Cossacks*.

A traditional love triangle, a woman and two young men, here a Cossack woman, a Cossack man and a Russian aristocrat. The Cossack and the Russian understand nature intimately, but each in his own way.

They are distinctive and well observed.

Love and the delight of love are depicted realistically, just as Olenin's delight in the mountains that gradually approach during their long journey.

Everything ends badly. The woman stays behind, at home with her lover.

She doesn't even look at the dust of the departing carriage, maybe Maryana hardly ever recalled the strange visitor, the strange soldier with his two servants, excellent guns, good hounds and almost incomprehensible speech.

The great short novel *The Cossacks* was written and published with the usual apology from its author for not being finished, and had it not gotten printed, the manuscript could have been used for covering cracks on the back of the bookcase, to prevent moths from getting in.

This is serious; we are talking about understanding literature, whether it can overcome all obstacles, whether it's supposed to do that, and what those obstacles are—aren't they perhaps the same as those in life? However we shouldn't doubt the existence of truth.

In the various drafts of *The Cossacks*, the Cossack dies first, then the officer, and then, in another version, they both die.

In one draft, the Cossack kills the officer; the Cossack is taken to be hanged, and right before his own death, he calmly adjusts the noose around his neck. This isn't unintentional.

It's as though young Tolstoy is recalling how he tried to free literature from things that had become ordinary.

■

Among his great works, Tolstoy has one that's the best.

It's *Hadji Murad*.

He worked on this short novel from 1896 to 1904.

But even when he was sick and close to death, Tolstoy was still doing research for this novel.

He demanded books, checking the details in them.

Let's return to the artistic detail once more.

The great and versatile Picasso was already old when he read *War and Peace*. At first, he didn't like the epic, "there are too many details," but then he understood that "every one of them is necessary." In other words, he understood someone else's art through the principles of his own art.

When a painter depicts objects, he doesn't just paint what he sees, but he also incorporates his own knowledge and experience. In architecture one doesn't rely solely on vision, but also knowledge, a multifaceted knowledge of the ingredients.

Detail allows one to perceive the world as a change, not through a colorful curtain, and not through colorful shutters, and not through tinted spectacles.

It's what we perceive through detail, it's when we can draw a line adjacent to the other lines of a figure, seen as if from various angles and perceived differently for that reason.

Art must be understood in multiple ways. Art makes it possible to get a relatively complete, although often contradictory, representation of the world.

We walk in this world without any guidance, and very seldom do we ourselves become the guides.

The Abrek—Hadji Murad—is a hero of the Caucasus, one of Shamil's first comrade-in-arms, a man, whose mother didn't tear him away from her bosom when she was ordered to go as a wet-nurse for a Khan's child; she fought for her motherhood, she fed her son with the milk of courage— there is a song about this.

Besides Shamil, there is another leader in the novel—Nicholas I. They both have their followers, they both have their women.

Shamil and Hadji Murad can't live together without a conflict.

In his heart, Hadji Murad re-conquers the Caucasus from Shamil.

There is an agreement between him and the woman, whom the soldiers affectionately call "the captain's daughter"—she is the wife of the captain of the fortress where Hadji Murad was held as an honorary captive. Shamil has taken Hadji Murad's son as hostage, he threatens to kill the boy, blind him, and the brave man wavers between the two powers.

The woman living in the fortress—she is very poor—is the captain's daughter. She is not unfaithful to her husband, but she walks with the young officer under the moonlight, and Tolstoy sees with the meticulousness of a physicist how the light envelops them as if with laces or layers of silver.

Hadji Murad's attraction to this woman is very pure and understandable, she pities him, pities his family.

Those streams of light that wrap the artistic figure, they are the same lines that later Picasso, who is almost our contemporary, would trace, shocking and irritating the viewer.

Painting involves cognitive work, and *Hadji Murad* isn't just a subject that evolved from *The Cossacks*, it isn't just a pared down theme that emphasizes differences in origin, differences in culture. It's a long journey along the paths of art.

It demands a great deal of energy, it takes from us currency that's irreplaceable, we pay our dues to art with years, with time—the time to convert the facts of life into art, let's say, through a new, multi-dimensional consciousness. It includes the energy of not just one person, but a succession of generations.

■

Shamil has two wives, one who is well respected and probably not so old, and a second one, who is very young. The husband brings a present not to his young wife, but his older wife, because he abides by custom. He loves in his own way; these are his moral values.

The young wife is hurt by this, she hides from her husband. He can't find her, and she laughs at him.

A very old game; a well-known game.

These are the accepted values of life—the difficulties of life.

Odysseus came to know many women, but when he arrived home to his wife, he tested her thoroughly with his well-designed questions. And he tied the necks of the slave women who didn't have any rights and lawlessly lived with the suitors of Penelope with a rope and turned them into a garland, which Homer describes with near tenderness; this is how the birds used to hang from a tree, glued to the branches—it was a hunting method many years ago.

There was no country for Hadji Murad.

The great man roamed somewhere between Nicholas' empire and the emerging despotism of Shamil.

He was fighting against an attacking army on that field with a small island of trees, plugging his wounds with cotton wool. Then he rose up against the bullets and sang.

He moved forward.

A shot was heard.

Hadji Murad fell.

The shooting stopped. There was a silence.

And the nightingales that had quieted down resumed their singing.

Heroes die, or they go mad. Cordelia dies, she is hanged by her sister; Ophelia goes mad.

I'll cite Chekhov's words once more about how we have only one kind of ending in drama—the hero either leaves, or dies.

The one who creates a new denouement will be a great person.

But we're bad at guessing the feelings of any great person.

"The Devil" tells about the temptations of life; in it Tolstoy doesn't even know who is guilty, who kills whom, or the other way around—who should shoot himself. The manuscript of this story was sewn under the upholstery of an armchair.

There was an incident: Tolstoy became infatuated with his cook, he asked someone else: Do you want to join me?—Only we shouldn't use force.

It's impossible to be a saint and eat ice cream at the same time.

Tolstoy was left in a world without solutions and wanted to escape somewhere with Makovitsky.[119]

All outcomes in works were conventional.

They progressed through a story.

It was necessary to resolve the plot.

The point isn't whether there is an end or no end at all, but that the nightingales that had quieted down during the shooting resumed their song.

The nightingales sang again after Hadji Murad's death.

A phenomenon of a different reality.

That world didn't know anything about Hadji Murad. It's as though he is cohabiting with them.

This was Tolstoy's story.

He wrote *Hadji Murad* all of his life, he wrote it better each time. More poetically.

He turned toward *Hadji Murad* trying to understand the mindset of his former serfs, the pupils in his school.

Let's not forget the art lessons that his pupils gave him. I'll remind you of the title of an article: "Who Is to Learn to Write from Whom: the Peasant Children from Us, or We from the Peasant Children?"

The "earthly, spontaneous energy that is impossible to invent" carried Tolstoy to his old age.

---

[119] Tolstoy's old friend and personal physician, Dushan Makovitsky, who was with him during his last journey away from home and was the one to close Tolstoy's eyes after his death.

Old age has its own laws.

Tolstoy died from pneumonia after having carried out one of his energetic decisions.

A decision somewhat similar to King Lear's.

He left his home, his estate, the small bath-house that stood by the old house among the huge trees; he left in an unheated, fourth-class train compartment.

He cast aside his fame and unfinished manuscripts in order to fulfill his dream of love, his dream of a different life. When Tolstoy finished *Hadji Murad*, he lifted himself up on the arms of his chair and said: that's how it should be, yes, that's how it should be.

And there he was, a mountaineer, heading straight toward the bullets.

He was singing a song.

■

Tolstoy attempted to pray many times; he had created his own perfected God, who was not related to the Church.

Tolstoy's truest prayer was the manuscript of *Hadji Murad*.

Through its endless drafts, endless corrections—this was a person paying service to his ideals, and to freedom, and to resistance.

17

DOSTOEVSKY'S "SUDDENLY"

They lived in the same time period, Tolstoy and Dostoevsky.

Their wives were acquainted with each other.

Dostoevsky's wife taught Tolstoy's wife how to publish books. Their husbands were supposed to meet, and there was an incident when both happened to be in the same place. But they didn't meet. Not only did they not talk to each other, they didn't even exchange a single letter.

And so, in this book that's more about Tolstoy, we are switching—"suddenly"—to Dostoevsky.

But first, let's try and understand what does "suddenly" mean.

"Suddenly" is an introduction of a new force, new qualities, and new proposals.

"Suddenly" is a discovery.

And of course, in art, "suddenly" is an important word.

The word "suddenly" should have been placed at the entrance of the temple of art—refuting the inscription above the Inferno, composed or found by Dante: "Abandon all hope, ye who enter."

The human mind that created eternal punishment later also created the destruction of the inferno—it created redemption.

■

Dostoevsky is the most predictable writer of our times.

It seems that he was born just enough years before us, so that if you had to speak of your own life, you wouldn't say: "It can't happen to me."

Dostoevsky is a person who has different answers.

The endings of his novels are conventional.

The comforting of his heroes is written with a skeptical hand.

I don't think that I will suddenly sit down and write a thick book about Dostoevsky, that I will suddenly understand him.

I respect Mikhail Bakhtin who showed Dostoevsky as a great writer with multiple voices that seem to contend one another and perceive themselves in their own ways.[120]

But the heroes' conflict with each another, their mutual misunderstanding is the simplest and oldest property of art.

A thousand years before the Bible, when even gods didn't know how to make pots, there lived a hero by the name of Gilgamesh.

He formed legions, made people obey him, felled woods; according to the text, he was first to set the battlements on fire when the enemy was jumping over the wall. They were supposed to encounter metal or glass there.

Gilgamesh had a friend, his right-hand man; he once lived among the beasts and ruled them.

[120] Mikhail Bakhtin's "Problems of Dostoevsky's Creation" (1929), renamed "Problems of Dostoevsky's Poetics" in the second, considerably revised and enlarged edition in 1963, was an in depth literary analysis of Dostoevsky's art. It focused on such questions as the role of the hero in Dostoevsky's novels, the way ideas are presented in the novels, the question of the genre tradition to which Dostoevsky was indebted or is supposed to belong, and finally the special use of language and dialogue in the novels. Bakhtin contended that Dostoevsky epitomized the "polyphonic" nature of the novel form, consisting of independent voices which are fully equal, become subjects in their own right, and do not serve the ideological position of the author. It is relevant to note that Bakhtin rejected the approach of the Russian Formalists as "material aesthetics" and diverged from the "mechanistic presuppositions" of the early Formalism.

This friend committed many heroic deeds, and when he came among people, he met a harlot.

He fell upon her—several days passed—and then they parted.

When he came to his senses, he found that the beasts that were following him had dispersed.

This was a complete "suddenly."

He was a character who was found and singled out from a conversation about a woman.

And she told him—ripping her dress (it probably was a very scanty dress) in two pieces—she told him: Take me.

—That's how we live. We wear clothes. Live among us, eat bread, that's our food, drink *sikera*.

In those days, vodka was called *sikera*.

—That's what people do.

And the man became Gilgamesh's friend and committed heroic deeds.

He tried to return to his old world, he swam across the ocean, they didn't have oars back then and he felled tall trees and made poles with which he pushed from the bottom of the ocean.

This was the awakening of consciousness.

∎

Dostoevsky loved the word "suddenly." In his conversation with the investigator, Mitya Karamazov repeats this word a few dozen times. A word about the torn nature of life, the unevenness of its steps.

And nobody can ever predict those steps.

The word "suddenly" means something unexpected; but surely there is an "other" standing next to one, let's say, a friend, a best friend.

"Other" means someone who suddenly appears next to you.[121]

[121] Shklovsky is playing with the words *drug* (friend), *vdrug* (suddenly), and *drugoi* (other). The new made-up word *vdrugoi*, is a linguistic anomaly in *zaum*, a transrational language invented by Khlebnikov and Kruchenykh that relies on puns, neologisms, and the free association of sounds and images. The device was used in

Suddenly—and from this unexpected incidence, a change in something big, something noticeable.

There used to be a marine command: "Turn suddenly!"—and the ships, against the resistance of the sails full of wind, would turn around, overcoming the inertia, leaving the stream of their previous course.

Suddenly—this is not only an unexpected change, but also an extensive or seemingly extensive change.

Tolstoy and Dostoevsky never had the chance to greet one another.

Two people lived—each in another world.

There is the world, but it should be another world: a powerful "suddenly" with a new force in the general movement. Tolstoy and Dostoevsky are the masters of the real "other" world that has not yet been conquered.

What did "suddenly" mean to Tolstoy? When he wrote novels, this great person, a man of unusually wide experience, would suddenly change the course of the novel.

He stopped the printing of *War and Peace*. It was difficult. It was costly. He had to argue, pay for the losses, but this was a necessary thing.

He realized that the "other" war, the one after the Battle of Shengraben, changed his relation to the heroes and the whole perception of war. Andrei Bolkonsky, the smartest of aristocrats with a good family name that was very similar to the name of Tolstoy's relatives, was the one designed to understand the war. This ordinary person, who was said to conduct himself as an "imperious prince," was suddenly moved aside.

In Tolstoy's plans Andrei Bolkonsky admires Napoleon. He wants to be like Napoleon. In the novel's original plan, the characters are generally described in their relation to the great commander.

---

poetry to communicate the inner state of the speaker more directly. Shklovsky's *vdrugoi* is an amalgamation of the three words *drug* (friend) + *vdrug* (suddenly) + *drugoi* (other) = *v/drug/oi* meaning all three things at once: an "other" who turns up suddenly as a friend, or any other combination, depending on the context, that represents a contradiction.

Then suddenly Tolstoy wants Napoleon to disappear.

The idea of a world ruled by him vanishes.

This world was replaced with another one that had its own inner laws. It was necessary not to hinder the materialization of those laws. The danger of crossing a street during traffic, according to Tolstoy, was an old idea.

The world's greatest danger was that it changed—suddenly.

He goes from the farmlands into the city. He resettles people in the city, and the horses, according to Tolstoy, have nothing to do in the city. People should use their own two legs.

Tolstoy had a carriage, but he walked from Moscow to Yasnaya Polyana.

The world should think—as a child does—in simpler ways.

Moral laws are simple; they aren't patriarchal. These laws, which Tolstoy tries to correct for himself, were created by the society of his youth.

He stops the printing of *Anna Karenina*; the woman has violated moral laws.

During the writing of the novel—as I said before—it's as if Tolstoy falls in love with Karenina, this strong, smart and prominent woman.

He recognizes, through Levin's eyes, that after Karenina, Kitty is trifling. But Kitty is his love. It's the love of a mature man, a person who has already created *War and Peace*.

Although the old truth had ceased to exist for Tolstoy. He wanted to resurrect her through his own laws. Maybe the laws of Chertkov. And suddenly Katyusha Maslova, who was seduced by a young gentleman, the muscovite "magdalene," a ten-ruble prostitute, is resurrected.

The hero—Nekhlyudov—must wait for Lev Tolstoy to write the second volume and perhaps in that book Nekhlyudov will also be resurrected.

But he isn't, the second volume was never written. Raskolnikov isn't resurrected either, although his resurrection is promised in a new book. There won't be a new book. There will be another "suddenly." All ships turn.

The contradictory nature of art, the contradictory nature of books and the contradictory nature of love for your own heroes. That's the theme of this book that you're reading.

Dostoevsky wrote in his *Diary of a Writer* that St. Petersburg was like a city in mist; it could appear, and then disappear.

Raskolnikov said that St. Petersburg was empty.

When Dostoevsky was asked whether he liked the city, he replied: "No —only the stones, palaces and monuments."

The city that would probably never be finished.

Was suddenly finished.

It was "suddenly" another city.

Many of Tolstoy's characters live in St. Petersburg.

But to them the city is a historic past that may change but never disappear.

It's made of columns that support nothing.

They're made of copper and painted to appear as marble. But they are painted under the cupola of a temple.

The columns have been added by Tsar Nicholas, and they make the structure look amateur, rather sinister in a dilettante fashion.

The arch that we see in St. Isaac's Cathedral is painted.

The cathedral is a structure that was nonetheless accepted by the city.

But it's a curious example of "theater" architecture.

There are scenes on the pediment that portray various characters from religious books who have the same names as the tsars.

The pediment, too, is made of metal—it's not marble.

This is one of the first metallic pediments in the world that was done by electroplating.

That's an eternity.

A new invention.

But it's as if it's fake.

In contrast to the Catholic Church, the Orthodox Church doesn't use sculpture.

But in St. Isaac's Cathedral there are sculpted heads, the faces of which are cut out and painted over the flat surface.

A bust with a painted face.

This trivial temple, a temple that's more like a sham, is at the same time a technologically advanced building.

Its massive, huge, monolithic columns were brought here as whole pieces; they were brought from the barge to the construction site by using wooden chutes with rolling balls.

It's important to mention that this was a period when the ball bearing first appeared.

Besides, these, as well as the Hermitage statues, were all made by a contractor who was Stanislavsky's grandfather.

■

The Admiralty building was built by the architect Zakharov. Before that he was an expert in quicksand, i.e., ground that has been liquefied by an over-saturation of water.

Zakharov knew how to stop moving quicksand.

The two huge statues representing the continents at the entrance of the Admiralty are made of alabaster, and because it's such a hard material, they stand unaffected under rain and snow. Meanwhile the massive granite statue of Alexander has cracks from top to bottom.

The middle part of the building is fashioned after the Nadvratnaya Church.

Atop its famous spire is a weather vane in the form of a bronze sailing ship.

The documents about the construction of the building are kept inside.

I remember the Admiralty so well because this is where Larissa Reisner used to live—she was the commissar of the Baltic Fleet.

I took the Admiralty from the White Army headed by Khokhlov, I think his name was Khokhlov, the general.

He telegraphed the Tsar: "I'm surrounded by Shklovsky's armored cars. Stop. I'm retreating."

He wanted to surrender to somebody, so he quietly tiptoed away.

The walls of the Admiralty were very thick. Take this fireplace, for instance, the walls there were as wide as that. Even the *Aurora* couldn't break its walls straight away, let alone my armored cars.

If we talk about St. Petersburg, it's gaining foothold only now; after the floods, they began to pour sand and soil; now they are building a dike.

The Winter Palace is saturated with underground water at its very bottom.

The conferences would take place in a building that used to be the Menshikov Palace, and so there is a whole floor there with big halls that are decorated with architectural detail and murals.

All this is being uncovered only now. They dug it up.

And so the first conference of the workers and military delegates took place in this building.

Tolstoy lived on Moscow Street in St. Petersburg, in a small hotel. Several Petrashev[122] members were also living in that same hotel.

It's not clear whether they talked to one another or not, but according to Boris Eichenbaum, and this needs to be verified, Olenin, who was leaving for the Caucasus, was in all likelihood associated or still is associated with the Petrashevs.

■

But in Moscow there was another hotel that was next to the telegraph office on Gorky Street, on the alley that's closer to the Manezh. Here lived students who were arrested and then freed.

Later they became students, or if you will, teachers at the school in Yasnaya Polyana.

If you come closer to the building, you'll notice that the windows are located so low that from the inside one can only see legs up to the knee.

[122] The Petrashevs were a group of dissident activists during the 1840s named after Mikhail Petrashevsky, who organized intellectual discussion on Charles Fourier and Saint-Simon on Friday evenings at his house. The story of the Petrashevs stretches from the critical months after the outbreak of revolutionary disorder in Western and Central Europe in February 1848, through the arrests which began in St. Petersburg on 23 April 1849, and on into the later nineteenth century.

One of the students said that Tolstoy used to enter the building through the window.

But we maintain our humble opinion that he wanted to come in through the window simply to avoid the porter.

Tolstoy knew the falsities of St. Petersburg and Moscow very well.

Dostoevsky wanted to believe in old Russia, but he couldn't. I think that even the exiles didn't believe in it. Everything was as it should have been, and there was going to be a coronation, and the Red Square was covered with a carpet, and they say that the carpet was stolen—it's not clear where they hid it, but it was very big.

Faith and disillusionment in Russia had become intertwined—not in the same way that they put the electric lines these days—and the only thing that could unite them, put them to work, was a discharge, a catastrophe.

The life of Dostoevsky and Tolstoy was a life in a country that had postponed a revolution for only a short period.

So, it means the word "suddenly" implies something co-existing and, therefore, unforeseen, but its being unforeseen can also mean being well-constructed, like the command to the ships: "Turn suddenly."

Disillusionment. Dostoevsky was close to all those who were cursed by Pobedonostsev.[123]

The name of Pobedonostsev still lives as a wound, as an accusation that never healed.

In exile, Dostoevsky lived next to soldiers who had wanted to express their indignation immediately and even killed their leaders.

---

[123] Konstantin Pobedonostsev (1827–1907) was a Russian statesman usually regarded as a prime representative of Russian conservatism. He was a gray cardinal of imperial politics during the reign of his disciple Alexander III of Russia. Pobedonostsev rejected the Western ideals of freedom and independence as the "dangerous delusions of nihilistic youth." He denounced democracy as "the insupportable dictatorship of the vulgar crowd." Parliamentary methods of administration, modern judicial organization and procedures, trial by jury, freedom of the press, secular education—these were among the principal objects of his aversion. He subjected all of them to a severe analysis in his *Reflections of a Russian Statesman*.

At first he wrote very submissively, he wanted to believe in old Russia.

Lev Tolstoy, too, wanted not only to believe in it, but also to preserve his country estate, which wouldn't conflict with the surrounding world, and yet he took payments from the peasants for the land that was acquired God only knows when.

In his great speech Dostoevsky wanted to reconcile everyone.

He was a revolutionary—he wrote novels in which he sometimes criticized the revolutionaries, calling them demons, but he had two Russias: the one that should be, and the other that was and that was never able to understand herself.

He published magazines, they censured him from every side. Here he was, with his own world that seemed to really exist. It was necessary to destroy it. Maybe that's why it was necessary to test oneself.

The person in exile, who had been wearing shackles for too long, who had been daydreaming for a long time, wanted to reconcile on common grounds, on Marei's faith, the kind peasant who comforted the frightened child. But Dostoevsky's father was killed by the peasants, he had a violent death.

The murder, of course, was committed publicly, but it was difficult to punish the assassins because they belonged to someone who was dead, and if they were put in prison, the inheritance of the dead man would be lost.

It was said that Dostoevsky's father was a good man, perhaps even a distant descendent of the Decembrists, a person who called the police "stinking demons." He was killed by people who had learned with him how to hunt, they were as close as friends, or as watch dogs.

The case was never investigated, such cases were usually hushed up.[124]

Platon Karataev was described differently, and so were the servants who

---

[124] Footnote by V. Shklovsky—I know that there is another opinion regarding the death of Dostoevsky's father, which is why I'm saying that mysterious cases were hushed.

stayed behind at the estate. That's how Tolstoy saw them, and evidently, that's how they felt.

Dostoevsky dreamed about another Russia. She was not another, but she was "sudden," unforeseen. It didn't come true.

But it was insinuated that Alyosha Karamazov, an almost saintly person, was supposed to become a revolutionary in the forthcoming chapters.

And Kolya Krasotkin, a boy who read widely, the future good person, was supposed to grow up into a revolutionary.

Dostoevsky ordered his wife to bury him in the Aleksandr Nevsky Monastery. This is where Belinsky was buried, and he wanted to secure himself among that rank at least in his tomb; about the Volkovo Cemetery[125] he used to say that this was where enemies were buried. Remember that this is where Gleb Uspensky[126] was buried; writers of various ranks, but mostly, the *raznochintsy*, people of no particular status.

Dostoevsky died when he was just becoming recognized, but fame, acknowledgement and even more—understanding, the understanding of his novel's structure as a construction of the soul, a soul desiring for change and freedom, the bottomless soul, the homeless soul, this recognition, it seems, is just coming now.

[125] In 1710 the Aleksandr Nevsky Monastery became the owner of the Volkovo lands. It was during the time when the cemetery was founded although officially it became a St. Petersburg cemetery only in 1756 by a decree of Empress Elizabeth I. The eighteenth century Volkovo was for the most part a poor man's cemetery. Because its "inhabitants" were poor, neither their relatives nor the state spent much money on the cemetery's maintenance.

[126] Gleb Ivanovich Uspensky (1843–1902) was a Russian intellectual and writer whose realistic portrayals of peasant life did much to correct the prevalent romantic view of the Russian agricultural worker. His first important work, *The Customs of Rasteryayevoy Street* (1866), is a series of narrative essays about poverty and drunkenness in the suburbs of Tula. For a time he was a follower of the Populists, but unlike them he refused to idealize the Russian peasant, whose primitive life became the main subject of his writing, as in *The Power of the Soil* (1882). After spending most of his last ten years as a patient in mental homes, he committed suicide.

18

BRONZE OF ART

I.

Lev Nikolaevich Tolstoy belongs not only to the Russian novel, the highest kind of literature, but also to the little known Russian memoir literature and the practical genre of travel prose.

It was Mark Twain who said that when you're writing a novel, you draw your material from one reservoir and fill another one with art.

Some of the material is discarded, it doesn't fit into the creative act. Tolstoy was creating something that was still unknown.

Russian practical and literary prose—Afanasi Nikitin's voyages, the travels of pilgrims to the Holy Land, the journeys of our explorers—is excellent prose well known to many writers including Lev Nikolaevich Tolstoy.

When Tolstoy lived in Starogladkovskaya, on the Terek, it's as if he had three voices.

Heraclitus the Obscure said that in order to have unity, there must be multiplicity first, which will ultimately unify.

I already cited an example, the lyre, i.e., there isn't just one string, but several, each one of which plays various notes; or the polyphonic songs that exist in folklore.

Tolstoy wrote with the English novel in mind—his love for Sterne. At the same time, he wrote practical prose, or no, he was preparing to write it.

The beginning of *The Cossacks* reads like the notes of a traveler; there is not a single fictional character in it.

Tolstoy loved travel books, originality even though it wasn't art.

In his notes, Tolstoy mentions Captain Vasili Golovnin:[127] Tolstoy relates to himself as one who has gone through a shipwreck and has been cast on an unknown island.

He is amazed:

—How is it that I don't know,

—Why is it that I don't know.

—Who am I?—he writes.

—Why am I here? I don't know.

Why he is reading Golovnin, he doesn't know either.

Captain Golovnin wrote a history of shipwrecks. He was a famous navigator.

This was a man who strove to change the world; he falls prisoner in Japan and bears himself with great dignity; he is a man from a different world, someone who experiences another culture and becomes only moderately captivated by it.

Golovnin describes shipwrecks, then analyzes what was right or wrong in the captain's actions.

It read like an observational novel.

The shipwrecked person is tossed out of life.

And here I must change the course of my thought:

—to a conversation with Friday that Defoe seems to be transcribing. I'll rephrase this. Defoe is transcribing his education of Friday. He

[127] Vasili Golovnin (1776–1831), author of *Memoirs of a Captivity in Japan, 1811–1813* and *Around the World on the Kamchatka, 1817–1819*. The voyage of the *Kamchatka* was one of the most notable Russian voyages of the early nineteenth century.

teaches Friday the English language and religion; he explains who the English god is.

At first the man begins to hunt, then he domesticates animals, but he doesn't have a dog and it's difficult to watch over the herd of goats; then he builds a boat that doesn't work too well, it's too big.

Defoe's half-documental, half-fictional book is preserved for us by children, like the ground holds onto roots.

Defoe enriched English literature with his uninhabited island—he showed the gradual emergence of culture.

Western culture is shown only by what has been saved from the ship; the first marriages, failures—the emergence of a new society. It seems that in order to have a new society there has to be a shipwreck. Defoe discovers this by accident.

The great author wrote daringly. He could have taught all those people who later wrote about him, but they weren't under his editorship.

Lev Nikolaevich wrote *War and Peace* in order to re-examine the history of war: the history of 1812. It's both a novel and a military investigation.

Here emerges the great commander of fiction, the commander of describing life through prose, the re-examination of life that becomes an artistic experience in itself.

Tolstoy spoke of Chekhov with great admiration. He talked about "The Darling" as though it was the world's greatest discovery—the discovery of life. The woman, who seems blindly to change her husbands because they are so available. They live in her house. The story ends with pure, unselfish and tender love for a young boy, a first-grader—the Darling had never experienced the joy of having children.

Tolstoy says that the Darling, the wife with many husbands, didn't ever change her life, she took them in as a forest, in winter, would take in a person on skis.

Tolstoy loved Chekhov gently, sometimes even jealously. He said that Chekhov created a new kind of realism, that even though his characters were drunks and foul-mouthed people, they were saints. He said: "I'll apply this to my book *Hadji Murad*," a book that was being written almost all of his life, a book that sometimes would change its title to "The Abrek."

The Abrek is a person who went away, who left the communities of the Caucasus.

Sometimes a Russian soldier could become an Abrek.

Hadji Murad is an incredible book.

I don't know how to write about it and won't even attempt to use the purely incidental fact that I'm still living.

Deserts appear because people trample the wild grass; they appear because of the goats and camels.

Tolstoy loved Chekhov. He didn't utter one bad word about him. Only regretted: "He wasn't religious."

But why wasn't Lev Nikolaevich impressed with Chekhov's dramaturgy?

And so, let's write: Chekhov's Prose and Dramaturgy.

It's not good enough to describe a person as kind or evil, it's necessary to look into his soul, weigh it in your hands, changing the ship's coordinates in the sea, changing the angles between the land and the sun.

Chekhov wrote stories without a beginning or an ending.

He wrote to his brother, Aleksandr, a talented man and the father of the ingenious actor Mikhail Chekhov, a person full of promise for the future, he wrote that after composing a story one should tear out the first five pages without reading them. He kept changing his own expositions and denouements.

According to Chekhov, ancient drama knew only one scenario—the hero either got married, or he died.

The old prose hadn't died yet.

But Chekhov was on a new road, on a road that hadn't been investigated, hadn't been trodden, not even seen.

He started off by examining Nature.

Nature—that's us.

He began with the small children, who embody nature and, therefore, don't see it.

If you think what I just said is contradictory, well, good.

Nature has been described thousands of times; it has been harmed not only by war, but also by people who stomped it in their search for refuge.

A lot has been crushed here since the erection of the Tower of Babel: while they were transporting clay and, later, during the departure of the building teams after their failure.

In "The Pipe," Chekhov wrote how the rivers were drying up and the forests changing.

The shepherd's pipe quietly mourned the sufferings of nature.

The old coffin-maker with his metallic nickname Bronze[128] was a cold-hearted egoist, a hard-working man to the point of stupidity—Bronze had never paid any attention to his wife, and only when she had reminded him of the infant with flaxen hair that had died a long time ago, he remembered in bitterness that there had been an infant, there had been a forest, rivers, birds. Everything had disappeared.

"What losses!" the hard working coffin-maker thought to himself.

"Had all survived, imagine how rich we could've been."

He composed a song on his old fiddle, a song about the dying earth.

I'll continue so that I don't lose my thought.

Rothschild the flutist heard the song when Bronze's dogs were chasing him away.

Bronze wrote down the song.

Chekhov wrote *Uncle Vanya* and gave it to the theater; for this play's set design he hung a picture, or as we call it now—a diagram of how many animals that used to live in our forests around Moscow, and how they all disappeared.

This was sort of the beginning of *The Red Book*.

---

[128] Chekhov's "Rothschild's Fiddle" (1894).

... Here is another subject: *The Seagull.*

These words appear on the signboard of the Moscow Art Theater.

It's the home of the seagull.

I'm writing about *The Seagull* in Peredelkino.[129]

It's snowing outside, and it's impossible to go out until the snow decides whether it's snow or rain.

It's not easy to enact a change of theme.

Not too far away from here, at the Lobnya Station, there is a lake that's been taken over by a kingdom of seagulls—all right, let's not exaggerate, a duchy of seagulls. There are so many of them that they even fly over the fields, they fly with the rooks after the plowman.

Well, these days—it's after the tractor.

The word "seagull" has no gender class.

The males of the flock are gulls, too; the form of their coat is identical.

A young writer by the name of Treplev is a failure, born to a talented woman who is greatly admired by the public, an actress who isn't very profound.

She will later become the mistress of the famous writer Trigorin.

I don't like to talk about prototypes, but generally speaking Trigorin's books are charming to read, he is an ordinary, successful writer, whose name might remind us of Potapenko.[130]

---

[129] Located in the town of Peredelkino, about eight miles from Moscow, the village was established in 1936 during the Stalinist era and served as a writers' colony. The novelist Aleksei Tolstoy, poet Yevgeni Yevtushenko, cellist and conductor Mstislav Rostropovich and his wife, opera singer Galina Vishnevskaya, all have lived here. It was in Peredelkino that Rostropovich gave refuge to Aleksandr Solzhenitsyn.

[130] Lydia Mizinova was a friend of Chekhov's sister Masha; her unrequited love for Chekhov drove her into the arms of the writer Ignati Potapenko. In 1894 the two ran off to Europe together, but when Mizinova became pregnant, Potapenko, who was married to his second wife, abandoned her in Switzerland. Mizinova's infant died three weeks following *The Seagull*'s St. Petersburg premiere, echoing the fate of Nina's child in a sad instance of life imitating art.

Treplev is his mother's illegitimate son, he is regarded as a Kiev provincial. His first name is Konstantin, like Balmont.[131]

Chekhov met Balmont in Yalta, in his summerhouse.[132] He brought Balmont to Gaspra.[133] It's close by.

Tolstoy respected Chekhov very much. But he didn't like Balmont's poetry.

He even waved his arm in disapproval.

Aleksei Maksimovich Gorky was telling me about this incident. But he said that Tolstoy's eyes were rather intent, he simply didn't want to admit to himself that he liked it.

Balmont recorded this episode too.

Treplev is the son of an actress, his kingdom hasn't been conquered yet, it has to be his own, his own art, but it's ruled by Potapenko.

Trigorin is his mother's civil husband.

The kingdom of the young prince belongs to a third-rate man, such a worthless man that each time he finished a glass of wine he would have the royal cannons fire.

Trigorin loves the thunder of fame.

Treplev did a stupid thing on the shore of the beautiful lake. He killed a seagull.

Treplev loves a woman like Hamlet loved Ophelia, only Hamlet's love was reciprocated, whereas Nina Zarechnaya doesn't love Treplev. Or more precisely, she fell out of love after she met Trigorin in his halo of fame.

[131] Konstantin Balmont (1867–1943), Symbolist poet, translator of Byron, Shelley, and Whitman.

[132] Chekhov's summerhouse in Yalta, known as Belaya Dacha, was a meeting place of Russia's intelligentsia; common visitors to the house were the writers Bunin, Gorky, Kuprin, Balmont, the painters Vasnetsov, Levitan, Korovin, the composer Rakhmaninov, the singers Chaliapin and Panina.

[133] Lev Tolstoy was being treated in the Russian resort Gaspra (west of Yalta) during 1901–02, where he was working on *Hadji Murad*. Chekhov was at this Crimean retreat in 1901, while visiting Tolstoy during a serious illness.

Treplev, like his old friend Hamlet, tried his hand at art.

He built a theater on the lake and gave the woman his manuscript so she could read it.

The audience consisted of Treplev, his mother, Trigorin, and another woman who loves Treplev.

The play is about the disappearing world, how the forests are being cut down and everything is dying away.

There isn't even a partridge left. Everything perished. Only the darling Zarechnaya[134] has a soul, but the Devil threatens her, it's an ordinary devil with human legs—I'm picturing him in a suit.

The Devil is a prototype of Potapenko and Boborykin—not bad folks at all.

They are the murderers of talent.

The dialogues between Treplev and his mother, which I'm not quoting here, remind us of the dialogues of Hamlet with the Queen, she doesn't believe in her son, she laughs at the Kiev provincial, a man who doesn't even own a suit.

■

And the audience bursts in laughter. Back then, in Brazil, the forests weren't destroyed yet, there were no cars and the air above the cities was cleaner, the snow was white.

Treplev is crushed.

He is suffering the failure of his play.

Arkadina is Trigorin's old mistress. For a brief moment she feels pity for Treplev. His wings are clipped.

This was Chekhov's great story about the destruction of the green world.

134 In Russian *zarechnaya* means the other side of the river, so the name of Nina Zarechnaya is also a pun possibly meaning nature that has been untouched by man, i.e., purity, or virginity. In the past, critics have also found this name as being derived from the Russian word *zarya*, which means dawn, the dawn of new possibilities.

Before *The Seagull*, Stanislavsky had produced one of Hauptman's plays. The scene was also set by a lake and the theater still had some frogs that croaked in chorus; when Chekhov's play was being staged, the producer left the croaking frogs on the stage.

Chekhov protested.

The producer said: "But it's realistic."

"Mine is a work of art," replied Chekhov.

There was a lack of agreement.

The croaking of the frogs was supposed to die away from the lake because all living creatures had perished.

Treplev continues writing; they publish him. The young woman who once loved him tells later about how he would receive copies of magazines, money, and how Trigorin arrived.

She says sadly how in Treplev's play nobody is allowed to suffer.

I'll quote the words from *Hamlet* used in the play:

ARKADINA (*reciting from* Hamlet): "My son!

Thou turnst mine eyes into my very soul,

And there I see such black and grained spots

As will not leave their tinct."

TREPLEV (*paraphrasing from* Hamlet): "Nay, but to live in wickedness,

seek love in the depths of sin . . ."

Everyone is in their places.

The king on his unsteady, disputed throne; he is also described as a bad decoration.

Then, while his mother is playing lottery for some petty cash, Treplev who represents the Seagull—the murdered Seagull—shoots himself.

In the end, it's good that Zarechnaya is still alive, but in all theaters across the world the play, in my sad opinion, isn't fully understood. Treplev shoots himself. He perishes like the Seagull that we see by the lake.

Yes, Tolstoy is alive.

And so is Pushkin.

And Chekhov, too.

Evidently, it's best to stage *The Seagull* by a lake.

But the point is that the play is of the imagination, a portrayal of ordinariness that's possible to show only to people who know how to look, people who know how to fly like seagulls, and don't walk on stones like sensible crows or common pigeons.

By the way, the word "pigeon" in Russian has a feminine gender, *golubitsa*.

She is a different kind of bird, from a different class; her voice is different.

II.

Works of art live on, constantly evolving.

Like it was once said and almost forgotten, no one can ever step into the same river twice—the water changes.

And it's not only the water that changes.

It can be the temperature of the water, the width and power of the current.

And besides, since this river originated from another kind of "slanting" rain, allow me a short digression.

I want to be understood by my country,

said Mayakovsky once in his remarkable voice,—

and if I'm not—

        then never mind,

I will pass

      over my native land

sideways,

                  as a slanting rain would pass.[135]

This wasn't at first published as a poem.

Now it lives on.

The slanting rain lives on; it is circulated along the way, passing through the native country, finally turning into water of the ocean, from where its path is also clear.

    ■

I'll repeat.

In other words.

Now those were clearly unnecessary words.

I already said that Treplev was from the same river on the banks of which Hamlet lived and died.

When Hamlet, the strong man who loves his mother and tempts the murderer with his play, who evokes our pity, when he becomes convinced through theater, when he believes through the play in the very thing that he didn't want to believe when he heard it from the ghost, he says that the world is being "dismantled."

The world can't be forever dismantling.

It is healed through literature; it grows a new limb.

But life, extended through art, changes how it's perceived.

The past is seen differently, the future envisioned differently, and the present suffered differently.

Hamlet summons his mother to the court of the present day, he criti-

---

135 From "Homewards" (1925). In his earlier book *Mayakovsky and His Circle* (1940), Chapter 25, Shklovsky wrote in regard to this poem: "He [Mayakovsky] hesitated printing these verses, and only quoted them two years after they had been written in a short piece in *New LEF*, which was an answer to some poet (the sixth issue in 1928). That was his last piece in *New LEF*."

cizes her, tells her about her shoes, the real shoes that the Queen is wearing.

She still hasn't worn out the shoes in which she walked at the burial of her husband and has already forgotten him.

It's quite clear that Treplev is the young Hamlet because Chekhov was a writer who wasn't acknowledged, they whistled at him for showing a new hero, the new hero of the new play.

■

This is a classical example of a traveling plot.

The theme of Orestes, who must revenge the death of his father who was killed at the orders of his mother. The theme passes onto Hamlet—and expands.

Just as the theme about the world being dismantled.

The theme is repeated and reinvented in *The Seagull*.

But for Madame Arkadina, her Hamlet, her son who despises Trigorin, his indignation is, if not comical, then at least trivial in her eyes.

A new view that clarifies and makes innovations on Hamlet's old conflict.

The theme is conceptualized in a new light; furthermore, it's tightly connected with the distinctively Chekhovian theme—man's unjust actions toward the surrounding world.

■

When Chekhov emerged as a writer, they received him in the waiting hall, they wouldn't let him in. He was getting published in *Zritel*, and *Budilnik*, whose editor was Nikolai Leikin, a man despised by everyone. He was told how long his pieces should be, then they were edited and made even shorter, since concision was connected not only to the writer's genius, but also the requirements of being published for the first time.

And on the bitter road of short editorials, sketches and plays he carved out a new literature, the end of which we couldn't have predicted because

he died when he was forty-four, and at forty-four Tolstoy was only starting his *Anna Karenina*.

It was Chekhov who changed the interrelationships in Russian literature, the interrelationships between fact and its treatment in literature.

Traditional plot and traditional denouement, as we know them, are ab-
sent in Chekhov, they're as unforeseen and sudden as Khlestakov's luck
that cheered up the sailors of the Baltic Fleet.

Forgive me. I got distracted and got ahead of myself.

Treplev's tragedy was that even Nina didn't recognize his talent.

The theater stormed and whistled at the discord between old and new
dramaturgy; it was like it would've been today, take for example the staging of Krylov's plays at the Suvorinsky Theater, which is connected to old
playwriting.

People gloated at the failure of a man who had brought a sword into the
world of Russian theater, he brought it like a new genius who is assessing
the world of art. And so this man fell into their hands. He fell into the trap
of the Aleksandrinsky Theater.[136]

The great actress Komissarzhevskaya[137] didn't have the right kind of
voice that would make sense to her audience.

[136] Chekhov's *The Seagull* was staged for the first time on October 17, 1896 at
the Aleksandrinsky Theater in St. Petersburg, the premier of which was not very successful and most traumatizing for Chekhov, as he suffered the worst literary failure
of his life. In response the audience booed and jeered, derisively laughed during
Nina's monologue in Act I. The press reviews were savage: a theater critic for the
Bourse News said the play was "not *The Seagull* but simply a wild fowl." Chekhov hid
in the actors' dressing rooms after the first act, fled the theater, and wandered
through the city in a daze, leaving early the next morning for Moscow. Despondent,
before he could leave Moscow for Melikhovo, his small estate, Chekhov wrote to Su-
vorin on October 18: "Stop the publication of my plays. I shall never forget last
evening . . . I shall not have that play produced in Moscow, ever. Never again shall I
write plays or have them staged."

[137] Vera Komissarzhevskaya (1864–1910) was the most celebrated Russian actress at the turn of the twentieth century. She played Nina Zarechnaya in the premiere of *The Seagull*.

Every success of *The Seagull* was a failure for its audience.

I'll dare say that even the friend and contemporary of Chekhov, Stanislavsky, wasn't able to understand him at the time. I'll try to prove this.

What is Chekhov's central theme?

I'll put it in words that will seem naïve.

It's ecology.

It's man in a world which he is destroying.

In "The Pipe" a shepherd is telling about the drying streams in the forest. It's as though the sun is shrinking from the sky.

A zoologist is showing how life is disappearing, how fauna is disappearing from the forests.

Chekhov decided to show this by hanging a diagram in the theater—statistical facts about the disappearing life.

This is the theme of many of his works.

Most importantly.

It's Bronze's theme.

It's relatively clear what Bronze stands for.

The story "Rothschild's Fiddle" begins like this:

The town was small—no better than a village—and it was inhabited almost entirely by old people who died so seldom that it was positively painful. In the hospital, and even in the prison, coffins were required very seldom. In one word, business was bad.

The town had so many shortcomings that he lamented that there weren't enough people dying.

The coffin-maker incurred losses.

In the long story "My Life," Chekhov wrote about a bad architect who designed buildings so badly, planned the interiors so poorly, the façades were all so hideous that people simply got used to the style of this person.

The style of a failure became the style of the town.

Chekhov hated expositions and denouements; he is the one who revived the two concepts.

I'll repeat once more about how he wrote to his brother saying that the plot must be new and a story isn't always necessary.

By plot he meant the false theater, the poetics of that theater, especially the expositions and denouements of plays—things that the viewer is anticipating with pleasure.

It's like a shot of morphine.

Literature became a place of false denouements, false expositions, false successes, the successes of individual people.

The young boys—the fugitive convicts who turned rich and cried on the graves of their comrades who didn't fall under the protection of the ancient plot, the happy ending.

Even Dickens, after his discovery of ancient plot, got so bloated that he resembled an old sunken boat.

Chekhov is the most desperate of all writers, he is the most straightforward one.

He doesn't want to soften, loosen the threads of life, he doesn't want to be capable of bending them to make a false happy end.

■

I was reading to my son—he was killed at the Neman River after surviving most of the war; he was an artillery officer, backing the infantry with close-range shots, and combating tanks.[138]

He was a little boy back then.

I was reading him one of Andersen's sentimental tales, "The Ugly Duckling."

Once upon a time among the ducks, in the hen yard an egg was laid, a different kind of egg, and the hatchling came out with a long neck, it was very large and ugly, meaning it did not replicate the old forms—I won't say of literature, the hen yard didn't know much about literature—the old habits of the yard, of the cats, hens, ducks, they all despised the ugly thing.

[138] Shklovsky's son, Nikita, born in 1924, was killed on February 8, 1945, during the last days of the war.

At the Aleksandrinsky Theater, Chekhov was an ugly duckling.

And I read—yet I don't like reading, I like telling stories, but I read him this tale, and the child, this plump little creature was suffering; soon the duckling would find out in the reflection of the water that he was a swan, a swan among swans, and then suddenly it turned out that the next page was missing.

I didn't think right away to make up the story, give the life of the little swan, I felt lost.

The page was missing.

My son started crying: what was I supposed to do?

—He turned out to be a swan—I kept reassuring him.

But they tortured the duckling anyway, it can't be undone, the way he suffered; this is how a Soviet boy cried; now, there is only three percent left from his generation.

Theirs was a compassionate generation.

They felt the falseness of happy endings.

Naturally, the dramas and tragedies of Shakespeare were performed in theaters, in courts, where playwriting was replaced with bearbaiting, where packs of excellent, well-fed English hounds would tear apart a bear.

Pushkin wrote about the viciousness and bloodiness of the national theater.

Chekhov wrote a short story called "Ward Number Six."

A conscientious, timid man is talking to another good person who somehow ended up in an asylum, and eventually he ends up in that same asylum.

The story made Lenin shudder.

A person who got entangled in the reality of his times.

The committee couldn't undo the fate of Chekhov's hero.

There was no god, not even an insignificant, or another, local god, who would arrive in his chariot to save him; not even a good doctor who would free him without charge.

We used to be young, we were known as the Futurists, I used to read with Khlebnikov, Mayakovsky, Aseev.

The audience was cultured, the usual Turgenevian crowd.

I hope some day I'll have such an audience again.

I'm old and I know how to talk with my contemporaries.

They were shouting from the audience: "Madmen, ward number six!"

Among other traits—I didn't have too many—I had a loud voice.

I said: You didn't understand Chekhov.

The person in Ward Number Six wasn't a madman.

Some other madmen, out of their own laziness, put him away.

This isn't about exposing a person who was locked up in an asylum.

Why are you shouting about Chekhov whom you don't understand? Think in silence.

This had an effect on the audience only because I talked in a loud voice and didn't shout.

But it helped them as much as a funeral service does a dead man.

Thanks to the excellent acting in *The Three Sisters*, *Uncle Vanya* and *The Seagull*, Chekhov was accepted in the world.

Characters spoke in words that weren't false.

Conflicts weren't getting resolved each time they occurred.

I'll just say, Chekhov's plays like tanks forged the road for Chekhov the belletrist.

It was one of Russian literature's greatest victories.

A kind of literature that has no opening, no denouement, a kind that brings forth new questions.

Chekhov entrusted his greatest tragedy to the coffin-maker.

Shakespeare often had jesters on his stage. They would pay the jesters more than any other actor, and in addition, they were allowed to improvise. In order for Shakespeare to allow someone to improvise—he was the owner of the theater—they had to be very good at it.

There were different kinds of jesters; there were jesters who were actually grave-diggers, and in an old Russian play there wasn't anything strange or accidental about having a prince die without rejecting his faith and then having the grave-diggers come and bury him with a merry song.

The point is that the selection of radically different values to study the world, through the examination of imagined extreme situations, makes the world more understandable than any article about art.

∎

Time, after all, wasn't cruel to Chekhov.

If we consider that he lived on his meager stipend while studying at the gymnasium and the university, then it's not so obvious. But he passed the beginning of his literary career, the beginning of his path through the worst kind of literature. The magnitude of his talent was already apparent. But the artistic influence that formed him as a writer was not so evident.

He obviously loved Gogol. Gogol, the singer.

Remember the steppe, the road, the road of men who sold wool, the middle-aged man, then the priest or coachman, the two horses, the broken britzka that strikingly resembled Chichikov's carriage. This couldn't possibly be a mere coincidence.

Chekhov thought of Gogol as the king, or better yet—the tsar of steppes. He came from the same region as Gogol.

You can already see this geographically.

Evenings on a farm near Dikanka,[139] by Poltavshino, on the shores of the Azov Sea. It was a small town.

Surrounded by steppes—the vast steppes—never described before Gogol.

But he didn't describe them as much as he praised them.

Chekhov had a feeling for nature, which, perhaps, we saw only in Pushkin or Tolstoy.

---

[139] The title of Gogol's collection of short stories. In 1831 Gogol met Pushkin who greatly influenced his choice of literary material, especially his Dikanka tales, which were based on Ukrainian folklore. *Evenings on a Farm near Dikanka*, written between 1831–32, was Gogol's breakthrough work, and showed his skill in mixing the fantastic with the macabre.

■

He is more read than written about.

I can tell you many things about him.

People knew Chekhov through his short humoristic feuilletons.

But when they read "My Life" and "The Steppe," they complained that "The Steppe" was too boring. They couldn't get back their subscription money, and, in the meantime—it took them years—they were trying to get used to Chekhov's style.

Let's return once more to the town, which had so few people dying that it was a pity, according to Chekhov, and it would have been better if everyone living in that unhappy town had died, and in this town lived a hard working coffin-maker who was good at trading; for some reason people had forgotten his real name and called him Bronze. Perhaps because he was the biggest man in town.

The fame of Bronze's name weighed heavily upon the town—he was not supposed to die. He reminded one of a living memorial.

Imagine a cabin with a workbench, coffins, a double bed, and Marfa, who was mistreated by her husband, although he never raised his hand on her. He simply didn't pay any attention to her.

Bronze made good coffins; for women or for men of good birth he made his coffins to measure; for the rest, he didn't bother with measurements.

He didn't like making coffins for children. And in the houses of crying parents he would say: "I confess I don't care much for wasting time on trifles." The commission for little coffins was in fact very small. The parents carried the coffin on a towel over their shoulders.

The towels were hand-sewn ahead of time, and when carrying the coffin, they would hold it up with their hand.

And so that you have a better picture, Pushkin wrote about this, too.[140]

140 The untitled poem Shklovsky is referring to was written in 1830 and ends with the following lines:

In Chekhov's "Gooseberries" a man spends all of his life planning, he wastes his life on saving up for a plot of land where he can plant gooseberries.

The plan is realized.

When he tries eating the gooseberries, they turn out to be sour. Still he keeps repeating how good they taste. In the room next-door a fat heiress is cleaning the kitchen as if it's already her own.

In this story, the man who ruined his own life for gooseberries is satisfied with the way they taste—this is suicide. The narrator says how many people are content and that one needs to knock on their doors because they are dying and they still think they're happy.

This unexpected plot twist, the negative ending, is felt acutely because you were anticipating a positive ending.

The coffin-maker.

Bronze is conceived as a big bronze man.

People often die.

We all do.

I'm warning you.

This fact surfaced in literature.

Here is a finished piece of literature.

Bronze's wife was dying and she was content that she was dying because nobody will fight with her in the other world, nobody will shout, there is no Bronze there, perhaps there is a river there, maybe some trees, like on the road to the churchyard.

In her delirium she says to her husband:

"Do you remember . . . God gave us a baby with flaxen hair?"

"That is all your imagination," says Bronze, "we had nothing."

Oh, here comes a peasant, with two women behind him:

Bareheaded, a child's coffin under his arm;

From afar he shouts out to the priest's lazy son

To call his father and open up the church.

"Hurry up! We haven't got all day!"

The woman dies.

Bronze was an uncompromising worker, he was afraid of losing money, but he didn't work during holidays.

His wife would die, then there would be a holiday—one shouldn't work on holidays and the work would have to wait.

It was a holiday and Bronze went out for a walk.

By the river, there once stretched an oak and birch forest, now there was nothing, only the empty banks of the river, and indeed there had been a child, and it had had flaxen hair.

There had been flocks of birds, geese; he could have gone hunting, and then sold the meat and feathers.

He could have made a fortune from the forest.

Why had they cut down the forest?

What terrible losses!

Why do such terrible losses occur? Why can't man live without losses?

Why did he have to shout at his wife?

Before this we are introduced to Bronze as a musician who played in a Jewish orchestra. What kind of an orchestra can there be in a town where people died so seldom that it was positively painful?

He played on a fiddle. When Rothschild came to fetch him, Bronze had his dogs chase him away.

This was a funny incident.

After Bronze had counted up human losses—of the heart, monetary, universal, permanent losses, he was already dying.

It's as though he was dying while also being resurrected.

Bronze people die too.

The priest came, there was a confession.

After his confession Bronze said:

"Give the fiddle to Rothschild."

Rothschild was a musician in the worst orchestra in the world, he was the one who listened to Bronze play and cried.

When Bronze died, the Jew got the fiddle and the memory of Bronze's music as an inheritance.

He played about losses, about how man is destroying the earth, about human evils, how men are evil to women, and women, evil to men.

Mankind tramples the earth.

It's destroying itself. It can't even understand why.

Bronze understood little from life, but he was a musician and he didn't realize that he was a great musician.

A great artist can convey himself through simple words that will elevate his work to incredible heights.

The Jew tried to remember what it was that Bronze played.

He couldn't remember, but people did, they remembered in the small town during the weddings and funerals.

In this small town where there were only a few musical instruments and musicians, people tried to remember Bronze's songs. His music, the music of Bronze's fiddle.

The story is constructed on such realistic details that it's impossible not to believe.

This change of plan, the transformation of a bad person into someone great, the removal of someone's scabs is a noble task.

Although the act of unmasking is, perhaps, heroism too.

Chekhov showed the losses of life; he uncovered the lives of failed people who can't even talk to their wives.

People who can't—at all—communicate with each other.

I'm not going to define Chekhov's new forms.

They are very simple.

They are like unfinished works; or, better yet, works that have not yet been written.

And in these works there is place for the conscience and for the demands of happiness.

In the midst of jeering and protestation, Chekhov conquered our stage; the stage of Europe, the stage of the world; sometimes it so happens that in the same city they stage several of his plays simultaneously.

When Treplev spoke of new forms, he said that it wasn't about form but the purpose of art.

Gogol got involved with the private lives of the "old world landowners" and told about how a woman died without even having the time to worry about her "own poor soul," just taking the trouble to advise her husband whom she was leaving an orphan and unprotected.

An ordinary person. In an ordinary room. And her husband wasn't able to forget her—it was true love.

■

"The Steppe," of course, has no ending.

This is made absolutely clear.

I'm coming to the end of my own book.

I'm very old. I have seen a lot; sometimes I've had to squint my eyes.

I have read a lot.

I was lucky enough to pass by Ward Number Six and not end up there.

At times I was happy.

And unhappy, too.

I have lost friends.

It seemed everything was finished.

But it only seemed so.

Here is a man sitting in front of me, he is half my age.

He has his own road to follow.

This young man, a new friend, helped me.

Without him, without Aleksandr Stroganov, I would have probably not reached the end of my book, it came to me with great difficulty.

After all, I'm a storyteller.

My handwriting is bad.

When you are telling something, you look at your listener as if you are looking into a mirror.

And so. There is a variety of mirrors.

You get smarter in the process of work, you learn while working.

At least that's what I believe.

I'm quite experienced now.

And I finally understand simplicity.

How does one achieve simplicity?

It comes when you don't feel that you have done what you have done in order to prove what needs to be told.

But I watch how life changes. The life that Mayakovsky believed in.

The word "faithfulness" is derived from the word "faith."

He didn't die because he made a mistake.

III.

But Chekhov had a good predecessor: Chekhonte.

I'll say this: the pettiness of life can be turned into plot.

As in Chekhonte.

Karenin's hesitations as to whether to demand a duel, whether to kill the other man or himself, are tragic in themselves because they aren't resolved. They exaggerate the tragedy of the situation.

Chekhov's reasoning is the reasoning of a person whose wife has been unfaithful.

He wants to kill his wife.

He goes to buy a pistol.

They offer him a variety of pistols.

But then he begins to think.

Kill her?

Or maybe it's better to kill himself?

Or maybe kill both of them?

But he starts talking to the seller.

Then he doesn't know how to leave the store.

As a result he ends up buying a net for catching birds that he doesn't need.

What we call plot—the unexpected turns—are unique reversals that destroy the present situation through the introduction of a new structure.

We should note immediately that in his short pieces, which are almost like signatures under drawings, Chekhov emphasizes shifts in meaning.

A young woman asks a writer to write about her.

She tells how once she was poor, then got married to a rich old man.

The husband dies, she is rich and free, but she is faced with a problem.

—What problem?—naively asks the writer, whose name is Anatole.

—I have a suitor who is also an old man.

The original sentimental story is given a twist in the most simple way.

Two old school friends meet each other in "Fat and Thin."

One of them has been successful.

The other has remained poor.

He carves wooden cigarette cases to make ends meet.

They talk like good old friends.

But then it turns out that the fat man is a very high official.

Then the overwhelmed thin man introduces his family once more to his old friend.

It turned out to be a very difficult and yet simple meeting, it's as if one of them jumped out of the window.

We see how a negation of the ordinary through the ordinary creates the most extraordinary collisions.

A hungry dog ends up in a circus because it's talented.[141]

Then it returns home where it was kept hungry and will always be kept hungry.

The dog's faithfulness is pathetic. When people pass it down from hand to hand it's perceived as the author's faithfulness—his own talent is being passed down from hand to hand.

It's Chekhov who wants to break free from the ordinary.

It's he who is being passed down from hand to hand—he has a talent.

It's Chekhonte.

141 Chekhov's "Kashtanka."

The dog is unhappy because it has returned to its ordinary life.

Playing lottery was a children's game; it tragically turns up in *The Seagull*. A man shoots himself, while everyone else is playing lottery.

Meaning, they are busy with nothing.

A journey to Sakhalin;[142] it's as if Chekhov meets his characters there.

And there is nothing romantic about prisoners.

This is not a journey into exotic lands, although there are instances of crossing rivers; there are no roads—absolutely no roads—and *such* a wilderness, that neither Cooper nor Mayne Reid had ever known.

Mark Twain wrote about this wonderful place in Russia called Siberia. He wrote an interesting novel that nobody remembers.

He says that the best citizens of Russia are those who died in Siberia. If you resurrect them, it would be the best thing in the world.

Chekhov was convinced that daily occurrences were rich in plot; in parts they were even romantic.

He has a story: a peasant is leading a tramp, a lost person who once used to walk among people.

A former romantic, he is now completely crushed.

A man of the past, the peasant is talking to his former friend. He is in despair that his friend is no longer a romantic, he has given up hope.

These are people who were called *melyuzga* or the "little people," Chekhov tells their stories with great respect; even the "book of complaint" is tragic, there is nobody one can complain to.

A pious bishop who was fasting wasn't able to find food without meat; the answer is: "Eat what they give you."

What a terrible resolution.

Chekhov is not very well understood.

"Anna on the Neck" was staged quite a few times, it was even made into film.

---

142 The title of Chekhov's treatise describing his visit in 1890 to the Russian penal colonies on Sakhalin Island and Siberia.

A woman is saved from poverty at her father's house, a penmanship teacher, who has nothing but a harmonium.

This woman, after she becomes noticed by high-ranking officials, instills her husband with fear, the man who thought that he'd done her a favor by marrying her, she tells him: "Go away, you blockhead."

In Chekhov, she is the kind of woman, mistress, whom Saltykov-Schedrin used to call "de Pompadour"—she is at the same time frightening and pitiful.

On film, she is presented as the object of everyone's envy, the woman who made a career.

But Chekhov also has the triumph of beauty.

He enters the world of outcasts as an insider. He is one of them, he takes responsibility for them.

He tells about a professor and a young boy who works for him, the boy corresponds with him and talks to him; the boy is hungry and cold, but he isn't being reproached for not having enough lines per page.

The professor almost loves this boy.

He is the only one who pities him.

A poor prostitute is being humiliated, she is passed down from hand to hand—among students.

She is in a shirt, a student is drawing the internal bodily organs on her shirt so as not to flunk his exam. He talks to her arrogantly. She returns him his change, some coins from things she had bought.

This is almost like not being guilty at all.

The oldest daughter has been married off.

The father says to his wife, "I couldn't sleep all night because of the bedbugs."

It's not because of the bedbugs, it's out of happiness because they married off their daughter.

They are uncomfortable with their own happiness, so they blame the bedbugs.

In this way, pettiness and hypocrisy can be used in plot construction.

Turn the telescope around and it will become a microscope.

The whole of Antosha Chekhonte, perhaps subconsciously, is a giant plot.

The britzka resembles the britzka of Chichikov that carries a priest, and a boy who is going somewhere to school for a small amount of money, and the steppe is seen through the eyes of the child, the steppe—not romantic but terrible in its uncontrolled power.

Chekhov talks about the writer's responsibility toward the beauty of nature.

He is against oversimplifying reality, against turning plot into a story, into a conventional sign.

■

His father, a small grocer, used to flog him as a child—the son would never forget this; he was forced to sing in the church choir—the brothers were praised, but they felt like they were little prisoners; and nobody has ever portrayed the graciousness of those children, the poor man's children who would repay their parents for the tears and beatings by fulfilling their dreams.

In Lopasnya, he builds a farm for his father, and then in a peasant church he sings an old church song in his father's presence, he also plants a garden for him—he makes his father's dream come true.

When someone asked Chekhov's mother and sister if he ever cried, they thought for a while and then remembered: "Not even once."

■

Chekhov said that he had two periods in his life, when they whipped him and when they stopped the whippings.

He was the grandson of a serf.

The son of a grocer who loved the church choir, a cruel, reticent man who had blinders on.

It's as though in the history of literature you won't come across a story that's more moving or decent as Chekhov carrying his large family on his back.

Someone so free in his judgments, who loved Tolstoy, who strangely never noticed Dostoevsky, and who freed literature from the slavery of old forms.

That was Chekhov.

He reproached art, especially the theater arts, saying how the endings had been reduced to either:

—the hero leaves,

or

—the hero dies.

This accusation and remark about the fate of heroes can be applied even to Shakespeare.

Everyone died in Hamlet.

They were all killed and poisoned except for Horatio.

He must tell what has happened.

But Chekhov has only one teacher in dramatic art—Shakespeare.

Only Tolstoy noticed this because he disliked Chekhov's plays as much as he disliked Shakespeare's.

He was jealous of Chekhov's love for Shakespeare.

This love came between them.

The infuriated audience was watching *The Seagull* in St. Petersburg. Among them were Chekhov's friends. They couldn't understand how he grew so fast, how he moved away, how he became so well known. So they joined their voices to the jeering and whistling of the audience.

Chekhov left.

They wrote about him profusely, then they pardoned him, but until today nobody has noticed that the young Treplev—the Kiev provincial, the son of a famous actress who plays mediocre roles, lives a senseless life and fails to notice her own son—is a man who sees through everything, sees things that others don't—the pettiness of one's surroundings.

Chekhov said that Tolstoy's greatness was in the way he described everyone except for the main hero, his Hamlet—Nekhlyudov—the hero who wanted to understand everything on his own, who wanted to change the world by himself.

And in the meantime, at the beginning of the play, the new hero Konstantin Treplev, or Chekhov's Hamlet, has built his own "trap" on the lake, like Shakespeare's Hamlet he has created his own stage for unmasking.

He is unmasking a crime.

But in order for the audience to understand who he is, the daring author quotes the direct words of Hamlet and the Queen.

On the lake, by the theater built for the purpose of showing something new, he reveals this something new using Shakespeare's words.

The matter here is about art, about the great kingdom that has no borders, that has had many conquests and many losses.

Art shows us how to see, but people sometimes want to sleep in peace, they do or don't want to look at themselves in the mirror.

A somewhat talented actress who is terribly stingy lives in her artificial world of art, sleeping perhaps with Potapenko, or maybe with the editors of the newspaper of those days, or with other fashionable people who patted Chekhov on his shoulder until one day they found out that he had grown and that it was almost impossible even to reach his shoulder.

There was the coffin-maker Bronze, who at first didn't see anything except the coffins, who didn't remember anything except for his music that he played on the fiddle and who used to be invited to play at weddings.

He was stingy and made profits from weddings.

He belonged to that guild that his predecessor, Shakespeare, described so well.

The grave-diggers' guild.

The fiddle music of Chekhov will play forever, awaking the steppe.

19

ON THE OMITTED CHAPTERS

GOGOL—WHY IS *DEAD SOULS* UNFINISHED?[143]

It's impossible to even try presenting Russian literature in its entirety, it's too rich; but it seems I omitted the most important part of what is important.

Gogol wasn't understood by foreign readers immediately.

A tree is cut down and floats on the river, during which time the wood dries, its sap evaporates and instead fills up with water.

Water evaporates from the trunk much more easily.

The wood then is stored according to size.

Then bonfires are made—not to burn the wood, but to dry it.

The wood is sawed into pieces.

Then dried again.

Then tied together.

These are the raw pieces for construction.

The pieces are dried again, then shaped into forms, planed and treated with oil.

[143] In his final years, Gogol struggled, as Tolstoy did later, with his work, repenting of all he had written, and in the frenzy of a wakeful night burned all his manuscripts, including the second part of *Dead Souls*, only fragments of which survived.

Then dried again.

After which the wood can be used to build something; in the old days it was usually a ship. It went on voyages, then got old. It was pulled to the shore and dried.

Then sawed into pieces.

Old frigates were used for making furniture.

In Old England they even knew which battleship an armchair was made from; an armchair in which a person who had earned his place would calmly sit.

But of all the conditions, of all the kinds of lives and deaths that a tree can have—the best is growth.

The wind bends the tree, dries it, transforms it, and the tree blooms.

Pushkin was the greatest of all trees and the greatest master of the woods of poetry.

He immortalizes poetry.

He would leave his drafts without changing them; they would ripen with time, then used in the construction, obtaining new contradictions in the meantime. He wasn't the only one.

Both *Eugene Onegin* and "The Kreutzer Sonata" live with contradictions like a tree lives with the earth, wind and sun.

I heard how Khlebnikov once made a bonfire in the steppe; the paper he used for the fire burnt cheerfully.

Velimir burned his manuscripts in order to make the future a better place.

The flame lives inside unfinished works, they need to be reworked; but they aren't complete yet.

More accurately, these are different works—they are the works of the future.

At the end of the week Mayakovsky would clean out his pockets, I have already said this or will say it again, it doesn't matter, he would empty his pockets and burn the drafts: so they would grow back again.

He had the excellent memory of a poet.

The editors of collected works sometimes rush while constructing, assembling the pieces that have already been composed; in the process, some of the truly valuable works get pushed aside, neglected.

When only a few people knew Khlebnikov, when his name wasn't so well known, he lived close to Piatigorsk, in a small settlement.

There was a telegraph office there and Khlebnikov worked as a guard. In that place there were logs, for registering and documenting each transaction.

Khlebnikov would ruin the book; he had nothing else to write on, and he didn't know any better.

In the book he would write down pieces that were still rough, as though not formed yet.

They should've been preserved.

Although all our archives are full.

They are usually overflowing with fresh water. But is that what we need in this world?

And so, they append those diary entries that contain the birth of the future to the collected works, they don't know what else to do with them, as though to go beyond some norm that was set by someone at some point in time.

I suppose I'm talking about something vague.

Tolstoy said the deeper you dig, the clearer it becomes.

Even the Russians and the Germans and the future will understand you.

He was talking about Dostoevsky.

The excerpt that you'll read is a diary entry—I'll present it to you like a coachman delivering wood.

It's torn from a draft-book.

No, not even.

It's taken from the night. Torn from the bosom of the night.

They have no idea where to put it in the collected works.

Precious stones can exist without being part of a pile; although they need to be cut, their chippings are used for the treatment of metal.

Here are the words of the great Gogol—a vow to the future: a sacrificial oath of labor that will go into the completion of the writing.

It's "The Prophet" of Pushkin.

A poem highly regarded by Dostoevsky.

He knew how to read it.

It seems as if it's telling about an attack by the strong on the weak, on something misshapen, something almost crushed.

Not at all.

In the life of the world, and even in the life of a tree, and in the life of prose and poetry, there is only one phase of accomplishment.

> He split my chest with a blade,
>
> Wrenched my heart from its hiding,
>
> And into the open wound
>
> Pressed a flaming coal.[144]

This is how poems should be composed.

And so the instants of creation hold up the entire construction.

It's very difficult to conceive them.

They mustn't be rushed.

Pushkin's entries are simply brilliant.

Tolstoy's diaries burn with great torments . . .

I'm presenting you with a small piece from Gogol's prose.

It's left out like a torn page.

But it contains a world that's still not understood by anyone.

The entrance into a great and mysterious expanse.

I'll hold the door.

So that you can enter.

[144] From "The Prophet" (1826).

Great, glorious Moment. God! How the waves of different feelings have crowded around and overflowed it. No, this isn't a dream. This is that fatal, irresistible brink between memories and hope. Memories that are almost gone, overtaken by hope . . . My past rustles at my feet, through the mist above my head flickers the unpredictable future. I beg you, my Genius. Oh life of my soul! Don't hide yourself from me, keep vigil over me in this moment and don't recoil from me in this year that's arriving ever so alluringly. What will you be like, Future? Will you be dazzling and grand, are you preparing great tasks for me, or . . . ? Oh, please be dazzling, productive, completely devoted to labor and serenity! Why are you standing in front of me so mysteriously, Year 1834? Be my angel. If idleness and insensibility come near me for even a second—oh, rouse me, don't let them triumph over me! Let your polyphonic [or polysemic; ambiguous handwriting—V.S.] numbers like a clock, like conscience [or a testament—V.S.] stand in front of me: so that each of your numbers strike my ear louder than the bells, so that like a galvanic rod it will shock me throughout my body.[145] Mysterious, unfathomable Year 1834! Where will I mark you with great labors? Among these buildings piled over each other, among these rattling streets, steeped in their mercantile mien— these formless piles of fashion, parades, officials, wild Northern nights, glitter and base dullness? [It's the city of Petersburg Stories—V.S.] Or in my beautiful, old, promised land Kiev, crowned with fruitful gardens, enveloped in my graceful southern sky, intoxicating nights, where the mountain with its harmonious cliffs is sprinkled with shrubs, and bathed by my clear, boisterous Dnepr. Will it be there?—Oh! . . I don't know what to call you, my Genius! Since my cradle you passed by my ears with your harmonious songs, such marvelous thoughts, thoughts born inside that are still mysterious even today, coddled such immeasurable and ravishing dreams in me! Oh, look at me! Beautiful one, cast your heavenly [clear—

---

[145] Footnote by V. Shklovsky—I hear the voice of Khlebnikov—regarding numbers and time.

V.S.] eyes upon me. I'm on my knees. At your feet! Oh, don't part with me! Live with me in this world ... my handsome brother! I will commit to you ... I will commit. Life is boiling inside of me. My works will be inspired. Divinity inaccessible to this world will drift over them. I will commit ... Oh, kiss me and bless me!

When you read this, you think that Gogol is addressing "genius" as though it has a life of its own.

Like Pushkin's Prophet.

■

Foreign readers didn't understand Gogol immediately.

He was translated by Louis Viardot.[146]

They wrote about him—the author is talking about provincial simpletons, who are, on top of that, Russian, and "that's always interesting to the French reader."

There is a new translation of Gogol. I haven't seen it yet, it's a brand-new publication.

I know that it's illustrated by some famous contemporary artist.[147]

Gogol is astonishing.

He astonishes the reader; "it's not gold, it's jasper."

It's an unusually dense, as though naturally born, heterogeneous portrait—it's his own world.

Gogol emerged rather organically.

He emerged right after a period of great poetry.

146 Louis Viardot (1800–83), French writer, critic and translator, who translated Gogol's *Taras Bulba*.

147 Shklovsky is probably talking about the edition of *Dead Souls* illustrated by Marc Chagall. The famous dealer and editor, Ambroise Vollard, invited him to do some book illustrations and the artist requested the book to be the Russian author Gogol's *Dead Souls*. Between 1923 and 1927, Chagall engraved 107 etchings on this theme.

After the depiction of an individual or people who can be called "heroes not of their own time."

It's as though people didn't fit in with that epoch.

Great Pushkin knew this.

Lermontov was beginning to understand it.

Gogol, too, knew it well.

In Gogol, the backdrop isn't next to the hero, but behind him, yet it's so substantial and precise that it seems to be both at the forefront and the back.

It's the yet undeveloped vein of the precious vision.

The Nevsky Prospect isn't a backdrop for heroes, it's not a backdrop for the poor man who doesn't have a coat in order to look like a privileged man, it's not a backdrop for someone with the strange name Akaki Akakievich.

Akaki Akakievich is a person of great humility; hence, St. Akaki stands out among the other saints.

His elder, spiritual master tormented the silent subordinate.

When Akaki died and they buried him, the elder addressed the dead man from above:

—What are you lying for, Akaki?

And the dead man replied:

—Blessed are the poor in spirit, for they will see God.[148]

Right before his death, with a last breath, Akaki Akakievich rebelled, he began robbing people of their overcoats and cursing like a cabman.

He wasn't trampled.

He was still alive like a crushed rye stalk that can't help but rise up.

He arose in Dostoevsky.

[148] A quote from the New Testament, Matthew, synthesized from two sayings: "Blessed are the poor in spirit, for theirs is the kingdom of heaven" and "Blessed are the clean of heart, for they will see God." In the Old Testament, the poor in spirit (*anawim*) are those who are without material possessions and whose confidence is in God (the word is also translated lowly and humble, respectively, in those texts).

Poprischin had declared himself King of Spain, because the throne in Spain was vacant, there was a confusion as to who should occupy it; this person to whom the lackeys offered their snuff-boxes, who had a truss of hay instead of hair, he had no place in this world.

He loved the daughter of his office director.

He was the unhappiest hero of the novel.

The vast spaces of Russia weren't yet filled with self-consciousness.

The great steppes, native to Gogol, but as though seen by someone else, stretched behind his oppressed heroes.

This hero, Poprischin, let other people, also poor like himself, wipe their shoes on him, they wiped their shoes as though he was a doormat.

His soul revolted.

His head was full of hay instead of hair, which made women laugh, but in his chest this man had something solid, like the description of the Dnepr.

An incredible description; because often only the incredible can describe the ordinary.

An extraordinary painter who fascinated Pushkin.

This man didn't know his own worth and was Taras Bulba and Akaki Akakievich both at the same.

Who, like Akaki, only loved his own handwriting and sometimes lost himself in the middle of the street thinking he was in the middle of a line, and himself—a single letter in a line the meaning of which he couldn't understand.

Gogol writes about the nobodies of society as though they were the greatest people.

He sees the roundness of the earth in the landscape. When Taras Bulba is departing from home with his sons, the house gradually disappears.

It hides behind the curvature of the earth.

And that's the Ukrainian steppe.

That's the steppe of *The Song of Igor's Campaign*.

The steppe that Chekhov thought no one had really described yet. He became convinced that it was possible to convey it by recording the impressions of a child.

That very person is the one who wrote *The Inspector General*.

Khlestakov was hungry and acted like all hungry men do.

He was frightened by another frightened man. One was shouting, the other was apologizing. Then the person who was apologizing fed him and gave him something to drink from a bottle.

Khlestakov started vomiting the truth. He was uttering things and at the same time getting surprised at what he was saying. He was growing on lies, getting bigger and bigger.

He was turning if not into the emperor himself, then at least into the frightened shadow of the government that will soon behold the enemy ships not too far off from St. Petersburg.

The grandeur of the nobodies, the stony hair, the brightness of cheap jasper that's not good for even carving a portrait.

Khlestakov is tragic because he is frightened.

He lies like a person who wants to delay the tragic moment of punishment for at least three more minutes. And he falls into a whirl of lies, piling one lie over another, like pillows in the house of some old-world landowner.

He gets drunk; after sobering up, he is overcome with a desire to stand in front of someone like a cock stands with spread wings in front of a hen.

He dances *pas de trois*. He is compelled to declare his love for both the daughter and the mother, and both are complaisant.

And both aren't there, they are only the shadow of the smoke.

The senselessness of people's behavior, their fears, their inability to bribe others is all born from their own ability at getting bribes.

These are people with only one hand.

And they have forced others to obey them—cure this person, bribe that person.

I've seen such whirlwinds on the roads that stand up like little moving grey towers, like chimerical witches.

Shakespeare's witches were made from earth; they were the bubbles of the earth.

Khlestakov is the cough of the earth when it's choking; it can't breathe.

He is grandiose, nonsensical and leaves right on time, apparently on a troika; the reader already had time to pity him.

Osip, the servant of this Don Juan, has witnessed the successes of his master. He despises Khlestakov from his little shop in the basement.

■

Gogol wrote of his discontent with the famous actor Nikolai Dyur, who played Khlestakov's part.

He wrote after the production of *The Inspector General*:

> The major role was a failure—as I had expected.
>
> Dyur didn't understand what Khlestakov was for even a second. Khlestakov was turned into someone in the fashion of Alnaskarov,[149] someone from the ranks of those vaudeville rogues, who have come to us from the theaters of Paris to flit about our stages. He became a conventional bluffer—an insipid figure who has appeared in the same guise over the course of two centuries.

The actor A. Diky remembered how M. Chekhov played the role of Khlestakov:

> A young pup, a boy, an unheard of belligerent nonentity, not "without a tsar up in his head," without brains—but someone conniving, who puts his logic to use—and yet with the help of the stupendous irrationality of Russian life he is raised to the rank of "lawmakers," is received as a "figure" invested with imperial powers. And you should've seen ... how this nonentity was swelling and puffing right in front of the audience ... squealing and fervently asserting his overblown vanity, shouting in frenzy: "I'm everywhere, everywhere!!"

[149] Footnote by V. Shklovsky—The main character from Khmelnitsky's vaudeville *Air Castles*.

And he would immediately assume the posture and bearing of the emperor.

What they say in regard to Khlestakov, from a somewhat estranged position, but at the same time generating the same general ideas: a person in a successful role expresses himself best during changing circumstances; he becomes erratic, unexpected, even astonishing to himself.

When a theater connoisseur watches the play, he sees Erast Garin, an actor of the Meyerhold Theater,[150] but simultaneously he sees the actor as a person who is playing a role, and he knows that this isn't Khlestakov. And he might love the changing of the actors because each actor is acting himself—this is the possibility in which that other person, the real person can exist.

An analysis is the result of a complex understanding of what is actually happening.

Merely listing the characteristics of an object is not enough.

There can be various qualities under each listing.

When Velimir Khlebnikov talked about the production of his play, he said that it was a "redressing of nature."[151]

The play was staged only once.

[150] Vsevolod Meyerhold (1874–1940), the most innovative actor and director of the Russian avant-garde theater between 1907–17 who staged classical works in controversial settings and introduced the plays of new contemporary writers like Zinaida Gippius, Aleksandr Blok and Vladimir Mayakovsky. In these plays Meyerhold tried to return to acting in the traditions of *commedia dell'arte*, rethinking them for the contemporary theatrical reality. In subverting Stanislavsky's traditional methods of acting, Meyerhold melded the character with the actor's own personal memories to create a character's internal motivation. In the later years, and especially during the 1930s Meyerhold's art was condemned by Stalin's fanatics and his theater was closed in 1938. A year later Meyerhold was arrested, brutally tortured, and executed by firing squad.

[151] From Khlebnikov's prologue to *Victory over the Sun*: "*Smotrany napisannye khudogom, sozdadut pereodeu prirody*" [Seens written by an arter will create a redressing of nature]. The word *pereodea* is a made-up phrase in zaum, which is a

On one occasion Belinsky wrote a strange review of Mochalov.

He watched Mochalov in the role of Hamlet eight times and gave eight different reviews of each performance.

A good actor's performance can be described not only in terms of how realistic it is, but also how unrealistic, how fragmented or even analytical it can be.

Take the riddle, for example.

You're given some clues that characterize an object—then you are asked: what is it?

A process is initiated where you begin assembling things that are similar.

The assembly of various signs of various possibilities.

What you are doing is climbing step-by-step toward a perception of the whole.

Introduced rather abruptly at the outset of the novel, and even as parody, Don Quixote is defined in several ways.

He is a "madman."

He is a "wizard."

Sancho's definition of Don Quixote: "He is the bravest man."

A person who believes in the possibility of the impossible.

We see Khlestakov at the theater.

We see who he can turn into under various circumstances. And Gogol's words uttered by Khlestakov: "Even the Imperial Council is afraid of me," introduces Khlestakov as a possible contender to the throne.

The possibility of a multi-layered polysemy—this is the nature of art.

The peculiarity of literary analysis, including folklore, is the existence of various answers to one and the same question, that is, different ways of describing a situation.

---

derogatory variant of the word *pereodet* [to change one's dress; to disguise] in association with another word, *idea*, which could possibly mean a conceptual change.

I'll repeat, with great delight: Sancho Panza said that he preferred it when they gave him the answer before the riddle.

In serious or popular literature the answer can sometimes be found in the title.

The analysis and the non-coincidence of its results is the multiple perception of an occurrence (in literature) as various truths; the numerous characteristic qualities of the object aren't enough, and each observation can result in a different answer.

The reversals in plays and novels intersect; their heterogeneity appears in the same light as the multiplicity of answers to a riddle that made Sancho so anxious.

And this multiplicity is characteristic of art itself. Gogol's indignation at the actor who played Khlestakov was his indignation at a problem that had a simple solution. Meanwhile, Khlestakov can be interpreted variously in various situations.

The great actor Mikhail Chekhov said that one had to play him neither as a boaster nor an impostor, but as someone who has turned as if into an echo, he serves as various echoes to various voices.

The things that Khlestakov says and the types that he casts himself in are different.

He is a coward.

He is a boaster when talking about the Imperial Council being afraid of him.

He is in love with two women at the same time.

Khlestakov's multiplicity is Gogol's riddle, the man who created this character.

These are all traces of multiple perceptions of one and the same situation. The characters in the play are riddles even to themselves.

They are puzzling and variously characterized in the play.

When Tatyana Larina says that she was younger then, hence better-looking, this is an assertion about the difference of the object itself.

It's as though the character is shot from various cameras, from various angles; Pushkin's doubts in regard to who Onegin really is appears when he lists several names and ends with the thought: I think that's him.

This was prevalent in Tolstoy, he said that people weren't smart, stupid, brave or cowardly—people were like a river that passes through various valleys, narrow and wide, shoals, and waterfalls.

A person flows and he has all this potential within himself: if he was stupid, he can become smart, if he was angry, he can become kind, and vice versa. Herein lies the greatness of man. And one mustn't judge him for this. Why not? While you are judging, he has already changed. You mustn't say, "I don't love," either. As soon as you have uttered it, it's already something else.

... How marvelous would it be to write a fictional piece that would clearly express a person's fluidity: the notion that he is one and the same —evil, angelic, wise, foolish, fierce, or the weakest creature. [From Tolstoy's diary, February 3 and March 21, 1898—V.S.]

"The literary character" is a literary riddle even for the author himself, the creator.

Dostoevsky typecasts his heroes for himself in various ways.

By way of digression, let's say that the reversals of the heroes in *The Iliad* simultaneously characterize them in different ways. That's Homer under various circumstances.

So is Achilles.

Humankind in the multiplicity of its fate is typecast in contradictory ways; that's the chief method of developing a character.

The blacksmith in Pushkin (in Dubrovsky) locks the door of a burning house; then the same blacksmith risks his life to save a cat on the roof.

The method of art lies in the multiple analyses and the confirmation of the reality of various qualities.

Those people in Gogol's "Old World Landowners," they are as if deprived of feelings, they are as if images that have been hanging on the wall for many years and their owners have stopped noticing them. But the husband is comical when he is teasing his wife with the horrors that could happen to them. They are people who are in love with each other. And on her deathbed, Pulcheria Ivanovna is thinking about her husband more than about "her own poor soul."

An analysis increases its accuracy.

The life of Shakespeare's heroes is both tragic and comic.

Falstaff has the same qualities of a variously described character as you may find in an analysis of Hamlet.

Falstaff dies from becoming disappointed in his protector. He doesn't need anything from this protector. But Falstaff has many facets, his character recurs.

For this gradual, stepped analysis we must create compound and contradictory experiments.

The drawings of prehistoric man, the multitude of his drawings—accurate drawings—mystified people for decades after their discovery.

Because, to begin with, they were inside a cave.

It was impossible to see them.

They were invisible, but at the same time—numerous and accurate.

However their multiplicity was contradictory.

That's a feature of realism.

If they had brought in a lantern, the caveman wouldn't have been pleased; and even if he had been pleased, then it would've been for some utterly different reason.

If the caveman had good lighting, exact points of reference, a good camera, it would have helped him develop a theatrical perception.

I'm talking about conscious visualization.

The energy of delusion is the energy of search; and at the same time—the energy of analysis. The metamorphoses of life. It's interpreted by man in its multiplicity.

Which is why we constantly return to what Dostoevsky said.

He said, "2 × 2 is 4; but it also can be 5, a charming little thing."

The uncertainty then is tested in a thousand ways, but the ambiguity of a work is the most realistic premise.

Tolstoy showed Natasha Rostova as a naïve girl who asked her mother if it was possible to marry two people, but at the same time this is the reality of doubts regarding her relationship with Bolkonsky, Kuragin and her future object of affection, Bezukhov.

Complex perception then is connected with scrutinizing, squinting, bulging one's eyes and almost touching an object with them.

An album of Picasso's drawings was recently published in France.

In his works, Picasso shows unusual multiplicity.

The drawings give us something like a still image of Shakespeare—a not very young, calm-looking man.

In that book, as was already mentioned in one Georgian magazine by a Russian writer, there are different instances from Hamlet's life.

Next to those are sketches of grave-diggers, a man with a scythe, who is probably representing the notion of time.

It's not accidental that in one of his Christmas stories Dickens inserted a clock on which a bronze figure is reaping in some great field.

With the help of this device Dickens is giving a summary of all that has happened in the story.

The unexpected arrival of a person who was thought to be dead, the unexpected failure of a rich man who suddenly thought that he too could be loved.

The unexpected happiness of the main character, the kind, generous husband, the old man who married a much younger woman.

The bronze scythe cuts down every single occurrence.

Art shouldn't be compared with a mirror.

A mirror shouldn't be deprived of its ability to reflect.

Art's concern is not reflection but changes in reflection.

People on the stage wore masks, but they were perceived as human masks. It was possible to see and name who was being portrayed—yet it was a mask.

And the mask was a sign of the multiplicity and unity of human character, exposed by a comedy or tragedy.

The mask is a face without make-up, and at the same time, the mask is the old designation of the actor's and dramatist's craft.

Whereas the idea of changing masks was born from the idea of the mask.

The hero of fairytales is in a mask, the possibilities of which, the fate of which we knew or know from childhood, and this mask in a traditional story that's only slightly changed—

—it's often a parody—

—this mask is a means to experience the effectiveness of reality.

The mask, which is made so that it doesn't falsely suggest that it's a real person, the mask, which exists next to the person, is the result of analysis, it occurs from a shift.

Montage is also associated with this widespread phenomenon—the transformation of the meaning of a scene depending on where it's located (next to this or that scene) and on the moment of action.

Montage is a method of life.

A child, at first, sees the world as turned inside out, then he restores it, but the world has already been seen as a montage.

I didn't list all these instances in literature and phenomena in order to say that they are the same. No.

They describe in different ways; they exist as different portrayals.

The mask, the changing of masks on stage, and the revelation of a continuous stereotypical occurrence to the audience—all of these are the features of a single method in the birthing of art.

The novels of Dickens, the masks that created, that imprinted the mimicry of the English heroes, made them understandable to each other.

This is how we begin perceiving the hero.

Or the phenomenon.

In similar way, Gogol, through the changing images of the Ukrainian baroque, describes the Dnepr in "all kinds of weather."

He talks about the width of the Dnepr, and because the space between the banks is associated with the life of birds that fly over the vastness of seas and continents, he finally resolves to say that only a rare bird can reach the Dnepr's middle.

We know all the birds, but nobody can argue with the way the breadth of the river is described, and we can only feel joy from the power of this image.

Life is in movement.

The Nevsky Prospect in various seasons, the fate of both the painter and people—the dead souls, the peasants, described by Gogol after Chichikov's purchase—this is, without a doubt, a way of seeing, Gogol's method of envisioning things.

The multiplicity of analysis, the multiplicity of phenomena that are given in their analysis is the energy of delusion, it's the path to artistic truth.

It's simultaneously the energy of search *and* analysis.

In art, the answer "five" is also a "charming little thing."

This charming thing is revealed and as if turned into parody in the Arabic fairytale about how several people of different nationalities were being rightly reproached for the death of a man who in the course of the events is resurrected; the fantastic nature of this story is reflected in the fantastic description of foreign lands and turns into a real journey.

This charming thing is the essence of enlightenment of the universe, it is the difference in movements—art sometimes can enter places where the scientist hasn't yet been.

Wasn't it the alchemist who insisted that two times two or two times three is five?

Even in the changes as we age, just like in the change of seasons, there is a movement that we can't really discern.

I'm writing this after a number of attempts to define art.

I think that some of the lines in this book are rather clear, and wherever there is a lack of clarity—it's the path of examination of life itself.

Nothing is frivolous here, just as nothing is frivolous in art.

Tolstoy's drafts, the tons of paper that refuse to be typecast, the irony with which he presents not only Napoleon but also Kutuzov—the world, perceived as love is perceived—that's what life is.

Life is movement.

The methods and descriptions change.

The history of the changes in method is the history of art.

The condition of grasping the new as madness, as an escape, as the abandonment of a permanent home.

Maybe Gogol believed in the resurrection of dead souls and wanted it to happen in some peaceful way.

An impossible thing.

The search for paths on earth and in the universe seems to be the fantasy of a man who sat in a log cabin outside of Kaluga. He kept staring at the cheap wallpaper pasted over the logs.

And this person, with his hopes, with his right to make an attempt, didn't get deluded, just as those people on expeditions didn't get deluded in their own right to explore, and even died trying to reach the poles of the earth.

Which is why the author of this book is asking his reader to be kind.

And there's something else that he is teaching the reader.

The right to search.

Literature plays the role of a poker; it stirs the coals in the fireplace.

I looked through the photographs of various actors who best played Khlestakov's part.

They were as truthful as they should be.

Sometimes they were grandiose.

Perhaps the best of all was Mikhail Chekhov, because he knew that the world had been wasted, that it's worthless now.

The elegance, fear, and childishness of Khlestakov, his boastfulness, is our pity for a nonentity.

Since I'm a relatively old man, I can't pave a new way for myself. Anyway, this road—this road on its own—is still good for reaching big cities.

And it's worn from car tires puffed up like boasters.

This flickering of feeling is like hitting the heart with a rod to get out the dust.

The array of nonentities and their correlation to each other—their hopelessness—broke Gogol's heart.

He drew a picture for the cover of *Dead Souls*, there were some roasted chickens, some hors d'oeuvres, but he didn't show his own delirium.

There was no sensation of a man who lived in an endlessly vast country, journeyed along its endless roads, searching for the impossible, the resurrection of those who never really lived.

Dead Souls isn't finished because it would have been impossible to resurrect those souls.

■

Kotlin Island is located not too far from the shores of St. Petersburg; here once stood a steamship, one of the first steamships ever made.

There were houses, churches, docks from which the ships set sail for unknown lands, to the eternally unknown South Pole.

Kronstadt was a town of the brave.

From here you could easily see the dome of St. Isaac's Cathedral.

And the smoke over St. Petersburg seemed so beautiful, so frightening to Dostoevsky that it seemed to him the smoky city would vanish into the frozen sky.

I came to Kronstadt as a newspaper correspondent right after the October revolution.

They were playing *The Inspector General* in the theater—I can't recall the name, it was a small theater.

Khlestakov was a young sailor.

Not only do I remember very well, but I also know that I've told you about this already. But this is important and I must mention it one more time.

Khlestakov was a young sailor who could kneel down and get up with one quick movement.

He could outsmart even himself and, perhaps, do other impossible things.

The people in the audience knew each other; they sat in groups according to which ships they were on.

They were swimming to the unknown islands of an imaginary world. They liked Khlestakov and felt pity for him.

Isn't he a fool, after all, aren't they going to flog him?

And how glad they were when he left town. A town in which the people are afraid, they are even afraid to lie; at least one person in that town had a good time, and his servant was able to eat a full meal. They gallop away and before them expands the whole world.

And the horses gallop like those bronze horses.

Eternally moving, they stand over the buildings of the great city of Petrograd.

20

ANOTHER NOTE ON THE BEGINNINGS AND ENDINGS OF WORKS— COMPOSITIONS

I.

I'm almost near the end of my book. But I'm afraid of repeating myself and losing my fellow travelers along this journey.

Whoever you are, you probably already know or will learn the paths to art, or, if you will, paths of truth, the energy of knowledge. The energy that polishes stones, weaves lacey patterns in the air with a needle, in the air because there are no hooks here, it's created from threads, stone, memories, and desire. This isn't an easy road. The road itself isn't as important as is observation—multi-perspective, never-ending observation. Knowledge makes the world comprehensible.

Delusions are never-ending, they adorn and elevate one's life.

My short book is about to end.

But I am one of those people who learn as they write. So let's say instead, almost done learning.

Each person has a so-called preconception. They think that they know how to write something that brings all the threads together.

This is something I won't be able to do.

I can only make a circle.

Let's return to the note on the beginnings and endings of works—compositions.

The epic tells the reader about something that he already knows.

Perception is delayed through rhythm, and the detail plays the role of a guide to perception.

The Iliad has a perfect opening; it's like a chain of battles paid for by the rage of Achilles.

But we have already read *The Iliad*.

I'm not going over its contents again.

We see how the threads of the epic are concluded.

But the epic has no ending.

Neither does *The Odyssey*.

■

The preconception of our contemporary age, it would seem, is different.

Let's talk about something related, *Eugene Onegin*. At the very end of the poem, Pushkin says that there won't be an ending. It's as though he is glad that there is no ending.

And it's strange that his statement was repeated in the afterword of *War and Peace*. Lev Nikolaevich wrote that the traditional ending diminishes the meaning of the process initiated by the exposition. He was sorry that compositions had to end with a death, but he also pointed out how the death of one hero shifted the interest to other heroes.

He ends *War and Peace* without clarifying the future fate of the heroes; they are only predicted in the dream of Andrei Bolkonsky's son. Pierre Bezukhov and his friends will apparently perish at the hands of the law-abiding Nikolai Rostov.

It's as if the ending of the novel is unjust. But Pierre Bezukhov and his friends enter the circle of the epic. He must perish for the sake of his ideas.

I'll remind you that in the sketch "The Decembrists" Pierre Bezukhov, an old Decembrist with his wife, Natasha Rostova, and a grown son, returns to Moscow. He returns to the old city, where they respect him for his impeccable language and manners, but he is a person from a defeated army.

All I'm trying to say is that the death of the Decembrists is interwoven in the structure of the epic, even though it's not said in a straightforward way; and Achilles' death, even though we don't see how he is wounded and how he dies, this is the end of the hero and not of the epic.

The ending doesn't exist. There is no happiness.

Tolstoy knew of Anna Karenina's death from the very beginning. But he didn't know who would stay alive and how he would live among the living. He wasn't able to utter truthful words at her grave.

Dostoevsky was delighted by the scene where Aleksei Karenin makes peace with Aleksei Vronsky by Anna Karenina's deathbed. She is dying from postpartum complications. She is dying and praising her former husband, forcing Vronsky to wrest his hands from his face.

Dostoevsky says that there is no better ending than this because no one is at fault.

But this isn't the end of *Anna Karenina*, the story goes on.

Resurrection ends with Katyusha Maslova going to Siberia with her future husband across a great Siberian river. She disappears from the field of our vision and from Tolstoy's judgement.

In his drafts, Tolstoy assumed that it would be Nekhlyudov who would be resurrected, that he would marry Katyusha Maslova. But it turned out to be an impossible thing. There, in England, Nekhlyudov was supposed to be publishing books about land reforms based on the ideas of Henry George, reforms which concluded that land should be taxed but there should be no landowners.

At the end of *Crime and Punishment*, Sonya accompanies Raskolnikov to his exile. She lives outside the prison camps. The convicts respect her, though they don't like Raskolnikov.

Dostoevsky said there would be a new story about Raskolnikov but he never wrote it.

"There'll be no end," Pushkin would have said; or it could have been Dostoevsky.

I'm finishing this book, which I can't bring to an end.

Vladimir Mayakovsky didn't have an end, either—a friend whom I, and the rest of our friends, couldn't help in the last days of his life.

The unhappiness of Anna's love is connected to the unhappiness of Mayakovsky's love.

He constantly repeated these lines:

But that my life may be prolonged
I must be certain in the morning
of seeing you again today.[152]

Can't it be so that . . .

one could without torture
kiss, and kiss, and kiss?![153]

This was pure love.

Mayakovsky was afraid of death and wished for resurrection. He begged the future scholar, the future historian who will be going through his archives: "Resurrect me."[154] He was supposed to be resurrected.

Walking along the pathways of a zoological garden, Lilya Brik, the

[152] Lines from Onegin's letter to Tatyana, which Mayakovsky misquoted and distorted in his "Jubilee Poem" (1924).

[153] From "A Cloud In Trousers" (1915).

[154] From "About That" (1922). Both "A Cloud In Trousers" and "About That" were dedicated to Lilya Brik, the wife of Formalist critic Osip Brik and Mayakovsky's life-long love.

woman who loved animals, the woman whom Mayakovsky loved, was also supposed to be resurrected, and Mayakovsky thought this would be fair.

Lilya Brik died recently.[155]

Death doesn't apologize. Maykovsky knew this.

Mayakovsky Vladimir—a name, a memory without which I can't close this book because I'm not sure if I'll write another book about him. In a poem, Mayakovsky described his own death, and he described his resurrection; he also resurrected the woman whom he loved.

The speaker—the author says:

The gleam that glittered
and that
was then
called the Neva.[156]

The Poet, the resurrection of the Poet, his vigilance, the sensation of a finished task can also be integrated in contemporary poetry.

Now it's only fitting that we return to *The Decameron*.

In the last part of his book Boccaccio says that the wind strokes only tall trees.

The Decameron—a large assembly of people who have gathered to investigate the question of familial happiness.

The plague has eliminated social fears, everybody thinks that he is going to die, the conversations are frank.

And even so, Boccaccio has an unconvincing ending.

He tells a story about Griselda, how this peasant woman endures all the trials her husband inflicts on her.

The marquis tells her that he has killed their children.

That he is going to marry someone else.

[155] Lilya Brik committed suicide on August 4, 1978, at the age of 87 when she was terminally ill.

[156] From "Man."

That he is turning her out of their house without a single dress to wear. She implores that he give her at least a shirt.

This world ends at a big gathering with a case of a woman's constancy being put to a moral test.

This was the only story from *The Decameron* that Batyushkov translated into Russian.

The rest of it was considered improper for translation and was read only in French.

But in reality, the quality of the text is checked at the Assay Office.

Not every text is appropriate for all occasions.

This joyfulness of the quality inspector ends with him writing as an old man about a woman who, apparently, was connected to him; she demanded food and quails, got fat, and didn't love him.

That's despair, that's a rejection of humaneness.

In *The Decameron*, the stories argue with each other, it's the great argument of the Renaissance era. This is the joy that one feels when old systems collapse; it was assumed that there would be a different kind of joy—a great one. But even though he knows this joy, Boccaccio can't find it.

And instead he produces a woman martyr, the peasant whom an aristocrat made his wife. The last story is probably the most terrible one; a marquis taunting a peasant woman.

She must endure all her trials. And, surely, this is the most immoral story of all the stories collected in *The Decameron*.

The book is a reexamination of the old world and, at the same time, it's a collection of memories that are free from judgment.

And yet, this book stands alongside Dante's *Inferno* in which the same behavior is treated as a system of crimes.

They are condemned to eternal flight; they won't ever be forgiven.

Dante, guided by Virgil, faints; he rejects this argument, this judgment. He refuses to become a witness to the punishment of the weak by the strong.

But what happens next?

Boccaccio writes *The Raven*, and excludes *The Decameron* from his bibliography.

Tolstoy does something similar in his proposal against marriage: humankind still will survive, even if by accidents.

Great is the helplessness of the great ones before life.

People want to find the other side of the mirror, they touch the glass with their hands, but it won't let them through.

Chekhov's novels either didn't have an ending, or they turned into stories.

The hero of "My Life" has fallen out of society, he has become a carpenter, all his friends tease him and disapprove of his behavior, then they leave him alone, and even the governor is tired of trying to "correct" his behavior.

This was an emergence of a new plot.

At the end, the hero of "Gooseberries" is content with himself, which is a terrifying thing; it's terrifying that a person would be content with his life.

And this recurring plot appears in Chekhov, I think, three times.

It was a replacement for an ending.

About the heroes of "The Steppe" Chekhov said that they couldn't figure out anything. Only Dymov quarrels with the young boy, he comes to him and says: "Go on, hit me! I offended you."

Chekhov says: here is a person for the revolution, but since there won't be a revolution, Dymov will die.

But he didn't want to believe in this and took off to Sakhalin—maybe to find Dymov there?

Gorky wrote to Chekhov: "You ... killed realism"—everything after you will seem "written not with a pen, but a log."

Like Odysseus, Chekhov goes to countries that didn't yet exist.

Everything starts from a trifle, a bit of nonsense—a piece of amber attracts a piece of paper.

The power of surprise is enormous. But we still haven't solved its mystery.

We often mention that Gogol's poem[157] *Dead Souls* has no ending. It's an expository poem.

At the same time, the author in the poem is mourning his own fate.

At first, he talks about the lucky people, he talks about the poet who has "clouded people's eyes with illusion, he has flattered them by concealing all that is sordid in life, he has shown them man in all his splendor."

Then a sinister digression follows:

> But the lot and fate of the author who dares to bring all that he sees out into the open is otherwise. All those things that an indifferent eye fails to notice—all the slimy marsh of petty occurrences into which we sink, all the multitude of callous, splintered, everyday characters who swarm along the drab, often painful road of life—he shows them clearly engraved, thanks to the power of his merciless chisel, so that the whole world may view them . . .
>
> Yes, his lot is grim and he is doomed to bitter loneliness.

Chichikov drove in a two- or three-horse carriage, from which we see the steppe and which is very stark.

■

But this carriage, the britzka, is unusual—even supernatural, if you will.

Here goes my digression, let it go along its own path, the path of my thought, or perhaps even my feelings.

A rather smart, smallish carriage drove through the inn gates of the provincial town of NN. It was the sort of carriage in which bachelors ride—

[157] Shklovsky refers to *Dead Souls* as a poem because in the original Gogol had called it a "poem" on the title page.

retired lieutenant colonels, captains, landowners having a hundred serfs or so—in fact, those who are called gentry of moderate means.

Its occupant was a gentleman who was surely no Adonis but whose appearance was not too unprepossessing either. He was neither too fat nor too thin, nor could he be described as either old or young.

His arrival caused no commotion in the town nor anything special, except for a few comments exchanged between two peasants standing by the entrance to a tavern opposite the inn, which, as a matter of fact, concerned the carriage rather than its occupant.

"Look there," one said to the other, "look at that wheel! Think it'll hold out as far as, say, Moscow?"

"It'll make it," the other peasant said.

"And what about Kazan? I say it won't make it."

"It won't make Kazan," the other agreed.

And that was the end of the conversation.[158]

But here is something similar that is marked as if by the same hand.

Early one July morning a springless bone-shaking britzka—one of those antediluvian ones in which only commercial travelers, drovers, and the poorer clergy drive nowadays in Russia, clattered out of N, the chief town of the Z province, on to the country road. The vehicle screeched and uttered a loud scream at the slightest movement; the bucket fastened behind sullenly chimed in. By these sounds, apart from its woefully torn leather-lining dangling on the inside of its peeling interior, you might arrive at a conclusion as to its antiquity and readiness to fall to pieces.[159]

In the vehicle sat a kind priest, a sweet boy, a pushy tradesman and the rundown coachman.

But the places through which they pass are beautiful and Chekhov re-

[158] The opening lines of Gogol's *Dead Souls*.
[159] The opening lines of Chekhov's "The Steppe."

marks: "The ground, the plain, the grass, the horizon, they all demand a song."

Here are two beginnings that so strangely begin with the same repetition, the repetition of one single circumstance.

■

But let's return to the road of *Dead Souls*.

The world is portrayed as a dreadful place, as if condemned from the start, because Chichikov's encounters with people amounts to a proposal by one charlatan to another to commit a crime.

But the work is constructed as a poem; it has mountains, its own topography that offers a different perception. Chichikov is buying up dead souls. He sees the lost list of sold slaves. And within this reality, the simultaneously realistic charlatan recounts the names of living beings, portraits of living men. The portraits are rather poetic.

"Good heavens! What a lot of you people are squeezed in here! Wonder what you all did in your lifetimes? How you got along?"

His eyes kept involuntarily returning to one particular name—Peter Saveliev, Trough-Scorner, who had belonged to Mother Korobochka. Again, he couldn't help commenting: "What an odd one! Wonder if you were a skilled worker or simply an ordinary peasant, wonder what kind of death you chanced to meet . . . And you, Stepan-the-Cork, a carpenter of exemplary sobriety. . . . Yes, you're the giant who was fit to serve in the Guards. I'll wager you went all over the country with your ax in your belt and your boots slung over your shoulder . . . And how did death catch up with you?"

". . . And there's Maksim Telyatnikov, the cobbler. There's a Russian saying, 'drunk as a cobbler.' I've got your number, brother, and if you like, I'll tell you your whole life's story. You served your apprenticeship under some German who allowed you to have your meals with his family, who whacked you across the back with a strap . . ."

The bitter survey of human lives ends here.

But the author wants to show a different world.

And after the parody describes how the petty people of this world will perceive the story of a petty man, the author tells about how people will talk about other people: there goes Chichikov, Chichikov, Chichikov:

—and this will create the effect of bird chatter.

And from this chatter the author—the person—transitions to an apotheosis.

He describes the movement of the troika as the triumph of the country that he has created, as something magical—the troika of Gogol.

> . . . as though some unseen force has swept you up and is carrying you off and you find yourself flying, everything is flying: the milestones . . . the forest on either side is flying too, with its rows of dark pines, its thumping axes . . . and there's something sinister about flashing past objects that disappear even before they've come into focus; and only the sky overhead, with its clouds split by the moon, appears to be standing still. O troika! O troika-bird! Who invented you? . . . And to think there's nothing complicated about a troika—no screws, no metal; all it took to build it was an ax, a chisel, and a smart Russian peasant . . .
>
> . . . what unknown force drives these mysterious steeds. O horses, horses! Are there cyclones concealed in your manes? Do your sensitive ears transmit fire to your very veins?
>
> . . . And where do you fly to, Russia? Answer me! . . . She doesn't answer. The carriage bells break into an enchanted tinkling, the air is torn to shred and turns into wind; everything on earth flashes past, and, casting worried sidelong glances, other nations and countries step out of her way.

So let's not say that literary works often don't have an ending.

But let's say that works imply a tragedy, whether it's described or not.

Gogol wanted to glorify Russia. Maybe he felt that he was the new apostle of Russia and the Ukraine. You can certainly hear the Ukrainian baroque music in the description of the Dnepr, the inaccuracy of the description in itself is beautiful.

The troika-bird doesn't bring *Dead Souls* to an end. I'm not talking about the fact that the poem doesn't show the life and death of Chichikov after his search for dead souls.

No, I'm talking about genre here.

The author is justifying himself for not showing anything marvelous and exciting; it's as though he is cursing his own hero.

The poem ends not with a conversation about nothing, but with a prophecy about the future.

Gogol wanted to glorify Russia and write a different work where all the dead souls would be resurrected, every single one of them, even Plyushkin, he listed everything that would happen; and Belinsky said that there were too many promises, and no means to carry them out.

The flight of the troika is majestic in its passionate force, in its melodiousness. It's almost mad, it was previously foretold in *The Diary of a Madman*.

It's a brilliant passage.

I'll give an abbreviated version:

Why do they torture me? What do they want from one so wretched as myself? What can I give them? I possess nothing. I cannot bear all their tortures; my head aches as though everything were turning round in a circle. Save me! Carry me away! Give me three steeds swift as the wind! Mount your seat, coachman, ring the bells, gallop horses, and carry me straight out of this world. Farther, ever farther, till nothing more is to be seen!

Ah! the heavens bend over me already; a star glimmers in the distance; the forest with its dark trees in the moonlight rushes past; a bluish mist floats under my feet; music sounds in the mist . . .

He gives a pre-setting: "Give me three steeds as swift as the wind"; "gallop horses, and carry me straight out of this world." This is the hero's flight, and Gogol re-experienced it in his rush to finish *Dead Souls* in the middle of the poem.

He wanted freedom.

"Gallop horses!"

But neither Poprischin nor the great author was able to break free from this world. He couldn't give glorification to something that couldn't be glorified. He didn't call for changes, for a transformation of life; he didn't call for improvement, but for reinvention.

I don't know exactly what Gogol burned during the last days of his life, after the long fatal fasting. What was it that he burned, regretting and repenting his action, blaming the flames and at the same time not touching the pieces of paper, and they don't burn that fast by the way.

Art cannot change the world, even though it wants to because it experiences the world. But I'm afraid that among those papers that Gogol burned none showed the way out: this is why they were burning in flames.

The horses that appear at the end or almost the end of *Dead Souls* cannot raise the souls because the souls must believe in flight, they must get rid of their dead bodies in order to be resurrected.

You'll recall the Ukrainian carts.

I'll remind you of other horses. The horses of Chekhov that carried a priest, a boy whose name I've forgotten, and someone else, too, and the carriage in which they traveled was exactly the same kind of britzka as Chichikov's.

A few paragraphs before I was suggesting a juxtaposition.

Why?

I really don't know. I only wish for you to remember Chekhov who called Gogol the king of steppes. The familiar horses, the extended quote, the attempt to resurrect mankind is realized through the boy who sees the steppe, the great steppe, described by Chekhov anew—after Gogol.

The steppe implores that we remember it again.

It's very strange why Chekhov has to travel in Chichikov's britzka; but instead the britzka is carrying a child who is describing the steppe, who is seeing the steppe worthy of being the equal of the Steppe.

But look again at *Resurrection*. One of Tolstoy's most difficult texts.

Here is Katyusha after her resurrection.

The word *resurrection* here is uncapitalized because Tolstoy used the capitalized word as the book's title.

Here is Katyusha after her resurrection; and here is an amazing excerpt from Tolstoy's diary: "Katyusha, already after her resurrection, goes through periods during which she wears a coy and languid smile, as if forgetting the truths that she believed in; it's just that one wants to live happily, just wants to be" (17 May, 1896).

■

This is probably the only truly joyful ending in literature.

The last time I heard Gorky's memoirs about Tolstoy was in the Anichkov Palace.

On the windowsill with windows open sat Aleksandr Blok. The reflection of the light cobalt blue sky poured all around him; Gorky didn't finish his reading.

He went, as we might say, behind the scenes.

He was probably crying.

And everything froze forever, and even though the train has long departed, I would've liked to have hung onto the compartment door handle on that train in which you won't be traveling.

I'm uttering the words of an old person. Besides, the words aren't right. The trains of art never stop or leave. They have a life of their own, a time of their own.

II.

I have been writing this book for over two years. It has been constructed and reconstructed in many different ways.

And now, just like in any ordinary conversation, it's important to know where you began and where you ended. And whether you wanted to end this conversation at all.

But from the conversations about the fate of this book, this is how I began. First of all I started with Tolstoy's conversation about the "energy of delusion." This was a person who could spend decades writing one book, who could fight for the justness of his cause through various books.

He was and still is the greatest commander-in-chief of plot.

I've been in the back lines of his army and know his steed very well.

I love those places where books are born.

It was in the village Mikhaylovskoe.

Why was I so struck by that place? Because it was a montage, literature in the highest sense of that word, a montage of those elements that survive in literature.

A sublime revolution with its losses, successes, and cruelties had formed here.

That's how literature lives on, how it got montaged around Pushkin's house.

Art can be montaged. And so can the world.

We see it because life has taught us to see the world not as inverted, but in the way it's supposed to reach our process of thought; the observer's entire construction must stand on its own.

We don't know how Pushkin would've montaged his life to its end.

But we know that he had a small piece that wasn't finished. An epigraph about a man who is leaving—I am talking about the excerpt "At the corner of a little square."

This was not published during Pushkin's life. But it was very similar to one of the scenes in *Anna Karenina*. I can show you the corresponding lines if you like.

We defy time when we think through art.

The past returns—resurrected.

Let's look again at the book that's clearly compiled from various other books.

It's called *The Decameron*.

It was as if composed by women and men who are narrating to each other, simultaneously clarifying and eliminating things in the process, because of the plague and because they want to eliminate fear and resurrect hope.

We see how plot gets reinvented here, how it parodies itself, how it persists.

I still haven't defined plot.

Throughout my life and until this day I still don't have a clear idea about what plot really is.

I know that a book can have a plotted beginning, when people—like the ladies in *The Decameron* who haven't yet invited any men, who know how to get things done (like Boccaccio himself)—reinvent the old, incorporated in the new.

The old never dies.

■

The carpenters used to say in the old days: "The eyes are afraid, whilst the hands create."

The hands know what to do when there is a piece of wood in front of you, when you have instruments.

Most mistakes in literary criticism, I think, occur when people are too afraid and they are afraid without even approaching the material, or, on the contrary, they approach so close to the poetic horse—Pegasus—and mount it so swiftly that they miss the saddle and end up on the other side.

Then they get up, look around, the horse is still standing on the same spot, the saddle, the stirrups are still there, but the person is not in the saddle.

A literary theory, first of all, must know its correlation to literature, the inner laws that create literature, that is—actual literature.

It must mount the horse just like Lev Nikolaevich would mount his horse, never from a stump or a small bench, but by placing one leg in the stirrup, grasping the horse by the mane in one hand together with the reins.

And so, the old man in a heavy coat is on his horse.

What is plot and what is story?

Gogol is a great creator of new rules, an expert on old literature, because people who understand literature the best are those who know how things are written, what is paper on a desk, what is a theme; I'll restate my thought—

A. P. Chekhov wrote,

—and here I need this repetition—

he wrote to his brother Aleksandr, a talented man, but someone who constantly tried to climb up on his horse from a bench and on top of that—someone had to help him up—

—he wrote—the plot must be new, and the storyline doesn't matter.

Those two terms clashed with each other as they passed many times from hand to hand—we understand that plot is a device.

It's a device for description.

At the same time, the main character in a play was also called a plot.

And finally, in the conversational language of Ostrovsky's times, "plot" was a person who was chosen for love.

That's exactly how they used this word:

—Your plot is sitting in my office.

Meanwhile the story fell into the skillful hands of aimless people: why are you shaving, why are you cutting the wood? The story fell into skillful hands and they started calling it an "intrigue."

An intrigue is an old worn-out pair of shoes.

At the same time, shoes can be falsely elegant.

An intrigue usually suggests the same thing as the most elegant pair of shoes.

The plot of *The Inspector General*, as Gogol acknowledged, was given to him by Pushkin.

His plot was about a man whom nobody could figure out, a person not in his place.

A person who wants to find that place, a place where he belongs, but doesn't know yet, as Pushkin suggests—who he really is.

The plot in *Eugene Onegin* isn't just about Eugene Onegin, but about the Onegin who was studying the science of love—the way that Ovid did.

How to approach love, how to seduce her, how to give private lessons, in quiet.

But love turned out to be something else.

Something that wc can't define.

Plot is a device that exists in reality, or could have existed had it not been deflected by the logic of time.

The tragic Don Quixote, who wishes only good, who is brave—he exposes time by being mistaken about time, and by being mistaken about himself. These mistakes gave birth to a new kind of prose.

And Dostoevsky, after returning from exile, thinks that Don Quixote is the hope of the world.

Whereas an intrigue is the traces of various coinciding plots. It's something that could have been and seems to be there.

The old General Dragomirov wrote about *War and Peace* in a magazine, and later published a separate book.

He liked its structure. He agreed with the parts that could have been managed by a young officer. But he disapproved of the way in which the strategy of those higher in rank was shown.

What huge mistakes when one thinks about them!

But at the same time, how dull Dragomirov is! He understands old books and it's as if he teases Lev Nikolaevich that Natasha Rostova—he knows it right away—will become the wife of Pierre Bezukhov, not Andrei Bolkonsky.

The battle against intrigue—i.e., old traces that lead to wrong houses— that's a Tolstoyan plot.

In reality, the plot in Tolstoy remained as if unified, meanwhile the story kept sorting itself out and Olenin's departure from the woman who simply said: "Get away, I'm sick of you!" was the elimination of the story.

This is exactly what Chekhov meant when he wrote: the plot must be new, and the story doesn't matter.

But when did this happen?

Chekhov's plays from his earlier period are rather story-like and as if "unplotted."

After a while this became unbearable for the author.

Apparently, the hero either had to die or leave.

Because of this drawback Gogol made one of his characters jump out of the window.

So Chekhov in his "Cherry Orchard" made the person left behind in the locked summerhouse say: "They forgot me."

And he leaves us with a parodied story: in the humoresque called "The Bear" a man and woman prepare for a duel, they invite people to help assist with the terrible task, and then begin kissing each other in front of the amazed crowd.

So I'll repeat, the triviality of a story can be turned into a plot.

III.

An author needs a plot.

Plot is like finding a new love, a new faith—the loss of fear of an ending.

Which is why it's necessary to differentiate between the plot when beginning a work and the plot when ending it.

The plot selected for beginning a certain work, the device that introduces a focus to the work, is a choice of restrictions.

For example, Pushkin in his future work, but we should keep in mind that it's still in an embryonic stage, when the author begins like this—

The initial plot of *The Captain's Daughter.*

A gentleman keeps a gang of thieves.

He has probably fallen out of favor, but has good connections.

As the novel progresses, the hero is faced with certain impediments that he overcomes thanks to his father's old connections.

The second plot.

A disgraced gentleman with no connections, except for an old friend who is serving in some godforsaken place, sends his son to the frontier, to this friend.

On the way, the young man meets a stranger and offers him his services.

The stranger later turns out to be the leader of another social group. He helps the young man.

The old friend, whom the young officer is sent to, plays almost no role here: he is a stock figure, a retired old man who knows some German.

The stranger on the road becomes a leader, then the protector of the young officer, he saves the officer—then he is taken to be executed, he's killed; hence the so-called "hero" is not so much of a hero as a device to move the story along, he is in trouble and the girl, his bride, saves him, and he is saved by the new government.

In a conventional plot it's the old connections that come to the rescue—the old army group, people who are organizing the coup d'etat. Or one's hunting friends.

Here the girl commits a heroic deed and is elevated to the title of the work, while the young man remains on the side, away from the politics.

He doesn't attempt to use his connections with Pugachev for his own benefit. And later he doesn't use his connections with the people who granted him a pardon.

The outlaw "guide" saves the disgraced gentleman.

Through the changing plots, Pugachev and his revolt come to the foreground; from the old plot there only remains the pardoning of the lead character, his amnesty obtained thanks to the fact that the Empress became approachable.

■

Let's take the history of plot in Tolstoy.

A young woman has committed adultery and dies.

What happens in the development of this plot?

The young woman falls out of her social circle.

It's as though her husband is not her husband.

Her real husband is the person with whom she commits adultery.

He loses interest in her.

She, being ostracized from her society, dies.

Here is the plan of another story by Tolstoy.

The initial plot.

A young man seduced a young girl, he ruined her, she was ruined, then he saves her, returns her to society, she becomes his assistant, they go abroad. She has been resurrected.

I am talking about *Resurrection*.

A subsequent construction of the old plot.

The woman is going through a second stage of love, which rehabilitates the first experience of love.

This is pure love.

It's the one shown in the first scene, where the ice is drifting, at the house of Nekhlyudov's aunts.

This love resurrects the young man.

The old idea—a man who is satisfied with his deed,

—look how it was transformed:

—when he has already made up his mind, sitting on the windowsill with open shutters, hearing the bells, and then Tolstoy notes,

—the fact that he is already feeling good about himself, that he has changed his life, the fact that he is content, forces Tolstoy to say—no, that's not it.

The questionable guilt of the woman forced both of them to change their lives, and so she has rejected Nekhlyudov's sacrifice and is going into exile with another person, and had she returned to her old lover, accord-

ANOTHER NOTE ON BEGINNINGS AND ENDINGS

ing to some woman in the labor camps, then this would have been a worse disgrace than the first one.

The initial questions of both plots, i.e., *Resurrection* and *Anna Karenina*, can be called "storied." They are traditional. They seem to be incidental.

In Dickens, a boy, sent away by his mother, ends up in the hands of a cruel man who disinherits him. He is saved by a distant relative. The man who wants to break up and ruin his family is also a distant relative who for some reason wants to discredit and ruin the boy.

In another book by Dickens, this boy is associated with some documents, he saves those documents. I'm referring to Nicholas Nickleby.

These are all examples of stories.

■

Plot is a knot of given circumstances that lead to other circumstances, circumstances of a different structure, different style.

Which is to say, with these circumstances it's as if we are fortifying the plot.

The change in the characters' behavior and in the nature of the old mythological crime, committed several generations ago, along with the intercession of higher forces pardons mankind.

The myth ends in a myth.

What do we see here?

One example.

A person passionately tried to save up some money so that he could have a peaceful life with gooseberries.

He wanted to preserve his old way of life.

This cost him great efforts, but the gooseberries, for the sake of which he killed his wife, turn out to be sour.

The first construction of happiness is negated.

But at a second glance, the person gets his gooseberries, they are sour but he likes them all the same.

He is content.

The plot, the derived construction, is that one needs to knock on all doors.

There are too many people who are content.

The land is dying, and so is mankind, which was foretold in the past about the dying land.

The initial plot is overturned.

Another example.

Initial plot construction: there was a coffin-maker, a tall, unkempt man, he torments his wife. The wife dies. She is as if relieved by her death.

However, the person is a musician and even a composer.

His motif: life for people is a losing game. The key to this second plot construction is that he is playing about it on his fiddle.

A person who isn't an enemy, but someone who neglecting truth had been tormenting others, this ordinary person suddenly realizes that ordinary life is extraordinarily bad.

It's as if Chekhov sometimes excises pieces from someone's life without trying to beautify them.

The son of an architect, tormented by his father, isn't able to save his sister, he is left to care for her child; the daughter of a rich engineer falls in love with him, they live as if a happy life. Then she leaves him.

It rarely happens in a plot that a woman abandons her lover.

But can this be considered as plot?

She asks for a divorce.

Evidently, he grants it.

The woman is wearing a ring with an inscription:

—everything passes away.

The man says, he would have liked it to read:

—nothing passes away.

In the town in which the son of the architect becomes a house painter, they call him "of little use," he sells a bird for a kopeck.

He is as if a worthless person in their eyes, but this provincial town that agreed to adopt the style of his untalented architect father as its own, this town began to respect the son. These unruly people still understand the sublimity of his fate.

The story is interrupted by a change in the plot.

■

Originally, the plot of a classic novel was realistic, however its ending was conventional, repeated too often.

It was "storied."

People were saved in stories about suddenly found wealth,

—or most often—about inheritance.

In the Chekhovian ending, the person doesn't improve his social condition.

But he understands it.

The character (from "Peasantry") who wanted to find religion turns out to be an accomplice in a murder case. He refuses to denounce the murderer in exchange for a bribe.

In the labor camp, he comes to understand a simple thing about moral decency.

Chekhov asks—why was it so difficult to understand such a simple thing?

The ending is much more realistic than the exposition.

Or it treats people ironically who think that they are going to get something in the end.

These endings are sudden in their shift to a different angle.

In another earlier work, a woman tells a writer how she was poor, then married an old man, became rich, saw the world, was happy. Her husband died. She is rich.

But now she has a new misery.

She has a new suitor, another old man.

But what she considers misery or wants to believe is misery is in fact her profession.

Happy endings that calm the reader and allow the author to leave this world since it's so good even without him, they have become more tragic because the best among us are dying.

■

If a talented person tried to lie, said Tolstoy, his talent wouldn't allow him to.

Plot is what the author seeks; we can say it's the result of a discovery.

Plot is almost always a dream, a marriage with a loved one, it's freedom, occasionally—a happy family.

And at the same time, plot, particularly in drama, becomes a label.

The ending often alleviates a situation that's frightening.

In a staged story, witches—the bubbles of the earth—are as if the natural element of the world's evil.

They make semi-predictions to Macbeth, the predictions come true, but they become the main reason for Macbeth's demise.

Sometimes happy endings are dressed with irony.

As in one of Charlie Chaplin's pictures his friend, the millionaire, recognizes him only when he is drunk, but when he is sober, Chaplin is a stranger to him.

At the beginning of the novel, Karenina is reading an English novel about a baronet. She reads it through to the traditional ending, when the baronet gains his happiness.

Suddenly she is filled with shame.

She has already seen Vronsky.

This is the first hint of adultery.

It's not going to end like the novel about the baronet.

Tolstoy appended a detailed list of disappointments to his novel.

Anna Karenina dies.

Vronsky is headed toward his death.

He had already tried to shoot himself with the words "of course."

He feels he has compromised himself.

And, of course, he is going to war, to die with the brave man's tragic words about dying in physical combat. Since it's trench warfare.

He is as if cleansing himself of his disgrace, as people cleanse themselves with a duel.

Levin, talking about how he never squints, sees life as it really is. His own reality, that is.

But Anna, too, when she is a mistress on Vronsky's large estate—everything is false—she, too, is squinting.

Everyone knows.

Tolstoy tilled with a plow.

But T. Maltsev's system of deep plowing[160] was established only in the recent years.

It surely can't be widely adopted.

Tolstoy didn't just see the future.

He knew the future, like a plant knows why it loses leaves in the fall.

Now I need to say something about repetition.

But I'll make a digression before that.

When a person begins writing, he starts with someone. It's either a historic figure, or someone else, i.e., someone from a personal experience.

The historical aspect in "The Bronze Horseman"—Peter, Eugene and the woman who didn't say anything, who was only talked about—she's not alive anymore.

The name Eugene means someone of high birth. The text says that the family name of Eugene has shone throughout history.

Now Eugene is a poor official.

Peter is the person who created the city plan of St. Petersburg.

---

160 During the Soviet famine of 1931–33, under Stalin, peasants and others were forced onto large collective farms where the state dictated farming methods and production quotas. According to one of Stalin's agricultural "experts," Terenti Maltsev, the deeper that farmers plowed, the deeper the root structure of the plant would grow. These theories were later adopted by the Chinese communists, which led to the great Chinese famine in 1958–61.

The word *here* is uttered with a special emphasis: *here* will stand a city. The place of action is already determined.

To destroy the structure, a flood occurs.

The flood—two people are watching it.[161]

The bronze horseman, i.e., "the bronze Peter," sitting on his horse; the water doesn't even reach the horse's hoofs; and Eugene, he is sitting on a sentry lion by the Ministry of Military Affairs (the garden isn't there yet, it's demolished so that they can close the Senate Square, the place of the Decembrist rebellion).

The alternative heroes are presented in an identical posture.

As if both riders are made equal in their stance.

The Finnish huts are historically realized as abandoned houses on the Galerny Harbor.

Here is an example of a historical construction.

History's contradictions are underlined by means of art.

Peter's victory is presented through the heroic cityscape of St. Petersburg.

In order to preserve, to show how a construction in art lives, how it re-emerges again, fortified by historical analogy.

Art doesn't stand in one place; it keeps developing.

Which is why, in this book that you have been reading, you often come across repetitions that have been deliberately devised.

Put your finger on the page, as you read, and compare the traces of history one more time.

■

Plot is the full use of knowledge about a certain subject.

Even the names of the poetic subject; even Tatyana Larina's name is taken from history.

It's stated though that this name is introduced for the first time.

161 In "The Bronze Horseman," Pushkin describes the flood of 1824.

It's stated that this is a woman's name and it's a common name.

The concept of neighboring estates, their closeness, is not emphasized but given in the conversation of Eugene with Tatyana's husband:

I'm their neighbor.

Tatyana then says:

Yet happiness had been so possible
so near! . . .

The arches and buttresses of poetry appear through the perception of the real weight of feeling.

Now I'm going to stop in order not to repeat myself.

I have already passed this road in my book.

■

So what is a story?

It's a return to the old, conventional and familiar theme for the reader or the audience.

The story, same as an intrigue, facilitates perception, repetition, but like any verbal rhyme, it sometimes trivializes repetition.

Aleksandr Blok depicted Russian history and its repetitiveness through the following imagery:

The decorative needles weave
a pattern of loose ruts.[162]

Plot repetition and reference to one and the same subject, one and the same breath—it speaks not of the incidental, but of one of the rules of poetic expressiveness, which is one manifestation of poetic thought.

[162] From "Russia" (1908).

That's the search for a path.

Art itself is constructed on the notion that history isn't predictable, it's unexpected because it's not a myth.

Insomnia. Homer. Taut sails . . .

—wrote Mandelstam.[163]

The phenomena in art are as diverse as they are in real life.

I won't be able to end; I won't be able to fly across the whole width of my book.

Along the road to Yalta, at that section where you are going so quickly down the mountain, I've seen parts of the highway, it makes a bend and goes up by the side of the slope.

One should know how to slow down a speeding car.

They showed me a place on that road where a man, unable to slow down, lost control of his car and ran into the hillside.

The metal letters of typeset have stopped meaning anything today—they are being cleared out.

But they are weighed so as to know how heavy the sibilants are, or how heavy the vowels are.

We offered to do this a long time ago.

Seventy years have passed, and they still haven't finished the experiment.

And was the experiment necessary, anyway?—They still haven't figured it out.

And perhaps the car should have gone up, in order to slow down.

We can weigh meaning.

Just as we can weigh a poetic line.

And anyway, typesetting has been changed to phototypesetting, nothing needs to be weighed anymore.

163 The first line of "78" from Mandelstam's first book *Stone* (1913).

You must realize that the rules of something unfinished cannot be transferred onto something that has already been represented or finished.

This is worse than Penelope's task, who had to weave and undo her day's weaving.

I'll repeat what Tolstoy said, without citing any page number or volume, because I lived through those words.

He said that gold is sifted from the sand, but there is no need to return the golden granules back into the sand.

It's important to know the rules of cultivating a thought, which has no weight by itself alone.

But it's difficult to tear oneself away from the old road, it seems that the sea will finally glisten beyond the bend.

The observations that we make on Tolstoy, his method of juxtaposing ideas, his ability to actually *feel* the subject, lead us onto the great road beyond words.

Mayakovsky often ended his poems with the poet's death, and then his resurrection.

It was a struggle for life.

Chekhovian plots, I respect them the same way Sancho Panza respected Don Quixote.

Whom I believe more than I believe myself, and I don't hope to own an island.

Chekhov created unplotted fiction, and in the last lines everything was overturned, reinvented, retuned, re-experienced in a new way.

Try it on "Rothschild's Fiddle," "Gooseberries" or any other story that is like a biography; it contains a road going upwards, and a glance back.

It turns out it's reconstructing itself.

Farewell, my friends.

PETROS ABATZOGLOU *What Does Mrs. Freeman Want?*

PIERRE ALBERT-BIROT *Grabinoulor*

YUZ ALESHKOVSKY *Kangaroo*

FELIPE ALFAU *Chromos* * *Locos*

IVAN ÂNGELO *The Celebration* * *The Tower of Glass*

DAVID ANTIN *Talking*

DJUNA BARNES *Ladies Almanack* * *Ryder*

JOHN BARTH *LETTERS* * *Sabbatical*

DONALD BARTHELME *The King* * *Paradise*

SVETISLAV BASARA *Chinese Letter*

MARK BINELLI *Sacco and Vanzetti Must Die!*

ANDREI BITOV *Pushkin House*

LOUIS PAUL BOON *Chapel Road* * *Summer in Termuren*

ROGER BOYLAN *Killoyle*

IGNÁCIO DE LOYOLA BRANDÃO *Teeth under the Sun* * *Zero*

CHRISTINE BROOKE-ROSE *Amalgamemnon*

BRIGID BROPHY *In Transit*

MEREDITH BROSNAN *Mr. Dynamite*

GERALD L. BRUNS *Modern Poetry and the Idea of Language*

GABRIELLE BURTON *Heartbreak Hotel*

MICHEL BUTOR *Degrees* * *Mobile* * *Portrait of the Artist as a Young Ape*

G. CABRERA INFANTE *Infante's Inferno* * *Three Trapped Tigers*

JULIETA CAMPOS *The Fear of Losing Eurydice*

ANNE CARSON *Eros the Bittersweet*

CAMILO JOSÉ CELA *The Family of Pascual Duarte* * *The Hive* * *Christ versus Arizona*

LOUIS-FERDINAND CÉLINE *Castle to Castle* * *Conversations with Professor Y* * *London Bridge* * *North* * *Rigadoon*

HUGO CHARTERIS *The Tide Is Right*

JEROME CHARYN *The Tar Baby*

MARC CHOLODENKO *Mordechai Schamz*

EMILY HOLMES COLEMAN *The Shutter of Snow*

ROBERT COOVER *A Night at the Movies*

STANLEY CRAWFORD *Some Instructions to My Wife*

ROBERT CREELEY *Collected Prose*

RENÉ CREVEL *Putting My Foot in It*

RALPH CUSACK *Cadenza*

SUSAN DAITCH *LC* * *Storytown*

NIGEL DENNIS *Cards of Identity*

PETER DIMOCK *A Short Rhetoric for Leaving the Family*

ARIEL DORFMAN *Konfidenz*

COLEMAN DOWELL *The Houses of Children* * *Island People* * *Too Much Flesh and Jabez*

RIKKI DUCORNET *The Complete Butcher's Tales* * *The Fountains of Neptune* * *The Jade Cabinet* * *Phosphor in Dreamland* * *The Stain* * *The Word "Desire"*

WILLIAM EASTLAKE *The Bamboo Bed* * *Castle Keep* * *Lyric of the Circle Heart*

JEAN ECHENOZ *Chopin's Move*

STANLEY ELKIN *A Bad Man* * *Boswell: A Modern Comedy* * *Criers and Kibitzers, Kibitzers and Criers* * *The Dick Gibson Show* * *The Franchiser* * *George Mills* * *The Living End* * *The MacGuffin* * *The Magic*

Kingdom * *Mrs. Ted Bliss* * *The Rabbi of Lud* * *Van Gogh's Room at Arles*

ANNIE ERNAUX *Cleaned Out*

LAUREN FAIRBANKS *Muzzle Thyself* * *Sister Carrie*

LESLIE A. FIEDLER *Love and Death in the American Novel*

GUSTAVE FLAUBERT *Bouvard and Pécuchet*

FORD MADOX FORD *The March of Literature*

JON FOSSE *Melancholy*

MAX FRISCH *I'm Not Stiller* * *Man in the Holocene*

CARLOS FUENTES *Christopher Unborn* * *Distant Relations* * *Terra Nostra* * *Where the Air Is Clear*

JANICE GALLOWAY *Foreign Parts* * *The Trick Is to Keep Breathing*

WILLIAM H. GASS *The Tunnel* * *Willie Masters' Lonesome Wife*

ETIENNE GILSON *The Arts of the Beautiful* * *Forms and Substances in the Arts*

C. S. GISCOMBE *Giscome Road* * *Here*

DOUGLAS GLOVER *Bad News of the Heart* * *The Enamoured Knight*

KAREN ELIZABETH GORDON *The Red Shoes*

GEORGI GOSPODINOV *Natural Novel*

JUAN GOYTISOLO *Marks of Identity*

PATRICK GRAINVILLE *The Cave of Heaven*

HENRY GREEN *Blindness* * *Concluding* * *Doting* * *Nothing*

JIŘÍ GRUŠA *The Questionnaire*

JOHN HAWKES *Whistlejacket*

AIDAN HIGGINS *A Bestiary* * *Bornholm Night-Ferry* * *Flotsam and Jetsam* * *Langrishe, Go Down* * *Scenes from a Receding Past* * *Windy Arbours*

ALDOUS HUXLEY *Antic Hay* * *Crome Yellow* * *Point Counter Point* * *Those Barren Leaves* * *Time Must Have a Stop*

MIKHAIL IOSSEL AND JEFF PARKER, EDS. *Amerika: Contemporary Russians View the United States*

GERT JONKE *Geometric Regional Novel*

JACQUES JOUET *Mountain R*

HUGH KENNER *The Counterfeiters* * *Flaubert, Joyce and Beckett: The Stoic Comedians* * *Joyce's Voices*

DANILO KIŠ *Garden, Ashes* * *A Tomb for Boris Davidovich*

ANITA KONKKA *A Fool's Paradise*

GEORGE KONRÁD *The City Builder*

TADEUSZ KONWICKI *A Minor Apocalypse* * *The Polish Complex*

MENIS KOUMANDAREAS *Koula*

ELAINE KRAF *The Princess of 72nd Street*

JIM KRUSOE *Iceland*

EWA KURYLUK *Century 21*

VIOLETTE LEDUC *La Bâtarde*

DEBORAH LEVY *Billy and Girl* * *Pillow Talk in Europe and Other Places*

ROSA LIKSOM *Dark Paradise*

JOSÉ LEZAMA LIMA *Paradiso*

OSMAN LINS *Avalovara* * *The Queen of the Prisons of Greece*

ALF MAC LOCHLAINN *The Corpus in the Library* * *Out of Focus*

RON LOEWINSOHN *Magnetic Field(s)*

D. KEITH MANO *Take Five*

BEN MARCUS *The Age of Wire and String*

WALLACE MARKFIELD *Teitlebaum's Window* *
To an Early Grave*

DAVID MARKSON *Reader's Block* * *Springer's Progress* *
Wittgenstein's Mistress*

CAROLE MASO *AVA*

LADISLAV MATEJKA AND KRYSTYNA POMORSKA, EDS.
*Readings in Russian Poetics: Formalist and Structuralist
Views*

HARRY MATHEWS *The Case of the Persevering Maltese:
Collected Essays* * *Cigarettes* * *The Conversions* *
The Human Country: New and Collected Stories* *
The Journalist* * *My Life in CIA* * *Singular Pleasures*
* *The Sinking of the Odradek Stadium* * *Tlooth* *
20 Lines a Day*

ROBERT L. MCLAUGHLIN, ED. *Innovations: An
Anthology of Modern & Contemporary Fiction*

HERMAN MELVILLE *The Confidence-Man*

STEVEN MILLHAUSER *The Barnum Museum* *
In the Penny Arcade*

RALPH J. MILLS, JR. *Essays on Poetry*

OLIVE MOORE *Spleen*

NICHOLAS MOSLEY *Accident* * *Assassins* * *Catastrophe
Practice* * *Children of Darkness and Light* * *Experience
and Religion* * *The Hesperides Tree* * *Hopeful Monsters*
* *Imago Bird* * *Impossible Object* * *Inventing God* *
Judith* * *Look at the Dark* * *Natalie Natalia* * *Serpent
* Time at War* * *The Uses of Slime Mould: Essays of
Four Decades*

WARREN F. MOTTE, JR. *Fables of the Novel:
French Fiction since 1990* * *Oulipo: A Primer of
Potential Literature*

YVES NAVARRE *Our Share of Time* * *Sweet Tooth*

DOROTHY NELSON *In Night's City* * *Tar and Feathers*

WILFRIDO D. NOLLEDO *But for the Lovers*

FLANN O'BRIEN *At Swim-Two-Birds* * *At War* *
The Best of Myles* * *The Dalkey Archive* * *Further
Cuttings* * *The Hard Life* * *The Poor Mouth* *
The Third Policeman*

CLAUDE OLLIER *The Mise-en-Scène*

PATRIK OUŘEDNÍK *Europeana*

FERNANDO DEL PASO *Palinuro of Mexico*

ROBERT PINGET *The Inquisitory* * *Mahu or The Material
* Trio*

RAYMOND QUENEAU *The Last Days* * *Odile* * *Pierrot
Mon Ami* * *Saint Glinglin*

ANN QUIN *Berg* * *Passages* * *Three* * *Tripticks*

ISHMAEL REED *The Free-Lance Pallbearers* * *The Last
Days of Louisiana Red* * *Reckless Eyeballing* *
The Terrible Threes* * *The Terrible Twos* *
Yellow Back Radio Broke-Down*

JULIÁN RÍOS *Larva: A Midsummer Night's Babel* *
Poundemonium*

AUGUSTO ROA BASTOS *I the Supreme*

JACQUES ROUBAUD *The Great Fire of London* * *Hortense
in Exile* * *Hortense Is Abducted* * *The Plurality of
Worlds of Lewis* * *The Princess Hoppy* * *The Form of a*

City Changes Faster, Alas, Than the Human Heart *
Some Thing Black*

LEON S. ROUDIEZ *French Fiction Revisited*

VEDRANA RUDAN *Night*

LYDIE SALVAYRE *The Company of Ghosts* * *Everyday Life
* The Lecture*

LUIS RAFAEL SÁNCHEZ *Macho Camacho's Beat*

SEVERO SARDUY *Cobra* & *Maitreya*

NATHALIE SARRAUTE *Do You Hear Them?* * *Martereau* *
The Planetarium*

ARNO SCHMIDT *Collected Stories* * *Nobodaddy's Children*

CHRISTINE SCHUTT *Nightwork*

GAIL SCOTT *My Paris*

JUNE AKERS SEESE *Is This What Other Women Feel Too?*
* *What Waiting Really Means*

AURELIE SHEEHAN *Jack Kerouac Is Pregnant*

VIKTOR SHKLOVSKY *Knight's Move* * *A Sentimental
Journey: Memoirs 1917–1922* * *Energy of Delusion:
A Book on Plot* * *Theory of Prose* * *Third Factory* *
Zoo, or Letters Not about Love*

JOSEF ŠKVORECKÝ *The Engineer of Human Souls*

CLAUDE SIMON *The Invitation*

GILBERT SORRENTINO *Aberration of Starlight* * *Blue
Pastoral* * *Crystal Vision* * *Imaginative Qualities of
Actual Things* * *Mulligan Stew* * *Pack of Lies* *
Red the Fiend* * *The Sky Changes* * *Something Said* *
Splendide-Hôtel* * *Steelwork* * *Under the Shadow*

W. M. SPACKMAN *The Complete Fiction*

GERTRUDE STEIN *Lucy Church Amiably* * *The Making
of Americans* * *A Novel of Thank You*

PIOTR SZEWC *Annihilation*

STEFAN THEMERSON *Hobson's Island* * *The Mystery
of the Sardine* * *Tom Harris*

JEAN-PHILIPPE TOUSSAINT *Television*

DUMITRU TSEPENEAG *Vain Art of the Fugue*

ESTHER TUSQUETS *Stranded*

DUBRAVKA UGRESIC *Lend Me Your Character* *
Thank You for Not Reading*

MATI UNT *Things in the Night*

ELOY URROZ *The Obstacles*

LUISA VALENZUELA *He Who Searches*

BORIS VIAN *Heartsnatcher*

AUSTRYN WAINHOUSE *Hedyphagetica*

PAUL WEST *Words for a Deaf Daughter* & *Gala*

CURTIS WHITE *America's Magic Mountain* *
The Idea of Home* * *Memories of My Father
Watching TV* * *Monstrous Possibility:
An Invitation to Literary Politics* * *Requiem*

DIANE WILLIAMS *Excitability: Selected Stories* *
Romancer Erector*

DOUGLAS WOOLF *Wall to Wall* * *Ya!* & *John-Juan*

PHILIP WYLIE *Generation of Vipers*

MARGUERITE YOUNG *Angel in the Forest* *
Miss MacIntosh, My Darling*

REYOUNG *Unbabbling*

ZORAN ŽIVKOVIĆ *Hidden Camera*

LOUIS ZUKOFSKY *Collected Fiction*

SCOTT ZWIREN *God Head*

For a full list of publications, visit WWW.DALKEYARCHIVE.COM